Grayson's Art Club

the Exhibition

Volume II

Grayson's Art Club:
The Exhibition – Volume 2

Exhibition supported by Channel 4,
Swan Films and Grayson Perry

Catalogue: Bristol Culture and Creative
Industries team – Sophie Berry,
Steven Bradley, Emma Brown,
Michaela Butler, Julia Carver, Frances Coles,
Helen Dowding, Amelie Drewdun,
David Emeney, Simon Fenn, James Fry,
Ellie Hasler, Alice Rymill, David Singleton,
Miranda Temple-Smith, Finn White

Design: Alice Fraser, Craig Oldham,
Office Of Craig

Printing: TEAM

First published in 2021
by Bristol Museum & Art Gallery,
Queen's Road, Bristol, BS8 1RL.
www.bristolmuseums.org.uk

Image credits: Grayson's Art Club stills
courtesy of Swan Films. All other images
Bristol Museum & Art Gallery
unless otherwise stated

A catalogue record for this book is available
from the British Library.

ISBN 978-1-3999-0643-2

Welcome to Art Club

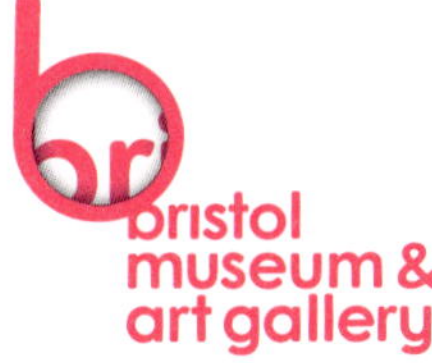

A glimmer
of Hope

Bristol is a vocal city. It is known for its activism, street art culture, dialect and distinctive identity. It is also a city now confronting its contradictions.

At Bristol Museum & Art Gallery we hope to support this process, and fuel creativity, through access to 4.5 billion years of Earth's history. Temporary exhibitions and events expand on our collections, forge dialogue, and celebrate diversity and well-being within our communities.

Having experienced a prolonged lockdown period where this passion and creativity has felt stifled and stilled by social distancing, much like *Art Club*, we have found new ways to express ourselves. We have used digital technology to keep in touch, watch theatre, visit exhibitions and experience talks. We have volunteered to help the people around us and we have protested with banners made in our own homes.

We now thank Grayson, Channel 4 and Swan Films for another opportunity to actively make and experience art through the second iteration of this phenomenal show. The current climate is a challenging one for all cultural organisations and creative people and we hope that this exhibition, with well-being and recovery at its heart, will play an important part in rebuilding and reinvigoration.

Lastly but certainly not least, we thank all of the artists that have contributed to the series and the exhibition and we also thank you, the visitor, without both contributions we would be witnessing a much bleaker 2021 than we see before us today.

Introduction
Grayson Perry

Art Club eh, who'd have thought?!

Looking back over the artworks that are included in this second *Art Club* exhibition I feel a glow of pride once more. Together we have achieved a wonderful thing, a lovingly made snapshot of the nation during the dark days of the second lockdown. By the spring of 2021 we were all getting very weary of the restrictions and our imaginations were banging on the gates to be let free and what a marvellous array of responses we have put together in this show. I think this catalogue will be a poetic record of a time that is seared into all our memories. A time of loss, sacrifice, of loneliness and boredom but also a time of great togetherness, hard work, reflection and of course creativity.

When we started making *Art Club* we had no idea of what a phenomenon it would become. How it would tap into a set of feelings shared by so many of you. Even now eighteen months after it all began, I am still trying to understand what it is that made *Art Club* so beloved. I think the recipe includes a great dollop of community, not just of those who make art but of those who help and share with those around them. One group of people who shone out were the carers, highlighted in the artwork by Lulu Willis 'Warrior Carer' and Lesley Woolvine's portrait of her friend Debbie Porter, who volunteered at the local foodbank. Two carers who I think warrant special mention are Fiona and Steve Tyler, the parents of Becky who made our lead image for the show. I had the great pleasure to go and visit Becky, "the girl who paints with her eyes", and I found her a remarkably moving and skilled artist. She let me have a go on her eye tracking digital art set up and I can report back it is very, very difficult to control and she is such an expert that the software developers use her as a tester. Visiting the Tyler home will stay with me as I felt a mixture of awe at the dedication of Becky's parents and carers and unbridled delight at Becky's joyful life force.

Mixed in with community is a good portion of fun, not just from our professionally comic guests like Mawaan Rizwan or Johnny Vegas but from you all, humour runs through a British person like raspberry through a ripple. I am thinking of Steve Nice's Dream Bar where he populated his own lockdown pub with his choice of celebrity guests or Francesca Simmons (Madam Ceski) dancing away in her suit of ribbons and bells to Covid ritual music in an attempt to ward off the virus. Once the lockdown had eased somewhat I had enormous fun getting dolled up with artist and aspiring drag queen Anthony Klej. We sashayed to the local drag club where we were welcomed by a phalanx of local drag celebrities including Grand Dame of the north eastern scene Ophelia Balls.

Sprinkled throughout the *Art Club* serving is a bit of technical information that may inspire you to make a chemist's shop out of felt (Lucy Sparrow) a crocheted beef burger (Sue Perkins) or burn your silhouette onto a frosty wall just using the sunshine (Andy Goldsworthy).

The main ingredient I think though is a generous helping of stories. Human stories that we can empathise with and that warm our hearts. In a word, love. I spent an afternoon making dumplings with Dora Lam and her parents Winnie and Sam. The very foodstuff that inspired Dora's artwork, a flotilla of ceramic dumplings, a modest monument to the perilous immigrant journey her parents made and a celebration of the food culture they brought with them. But it's perhaps mainly a sculpture about love, family togetherness round the table, sharing the preparation and enjoyment of delicious food.

Another story that stands out vividly is that of our youngest ever contributor to *Art Club*, Amira. Her parents Paul and Louise Weedon were encountering difficulties in conceiving. When visiting Bhutan they heard of a fertility ritual carried out at a temple called The Temple of the Divine Madman so they asked for the help of the monks. The ritual involved a lot of chanting and Louise carrying a large and ancient wooden phallus round the temple three times. It worked! A short time later Louise was pregnant and Amira Kinlay Weedon was born hours before appearing on *Art Club*.

I'm in Dominic Cummings' Whatsapp group!

To quote the title of Paul Weedon's artwork, thank you, thank you, thank you. I am so grateful to everyone who has sent in artworks and hope you will keep doing so. Especial thanks to all the artists who have let us glimpse into their lives. This exhibition would not have been possible without the support of Channel Four and the hard and skilful work of the teams at Swan Films and Bristol Museum & Art Gallery.

The main reason that *Art Club* started is of course the Coronavirus pandemic. Hopefully we are starting to see the beginning of the end of this global catastrophe. Hopefully by the time of the third *Art Club* exhibition we may be back to some kind of normal. But for now take care and enjoy the wonderful variety of ways that we have endured and I hope it may inspire you to make your mark and send something in for the next series.

Grayson

Fami

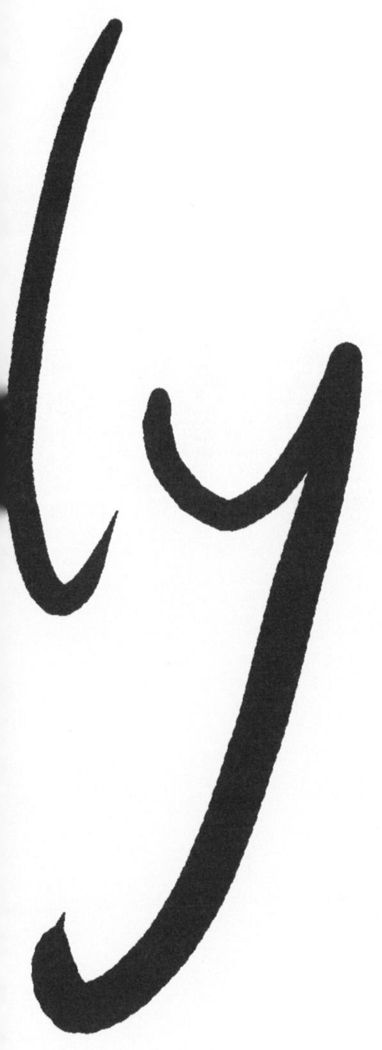

"Never in our lifetime had family been thrown into sharper focus than during the pandemic. Art can help us explore who we miss, who we're shaped by and who we truly belong with.

There are a lot of different sorts of families. There are gay families, straight families, nuclear families, imaginary families, long lost families and constructed families. When we're making art, we have to make decisions. Who am I going to draw? Who's going to be in this picture? Who is my family? We construct a family as we construct an artwork about it. I think that's a powerful thing to do."

Comfort Blanket

Amelia Mullins

Embroidery on cotton fabric
Courtesy of the artist

"Just before my wedding
I was diagnosed with what
is basically a premature
menopause. It was
devastating. I felt huge grief.
A chance of a biological
family had been taken
away in a second. And
then lockdown came and
I needed to distract myself.
I just started sewing little
memories: how I was feeling,
the people I missed, my
family. An escape which
became a place of comfort
and gratitude and filled with
hope and love."

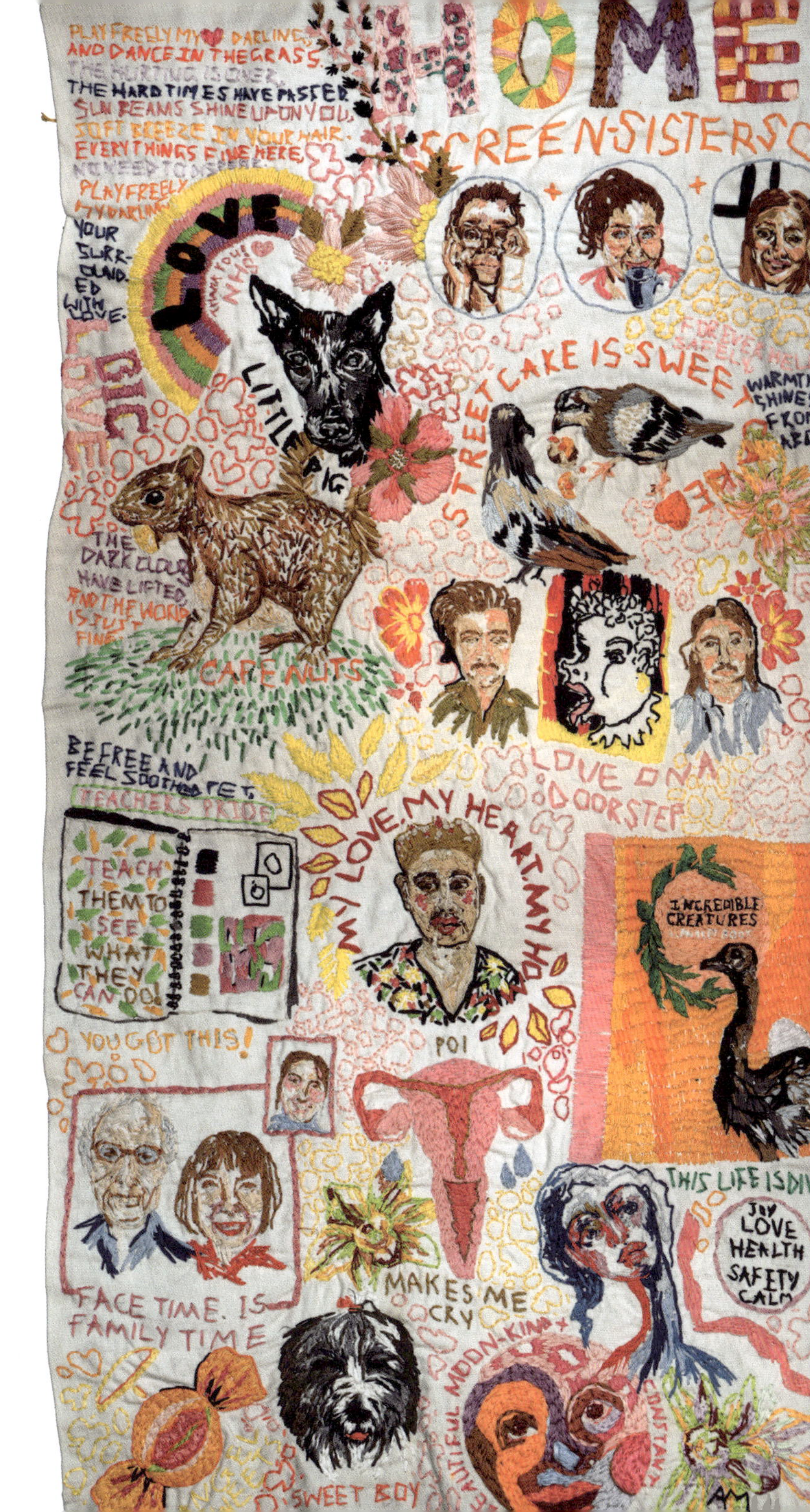

PLAY FREELY MY DARLING,
AND DANCE IN THE GRASS
THE HURTING IS OVER,
THE HARD TIMES HAVE PASSED
SUN BEAMS SHINE UPON YOU,
SOFT BREEZE IN YOUR HAIR.
EVERYTHINGS FINE HERE,
NO NEED TO SCARE
PLAY FREELY
MY DARLING
YOUR SURROUNDED WITH LOVE.
HOME
SCREEN SISTERS
LOVE
BIG LOVE!!
THE DARK CLOUDS HAVE LIFTED, AND THE WORLD IS JUST FINE.
LITTLE PIG
CAFE NUTS
STREET CAKE IS SWEET
WARMTH SHINES FROM ABOVE
FOREVER HELD SAFELY
BE FREE AND FEEL SOOTHED PET.
TEACHERS PRIDE
TEACH THEM TO SEE WHAT THEY CAN DO!
YOU GOT THIS!
M I LOVE MY HEART MY HO
POI
LOVE ON A DOORSTEP
INCREDIBLE CREATURES
FACE TIME IS FAMILY TIME
MAKES ME CRY
THIS LIFE IS DIVI
JOY LOVE HEALTH SAFETY CALM
BEAUTIFUL MOON-KIND
SWEET BOY

Tree Hug

Harry Hill

Video performance
Courtesy of the artist

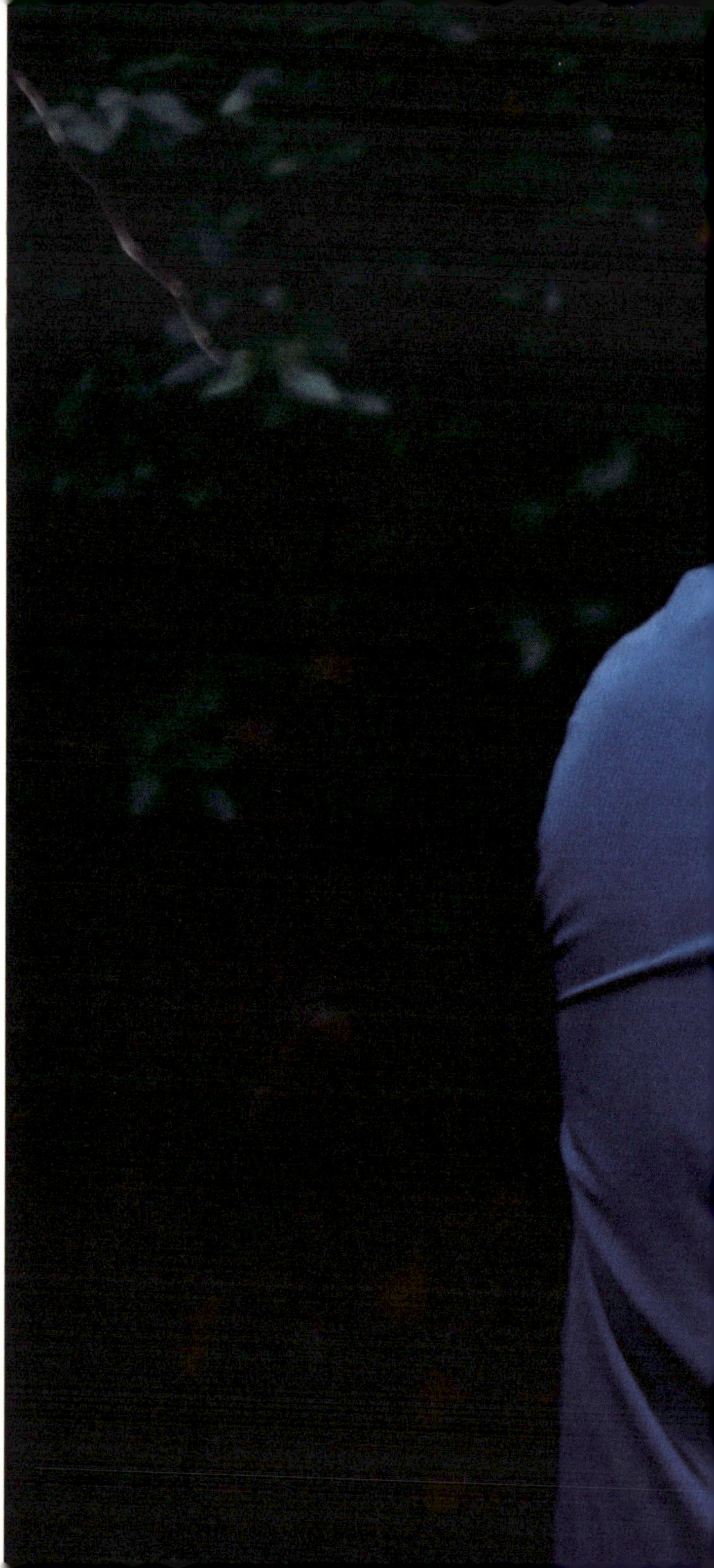

"I was inspired by a piece by
Marina Abramović. It seemed
to me that hugging a tree
with a photo of someone you
weren't able to hug due to
lockdown, might be the next
best thing."

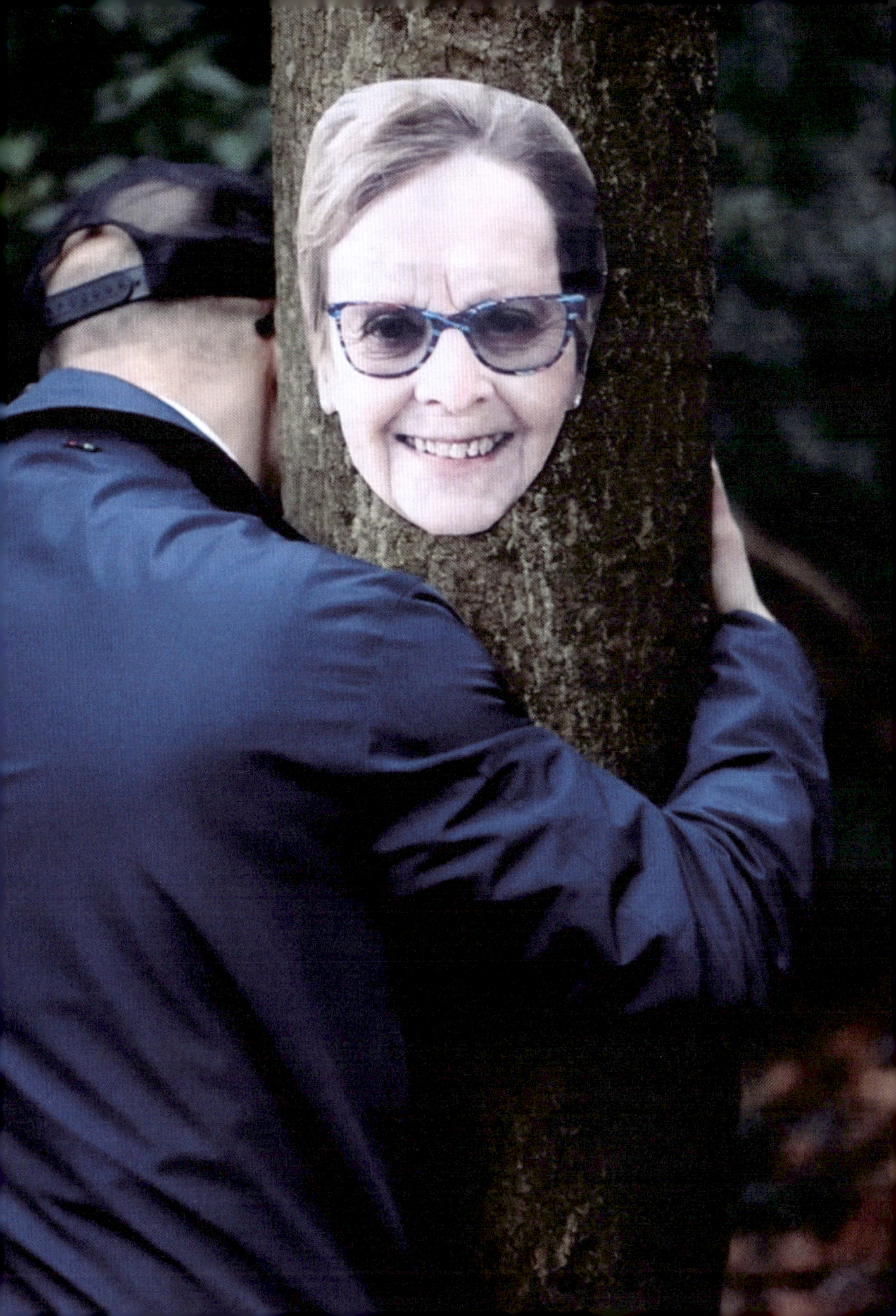

Dad's Children

Julie Bennett

Pencil on paper
Courtesy of the artist

"I was four when my Dad died.
40 years after his death, I met
one of my Dad's two sons.
I knew of their existence
but didn't know where they
lived. Out of the blue one of
them contacted me. I wanted
to explore how much of my
Daddy I would rediscover in
these men. I have spent my
life looking at photos of my
dad. Looking intensely at our
three faces for this drawing
helped me get to know our
dad better."

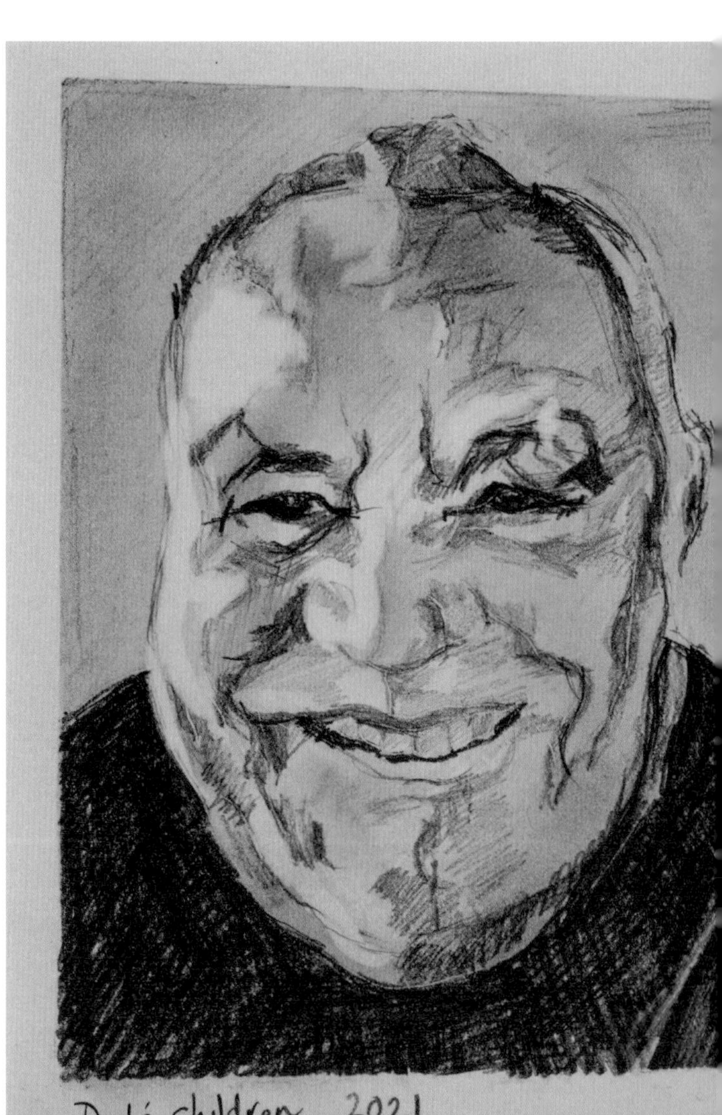

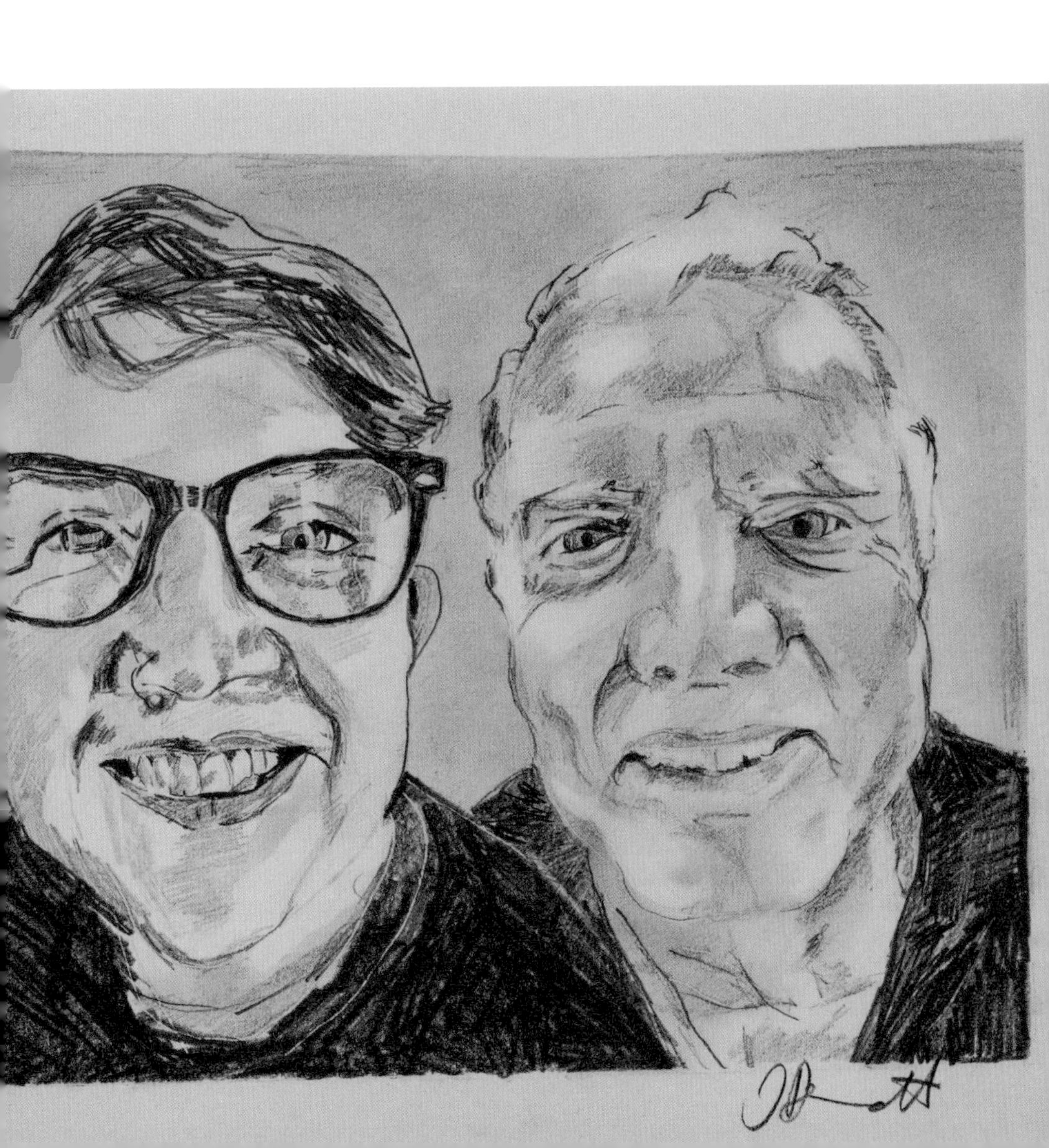

The Smells of My Family

Suzanne Bull MBE

Mixed media: glass jars,
paper, fabric
Courtesy of the artist

"I was shielding during the
pandemic and unable to
see my family. As well as
being disabled, I was also
diagnosed with breast cancer
when the UK shut down.
I asked my family members
what their favourite smell
was. I pretended to 'bottle up'
each smell for a permanent
reminder of them whilst we
were apart. Making art is a
huge part of my life and I'm
glad something great came
out of a bad situation."

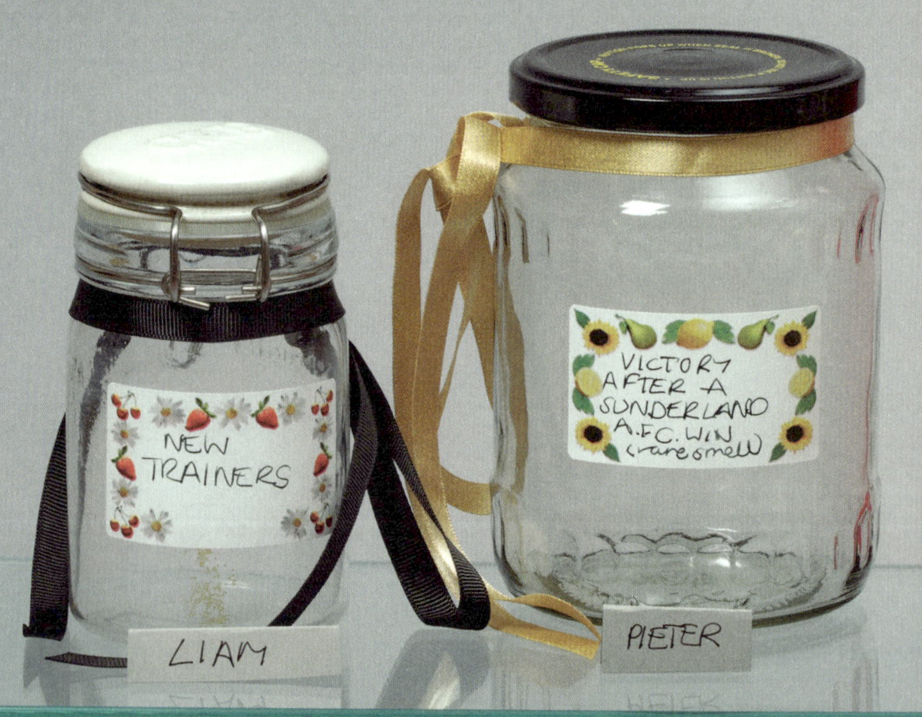

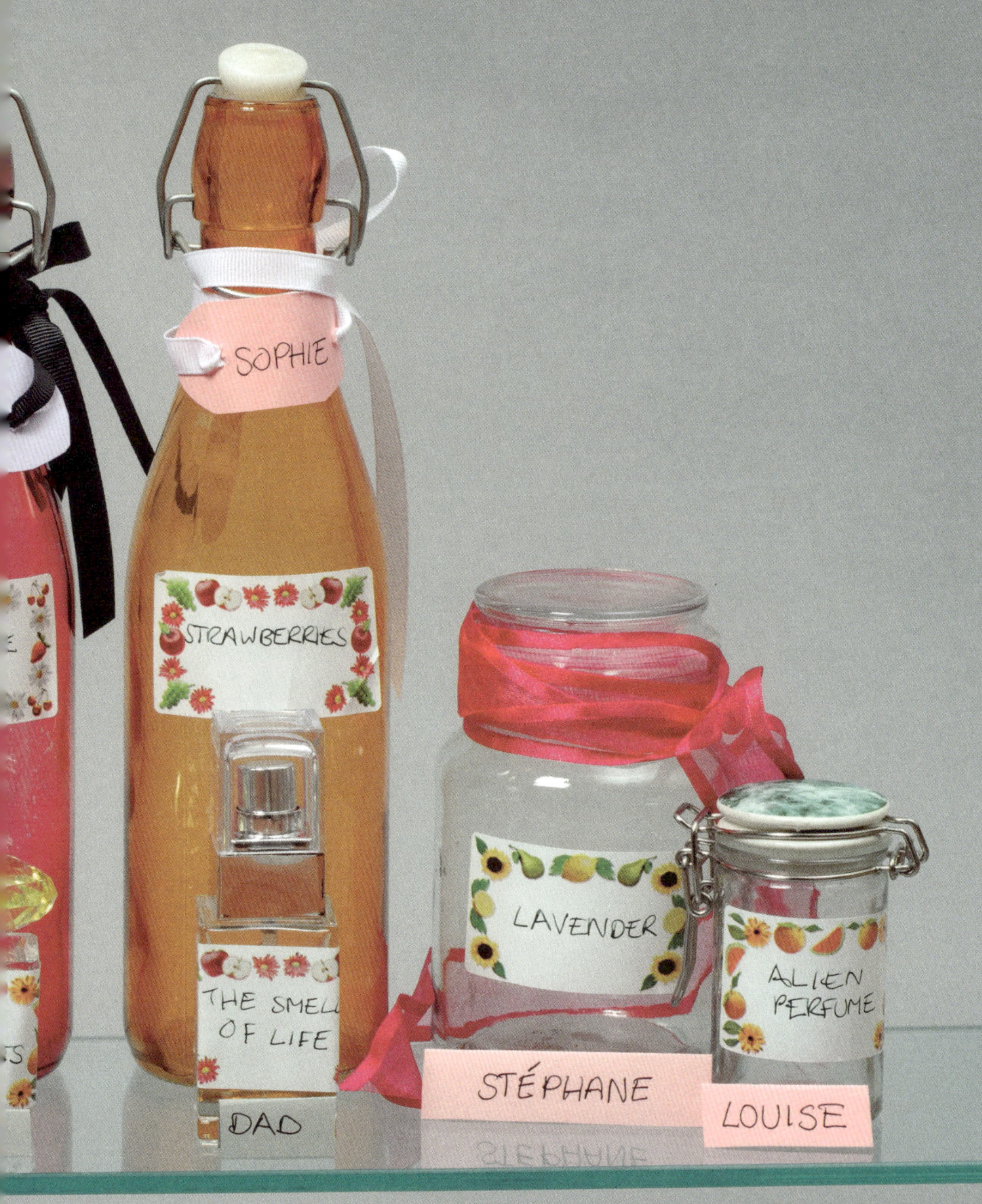
SOPHIE
STRAWBERRIES
THE SMELL OF LIFE
DAD
LAVENDER
STÉPHANE
ALIEN PERFUME
LOUISE

The Family

Boy George

Acrylic paint, beads, thread
and sequins on canvas
Courtesy of the artist

"You've got your family family
and then you've got your
disco family. When I got on
the train to the West End my
world became more colourful
and more bohemian. I'd
never been anywhere really
glamorous. We'd never
eaten prawns or courgettes.
We were quite a basic family.

This is the family that
I've created. My nightclub
family. My fake family.
My fellow weirdos.
My fellow exhibitionists."

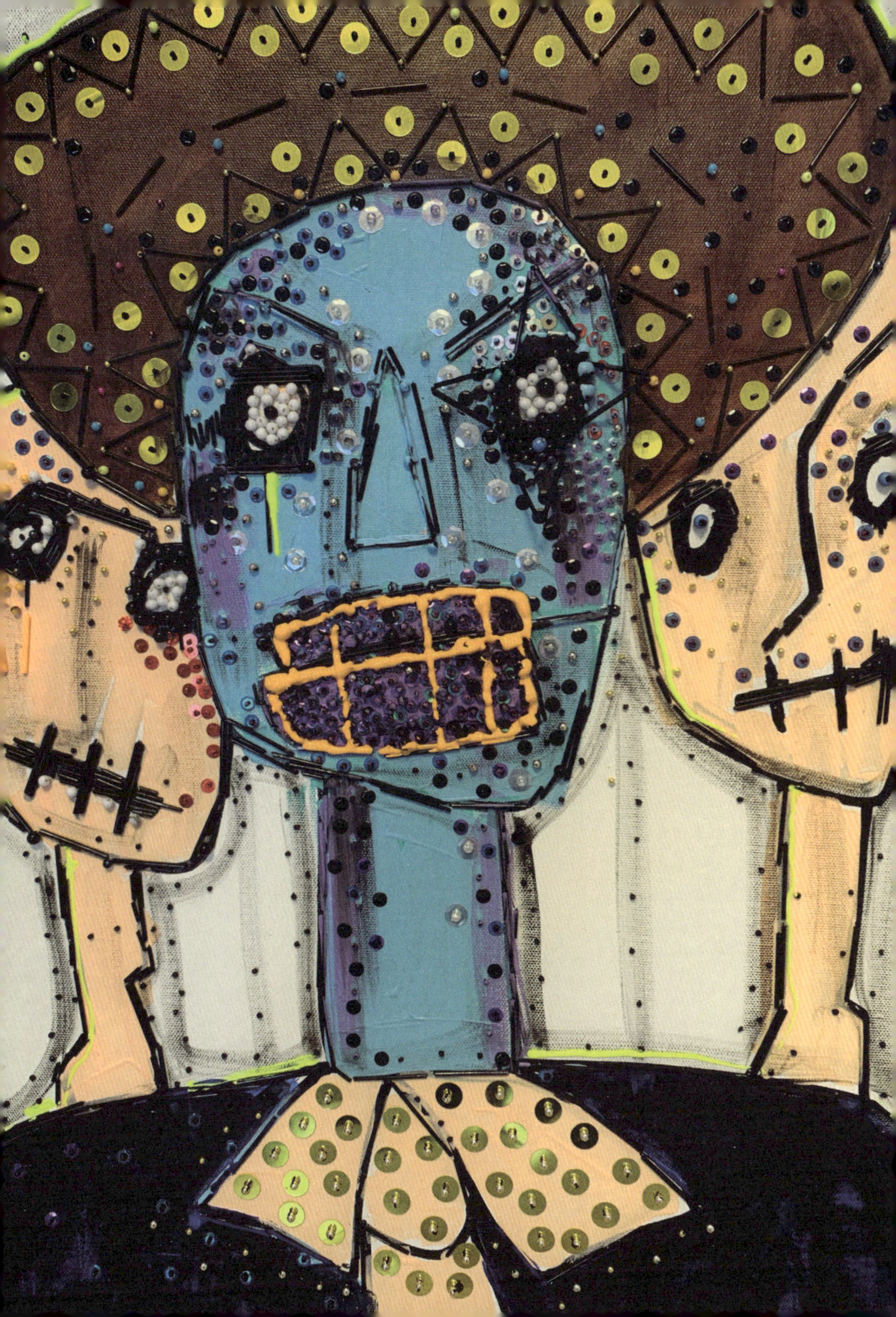

Family

Cian McLoughlin

Oil paint on canvas
Courtesy of the artist

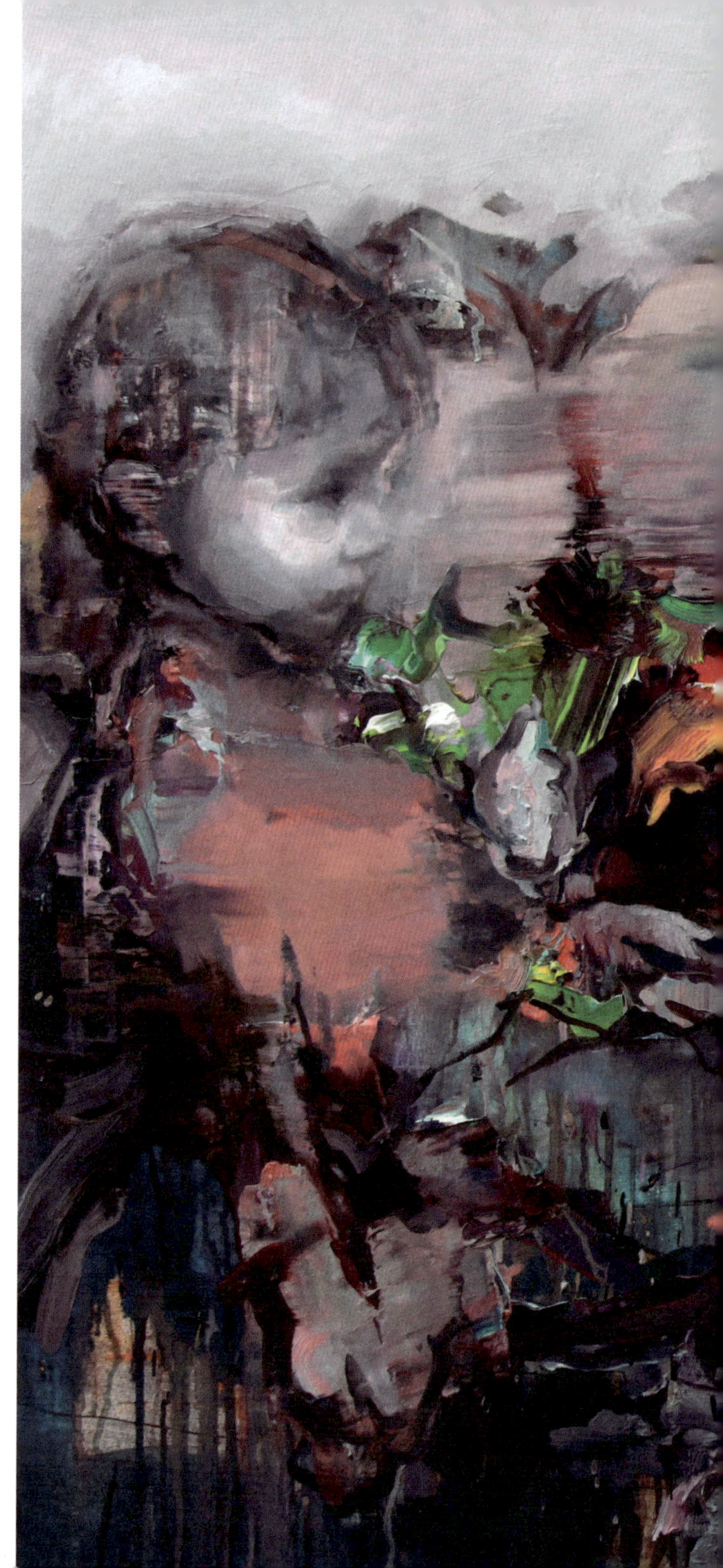

"I made this to mark the birth
of our second son, Culann.
The mother and two sons
are painted in a tight group,
each figure running into the
next. Individual, but a unit
at the same time.

During *Art Club,* Grayson and
Boy George correctly assessed
that there was a suggestion
of a delicate dynamic between
the brothers. Despite the
gentle rivalry at the outset,
I'm glad to report that the
boys get along brilliant."

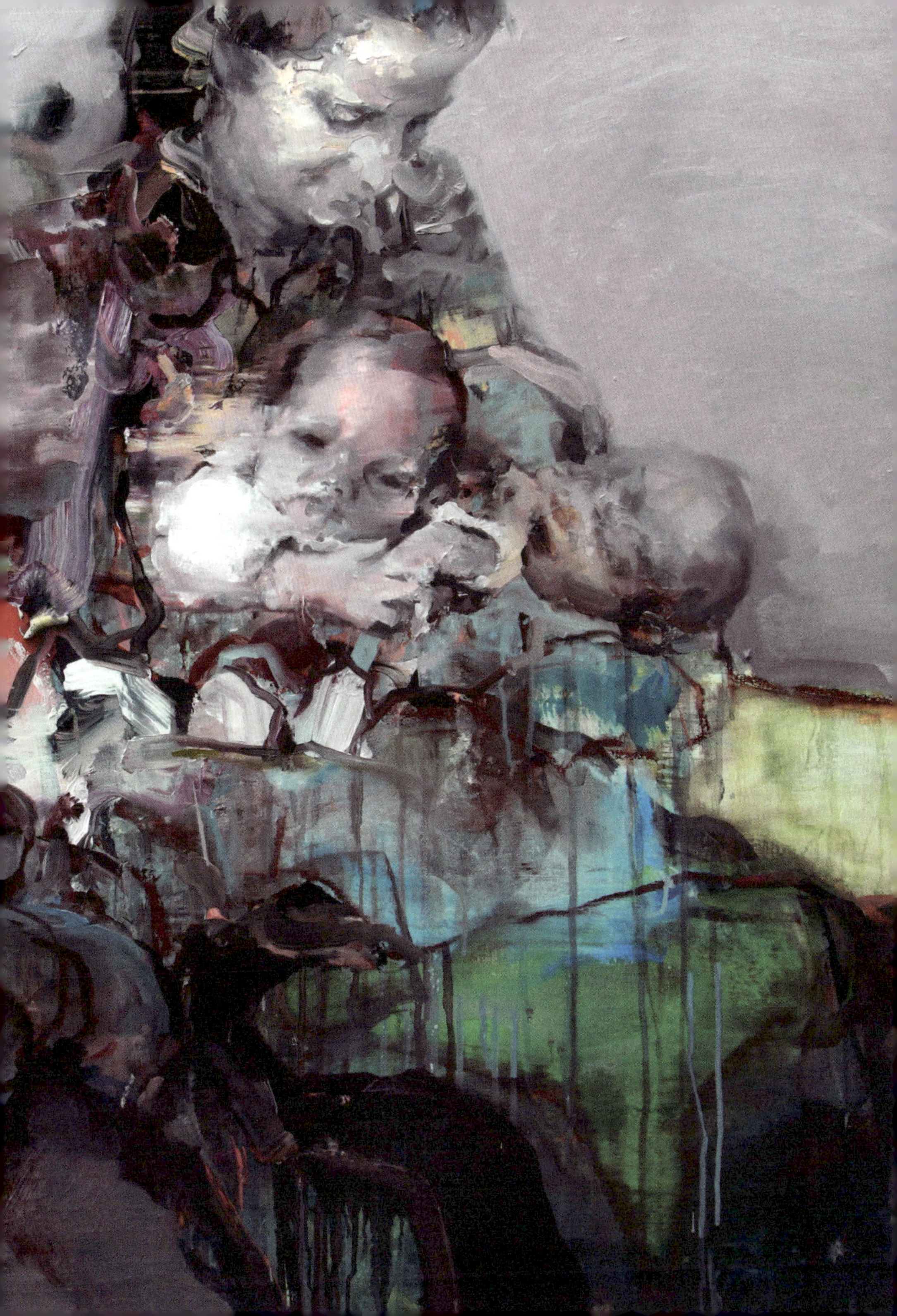

Helping Hand, part of
'If Chairs Could Talk'
2015

Yinka Ilori MBE

Wooden chair with painted
decoration by the artist
Courtesy of the artist

"There's so much beauty in
everyday objects. Especially
chairs. We sit on a chair,
we cry, we argue, we laugh.
These are objects that we
trust to hold our feelings
or emotions.

Being raised by Nigerian
parents, colour was a huge
part of my life. It's very
evident in my work. With
Nigerian cultures, families
always wear the same colour
and pattern. Fabric can give
you an identity. Colour gives
you a sense of pride and a
sense of belonging."

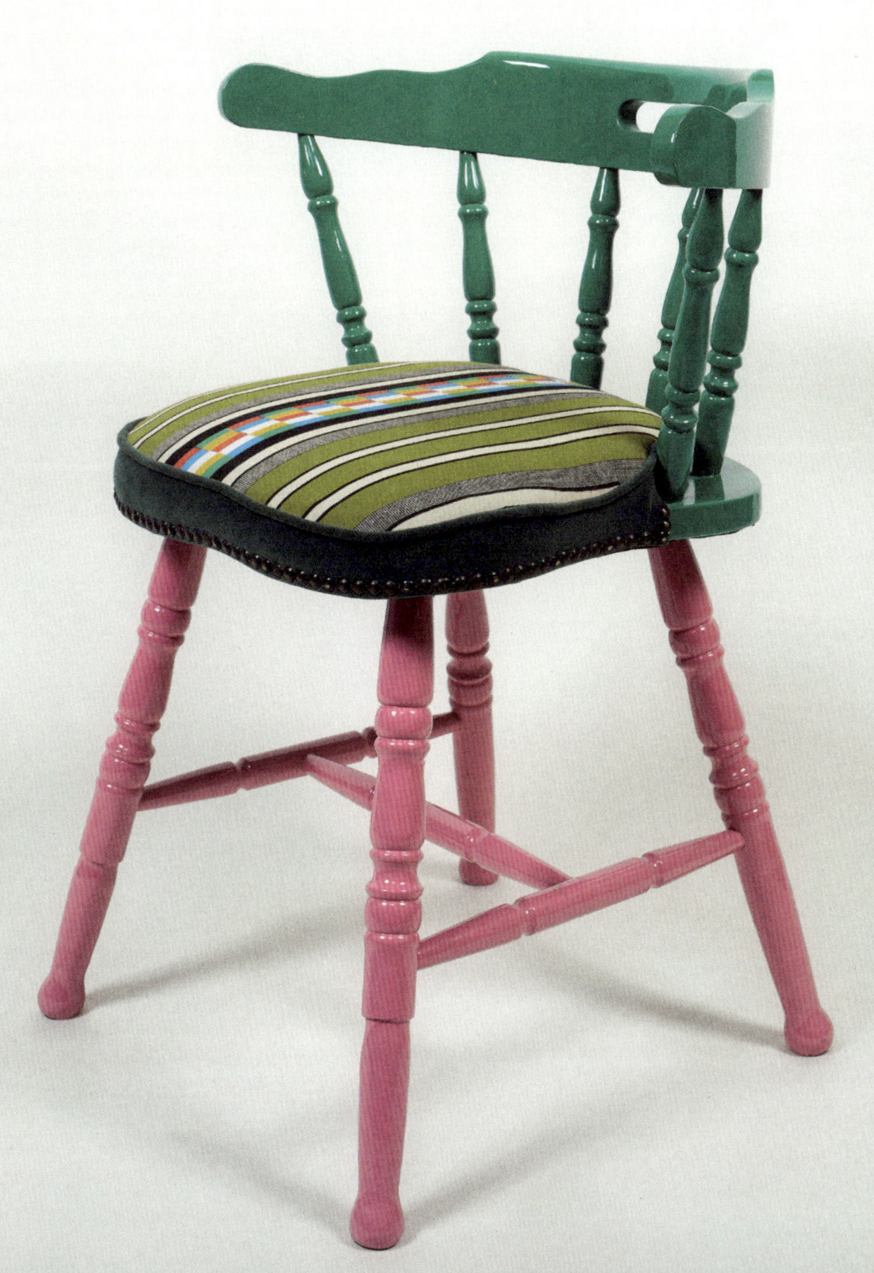

Unlikely Family

Zoë Pyne

Acrylic paint on canvas board
Courtesy of the artist

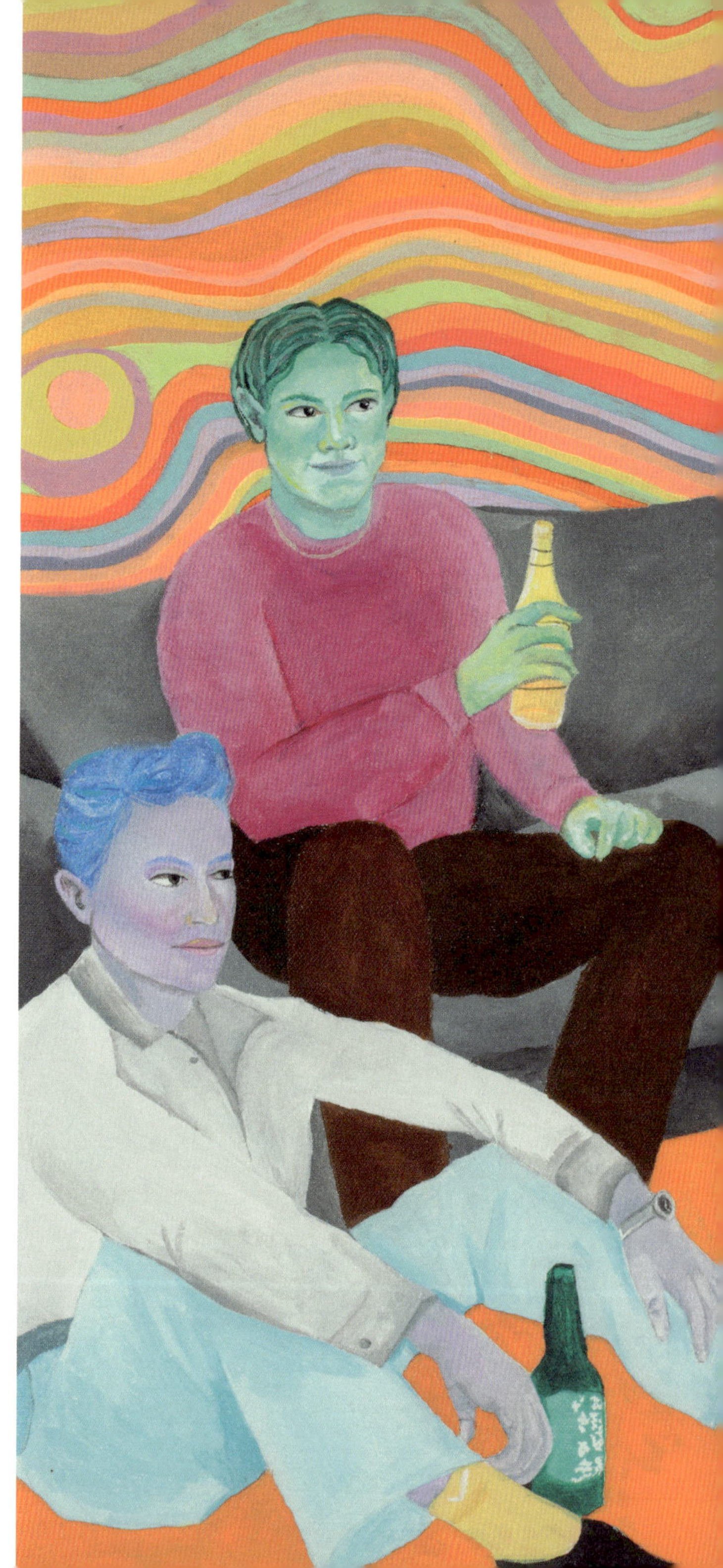

"At university, you might
live with complete strangers.
It's an eye-opening life
experience. You create an
instant alternative family.
My painting represents
the warmth and happiness
finding this family can give.
I've included elements from
a typical student house.
Tally charts on who puked
last night, people arguing
about who's turn it is to
take out the bins and
deep conversations on the
meaning of life. The bright
and vibrant colours represent
different backgrounds and
cultures of this family."

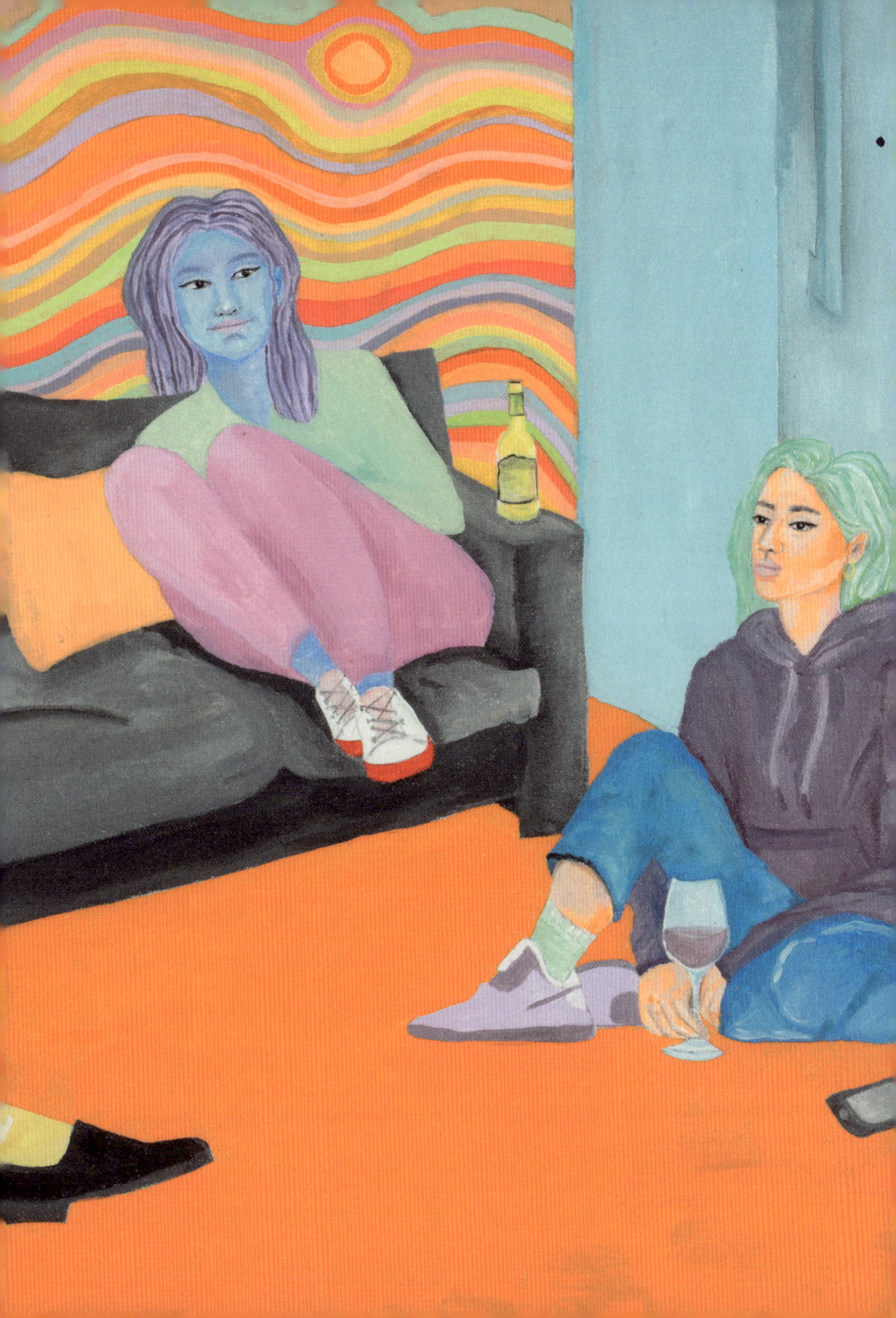

Ode to Phil Mitchell

Harry Rose

Acrylic paint on canvas
Courtesy of the artist

"When thinking of family,
 Phil Mitchell stood out to me.
 My own family kept shouting
'HE'S FAMILY' in their best
 Phil Mitchell impression.
 Phil has a gay son in the show
 and I wanted him to become
 the embodiment of misplaced
 anger towards the LGBTQIA+
 community. I am an openly
 queer man. My late father
 was accepting of my
 sexuality. My painting shows
 acceptance as well as past
 generations looking down
 in anger and disgust."

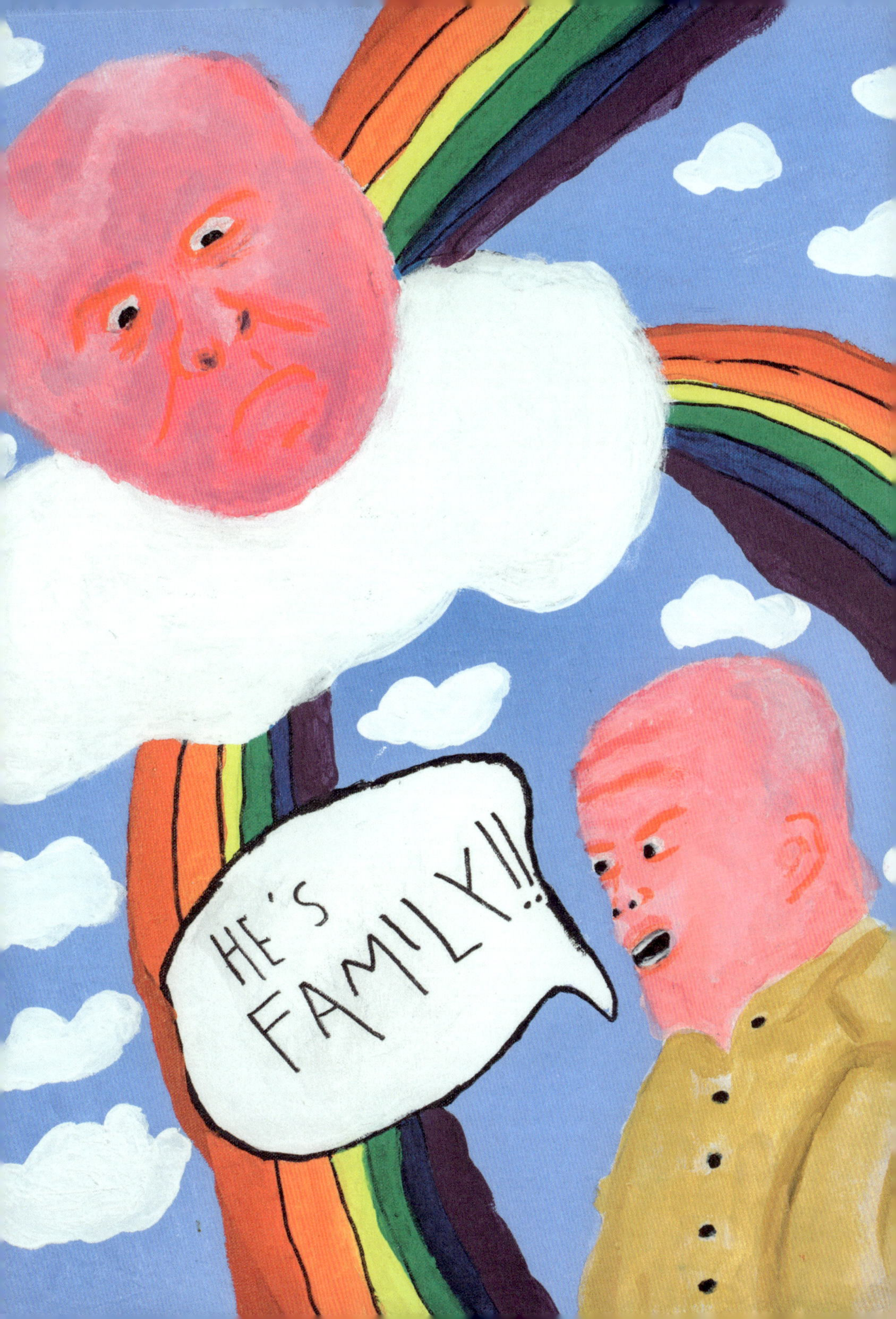
HE'S FAMILY!!!

Chagrin Sur L'herbe

Allegra Gordon

Lino print on paper
Courtesy of the artist

"This was inspired by
childhood summers at my
grandparents' home in
France. It depicts myself,
my brother and my parents.
My Dad died in 2012 and my
work has been influenced
by this. Grief, memory and
nostalgia are all themes
that appear in my prints.
Using my work to explore
these experiences has been
extremely cathartic. During
lockdown I found the lack
of routine difficult. Drawing
and printmaking gave me
a sense of structure but
allowed me to get lost in
my own fantasy world."

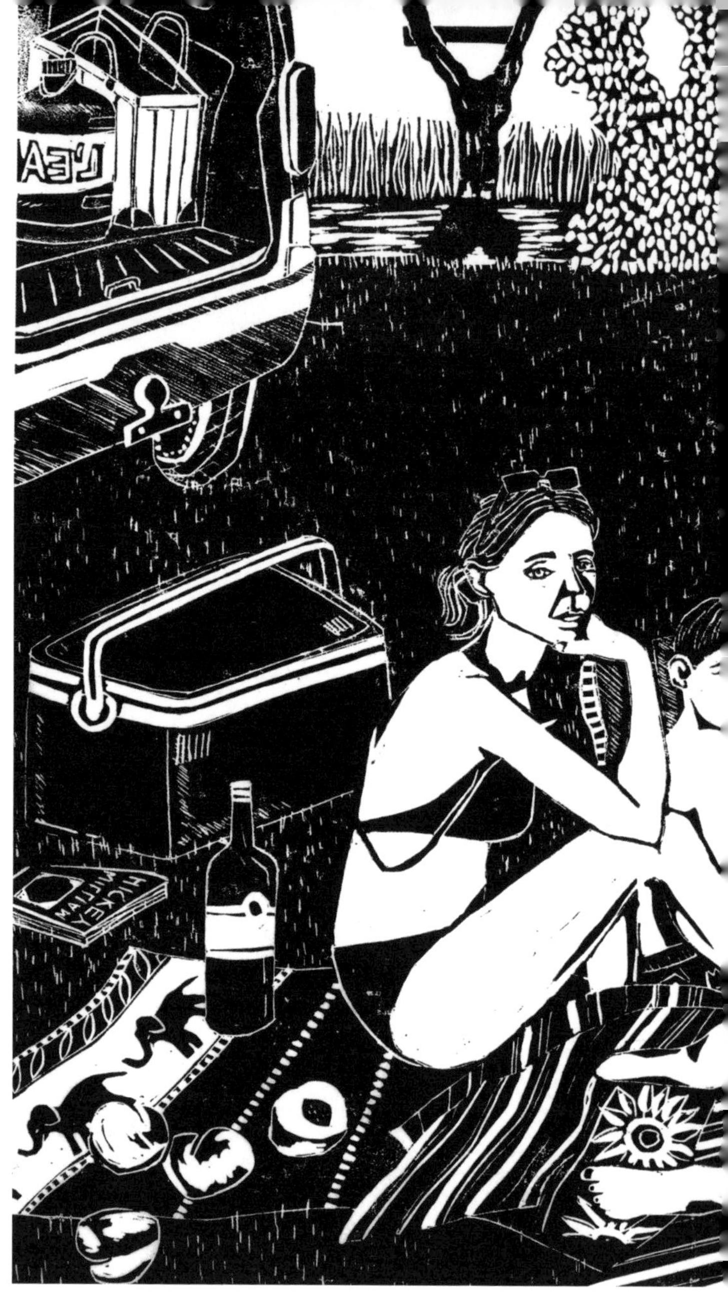

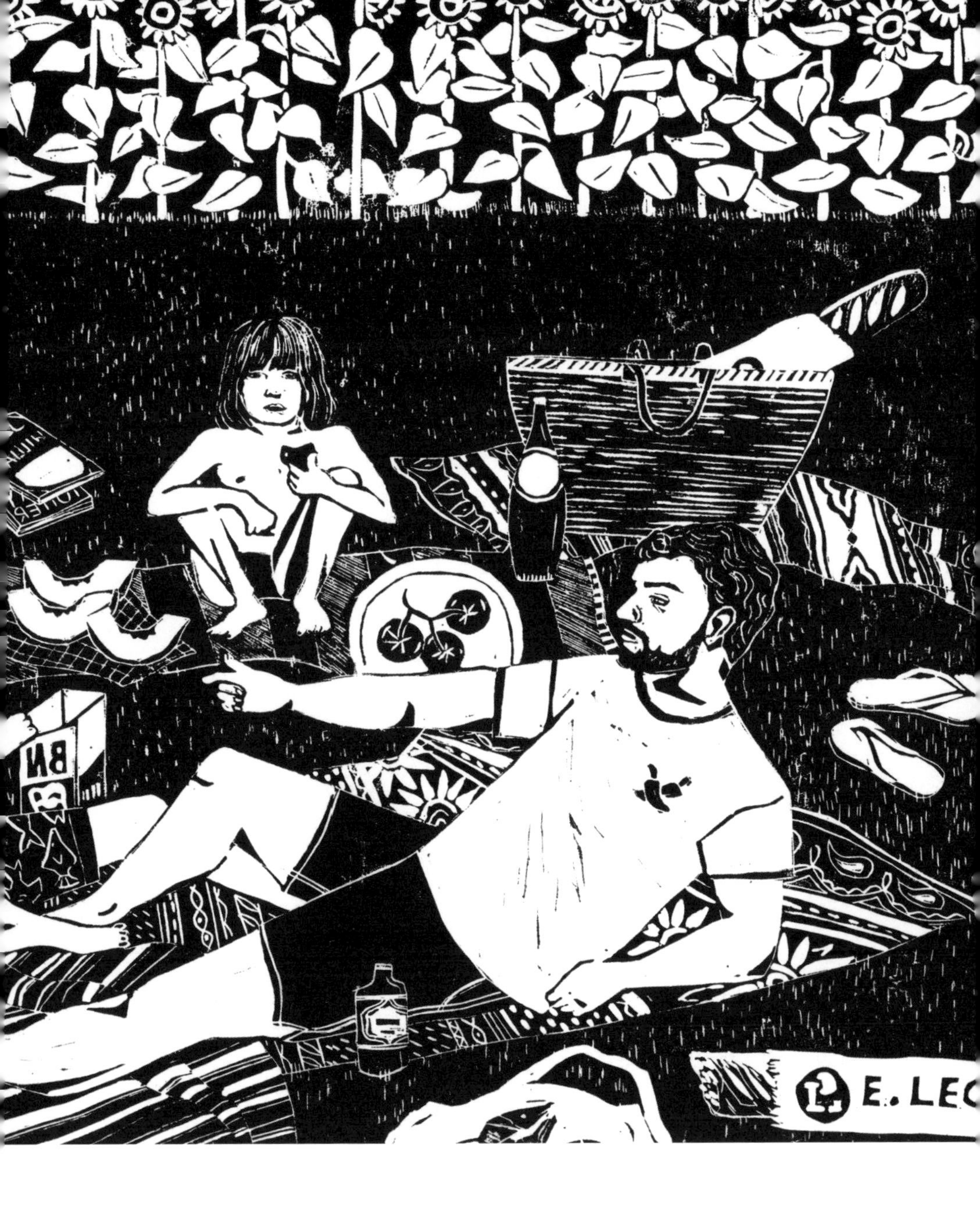
E. LEC

The Covid Captive

Andy Jeffrey

Acrylic paint on paper
Courtesy of the artist

"I was inspired by how well my
mother-in-law coped during
the first lockdown. Several
of her friends passed away
during this period. Being
unable to pay her respects
was incredibly distressing.
This painting shows her
looking longingly out of the
window with her 'essentials'
of life during that bleak time."

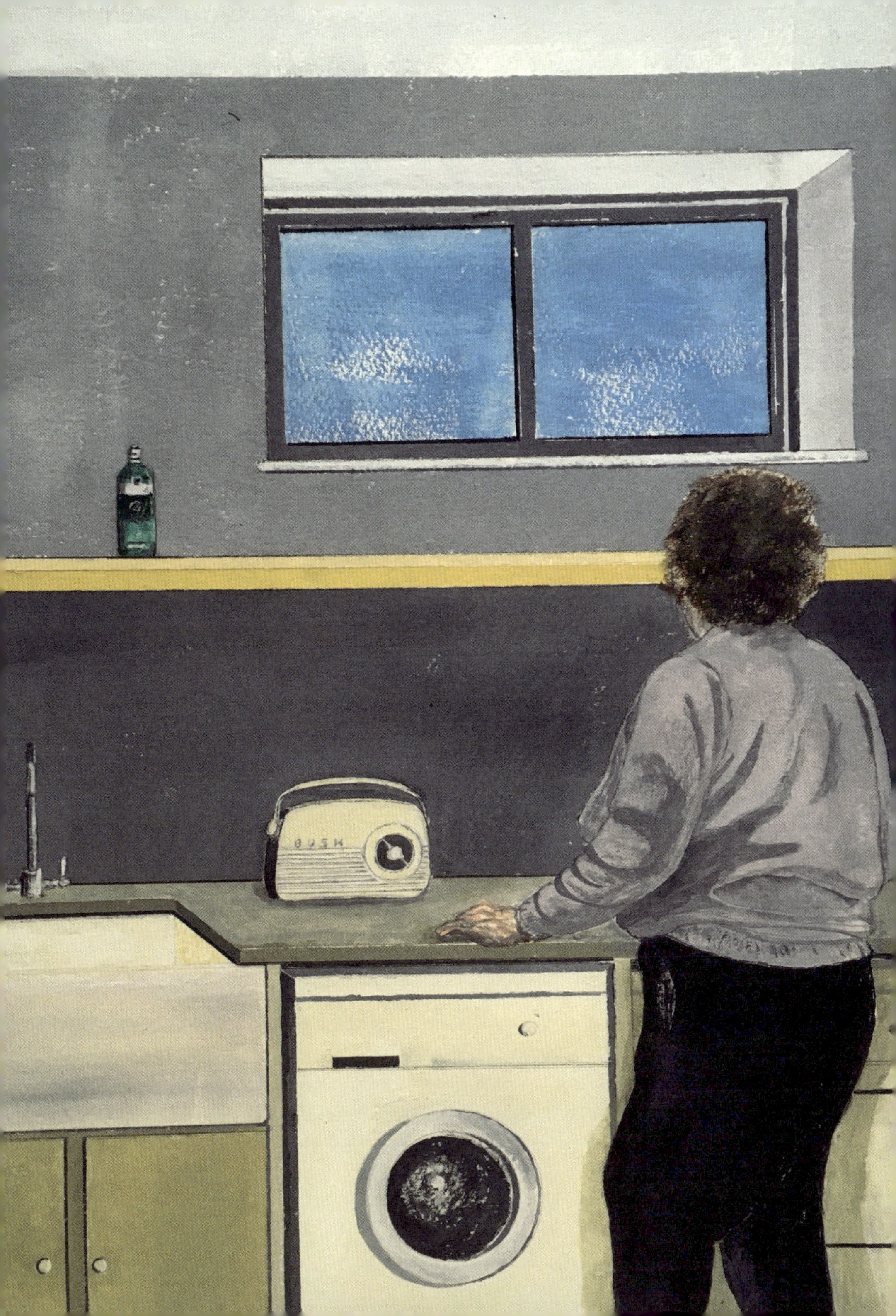

BUSH

JOKE ALPHABET

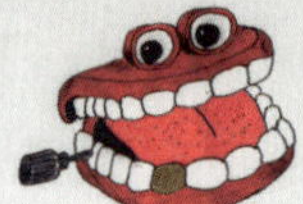
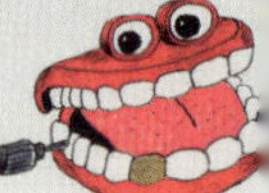

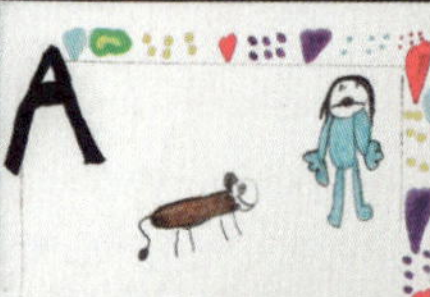

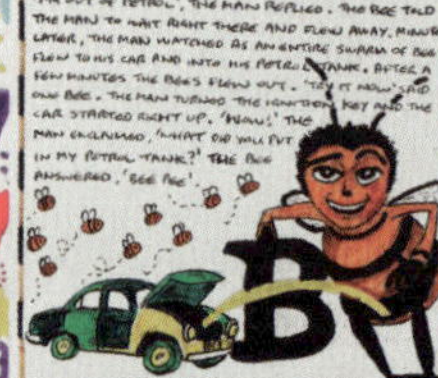

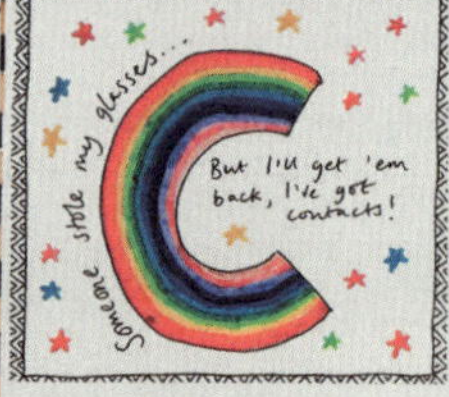

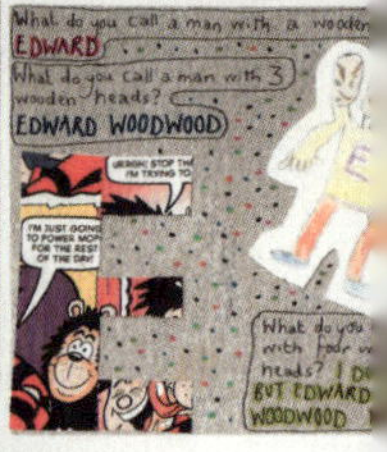

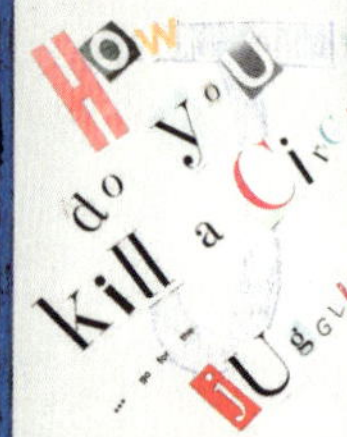

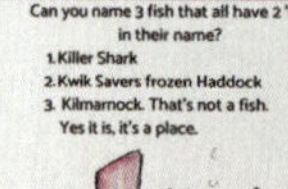
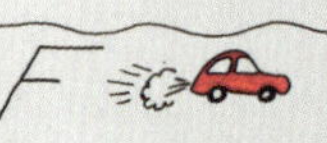

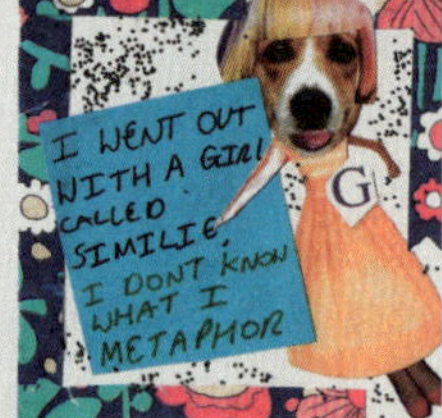

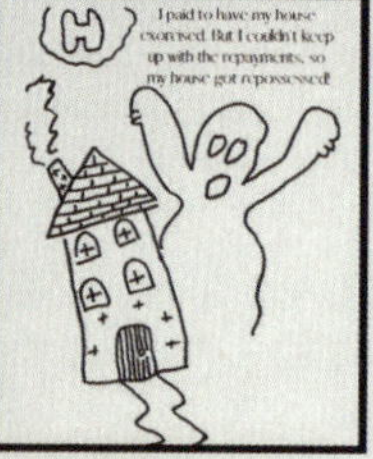

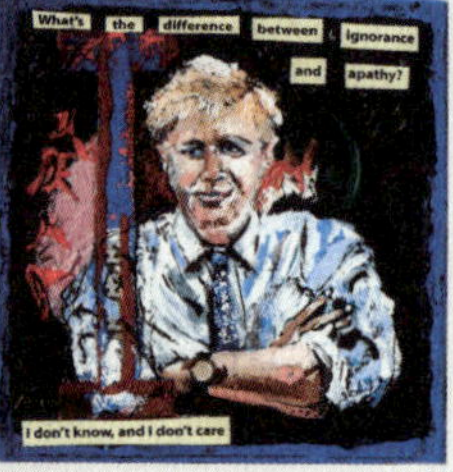

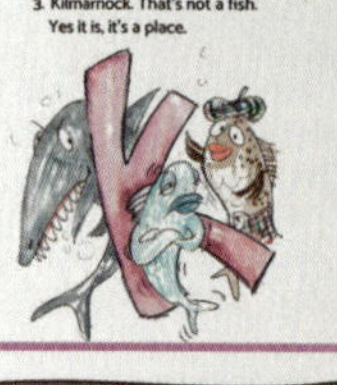
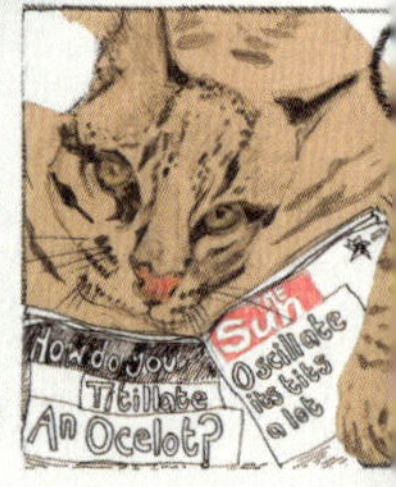

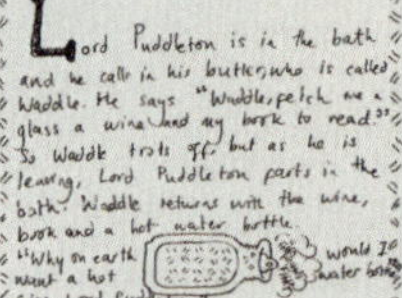
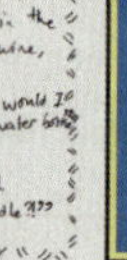

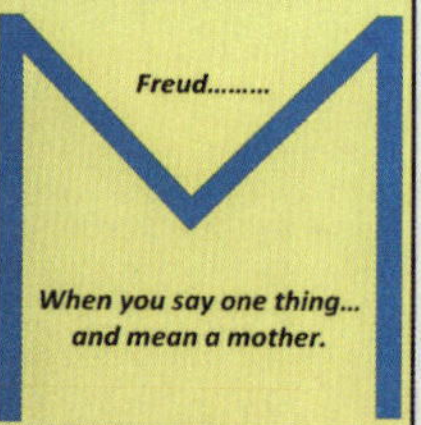

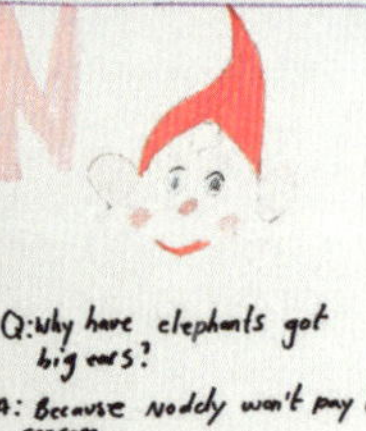

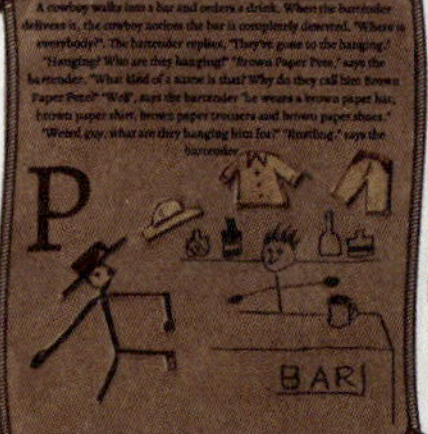

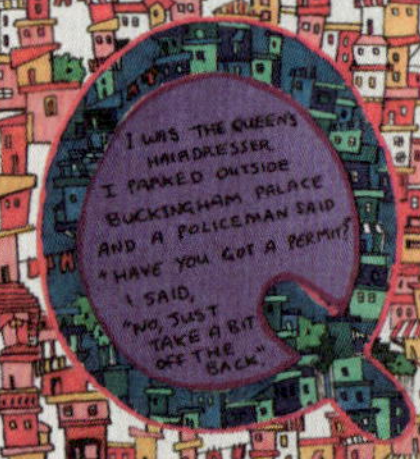

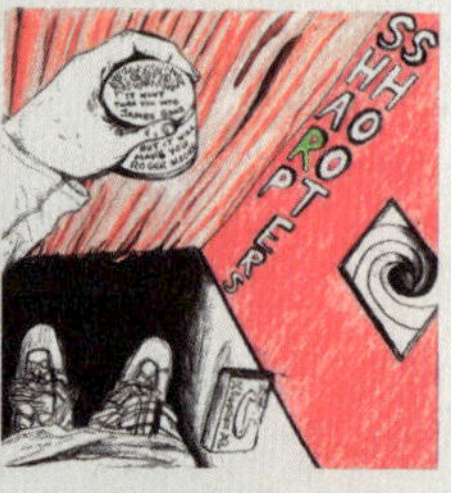

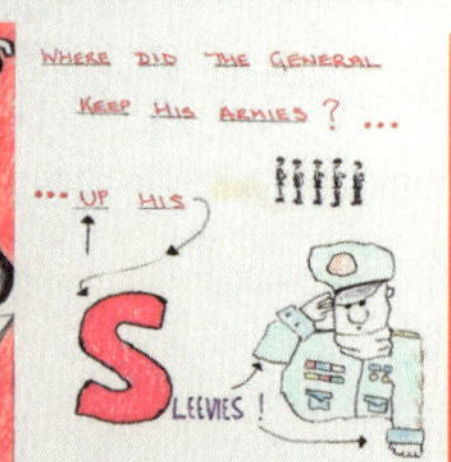

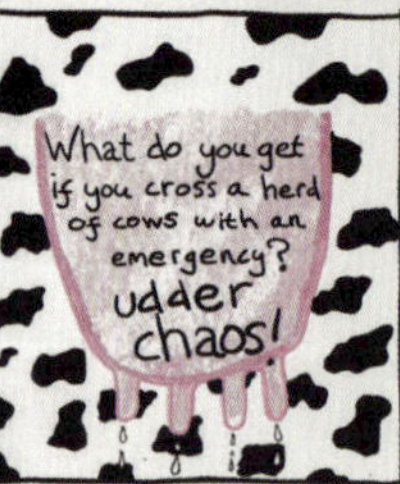

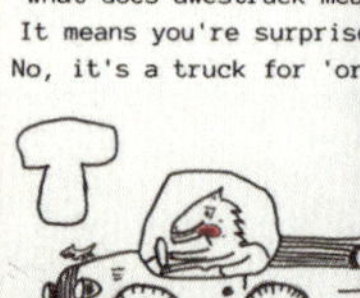

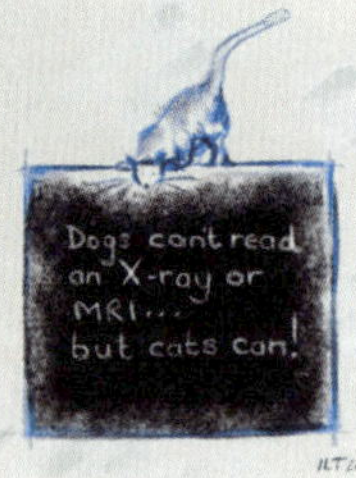

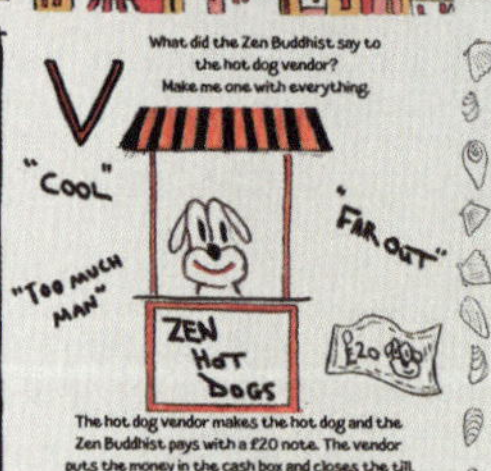

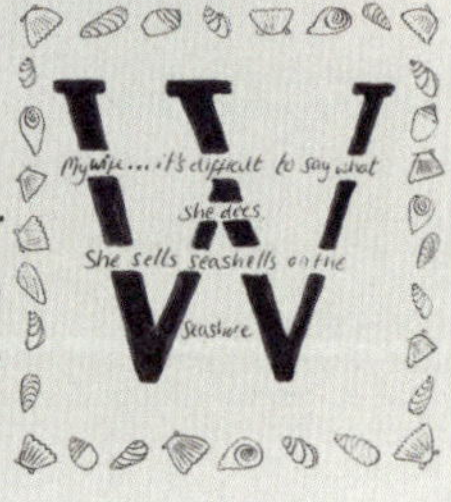

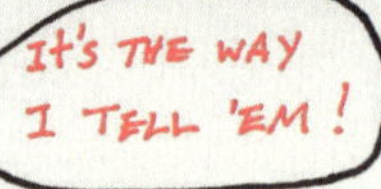

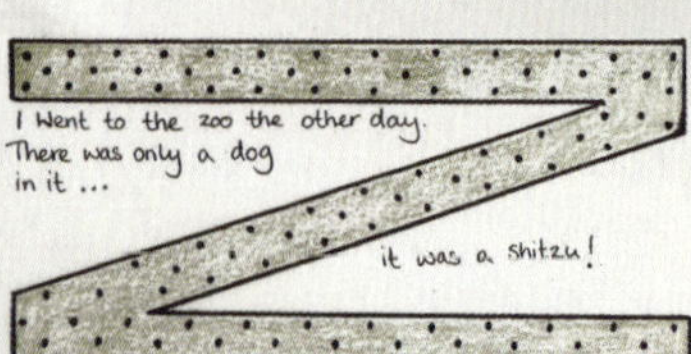

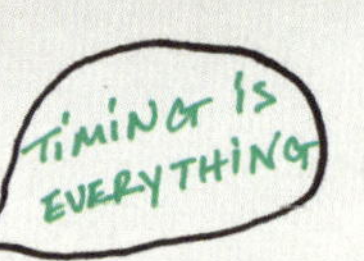

AS TOLD BY TOMMY THE POLE WITH ILLUSTRATIONS BY FAMILY & FRIENDS

Chloë
Häuchen-Garner

Tom &
Häuchen

"My dad loved life. He brought humour into everything he did. He was famous for knowing a joke for every letter of the alphabet.

My dad had lived with cancer for twelve years and had gone through a lot of pain. Last year, his health was deteriorating. I started to think about losing him. The thought of the void he would leave was unbearable. I had the idea to capture his spirit on a Joke Alphabet poster. It felt like I was preparing myself for what lay ahead.

Me and my dad went through his collection of jokes and picked out our favourites. I sent family and friends a 'joke pack' containing a piece of card, a letter of the alphabet and a joke. I asked them to create a piece of artwork in any way they chose. Me and my dad felt very supported and loved through this. Although we couldn't talk about death verbally we could through this. The following months were full of wonderful moments as the 'joke alphabet letters' arrived on my door mat.

My dad sadly passed away on 1st November 2020. But his spirit lives on in the Joke Alphabet! I feel a profound connection to my dad when looking at my dad's artwork and the marks that he made, experiencing the interconnectedness of life and death."

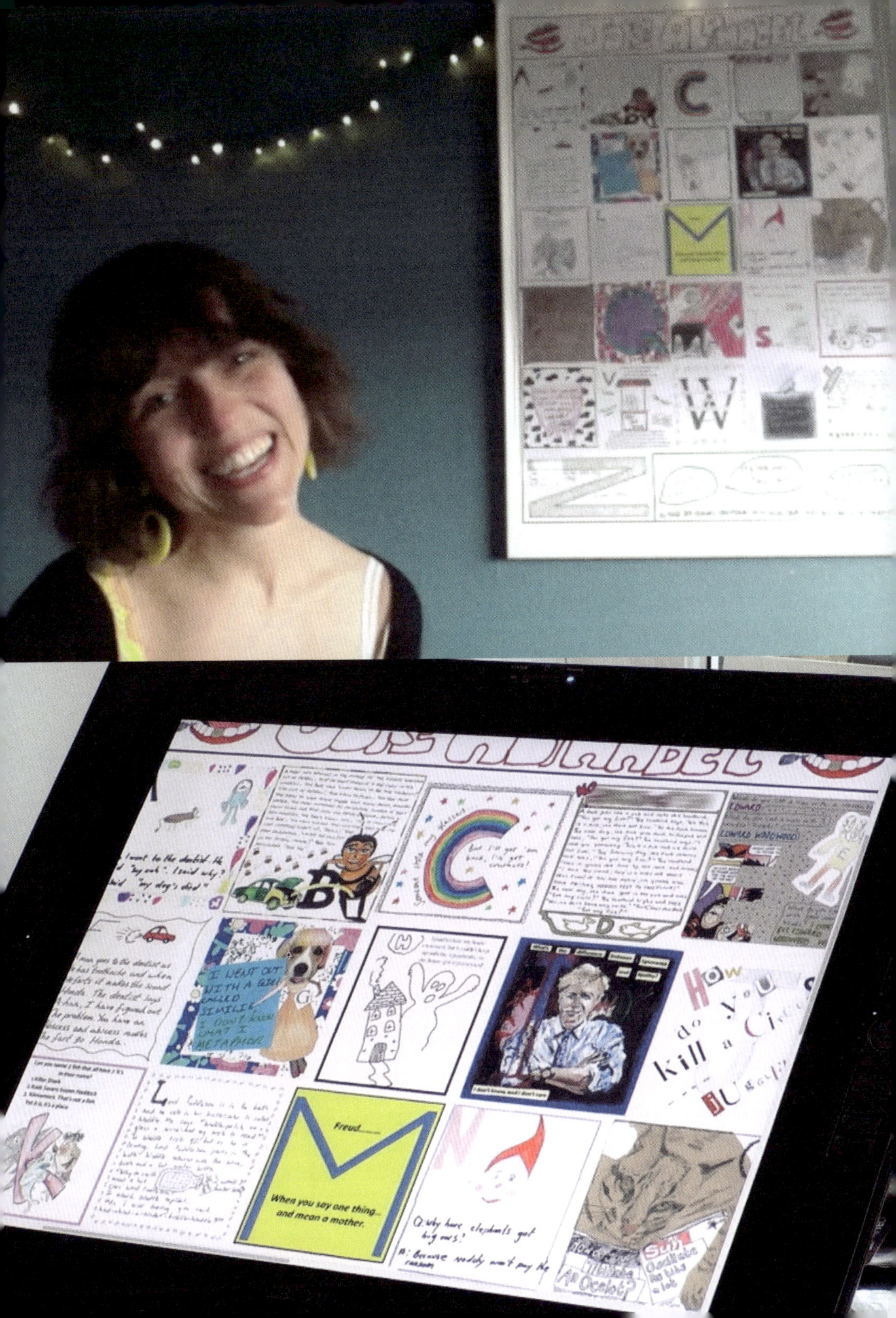

Family is Community

Anneka Rice

Watercolour on paper
Courtesy of the artist

"The word family is so
loaded for me. I grew up
not knowing grandparents,
uncles, aunts, cousins. Both
my parents were secretive
about their backgrounds.
It's left me with such a sense
of yearning. Throughout my
life I've created these tribes
of people. I thought I'd do a
frieze of some significant parts
of my life. It's been like 60
years of therapy! I realised my
family was about community
and people that I love."

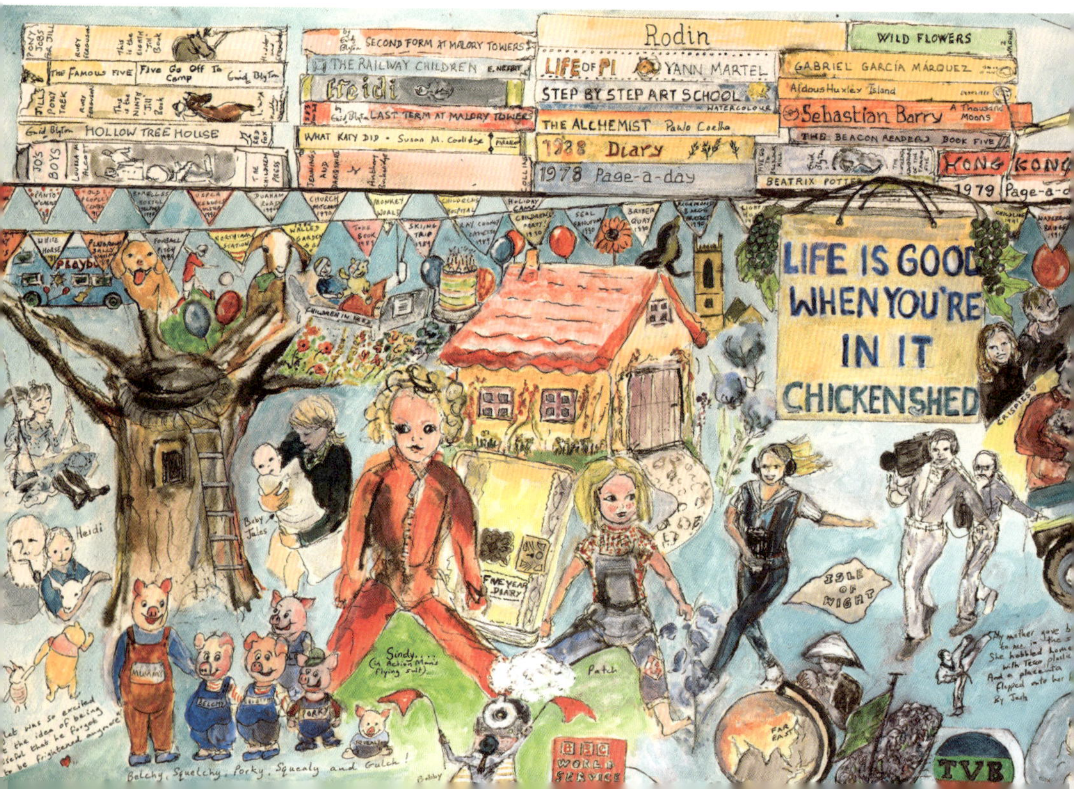

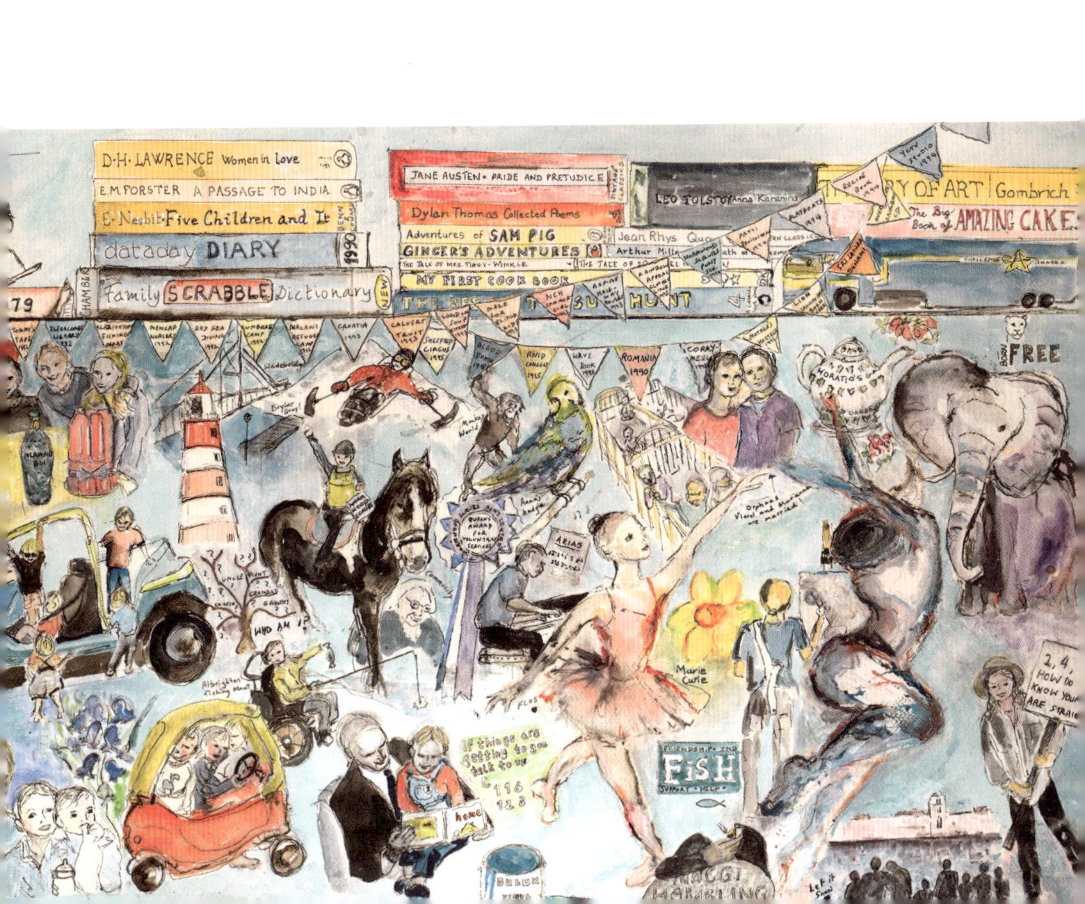

D·H·LAWRENCE Women in Love
E.M.FORSTER A PASSAGE TO INDIA
E. Nesbit Five Children and It
dataday DIARY
Family SCRABBLE Dictionary
JANE AUSTEN PRIDE AND PREJUDICE
Dylan Thomas Collected Poems
Adventures of SAM PIG
GINGER'S ADVENTURES
THE TALE OF MRS. TIGGY-WINKLE
MY FIRST COOK BOOK
LEO TOLSTOY Anna Karenina
Jean Rhys
Arthur Miller
THE TALE OF
STORY OF ART Gombrich
The Big Book of AMAZING CAKES
BORN FREE
WHO AM I?
Marie Curie
FiSH
SUPPORT · HELP
ROMANIA 1990

Grayson Perry by Bailey
2020

David Bailey

Photograph
© David Bailey 2020
Kindly lent by the artist

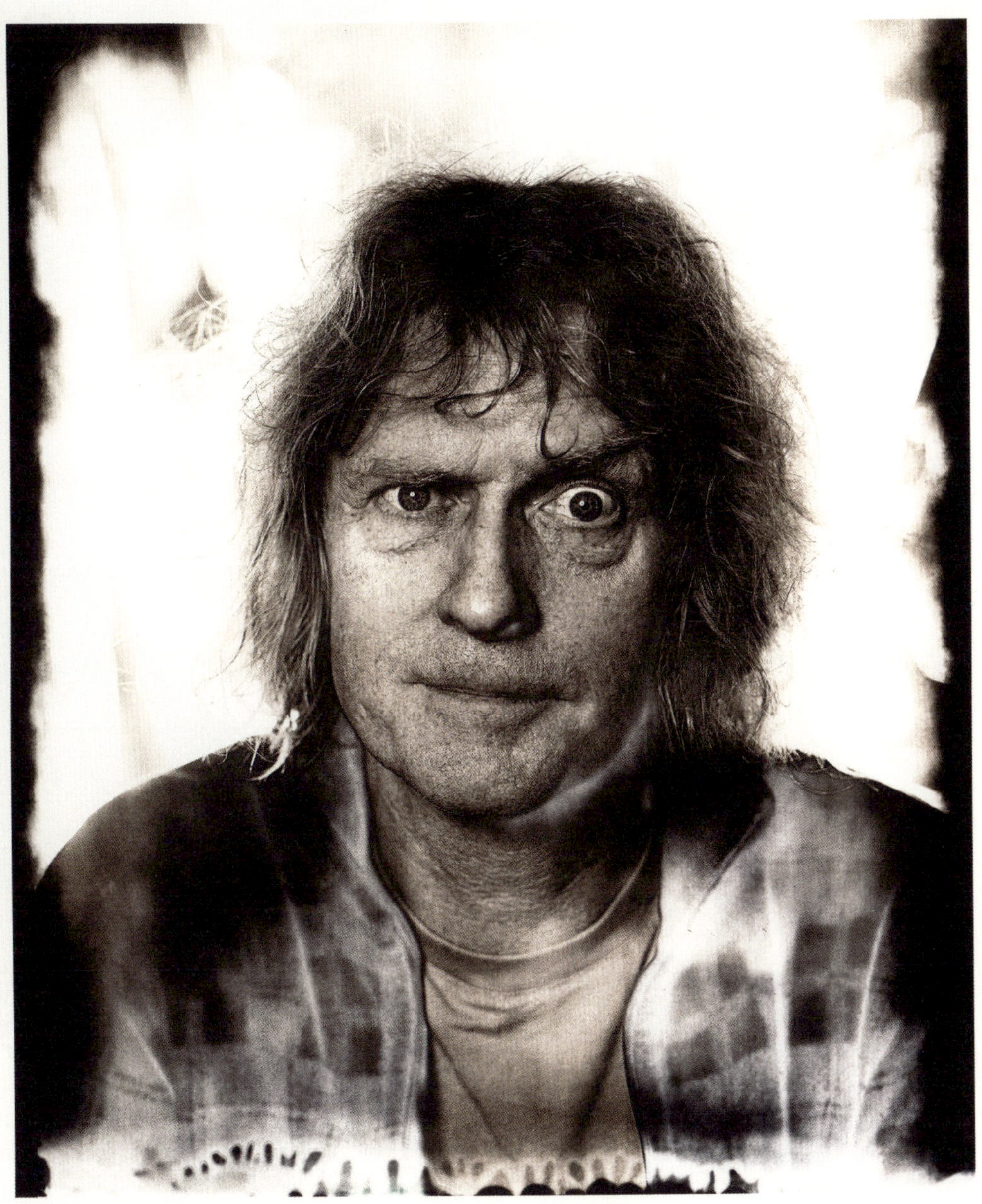

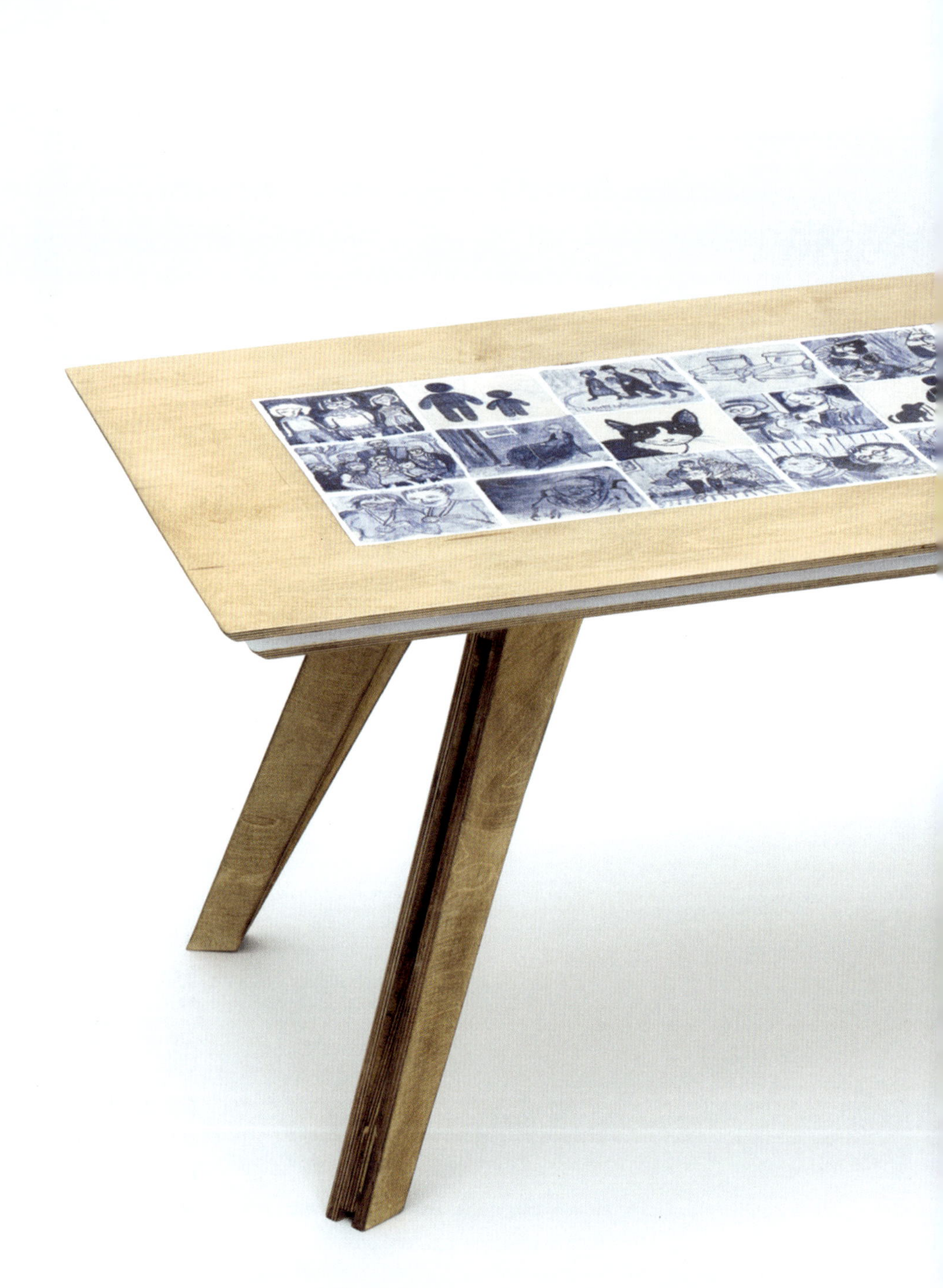

Family Table

Philippa Perry

Coffee table with glazed
ceramic tiles
Courtesy of the artist

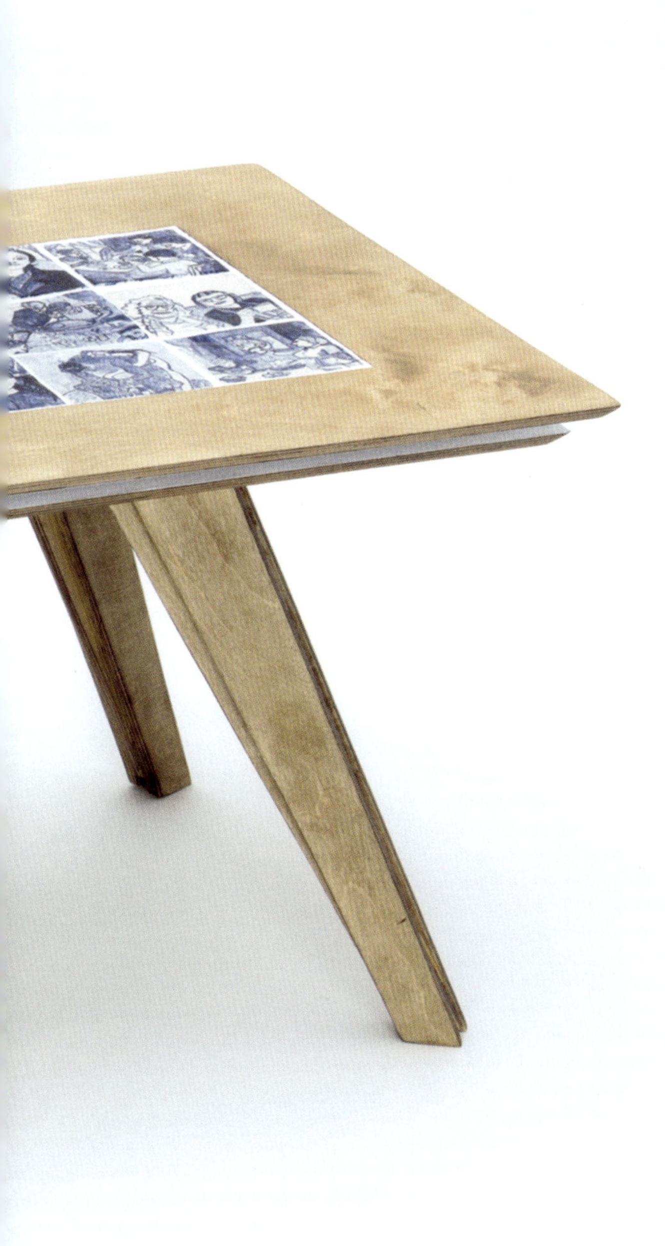

"Families are far more than
a mum and a dad and 2.4
children. They are a man and
his cat, a group of friends
living together, a lesbian
couple. I tried to represent
many different types and
different atmospheres of
family. The armchairs
represent where family
members once sat because
death is a part of family life.
Eilidh Brooker, my daughter's
partner, designed and made
the table, so I've kept it all
in the family."

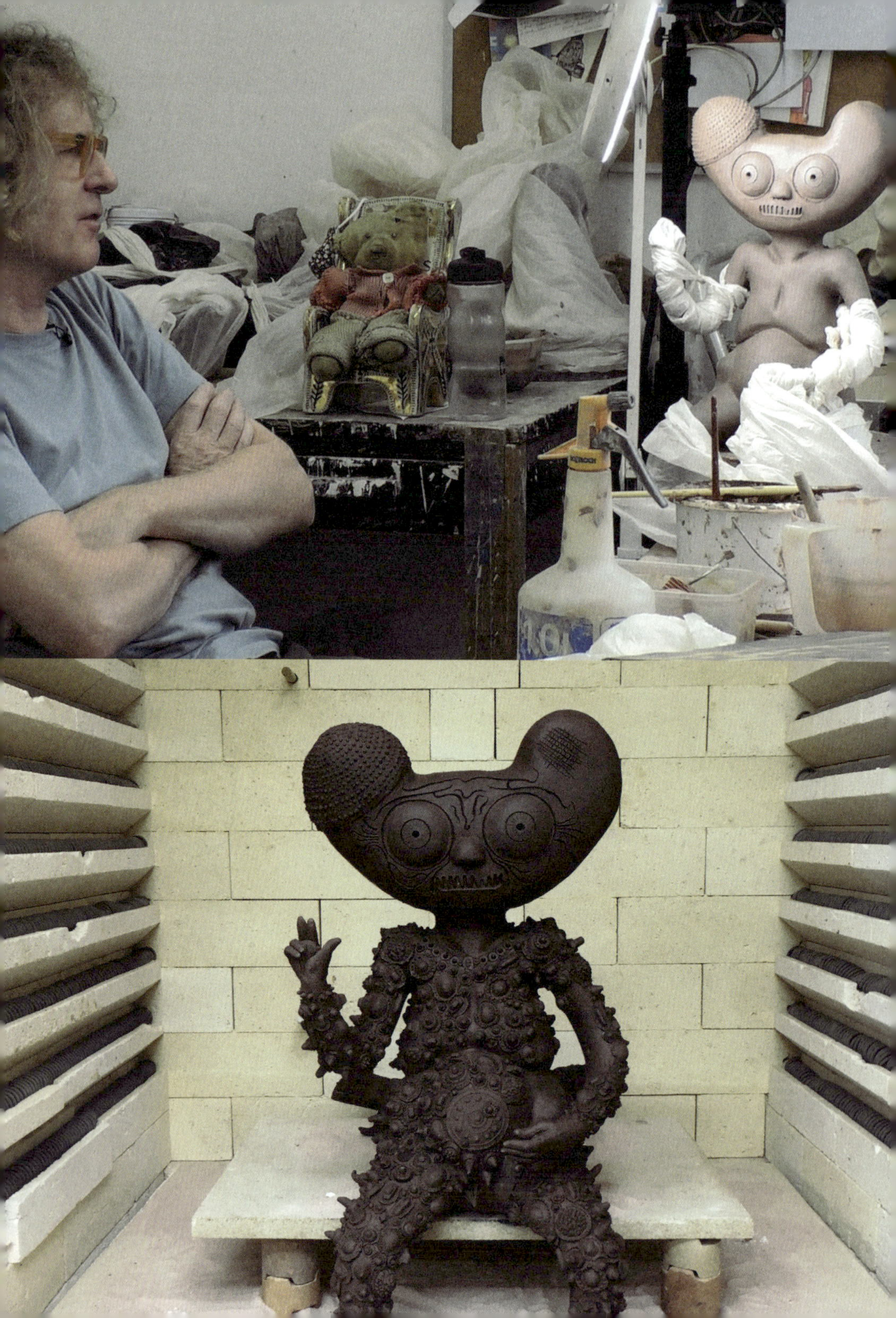

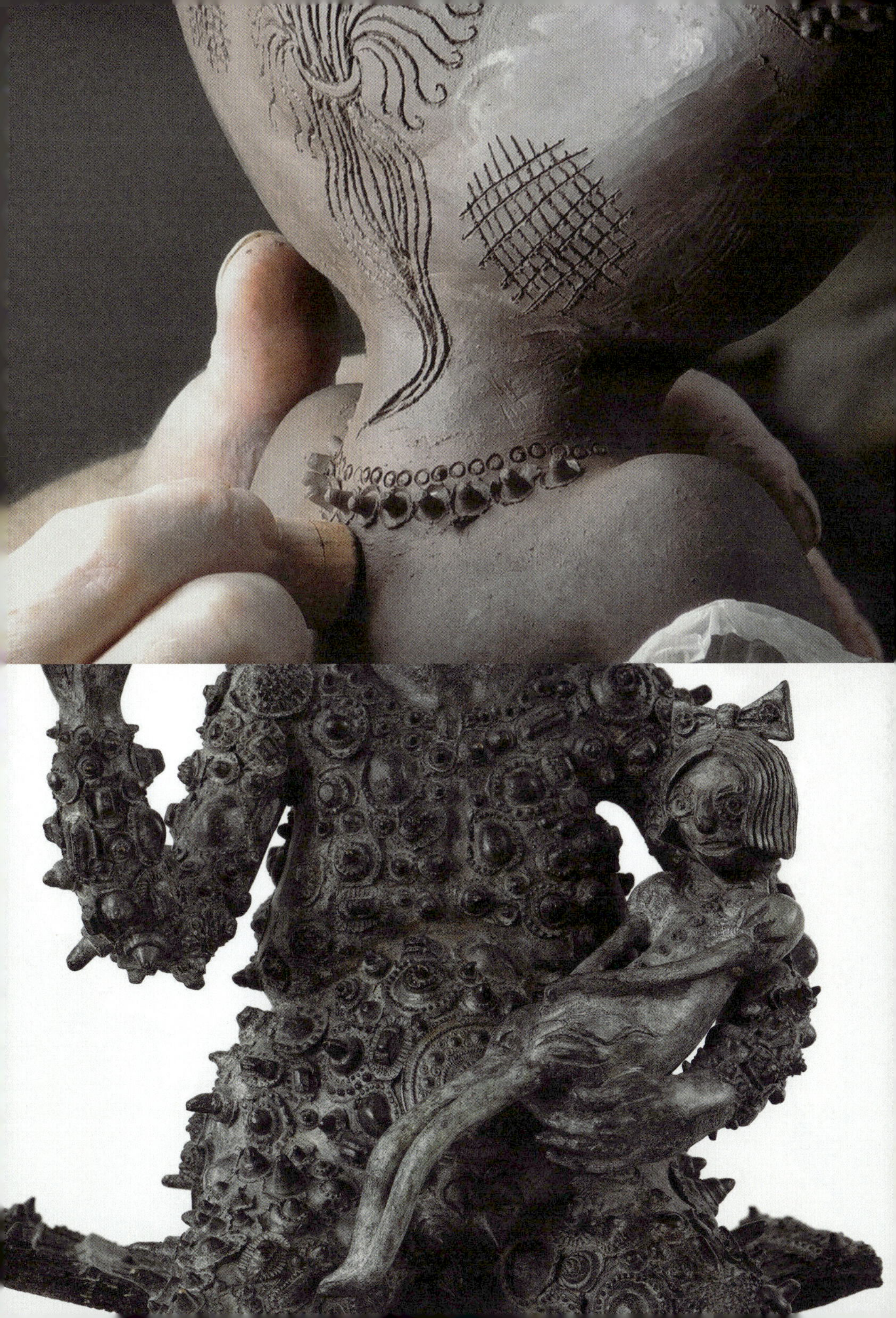

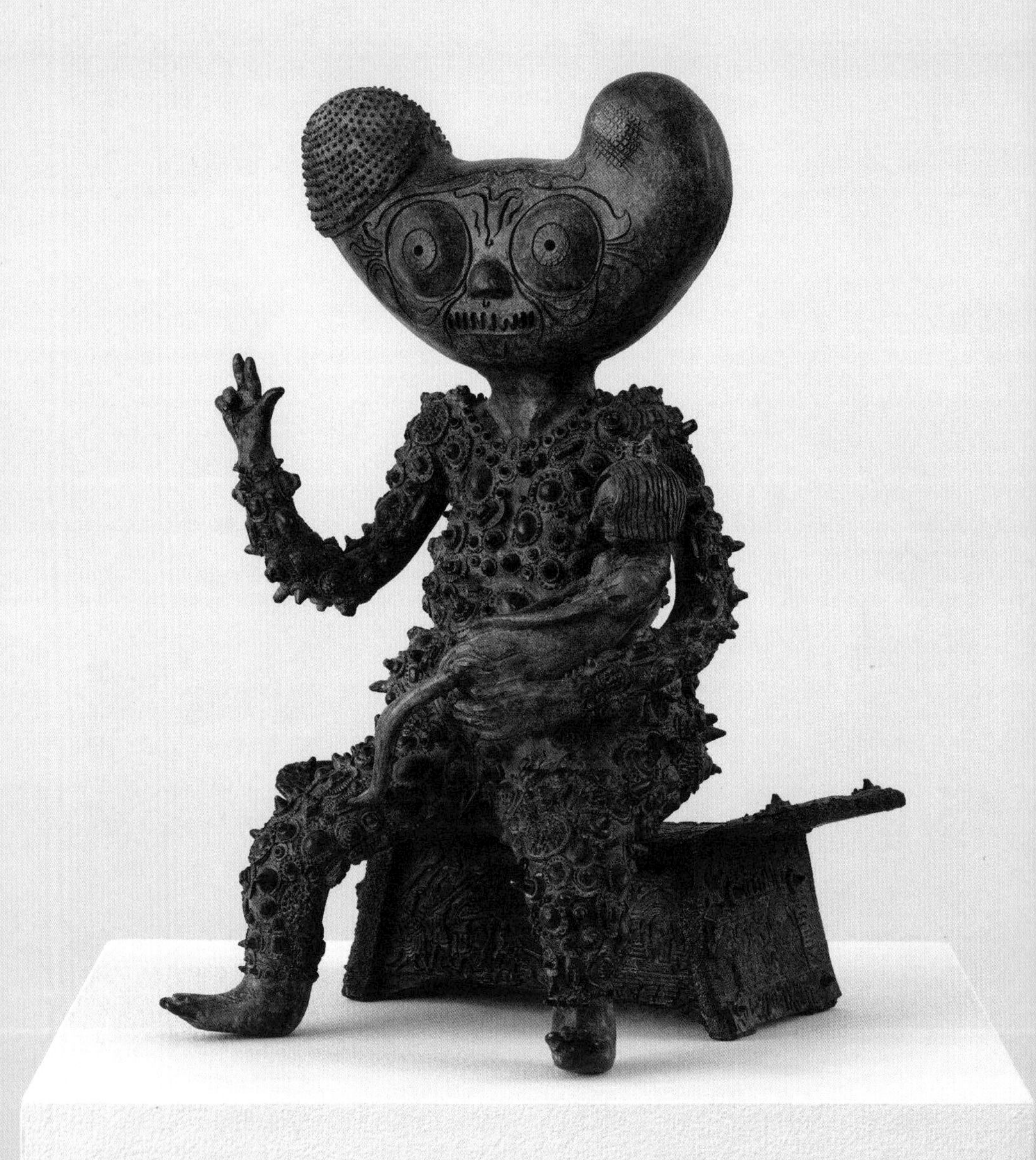

Alan Healing the Wound
2021

Grayson Perry

Bronze
Courtesy of the artist
and Victoria Miro

"I've turned to my childhood
teddy bear Alan Measles
for inspiration. As a child,
I projected a lot of stuff onto
him. He became a kind of
parent to me.

I like to take Alan into
different parts of world
culture. I've been looking
at amazing Chola bronzes
from Southern India. I love
the style. He's a kind of
Hindu deity mixed with a
Christian reliquary Madonna
and child. Alan the surrogate
father goddess."

Bill

is wat

Gales

hing me

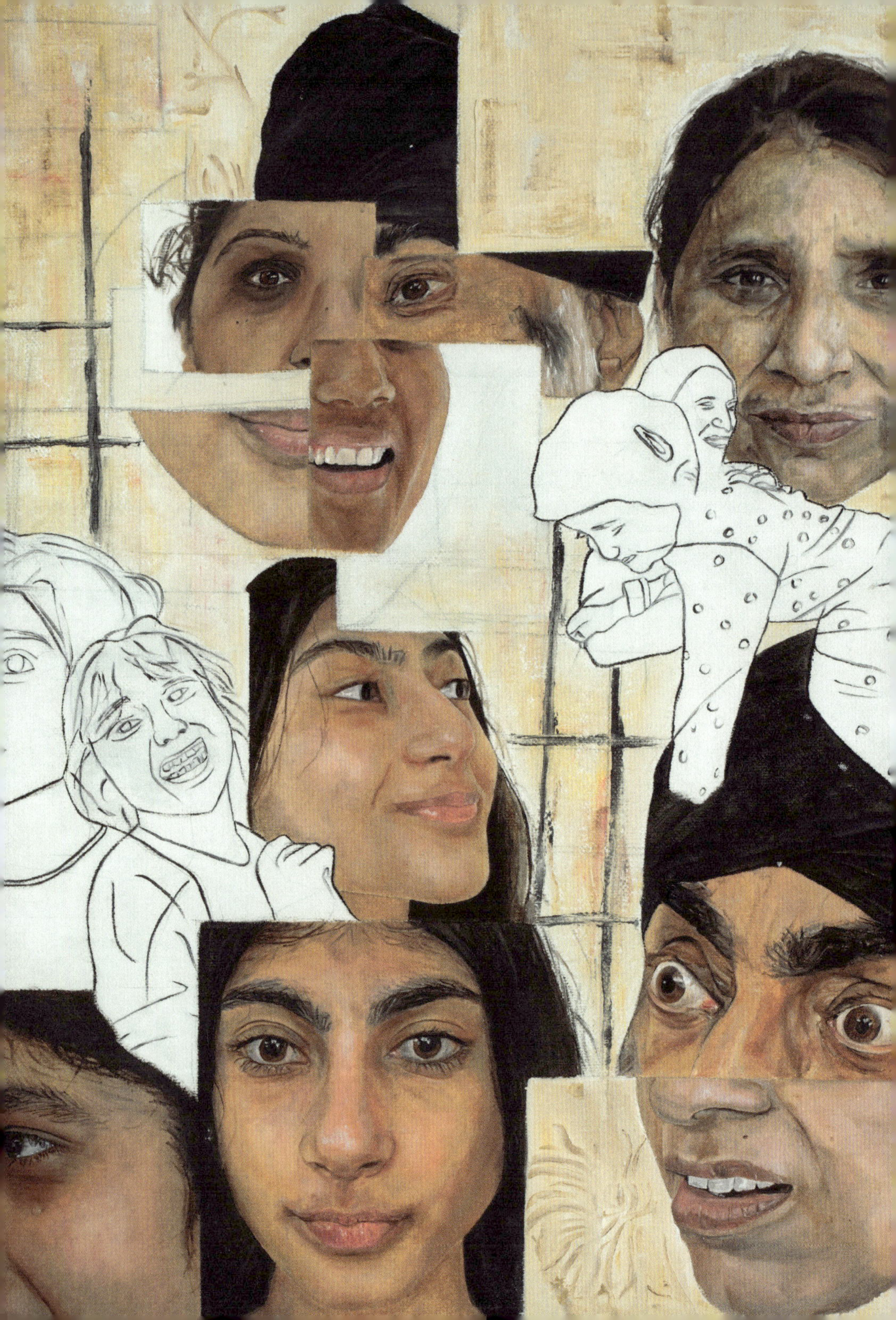

Prabhneet
Sondhi

"The concept of my painting was to explore the theme 'personal space'. I was keen on the idea of people invading each other's space and how they feel about it. As well as how they act in their surroundings. This led me to my subject matter: portraiture. I chose family, as they are close to me, and during lockdown their presence was more prominent.

Expanding on invasion, the idea relates to chaos. This flows throughout my painting through the disordered composition. This painting represents what the majority have been through: living on top of each other. There were times where I got completely irritated and frustrated. Holding on to the fact that I was surrounded by my family during this time helped me through.

Drawing and painting is so valuable to me. It gives me an outlet for when times get stressful. Online school, being stuck in the house and the repetitive daily walks; it was monotonous. Painting enabled me to express my feelings, let loose and free my mind. I painted a wide range of emotions which tell a story. Each interpretation will change for every viewer, as we all had different experiences."

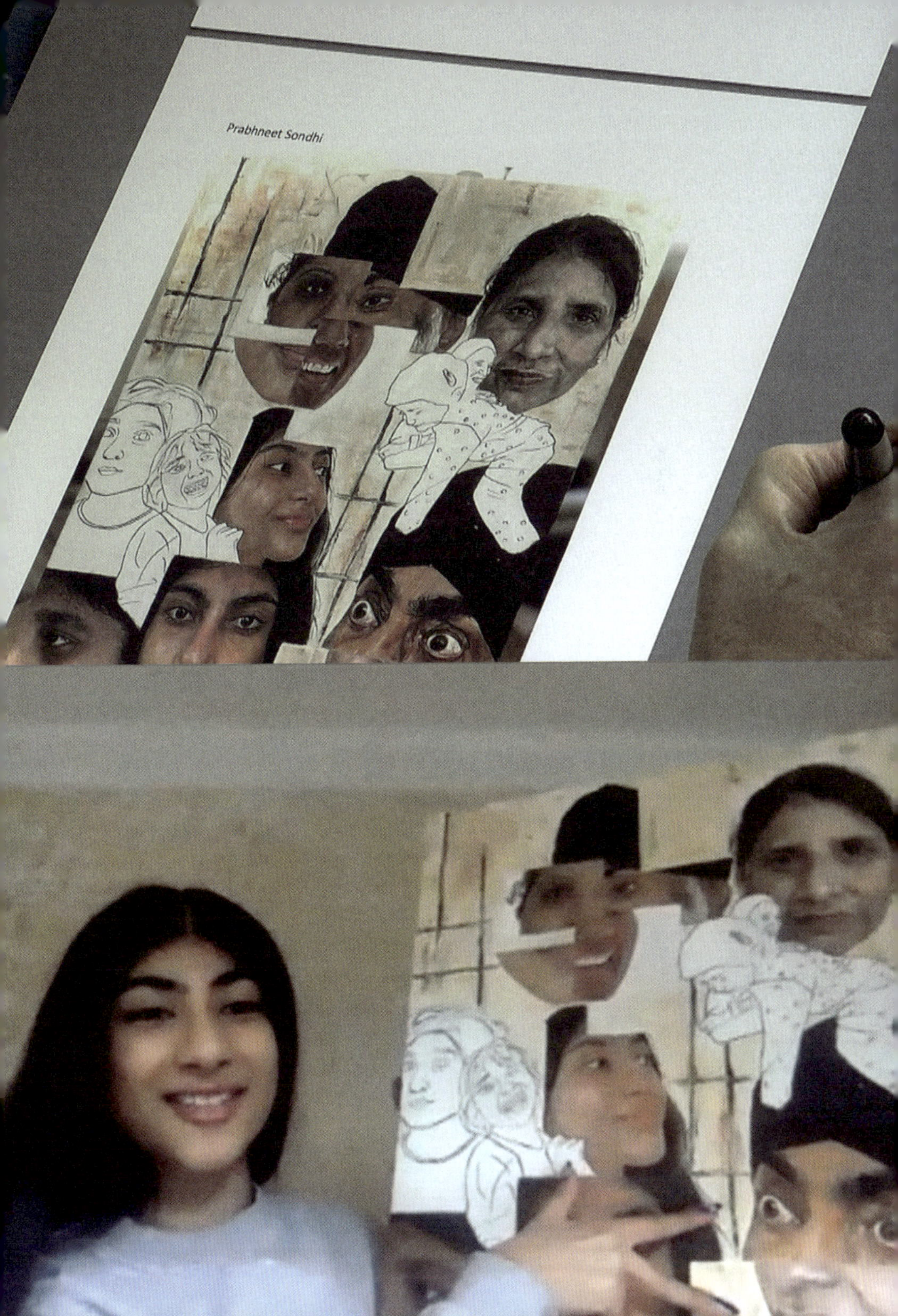
Prabhneet Sondhi

Natu

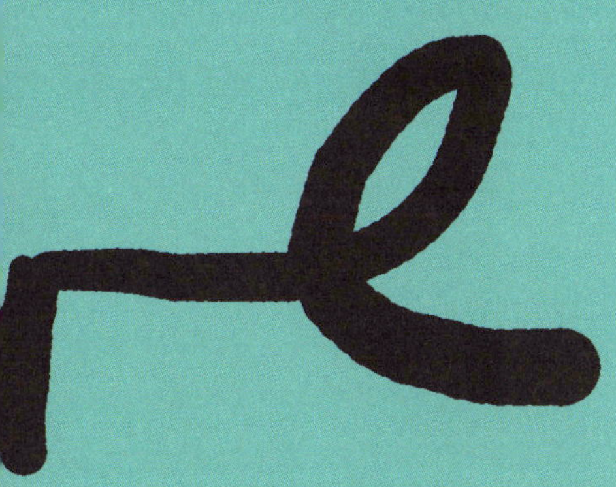

"The more we felt cut off from
nature during lockdown, the more
we became aware of how much
we're in its power. Art is a great
way of looking. It has a role to
play in making us see nature in a
more loving and more appreciative
way. Helping us to understand the
natural world and the part we play
in it is the first, and perhaps the
deepest, role of art."

Tape Loops

Toby Bain

Audio recording of walks
outdoors, mixed media:
hand decorated-cassettes
Courtesy of the artist

"During lockdown I would go
on walks and record as many
sounds as I could: footsteps,
crunchy leaves, birdsong. I
edited the sounds to recreate
the walk. I made dioramas
on the back of tape cassettes.
I'd stream it on social media
and invite friends to join me
on "an audio adventure into
the world of tape loops".
It was a way to go on virtual
walks with my friends and
family when walking together
was no longer allowed."

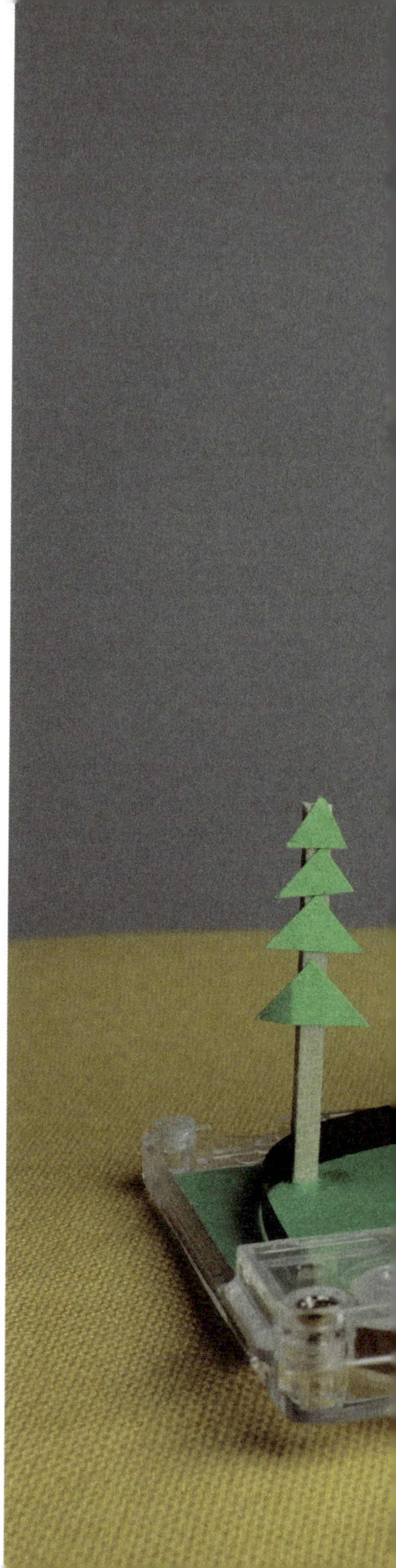

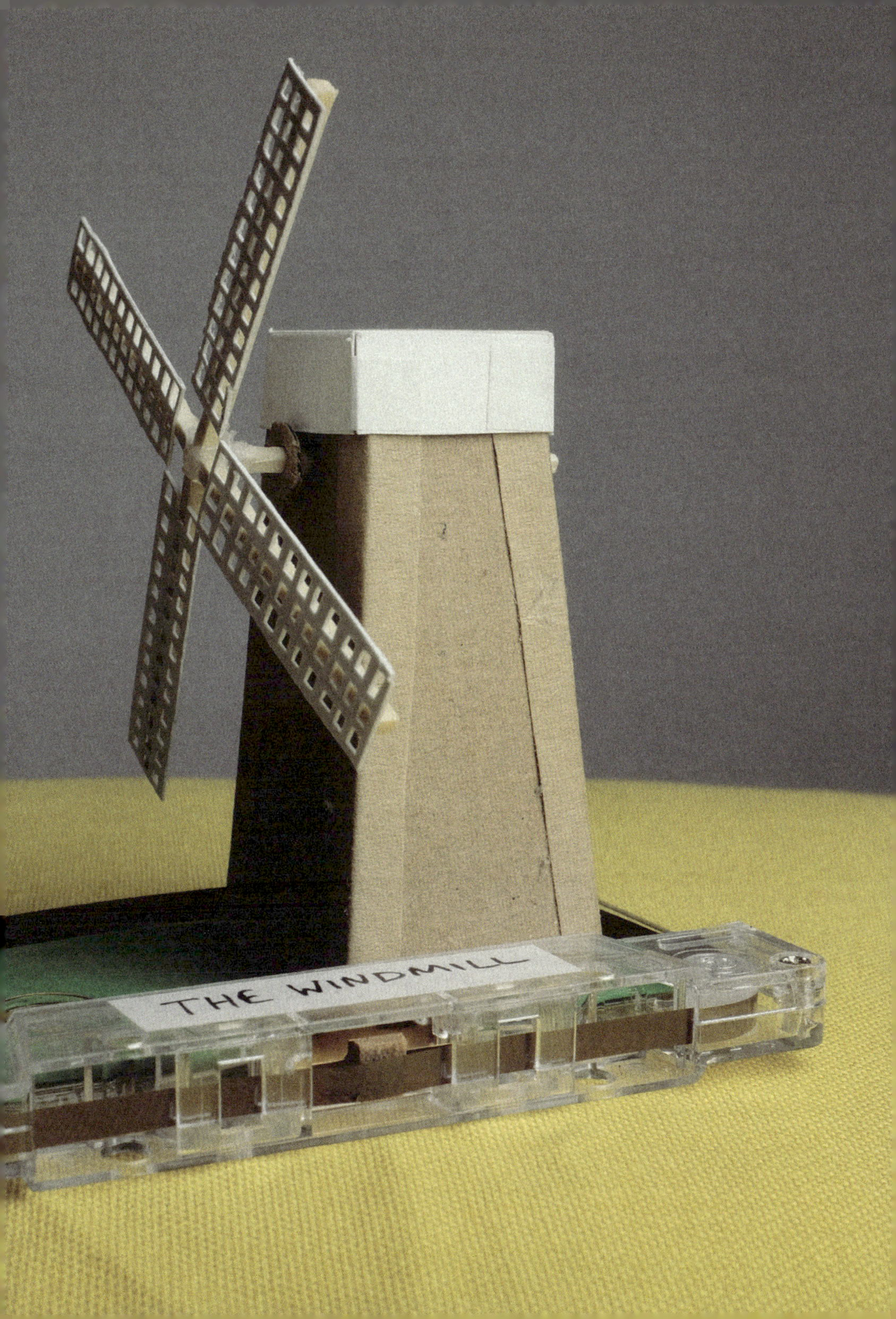
THE WINDMILL

Daily Exercise

Esther Jeanes

Acrylic paint on board
Courtesy of the artist

"I made this to help me
through the time of
unparalleled strangeness.
I was homeschooling two
young children, walking
every day for exercise.
We didn't know what was
going to happen but nature
carried on unaffected by the
enormity of our situation.

I decided to paint miniatures
of our daily exercise.
Celebrating the stunning
part of the world where I live
and marking the passing of
time. Recording lockdown
kept me creative and gave
me a few hours to myself."

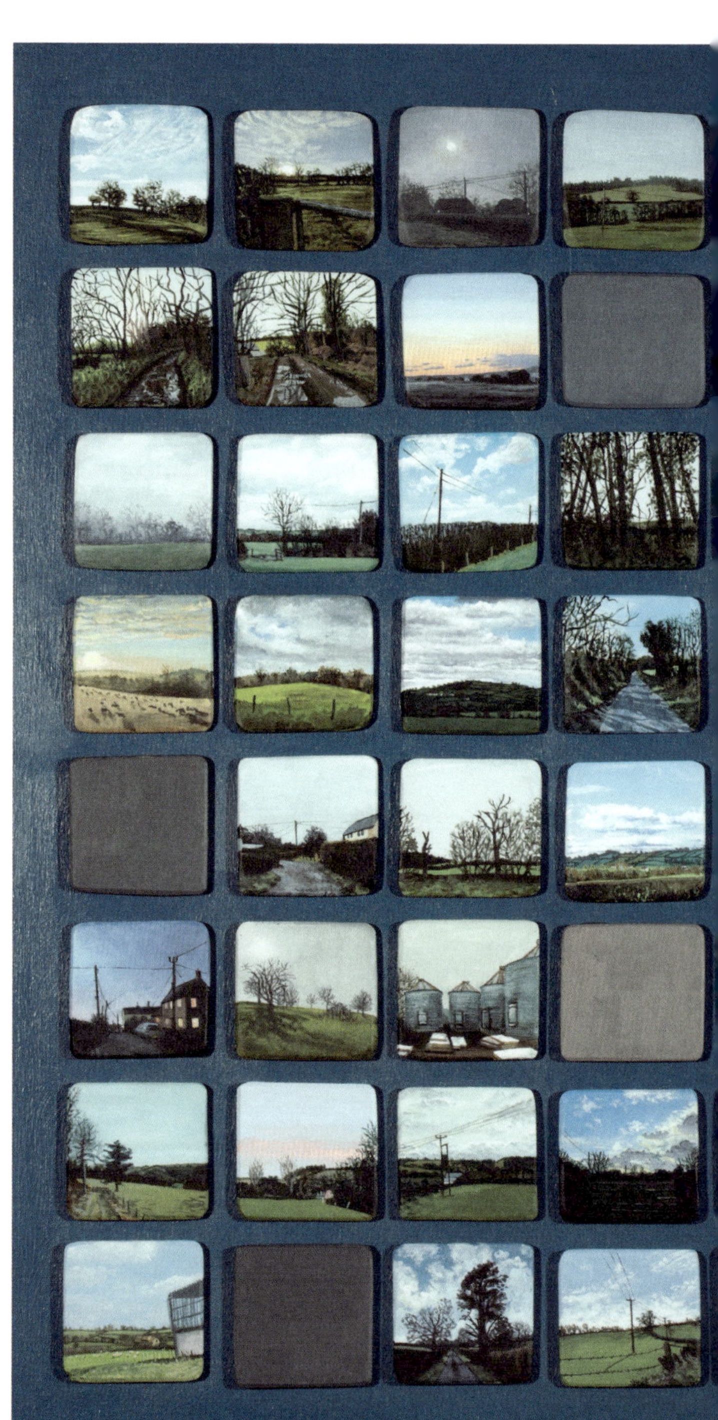

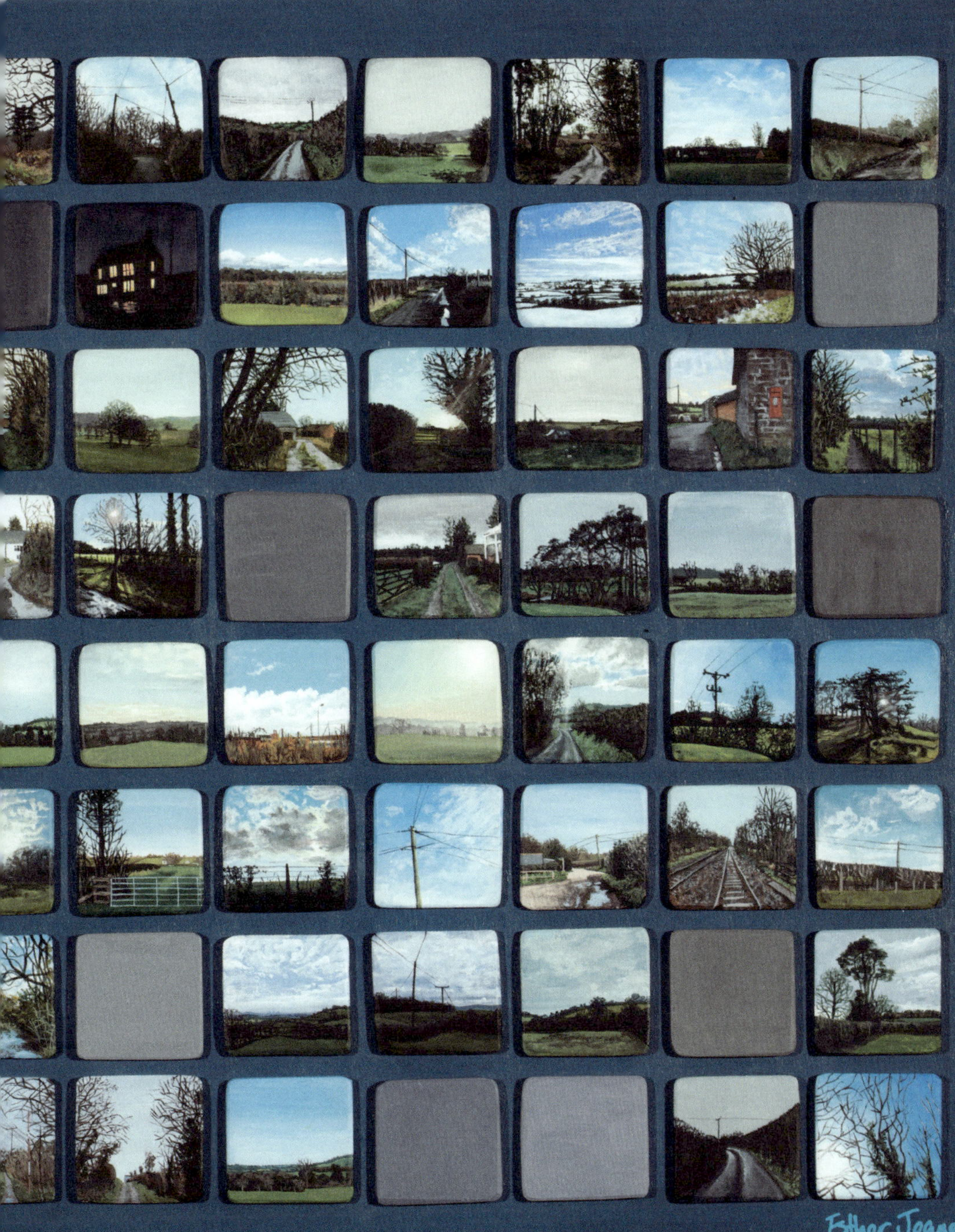

Esther Jeanes

Nature

Becky Tyler

Digital painting
Courtesy of the artist

"I need help with so many
aspects of my life. I love
art because I can be totally
independent with it. I have
an eye-tracker that can tell
where on my screen I am
looking. My eyes become like
my computer mouse. I love
to immerse myself in my
painting. This picture depicts
the dreams and opportunities
waiting for me beyond the
gates of my disabilities.
In my imagination, I can do
so much more than my body
will allow. Art makes me feel
less disabled."

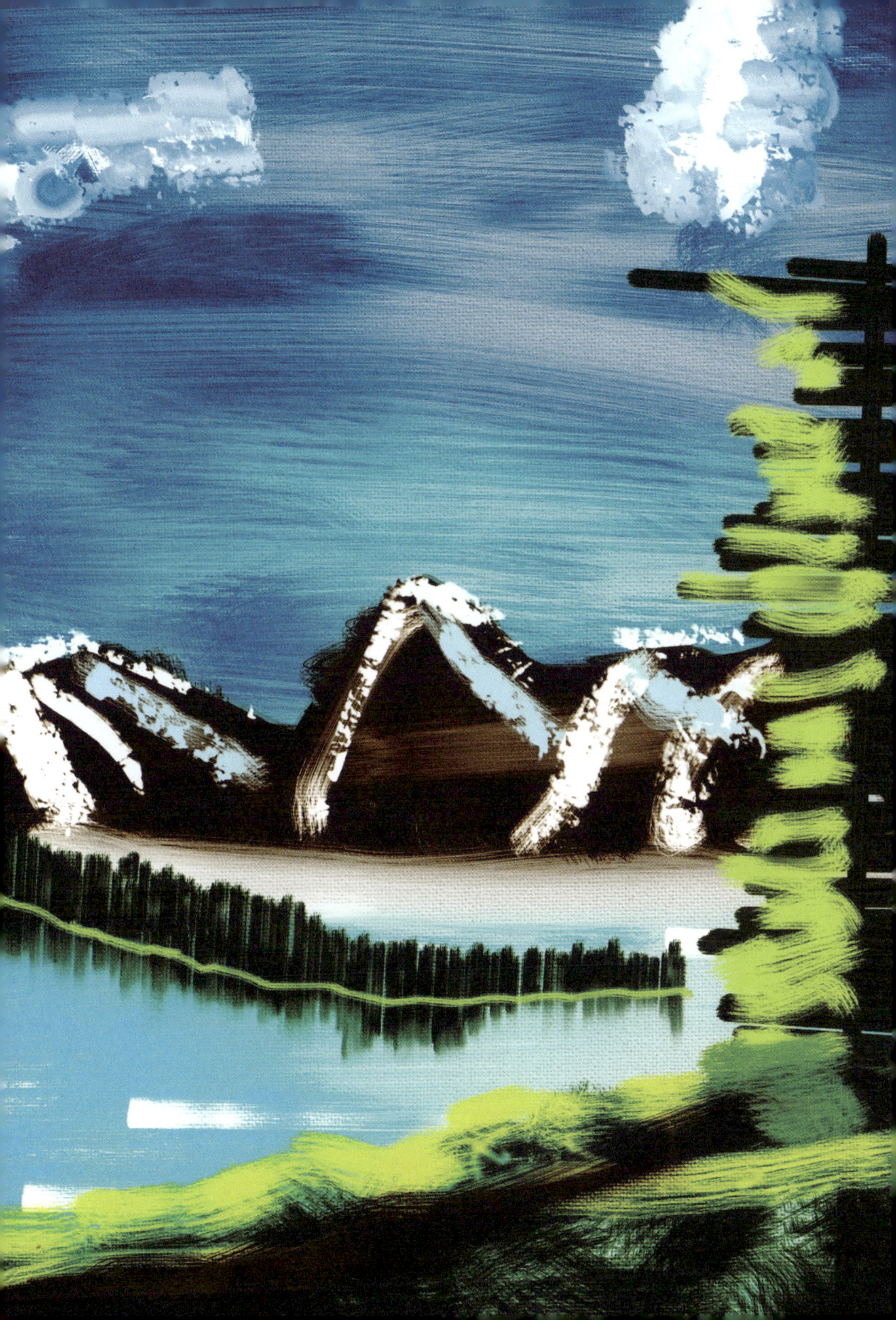

Portrait of Grayson

Becky Tyler

Digital painting
Courtesy of the artist

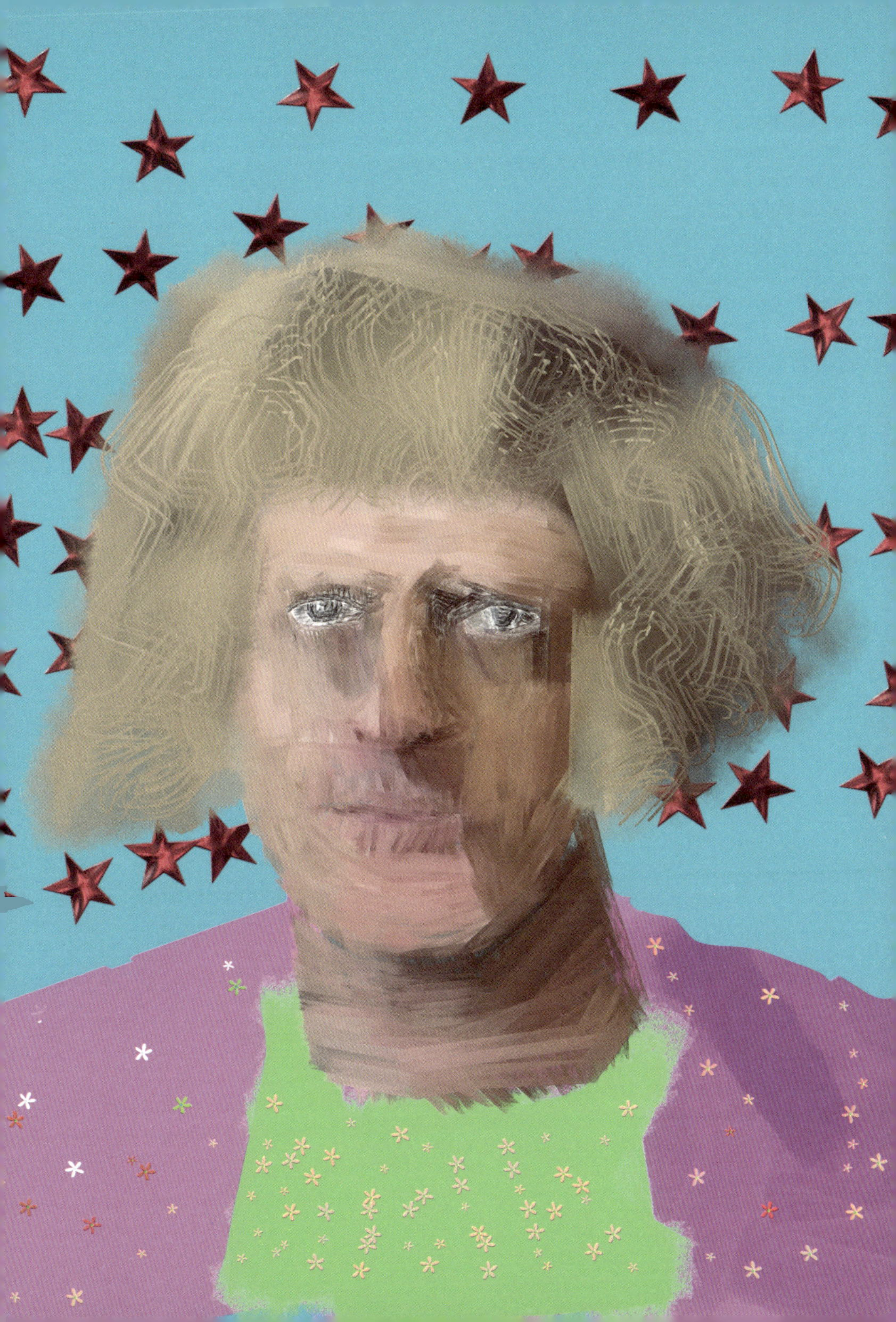

Old McDonald

Leonie Brown

Coloured pencil on paper
Courtesy of the artist

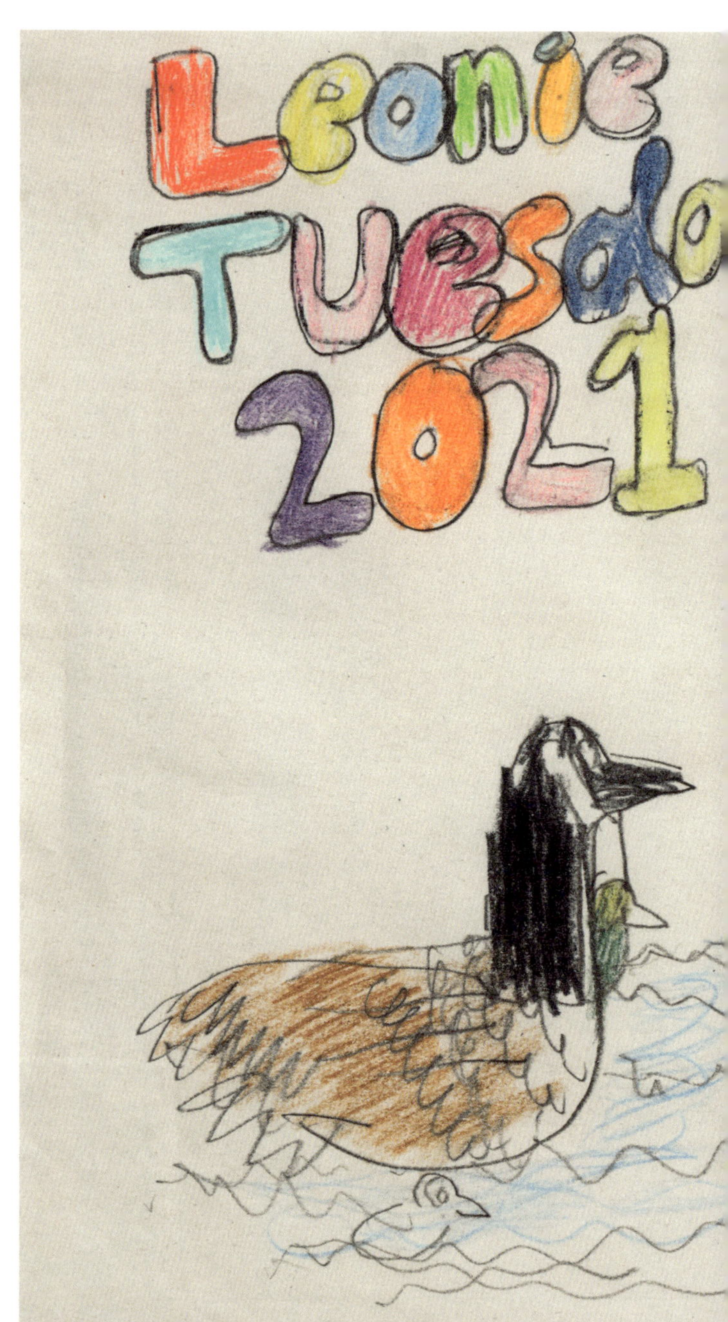

"My name is Leonie, I made
this artwork when I was
in lockdown. I really like
animals, I like seeing the
birds, pigs, sheep, cows
and more. When I was in
lockdown, making the
picture made me so happy
because I could not go to
the farm to see the animals."

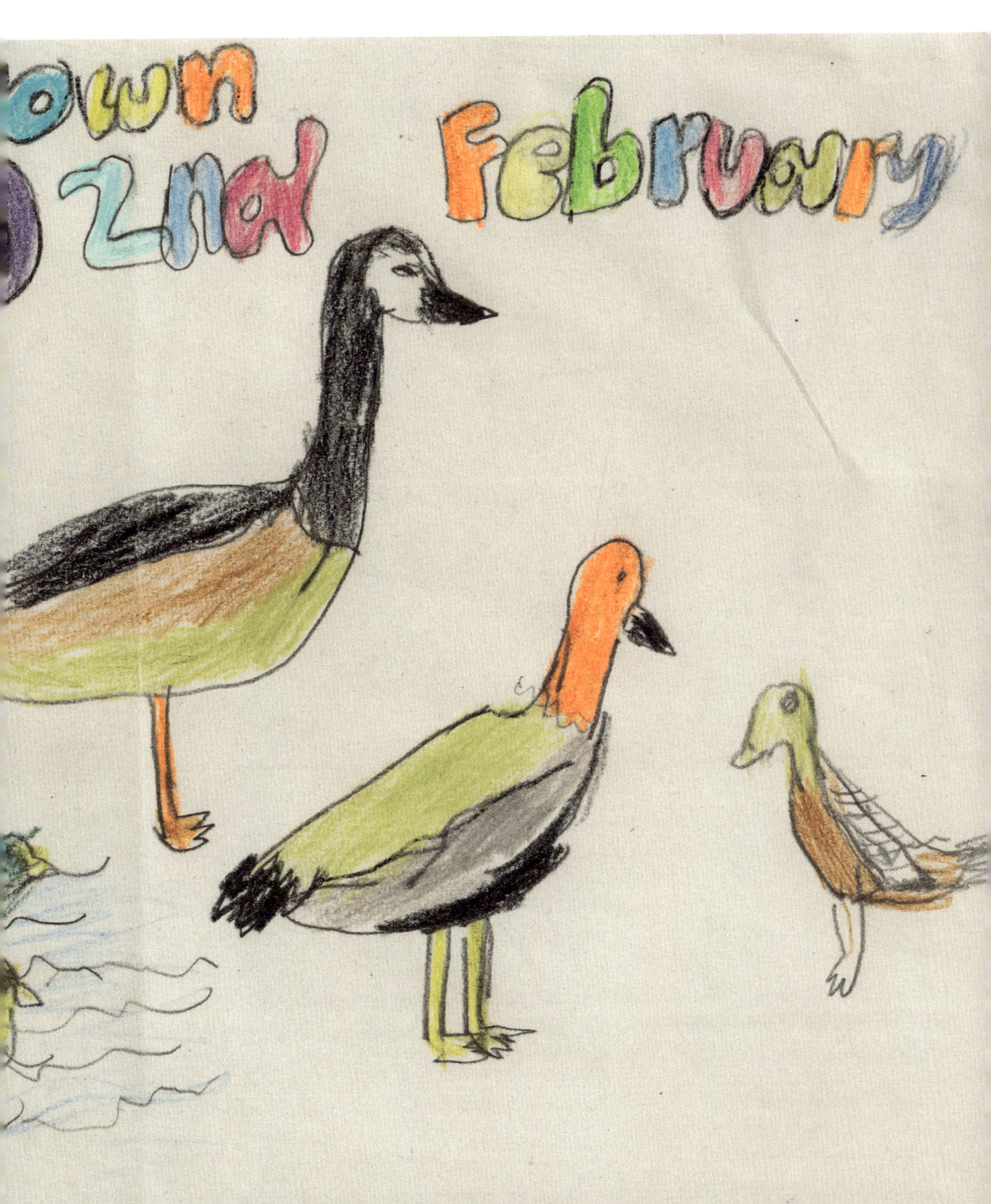
own
2nd February

The Human Destruction
of our Natural World

Emma Ridley

Acrylic paint, bark and
plastic on card
Courtesy of the artist

"My aim for the artwork was
to communicate each main
issue happening on our
planet today. I knew there
had to be at least one 3D
element to reflect our reality.
I used a piece of bark found
in a local park to resemble
deforestation. Throughout
the project I visualised the
Earth's body of water being
transparent, making plastic
the perfect material. A symbol
of the world's hidden threats.
We each have a choice today
of how we want our world to
look in the future."

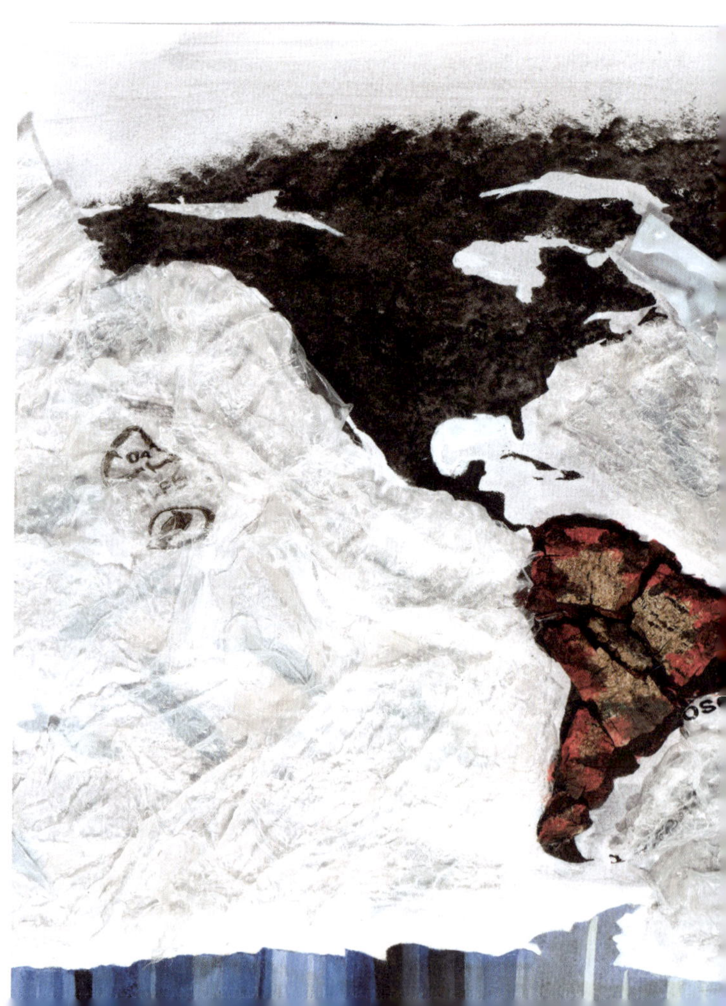

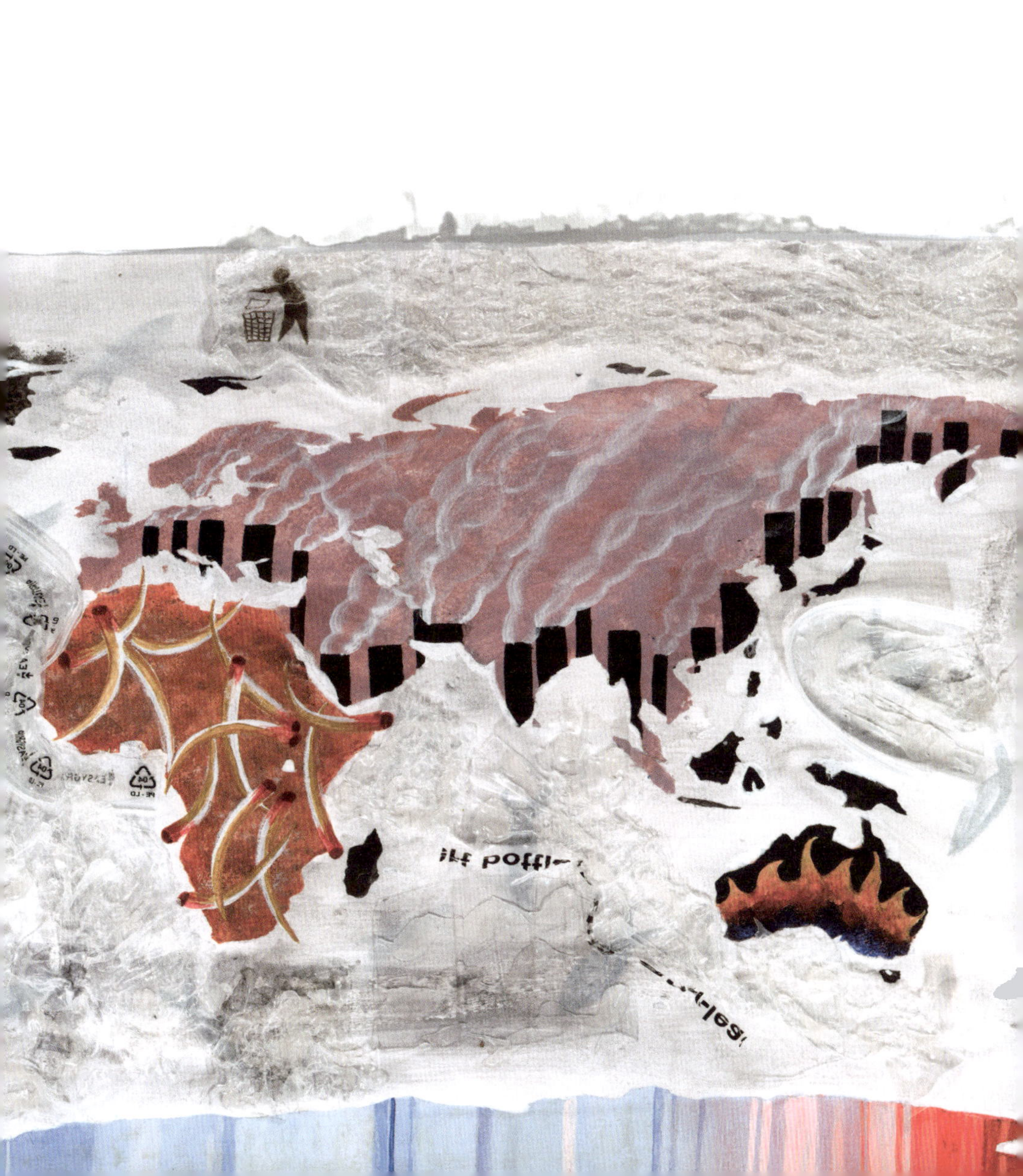

Polar Bears Swimming
at Sunset

Gillian Mather

Acrylic paint on canvas
Courtesy of the artist

"My painting is a statement
on global warming. It is
also a statement about love.
I believe in the saying 'All
You Need is Love' and my
paintings try to express this.
I paint all the time. Even
more so during lockdown.
I was blown away when
my painting was chosen,
especially when Russell Tovey
said it was about friendship.
He saw that it was about
emotion. I want my paintings
to make the heart sing."

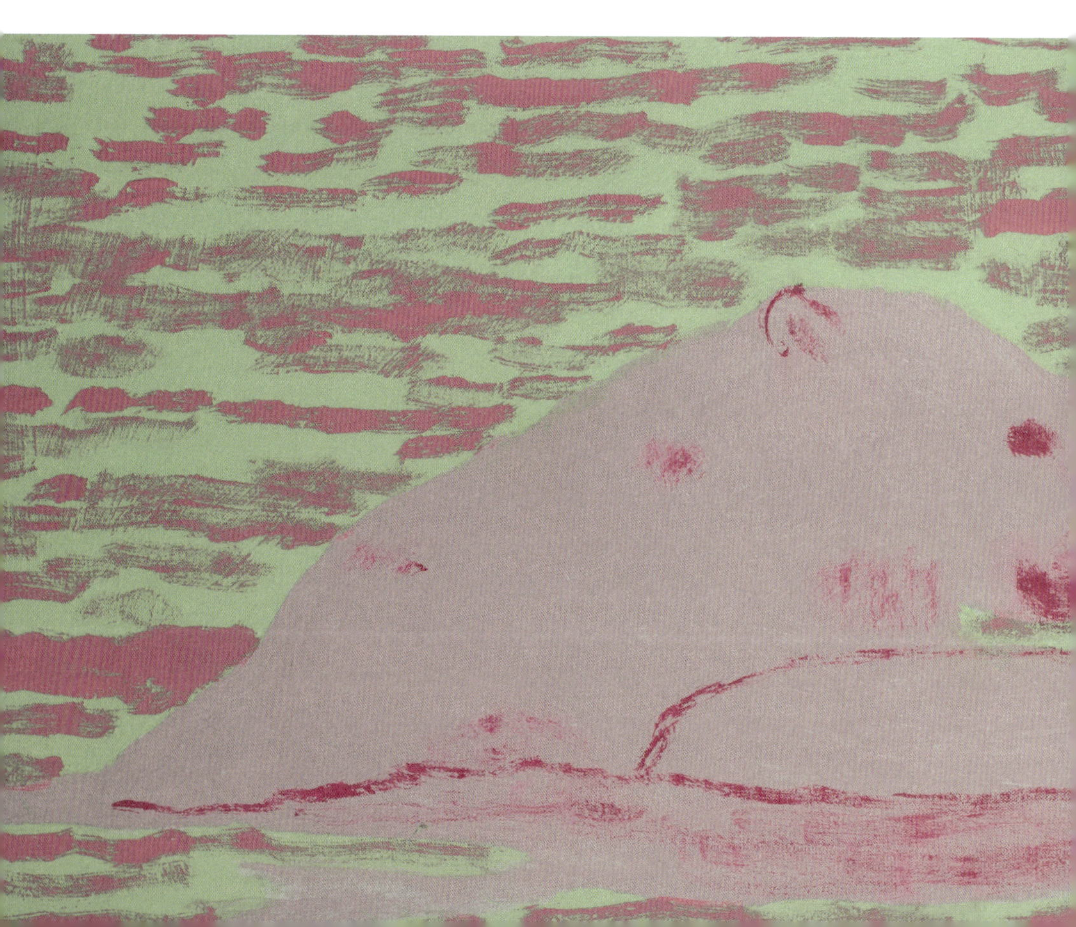

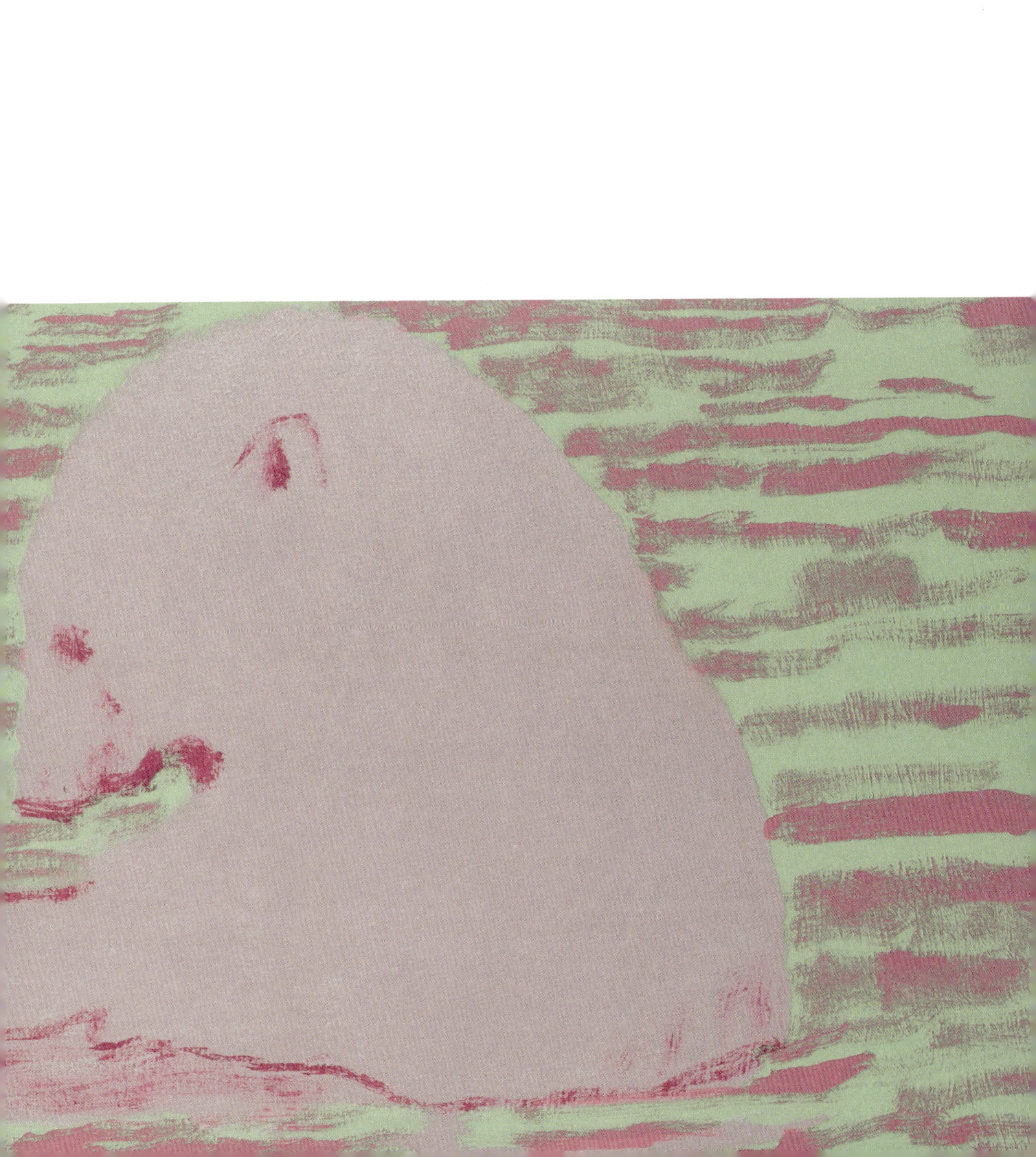

Housebound Houseplant

Laura Connelly

Acrylic paint on canvas
Courtesy of the artist

"My painting was created
at the start of the first
lockdown. I was 9 months
pregnant, self-isolating, and
living in a one-bedroom flat.
I was feeling pretty stressed
and anxious.

I chose to paint a houseplant
– my only connection to
the outdoors. Creating
something from scratch,
working through it, then
having a beautiful finished
result was symbiotic with my
pregnancy. A week later, we
welcomed our son Freddie,
my greatest creation to date!"

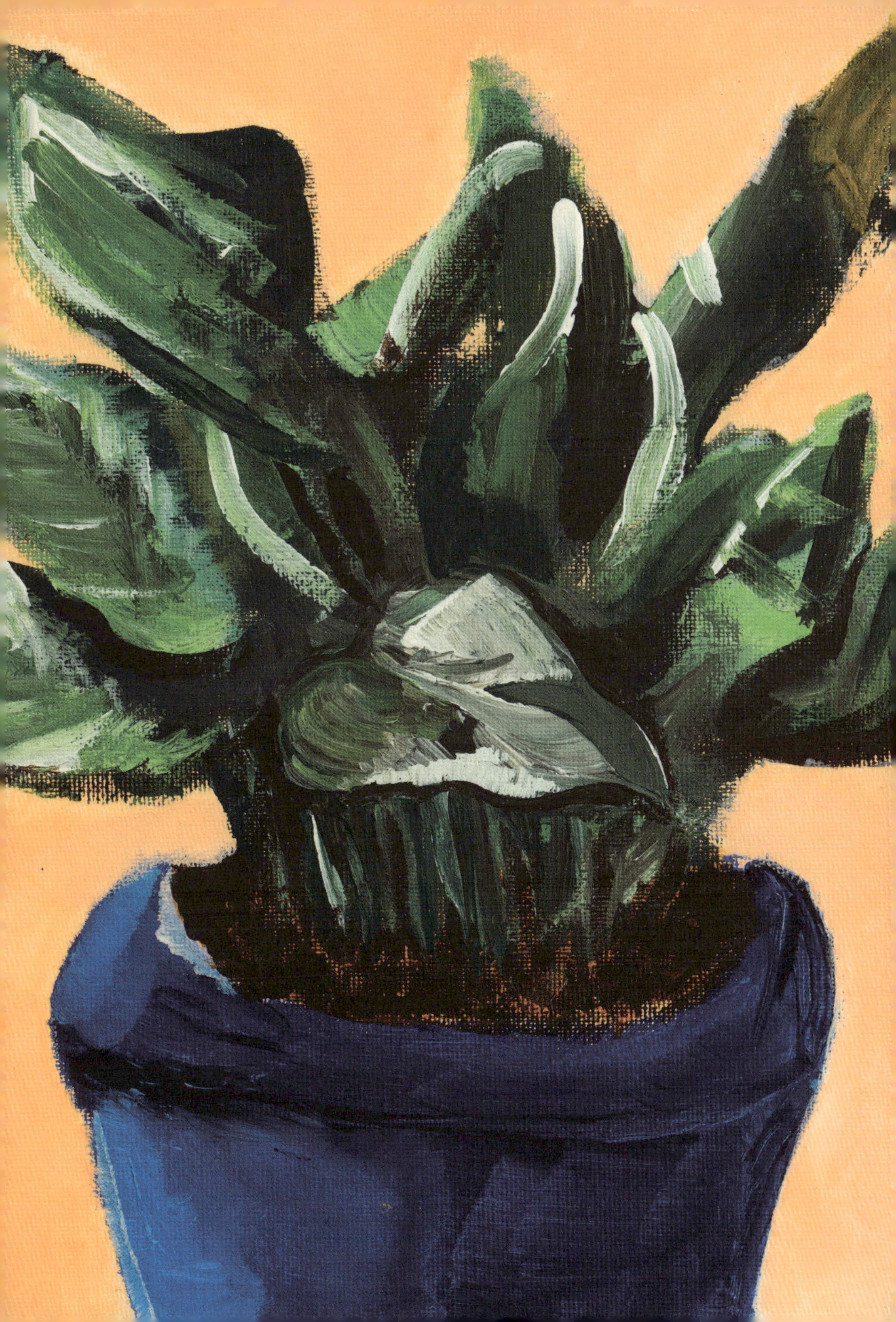

Social Creatures – Tiger

Imogen Paton

Plastic waste, papier mâché,
acrylic paint
Courtesy of the artist

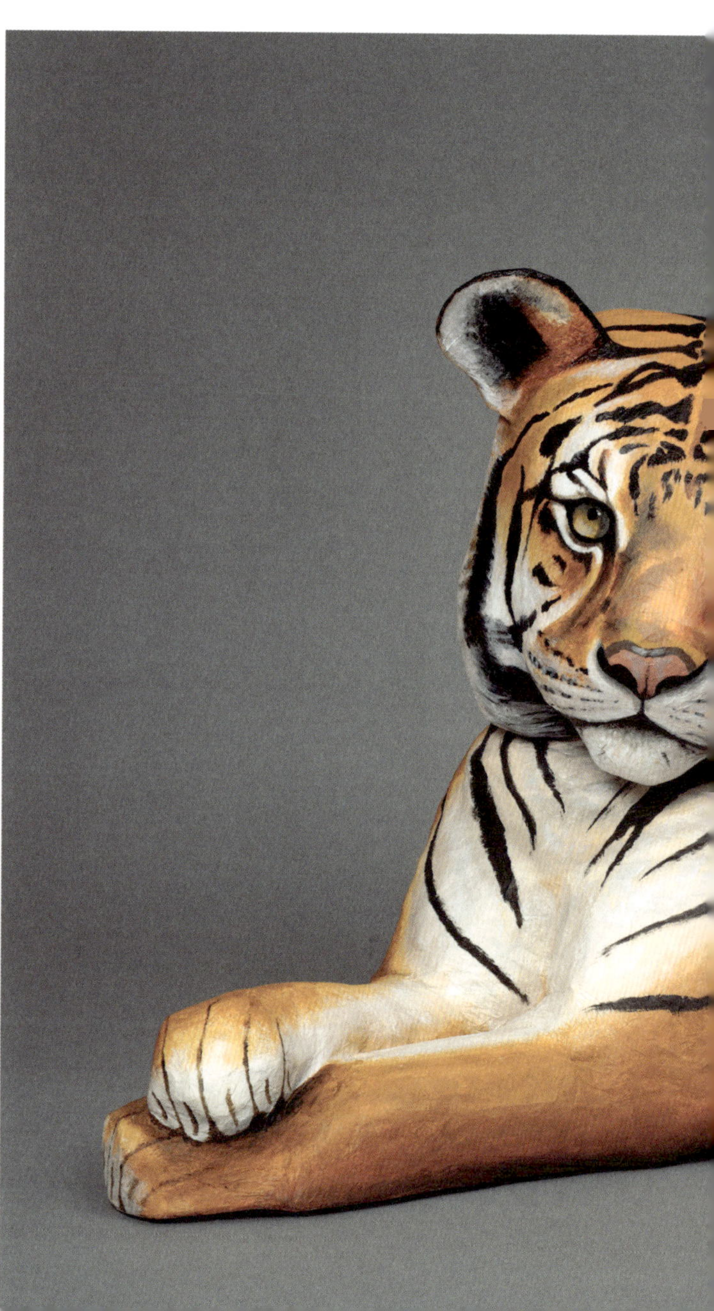

"Issues of sustainability are
more important than ever.
The arrival of COVID-19
meant choosing food
without unnecessary
wrapping became a dream,
especially as a single parent
in isolation. I began creating
sculptures of unusual
and threatened species,
constructed out of household
waste. My Social Creatures
are a message: protect,
conserve, enhance. Think
creatively, think sustainably,
and rethink your everyday
needs for the greater good
of ALL that need our planet
for survival."

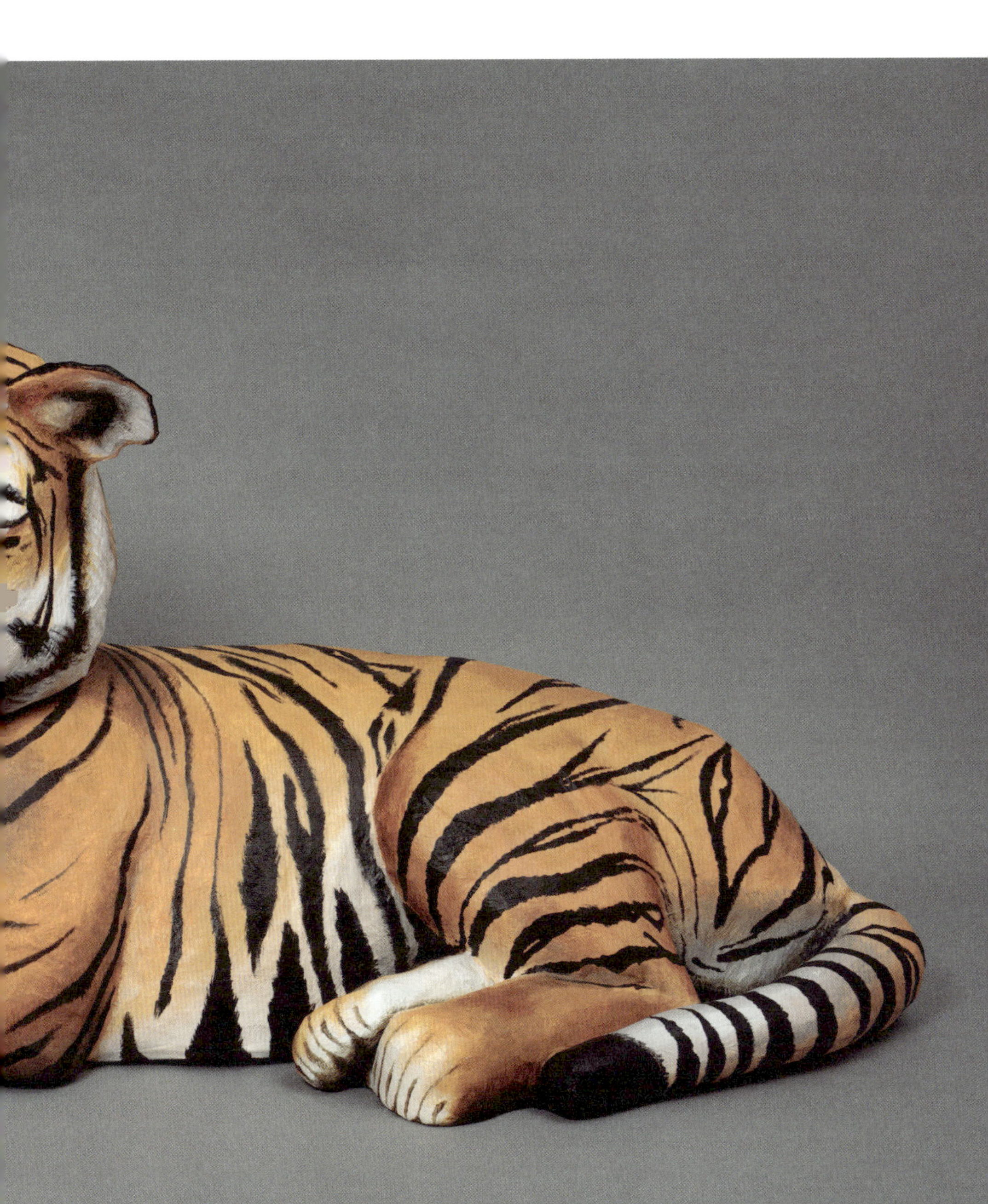

Joyce's Haring Bird

Russell Tovey

House paint on paper
Courtesy of the artist

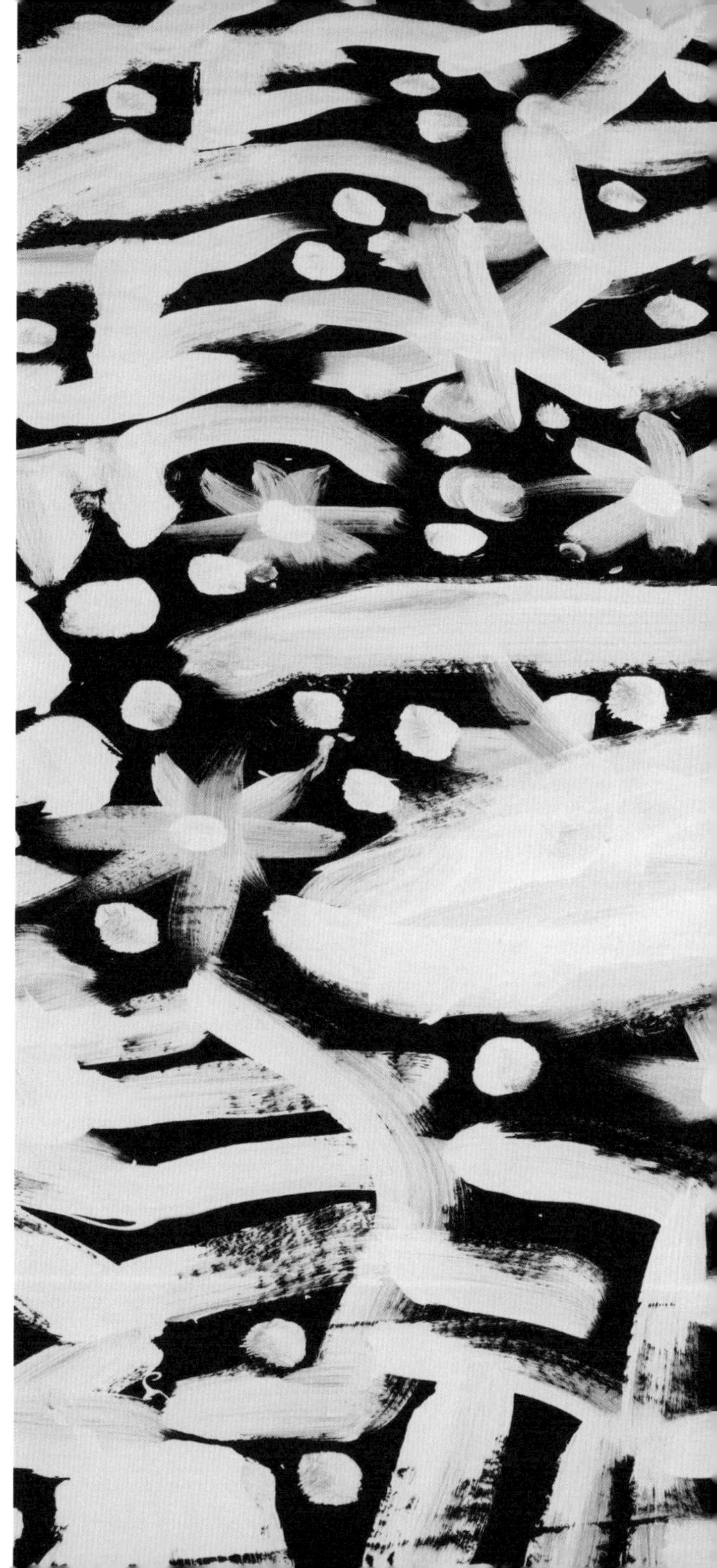

"I'm inspired by Keith Haring.
He started off as a graffiti
artist on the subways of New
York. I saw this video called
Painting Myself Into a Corner.
It was a performance piece.
He had this massive sheet of
paper and he automatically
painted. He didn't really
think about what he was
doing. I've done something
like that. I really like cartoon
imagery and channelling
my love of Joyce Pensato
with Keith Haring and the
presence of Henri Rousseau.
This big work just appeared."

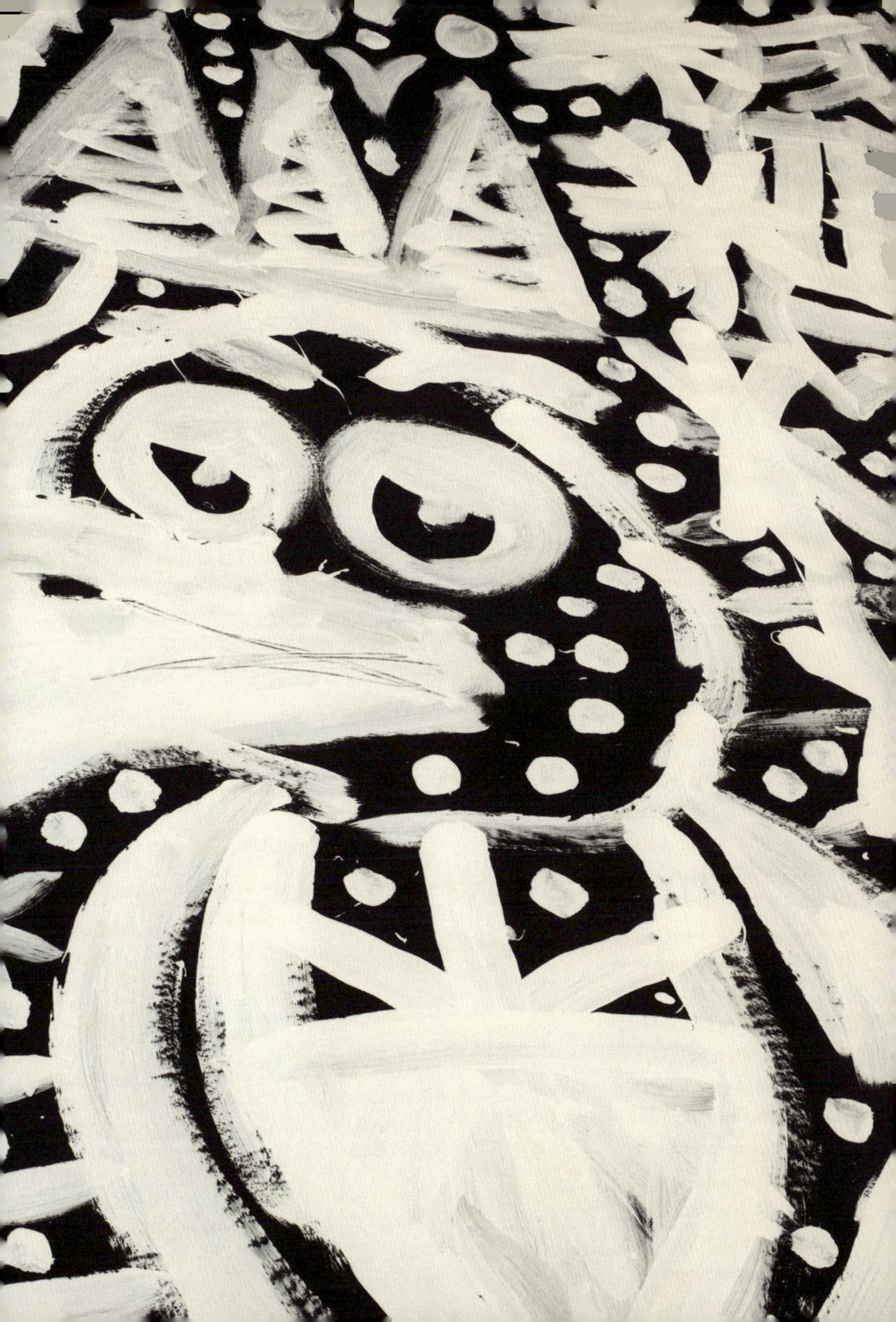

Tree of Fists

Holly Walsh

Tapestry
Courtesy of the artist

"I've become slightly obsessed
with pollarded trees.
They seem to express how
I feel about the lockdown.
There's something kind of
pointlessly angry about them.
I think they look like they've
got little fists on the end
and they're just screaming
WHYYYY? so I think they are
good subjects for my tapestry.
I'm very happy with the
finished result. The back
is an absolute mess."

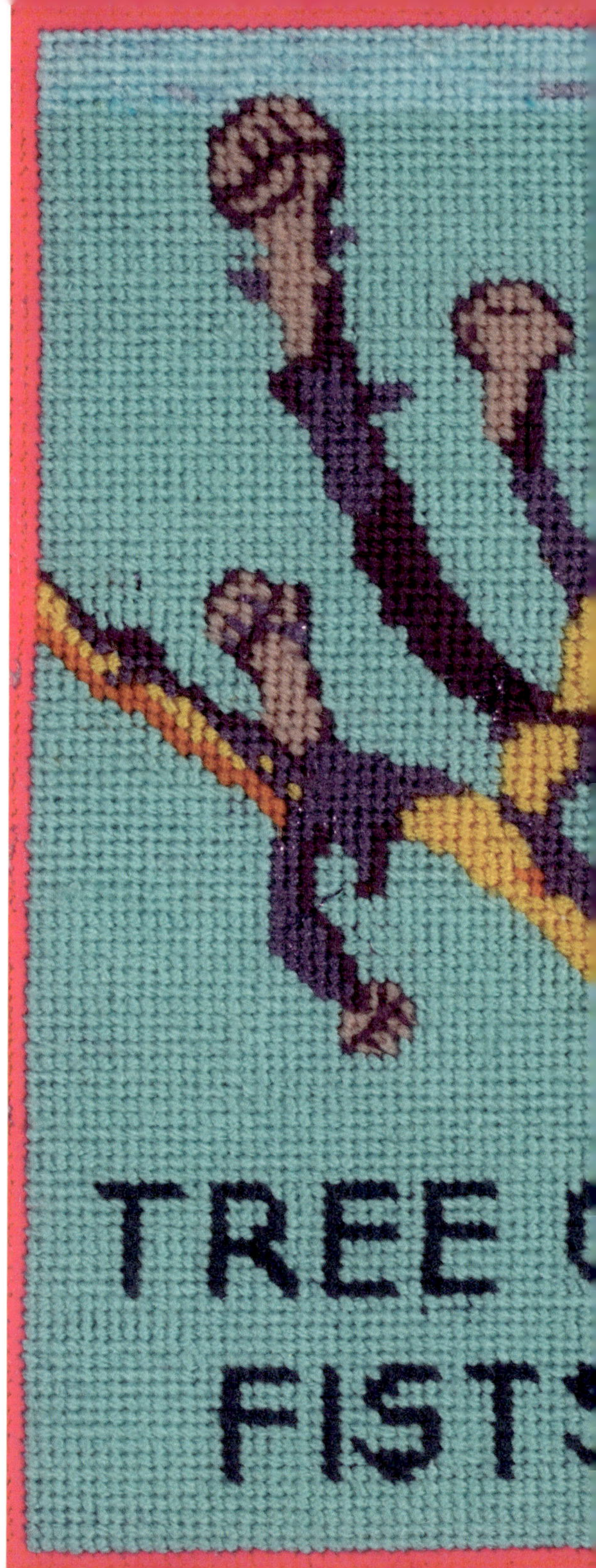

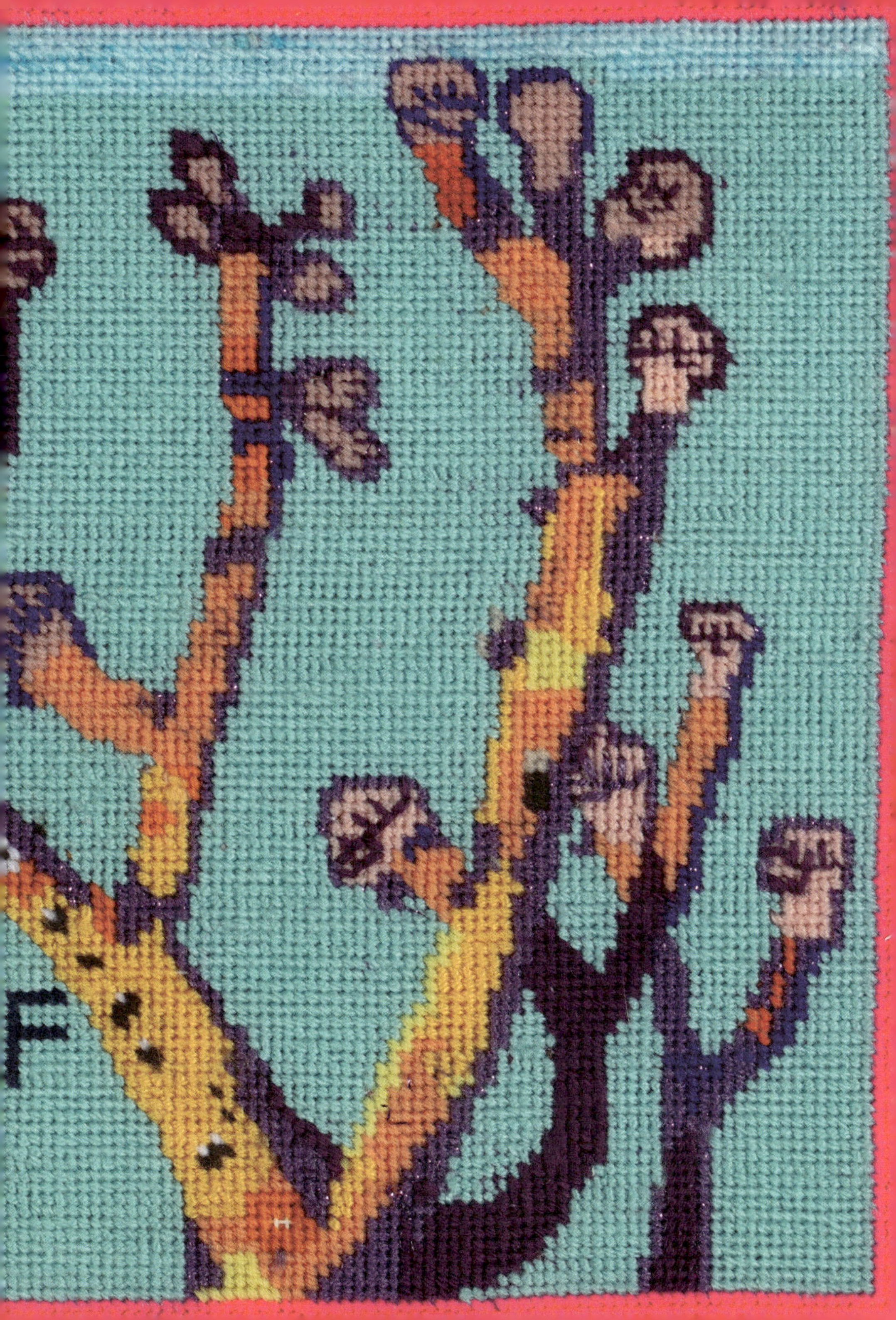

Andy Goldsworthy,
Shed shadow.
Standing still at sunrise.
Dumfriesshire.
22 January 2021,
still image (digital video).
Copyright Andy Goldsworthy

"I've been making shadows on the side of this shed when the sun rises. My shadow emerges very, very slowly. Very beautiful. I experience a whole range of thoughts and emotions. There is intense concentration in looking at the shadow as it begins to move. You feel all the landscape beginning to rise up as the light changes. That's the joy of art. It makes me see what's there. It opens my eyes and my mind."

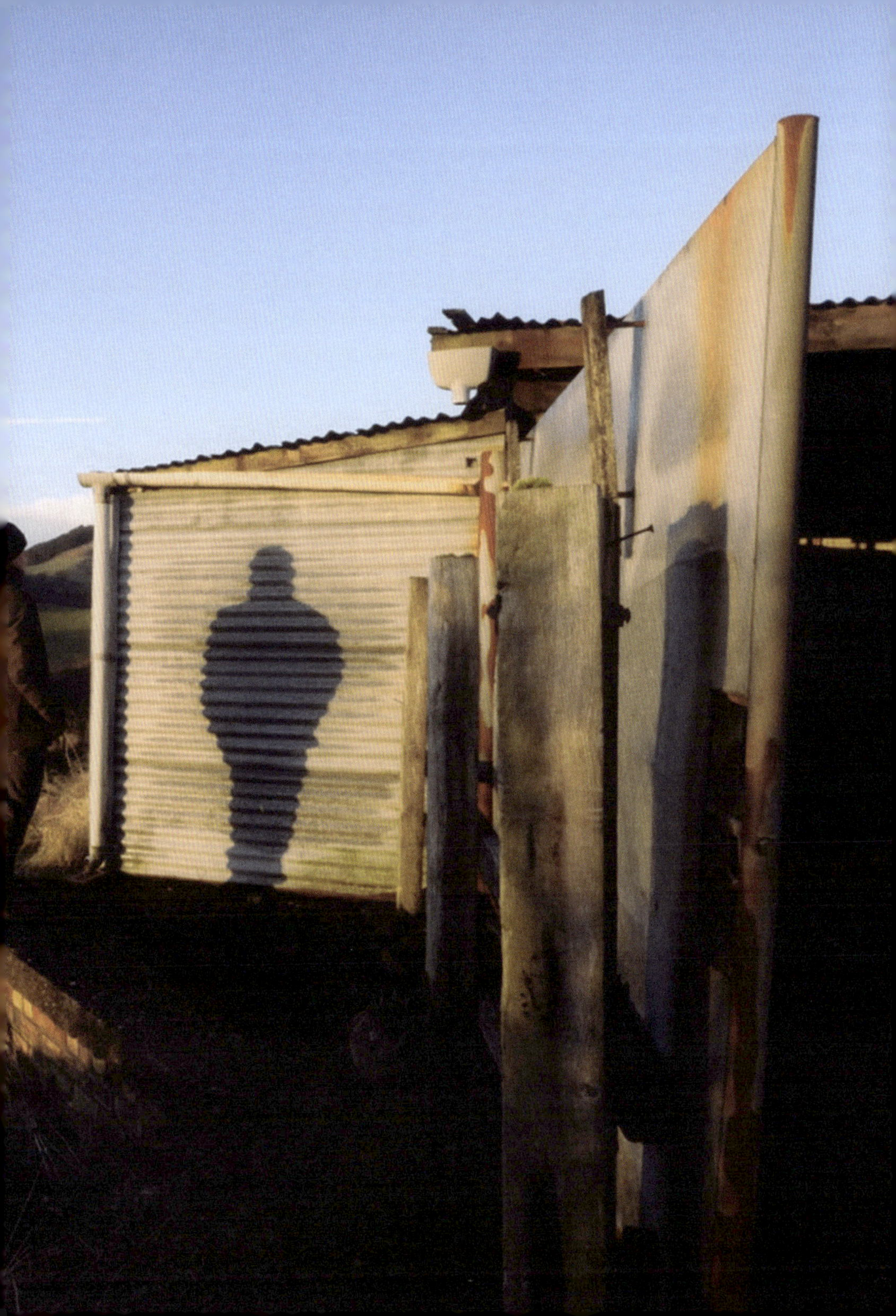

Love and Happiness or
Self Portrait with Priscilla
the Canary

Mark Gee

Digital collage
Courtesy of the artist

"Priscilla the canary came
into my life just before
Coronavirus. Being with
Priscilla was escapism from
the repetitive reports of doom
and gloom from television.
Priscilla changed the way
I viewed life. She represented
freedom, hope, love,
imagination and happiness.
I created this for a project
which explored my life.
I simply wanted to express
how much I loved Priscilla,
how happy she made
everything in my life. In May
2021, Priscilla sadly passed
away unexpectedly."

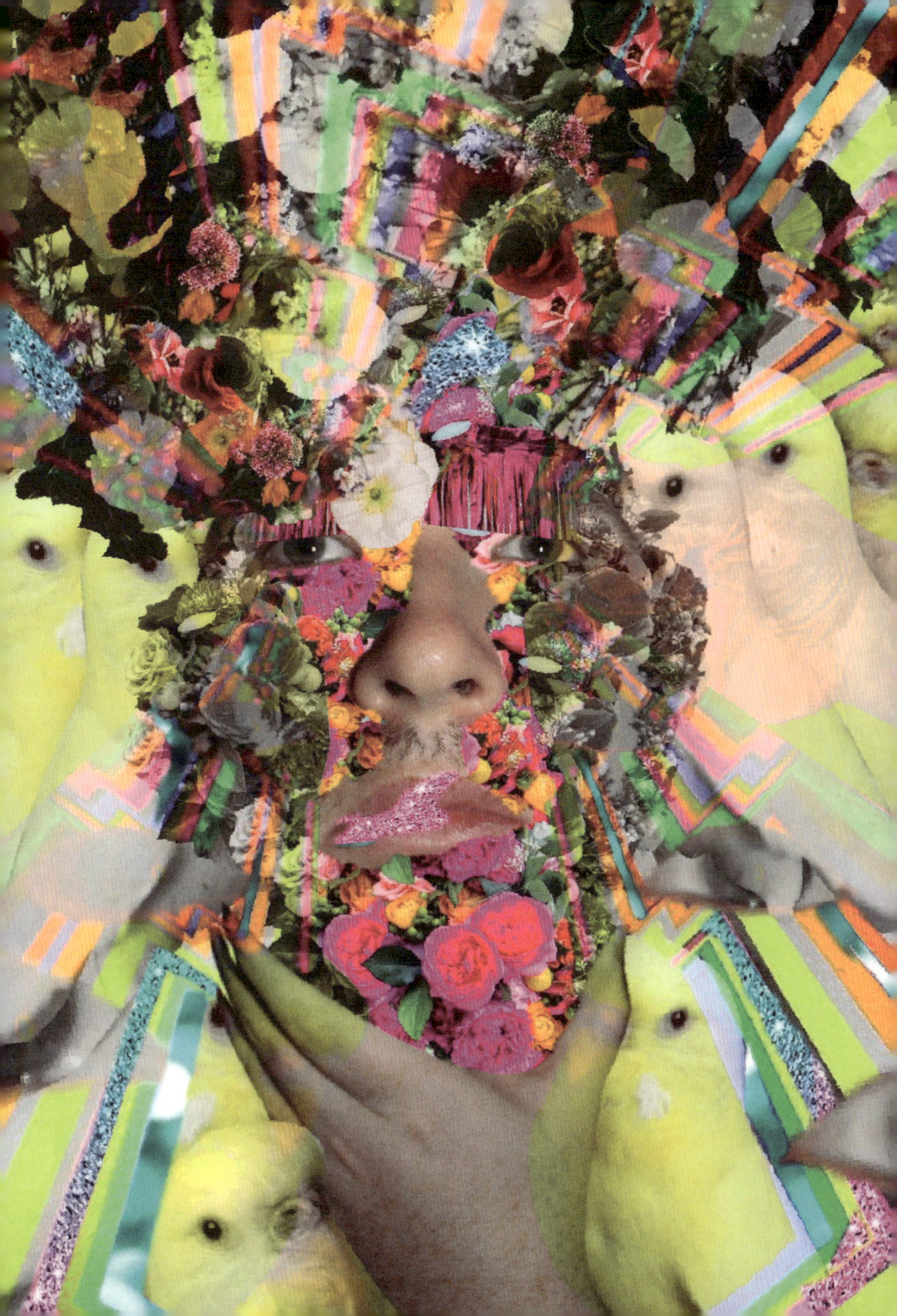

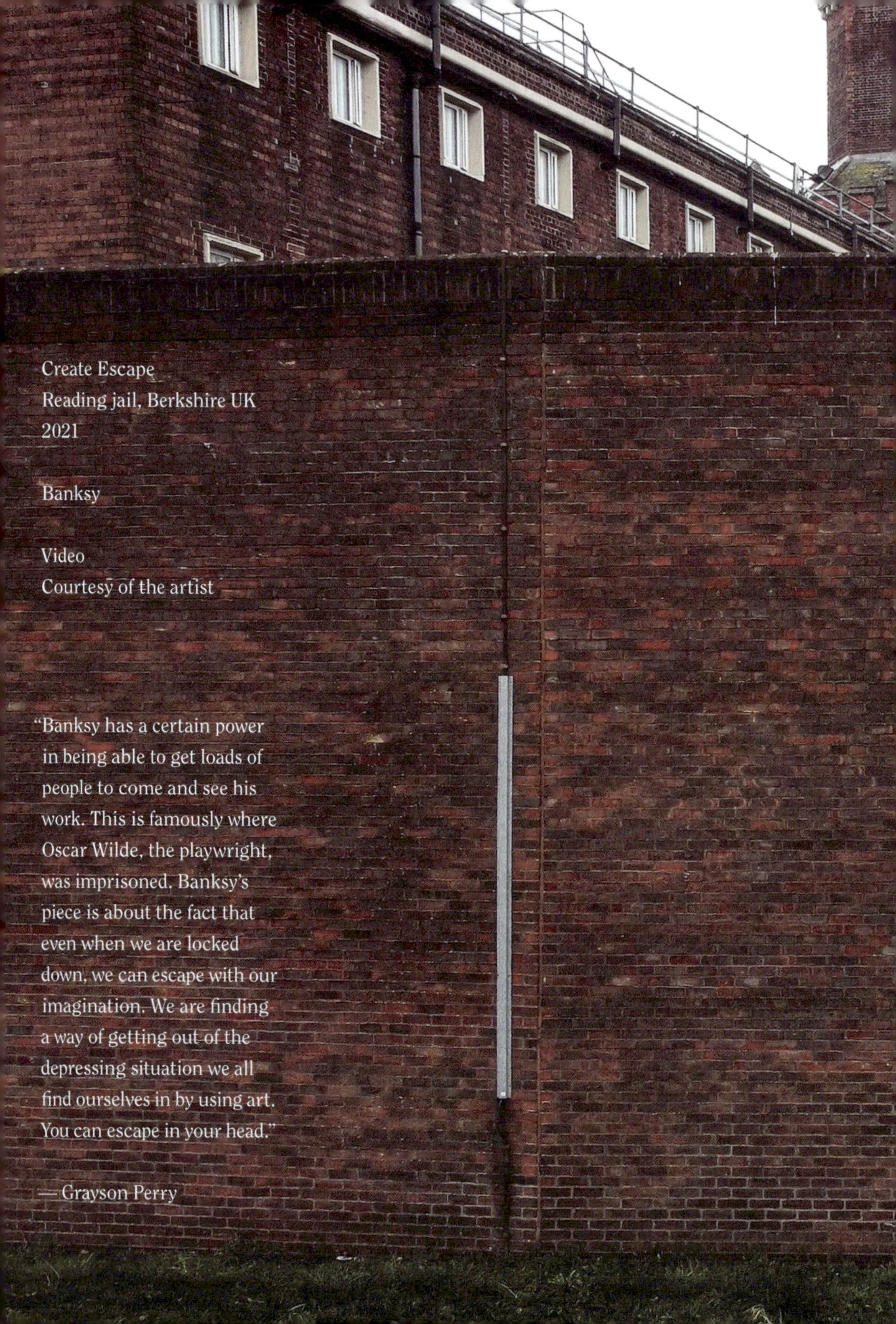

Create Escape
Reading jail, Berkshire UK
2021

Banksy

Video
Courtesy of the artist

"Banksy has a certain power
in being able to get loads of
people to come and see his
work. This is famously where
Oscar Wilde, the playwright,
was imprisoned. Banksy's
piece is about the fact that
even when we are locked
down, we can escape with our
imagination. We are finding
a way of getting out of the
depressing situation we all
find ourselves in by using art.
You can escape in your head."

— Grayson Perry

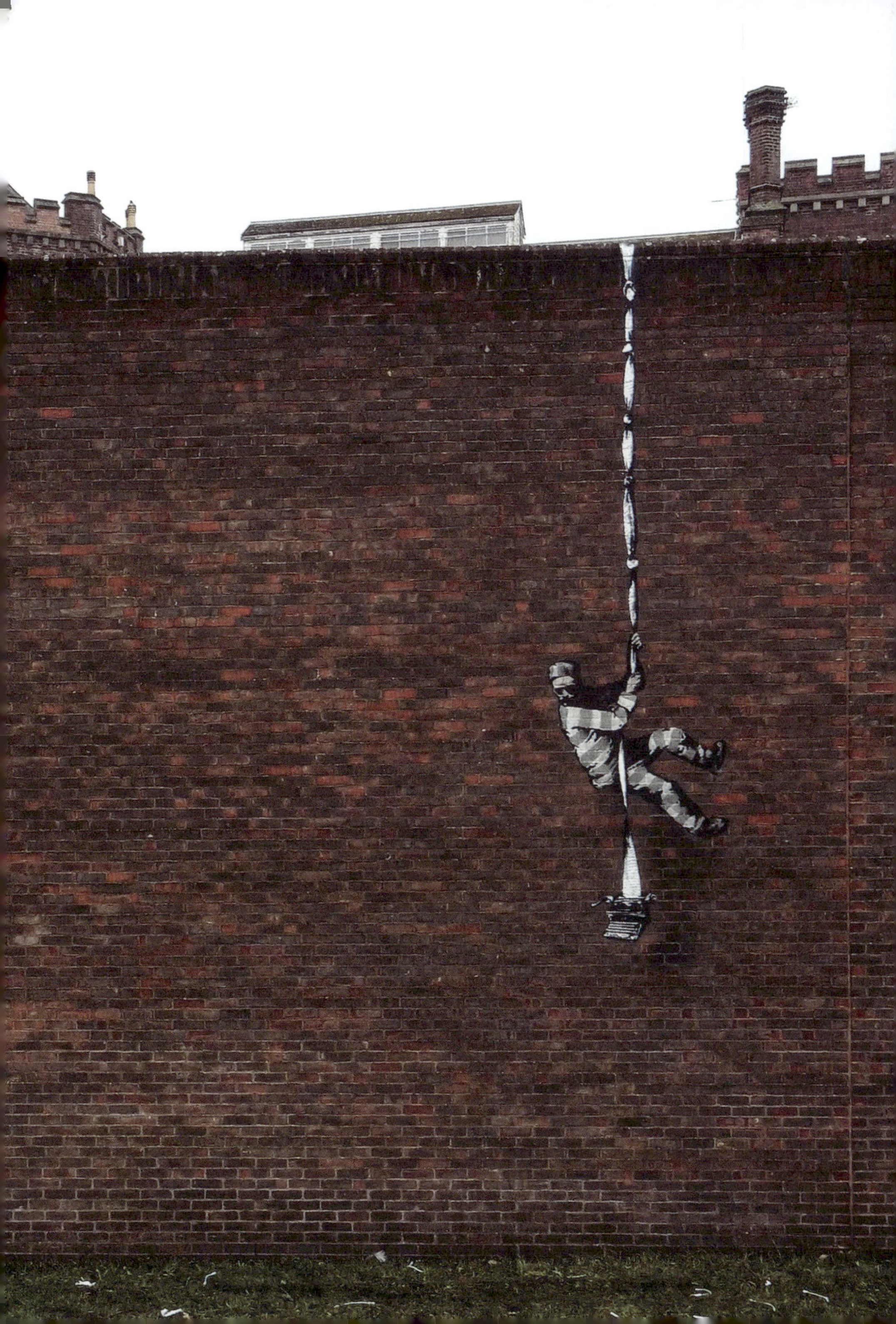

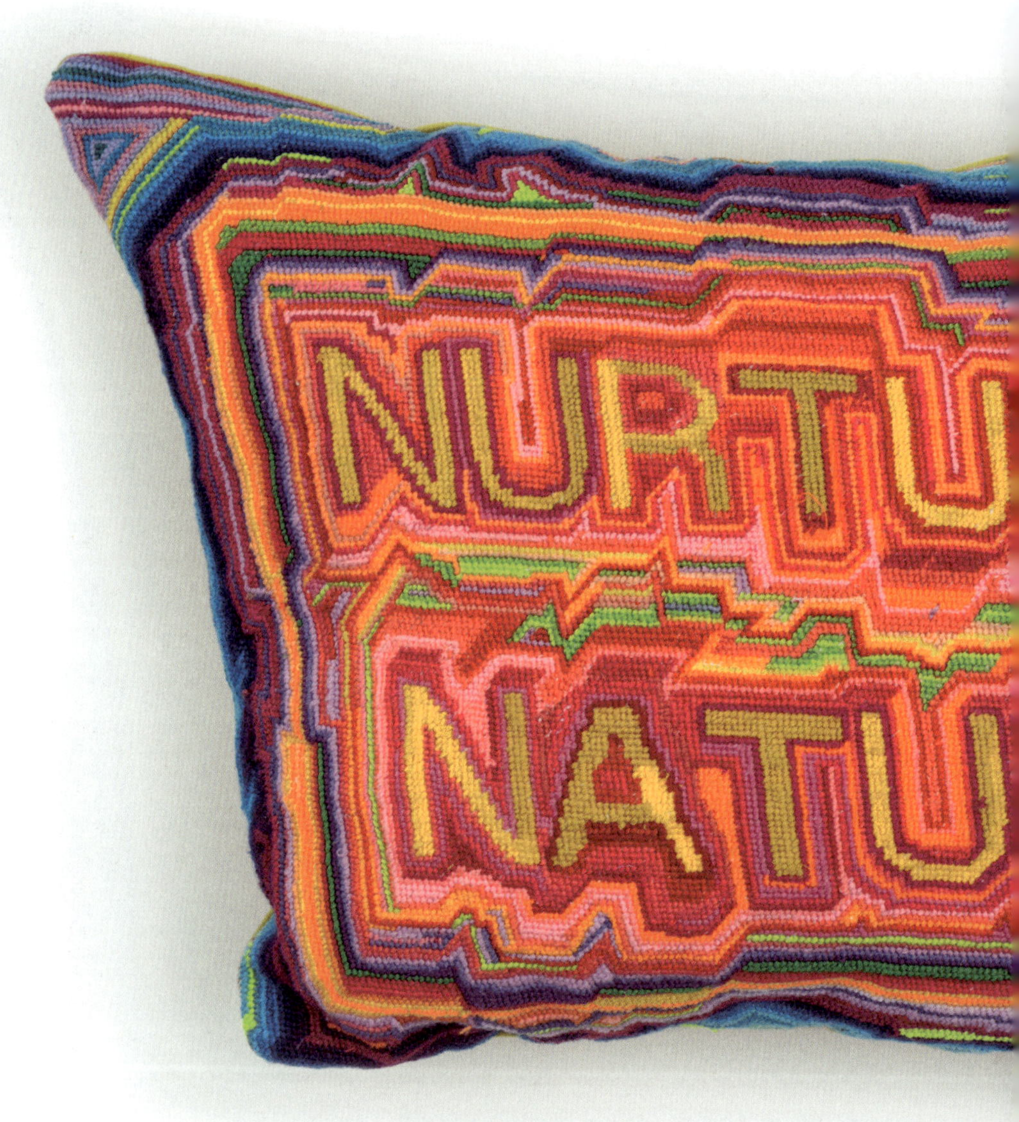

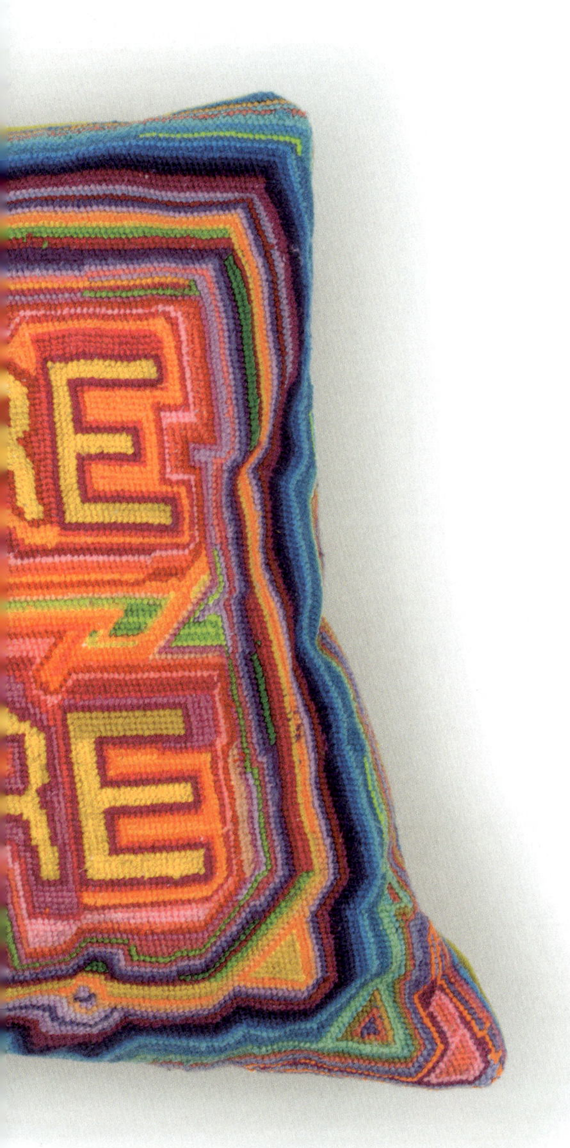

"We need to nurture
  nature. I love the backside
  of embroidery. It's chaos!
  Everybody sees everybody
  else's fronts and everybody
  else feels like this inside.
  So what we tend to do
  is compare our mess on
  the inside, to everybody's
  nurtured, outside appearance.
  You can no longer see the
  back of the embroidery.
  Like all of us, its true nature
  is hidden."

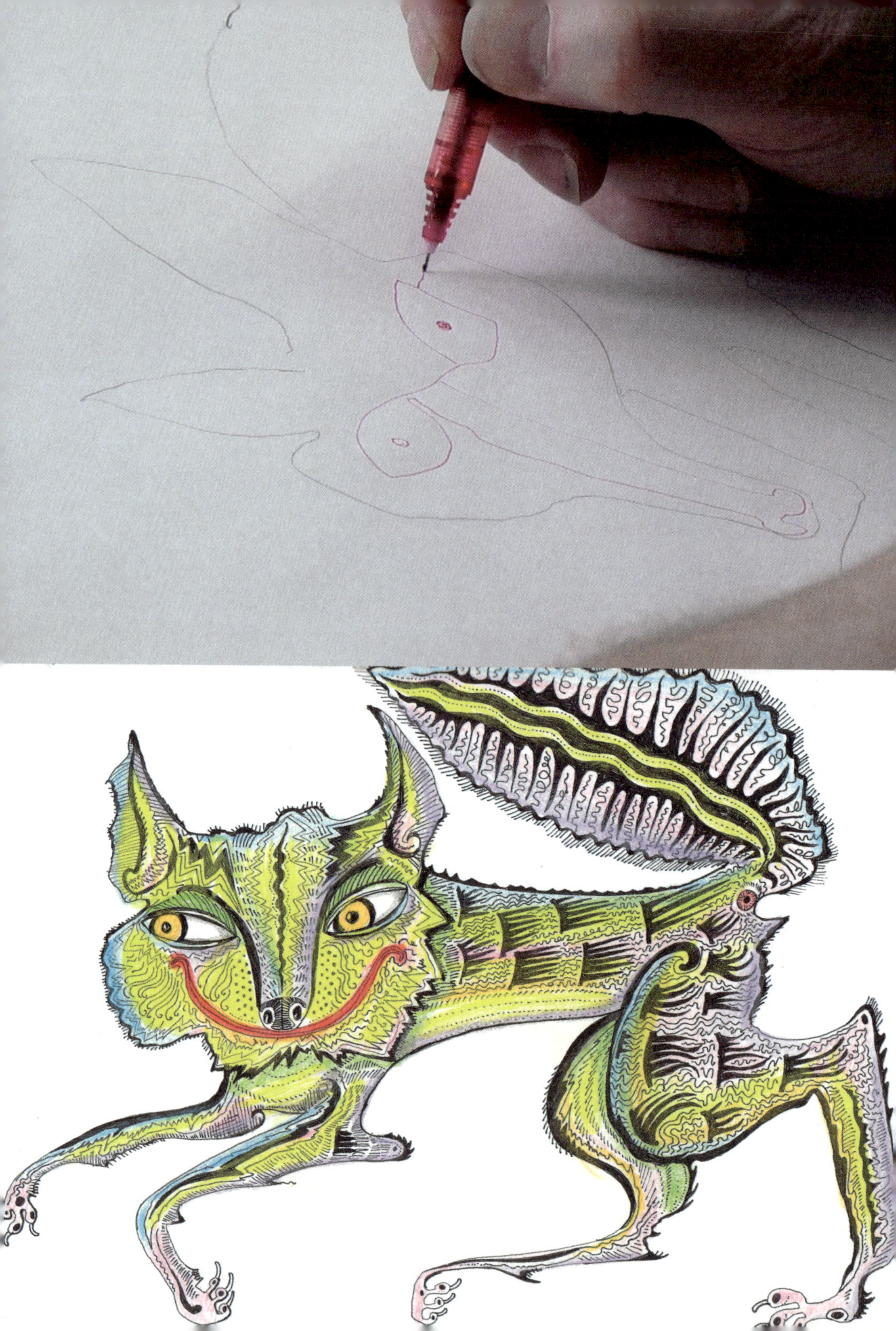

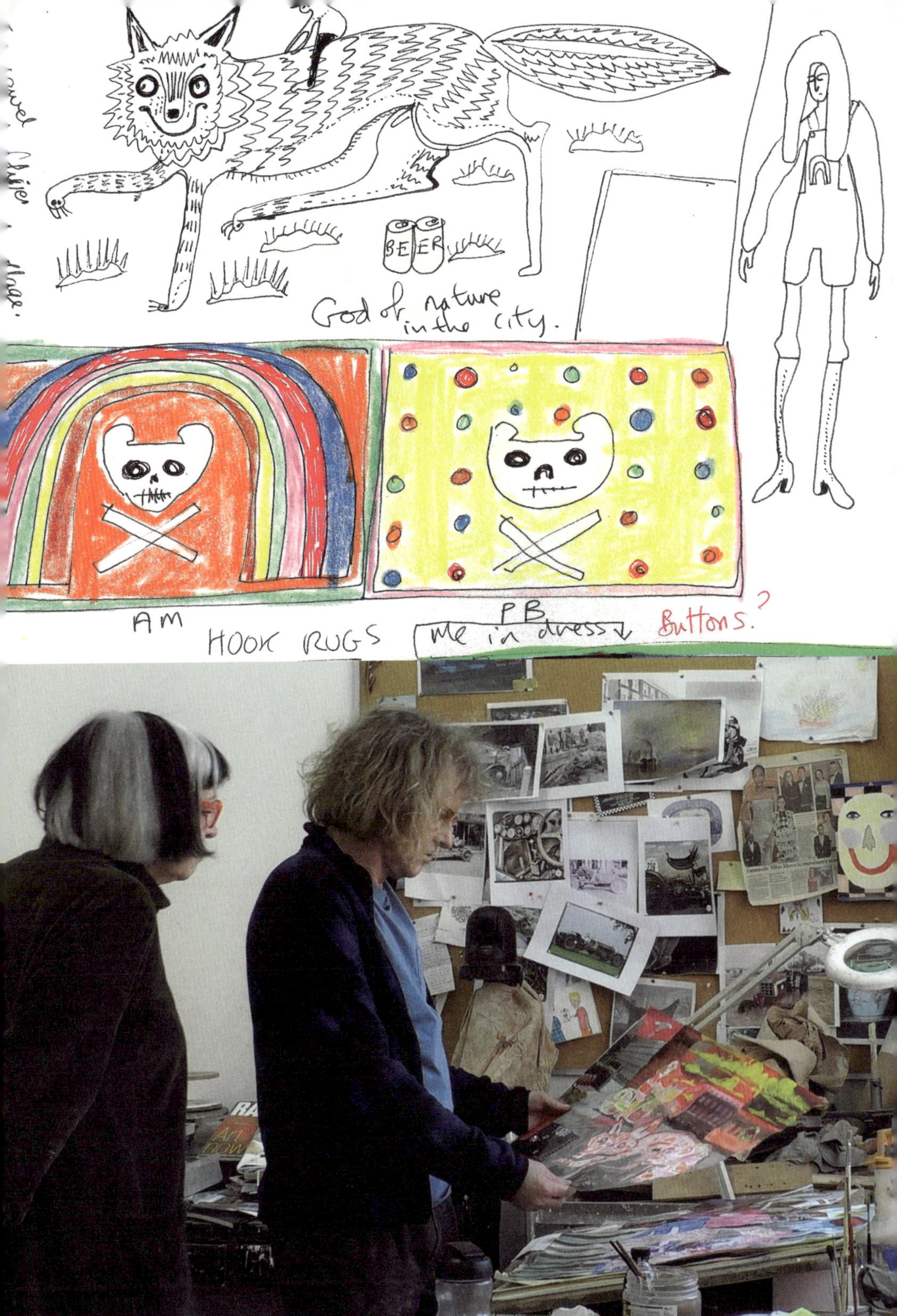
BEER
God of nature in the city.
AM   HOOK RUGS
PB
me in dress   Buttons?

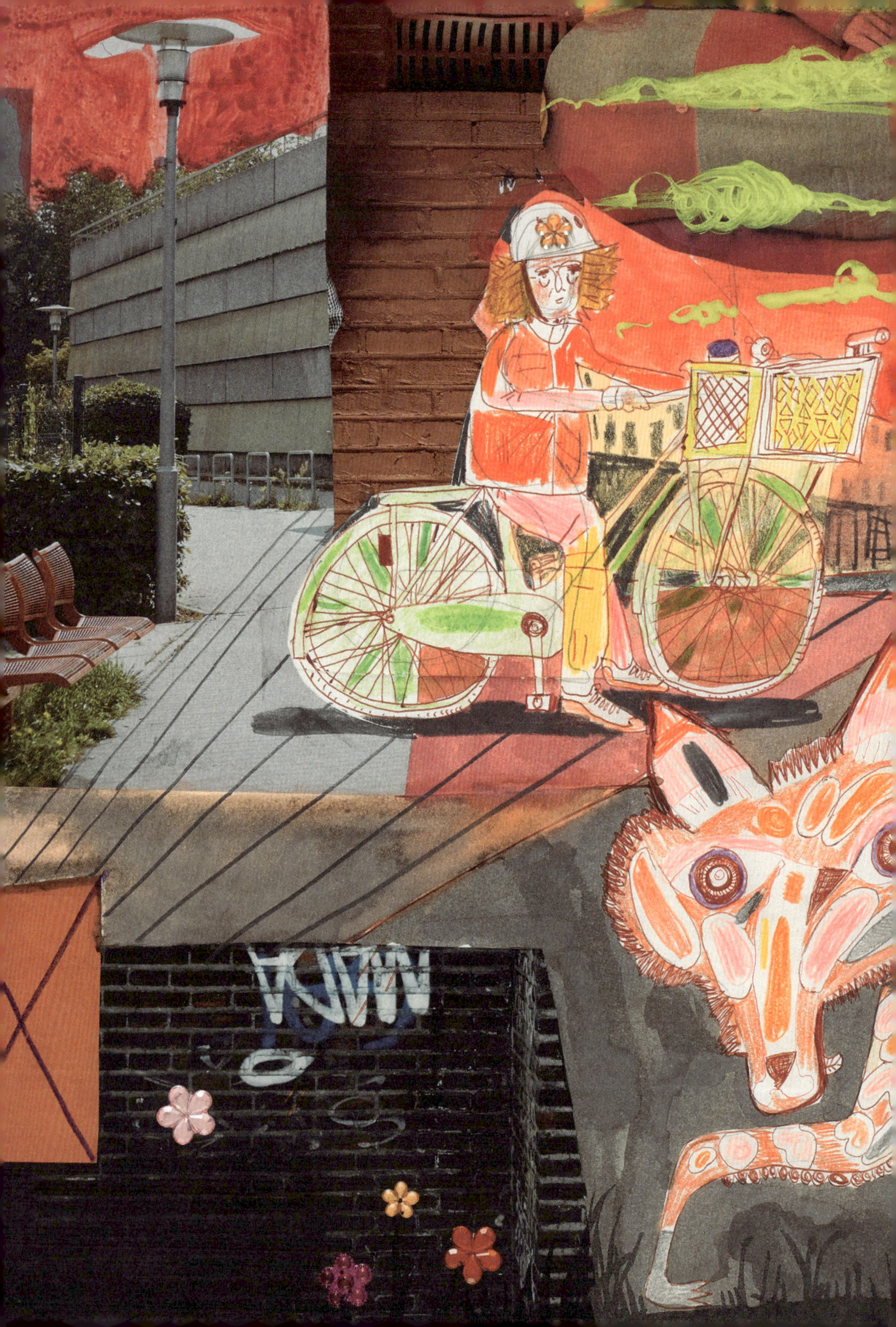

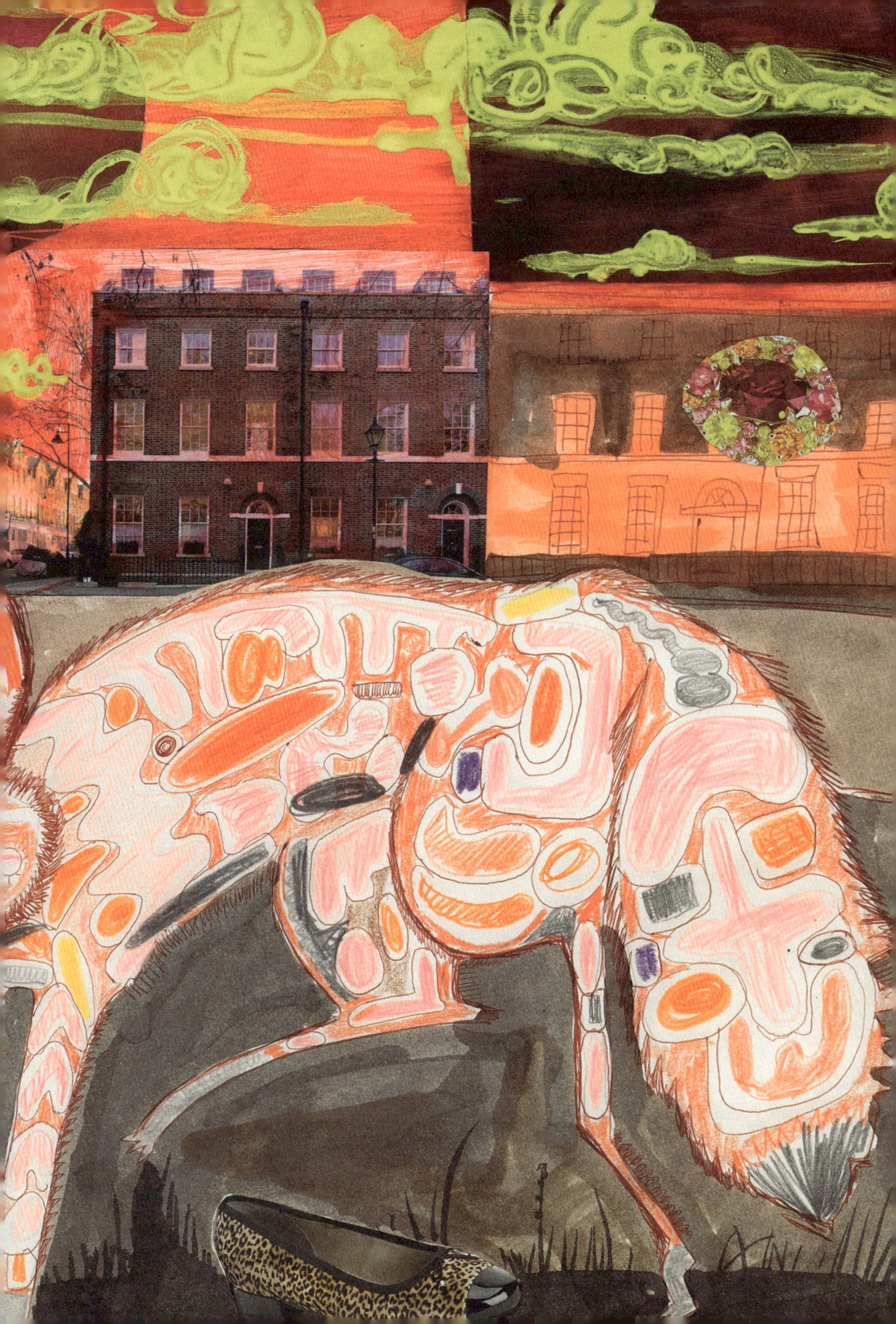

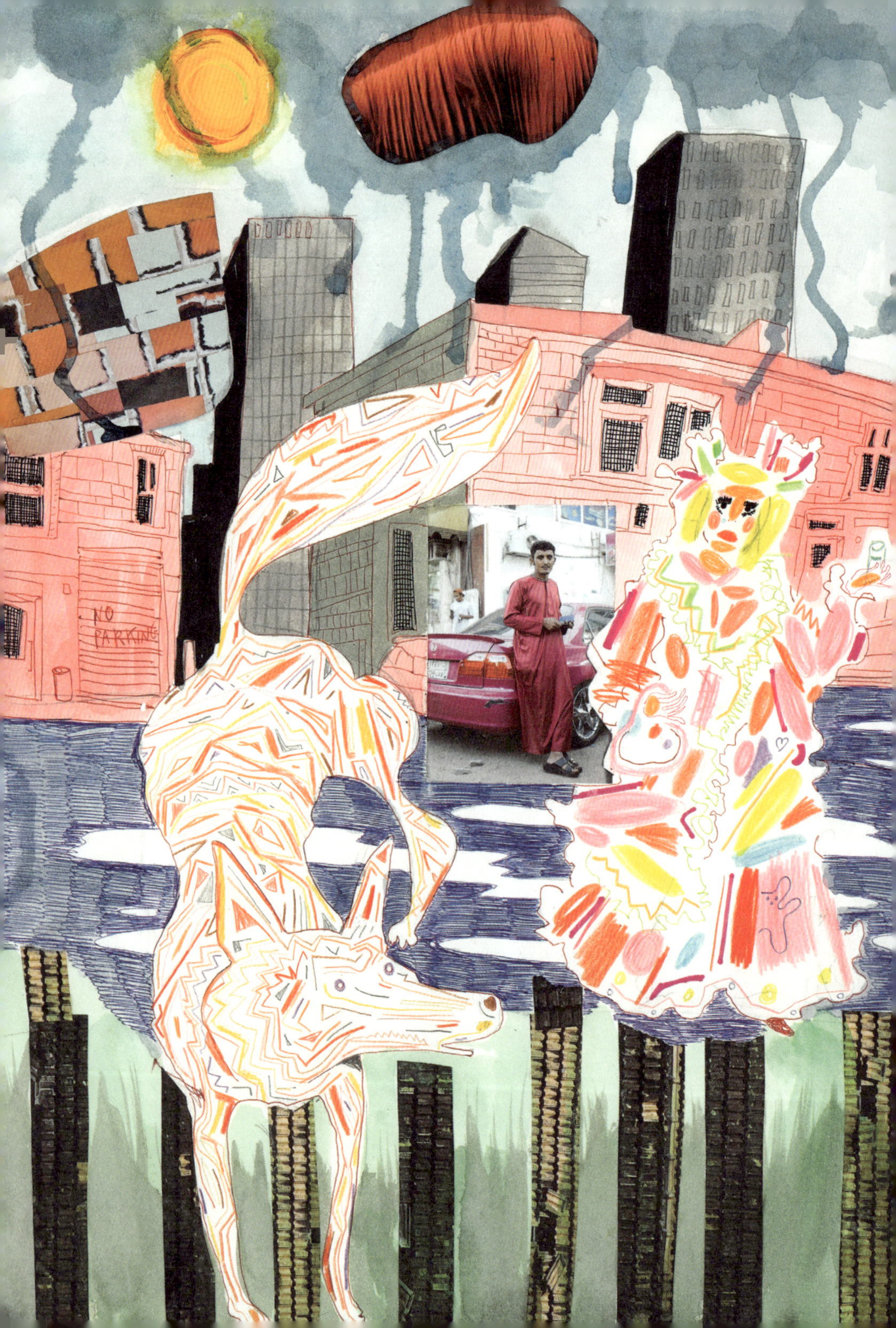

NO
PARKING

Previous:
Urban Fox 1
2021

Grayson Perry

Crayon, watercolour,
collage, ink, plastic jewels
Courtesy of the artist
and Victoria Miro

Urban Fox 2
2021

Grayson Perry

Crayon, watercolour,
collage, ink
Courtesy of the artist
and Victoria Miro

Please wear
a face covering

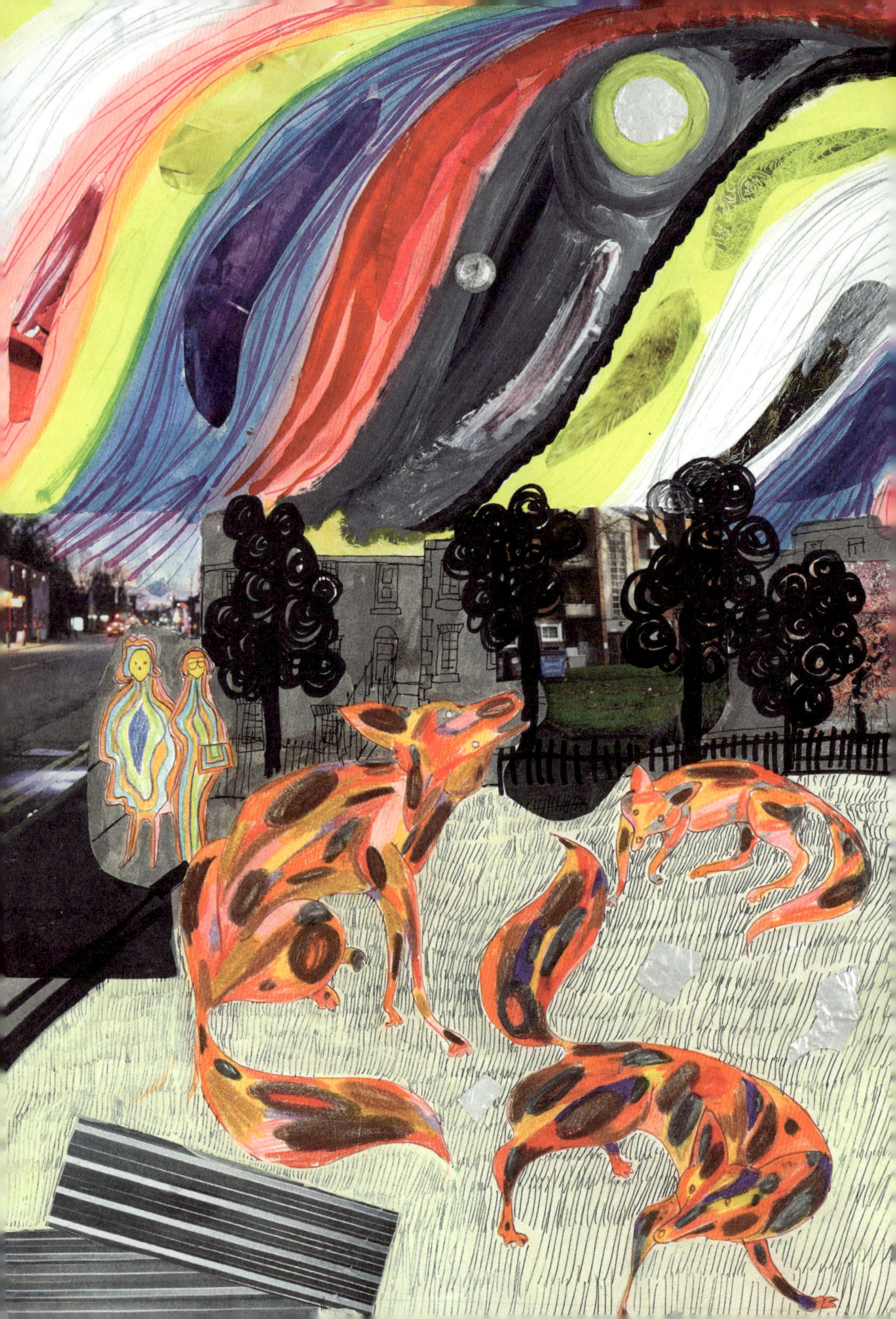

Urban Fox 3
2021

Grayson Perry

Crayon, watercolour,
collage, ink, silver foil
Courtesy of the artist
and Victoria Miro

"I can remember the first
time I saw an urban fox.
I was so thrilled to see this
piece of wildness wandering
across the road nonchalantly.
I like to go out on my bicycle
around the town at night.
They pop up all the time and
their eyes glow in my lights.
I have drawn, collaged
and painted my encounters
with Mr Fox."

I ♥ B

...ris' Flat

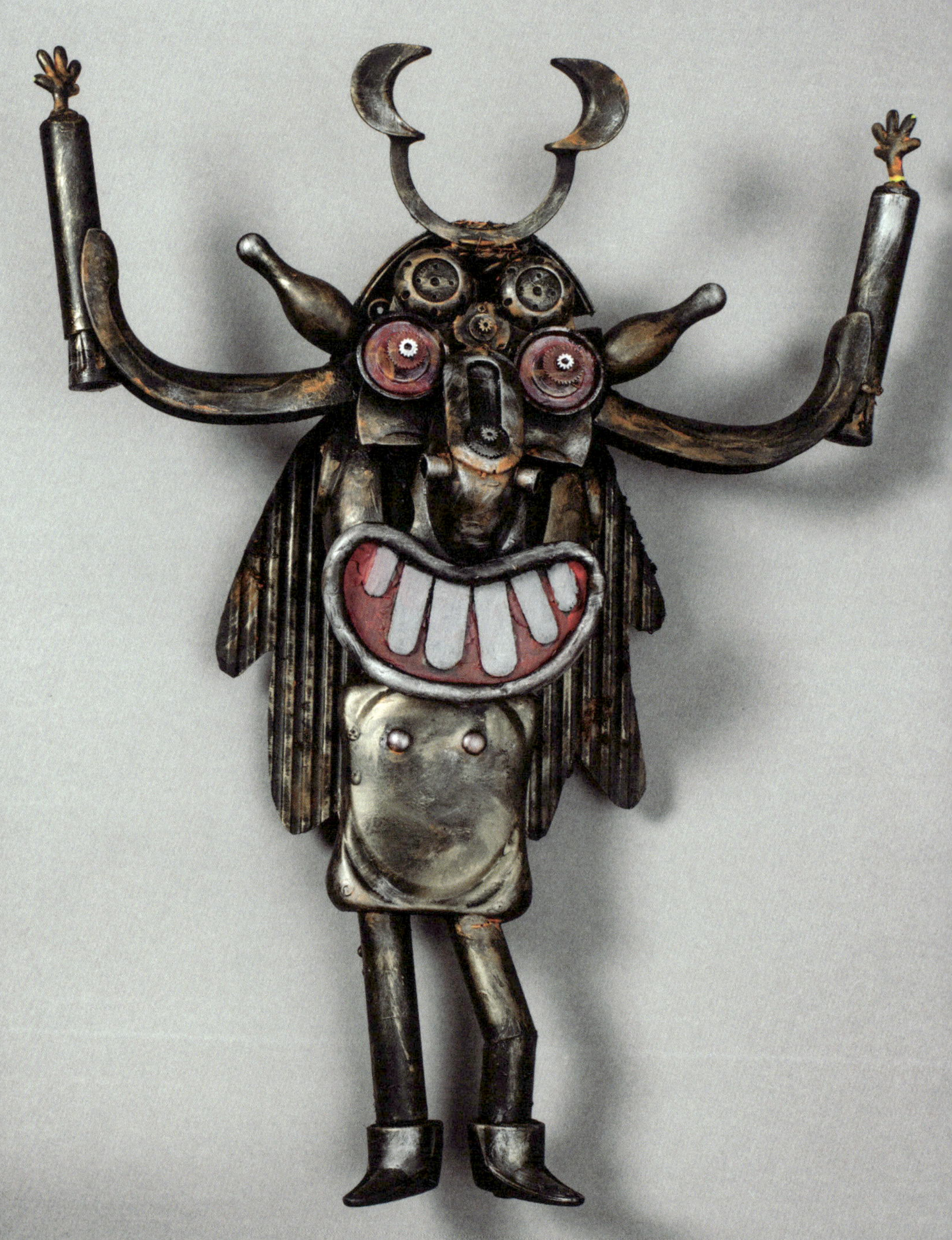

Stevyn
Colgan

"As we went into lockdown, I kept hearing neighbours saying that there was nothing locally for kids to do. Children preferred their screens. Going for a walk was 'boring'. I was also hearing a lot of talk about families' mental health suffering. I decided to try to do something about it.

I made a small set of monsters from recycled materials and hid them in some local woods. Then I waited. They soon got discovered and, all of a sudden, kids were dragging their parents off the sofa to go monster hunting!

As social media groups started to buzz, I suggested that kids make their own monsters. My initial six were joined by 95 more. The woods became too crowded and I had to find a new site. A local farm gave us a large space to set up a Monster Zoo. Many adults got involved too. The Zoo had over 360 exhibits and was attracting so many visitors that we put on a tuck shop. All profits were donated to charities.

I chose monsters because no one can ever tell a child that their monster is 'wrong'. All children can have a go.

I suspect that this will become my new day job!"

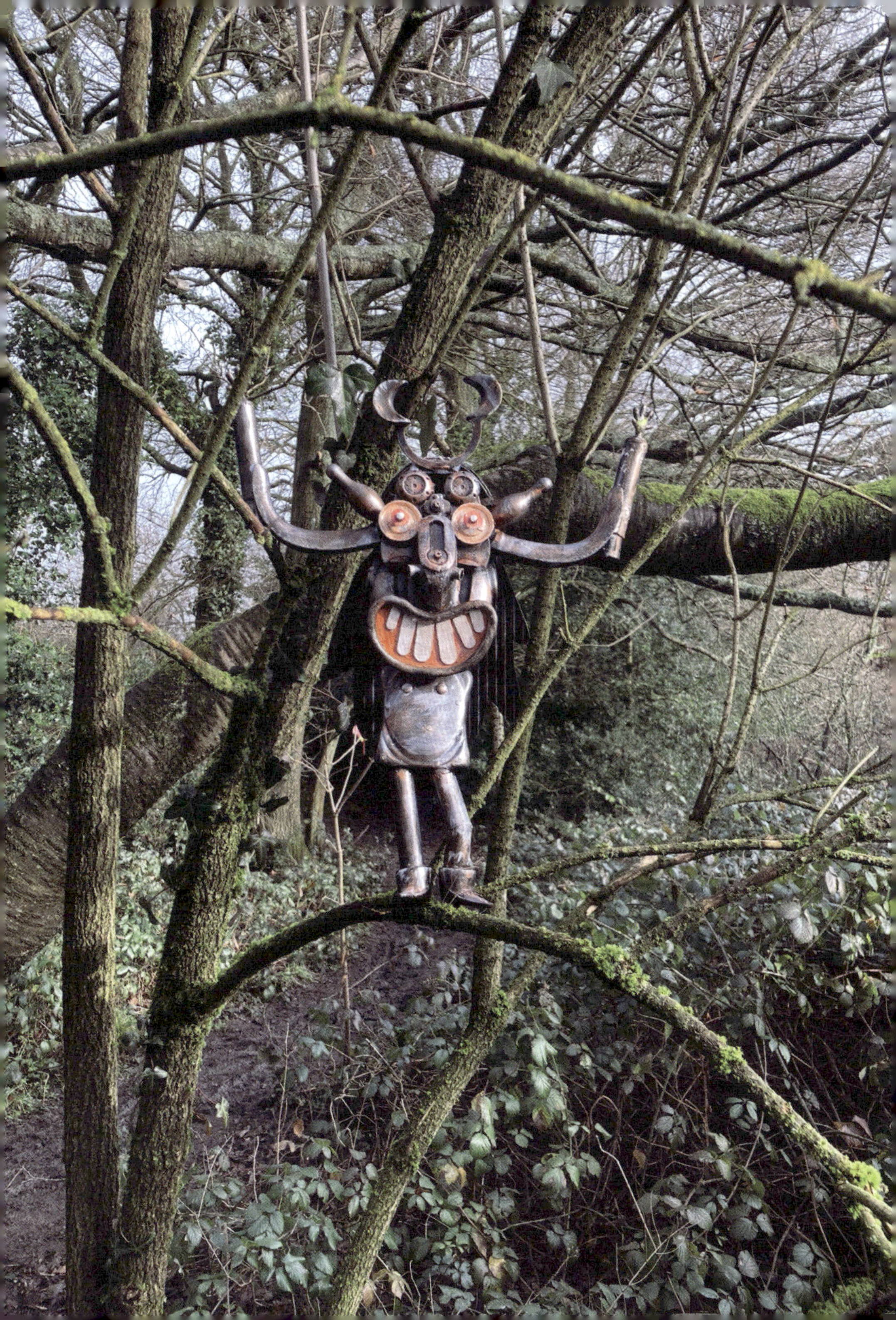

Food

"I doubt we've ever given the subject
of food as much thought as we gave
it during lockdown. Art about food
is so much more than a record of
what we've eaten.

Food is not just a biological need.
It makes our culture, it feeds our
emotions and it builds our identity.
Art about food tells us that food isn't
just this thing we eat. It comforts us,
it keeps us busy, it feeds us,
and it reminds us of who we are."

Clay Dumplings

Dora Lam, Winnie Lam
and Sam Lam

Air-drying clay
Courtesy of the artist

"My mum is from Guangzhou
and made the perilous
journey from China to Hong
Kong. When she landed
she didn't even have a pair
of shoes. I started thinking
about heirlooms and how
we don't have any. I said to
mum and dad 'let's make
clay dumplings', so we made
them together. Conversations
happened while we were
making them. You can tell
from the shape who made
which. I uncovered stories
about our family's past
which I never knew."

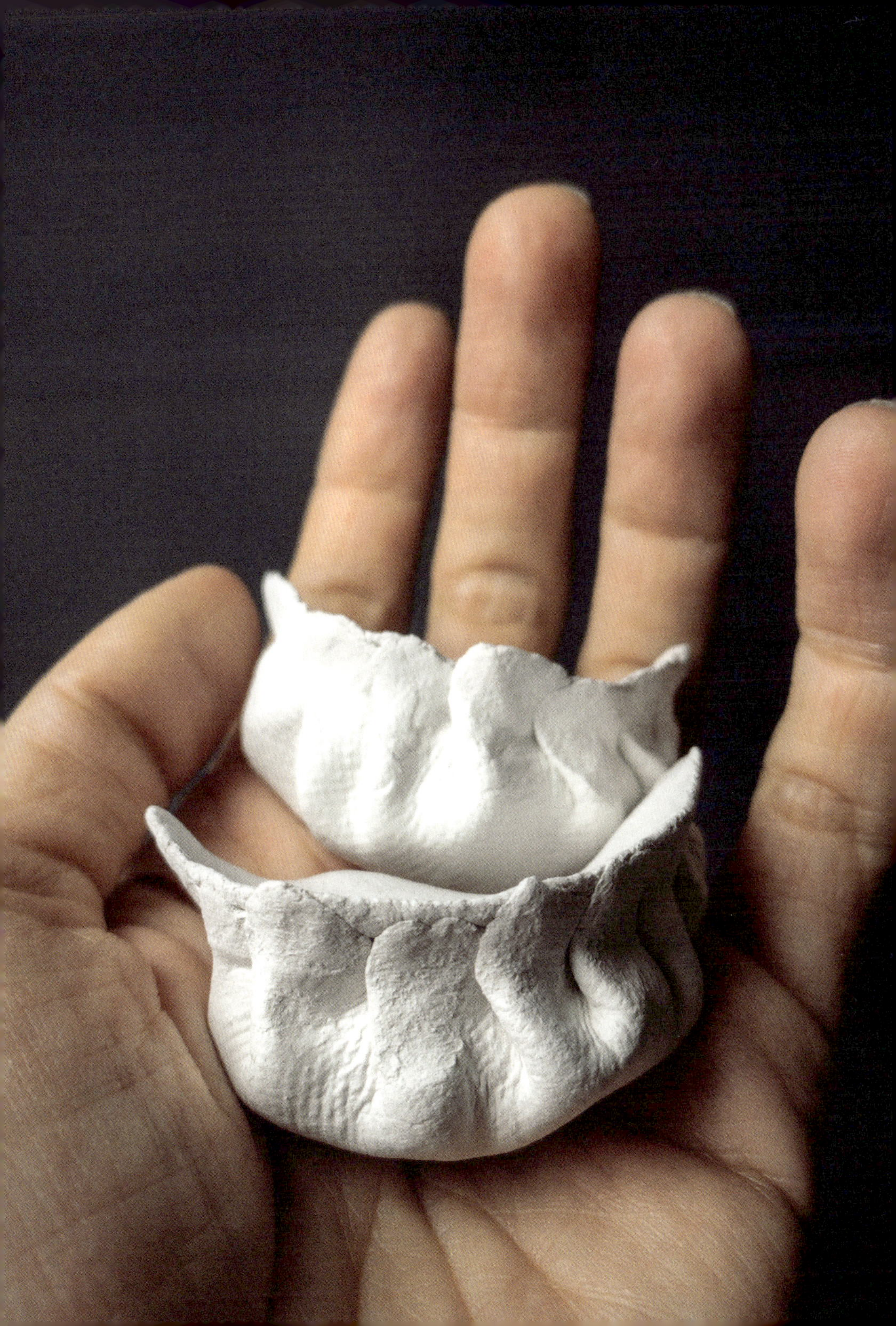

Dinner Date

Sweet and Maurizio
D'Apollonio
Maurizio Dining & Co.
Cambridge

Mixed media installation
Courtesy of the artist

"Dinner Date shows how
the pleasure of eating
together creates memories
and connections. Billy and
Antoinette are on their first
dinner date. They met on the
plane to the UK from Venice
and Billy invited Antoinette
for pizza. During lockdown,
we loved having Dinner Date
displayed in our restaurant
window. It made people smile
and for a fleeting moment,
remember what it was like to
eat out. It reminded us that
one day we would see our
customers again."

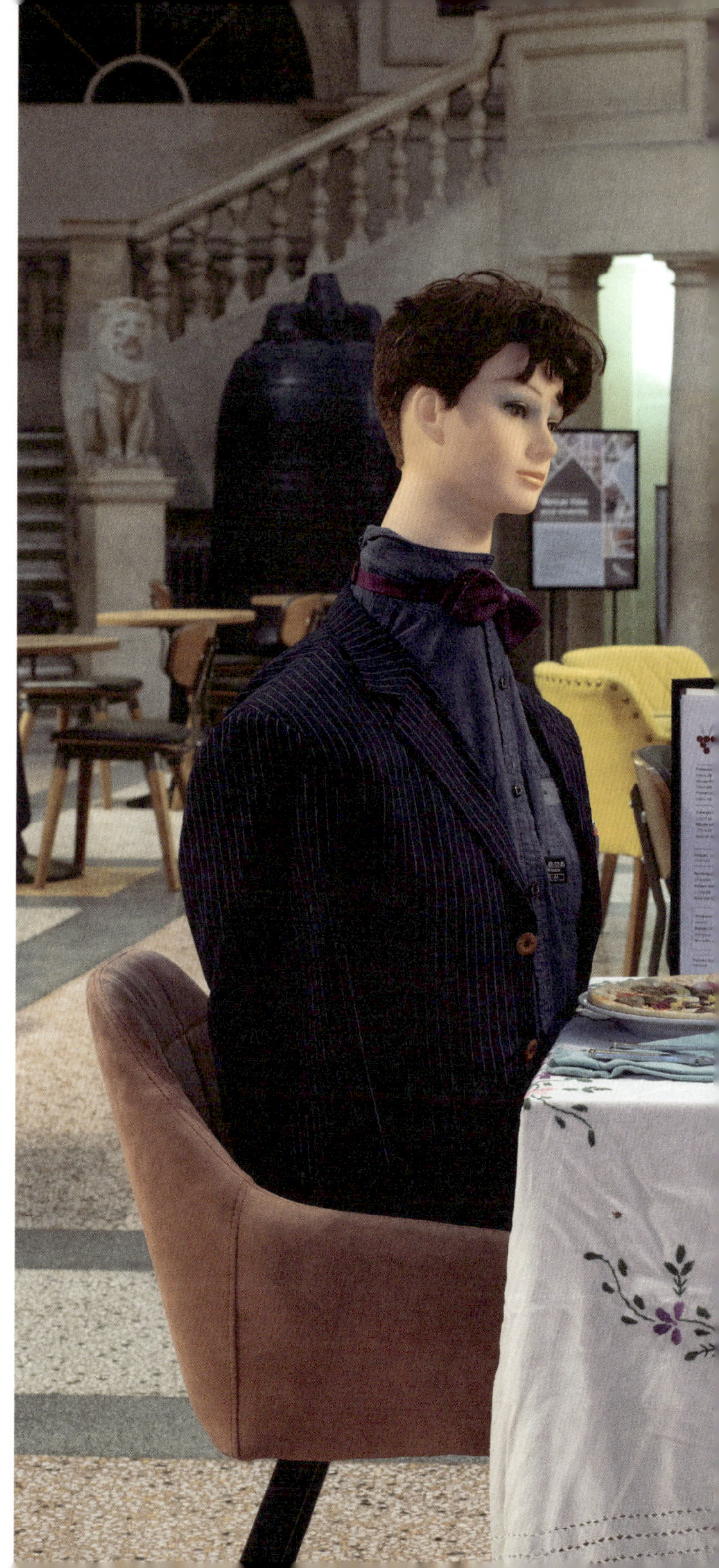

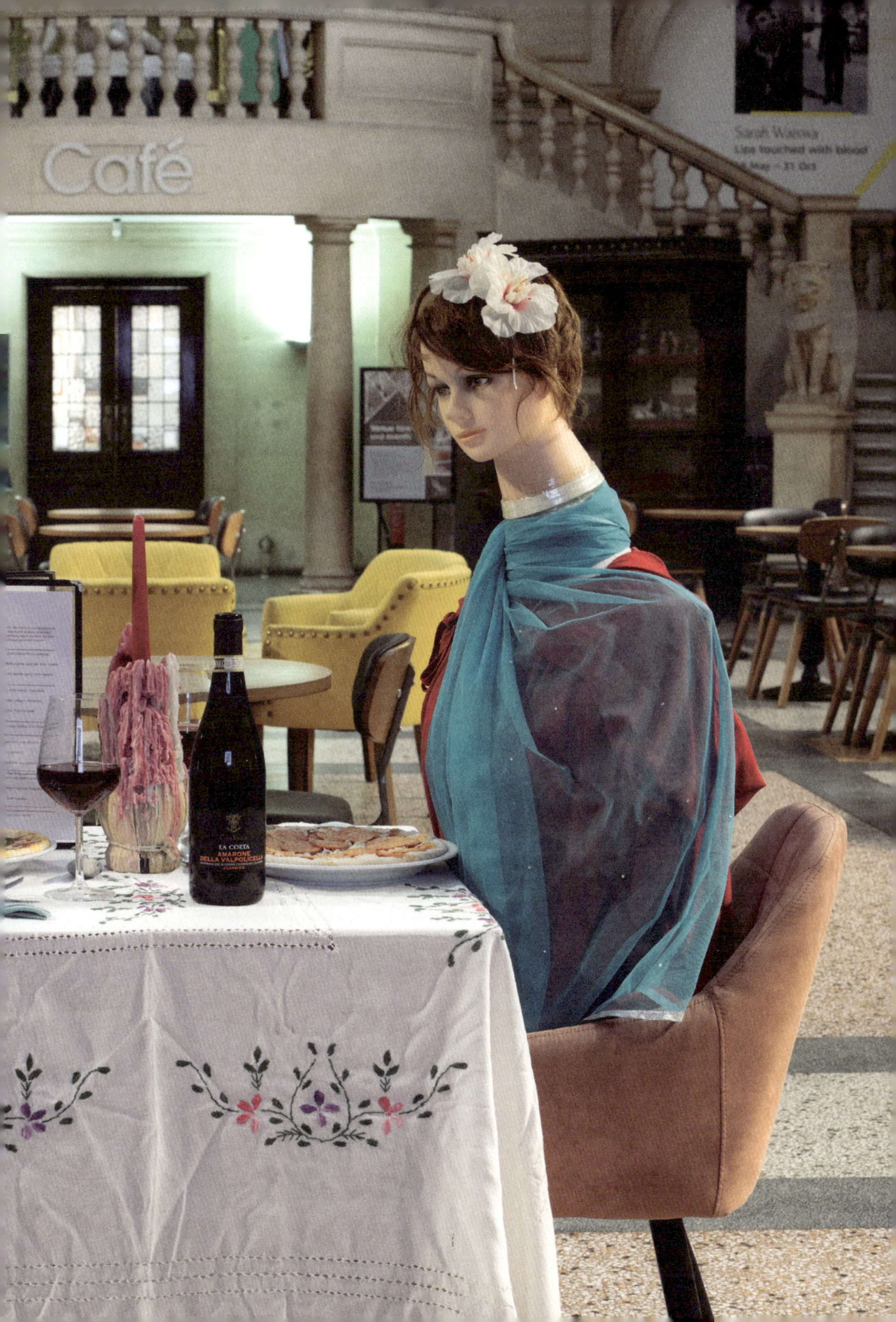
Café
Sarah Woolfson
Lips touched with blood
... May – 31 Oct
LA COSTA
AMARONE
DELLA VALPOLICELLA
CLASSICO

Debbie and the Foodbank

Lesley Woolvine

Coloured pencil and ink
on paper
Courtesy of the artist

"My artwork represents the
amazing work my local
neighbourhood centre has
done for the community
during the pandemic.
Supplying local people
with food hampers, clothes,
toiletries and so much more.
All the staff and volunteers
are absolutely amazing and
I am honoured to represent
them in this artwork."

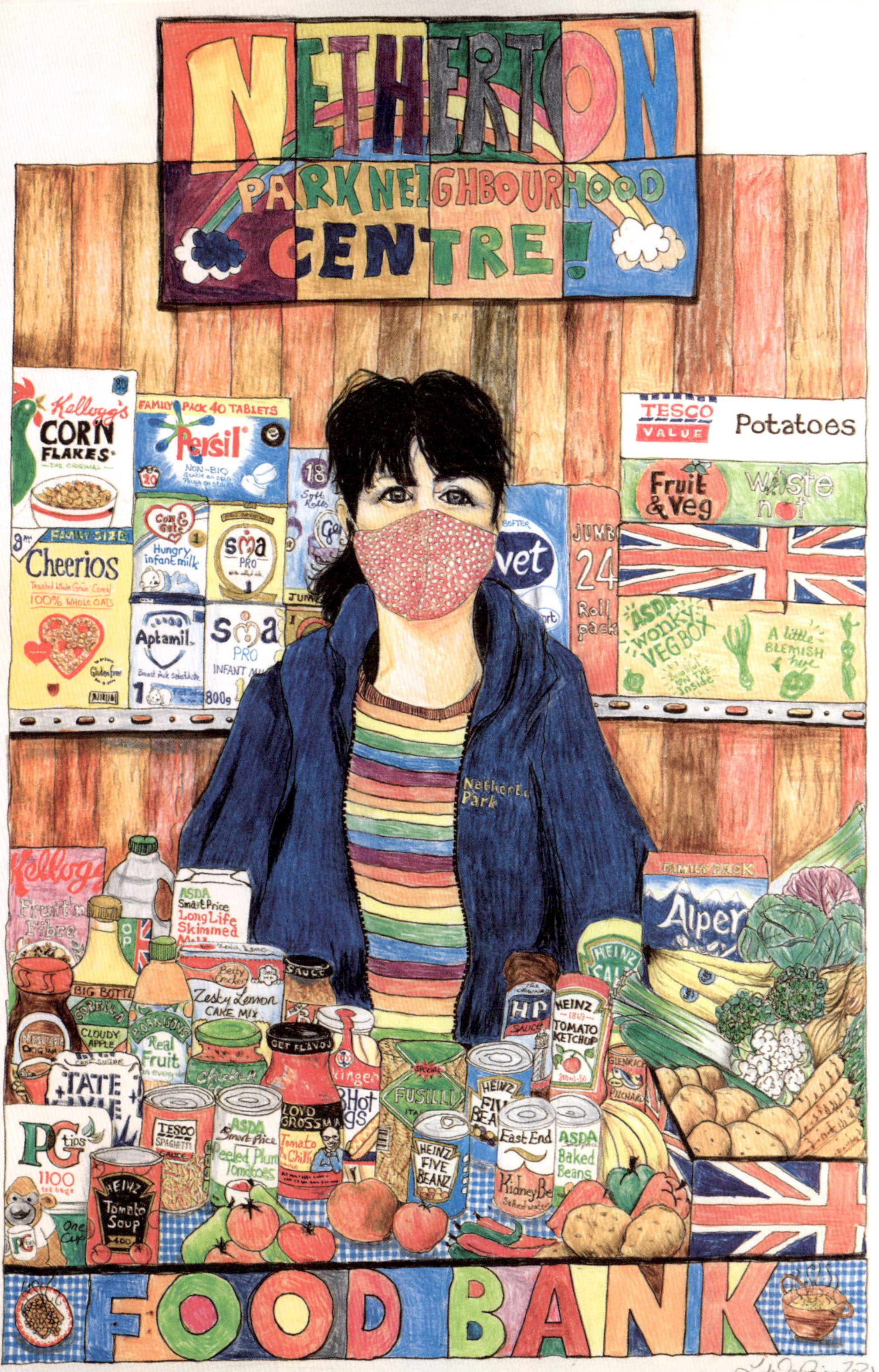

NETHERTON
PARK NEIGHBOURHOOD
CENTRE!
Kellogg's CORN FLAKES
THE ORIGINAL
FAMILY PACK 40 TABLETS
Persil
NON-BIO
TESCO VALUE
Potatoes
Fruit & Veg
Waste not
FAMILY SIZE
Cheerios
Toasted Whole Grain Corn
100% WHOLE OATS
Gluten Free
Cow & Gate
Hungry infant milk
sma PRO
18 Soft Rolls
Velvet
SOFTER
JUMBO 24 Roll pack
ASDA wonky VEG BOX
A little BLEMISH here
Aptamil
sma PRO
INFANT MILK
800g
Netherton Park
Kellogg's
Fruit 'n Fibre
ASDA Smart Price
Long Life Skimmed Milk
FAMILY PACK
Alper
HEINZ
BIG BOTTLE
Zesty Lemon CAKE MIX
SAUCE
HP SAUCE
HEINZ 1869 TOMATO KETCHUP
CLOUDY APPLE
ROBINSONS Real Fruit
GET FLAVOUR
GINGER
SPECIAL
FUSILLI
HEINZ FIVE BEAN
GLENRYCK PILCHARDS
TATE
Chicken
HOT DOGS
PG tips
1100 tea bags
One Cup
TESCO SPAGHETTI SAUCE
ASDA Smart Price Peeled Plum Tomatoes
LLOYD GROSSMAN Tomato & Chilli
HEINZ FIVE BEANZ
East End Kidney Beans Salted water
ASDA Baked Beans
HEINZ Tomato Soup
FOOD BANK

Sherbet Lemon –
A Memory of Colin

Sally-Anne Wilson

Ceramic and glass mosaic
Courtesy of the artist

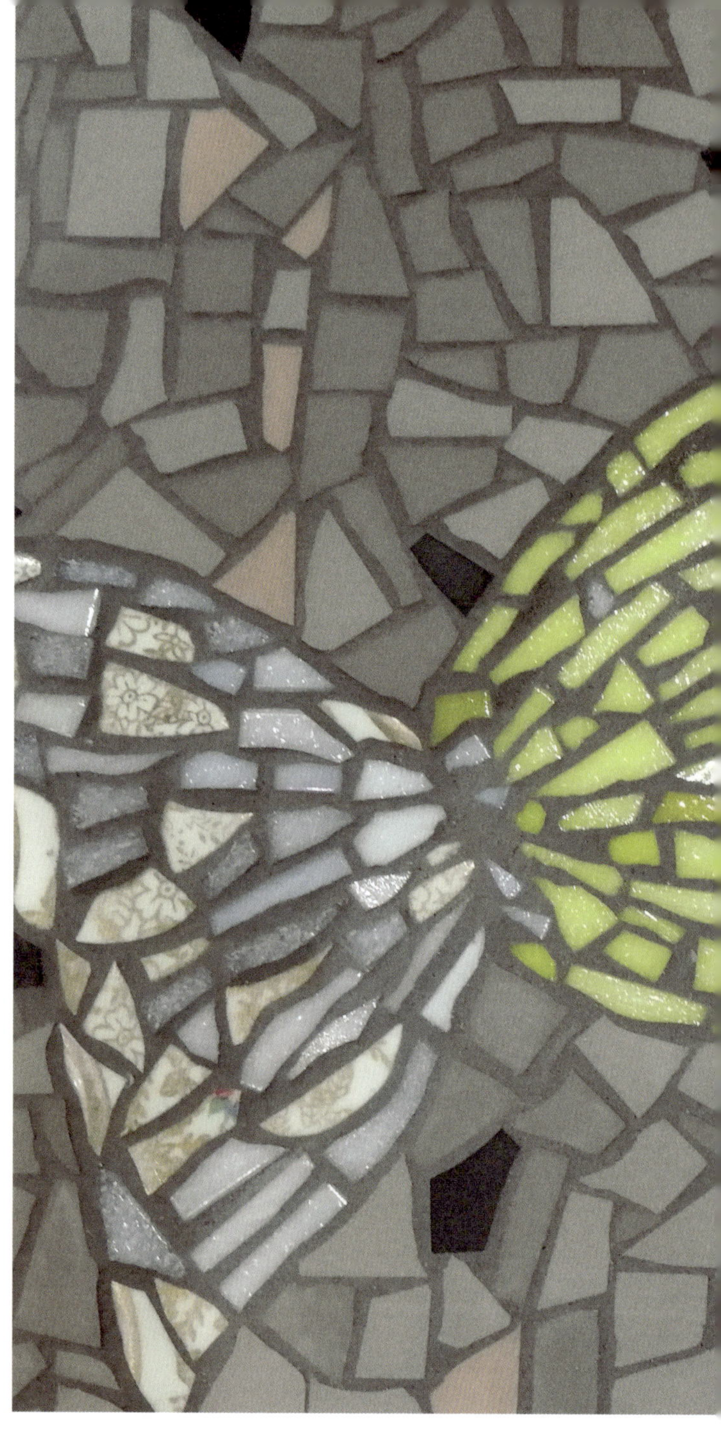

"I worked with Colin in the
Emergency Department.
He always made time to
check how you were. He
could win anyone over with
his big smile, beautiful laugh,
and a sherbet lemon. He had
an amazing ability to connect
with people. He would leave
you feeling that you mattered.
His death during the first
wave of the pandemic
was devastating to us as
individuals and the hospital.
He was never without sherbet
lemons. I created this to
remember him."

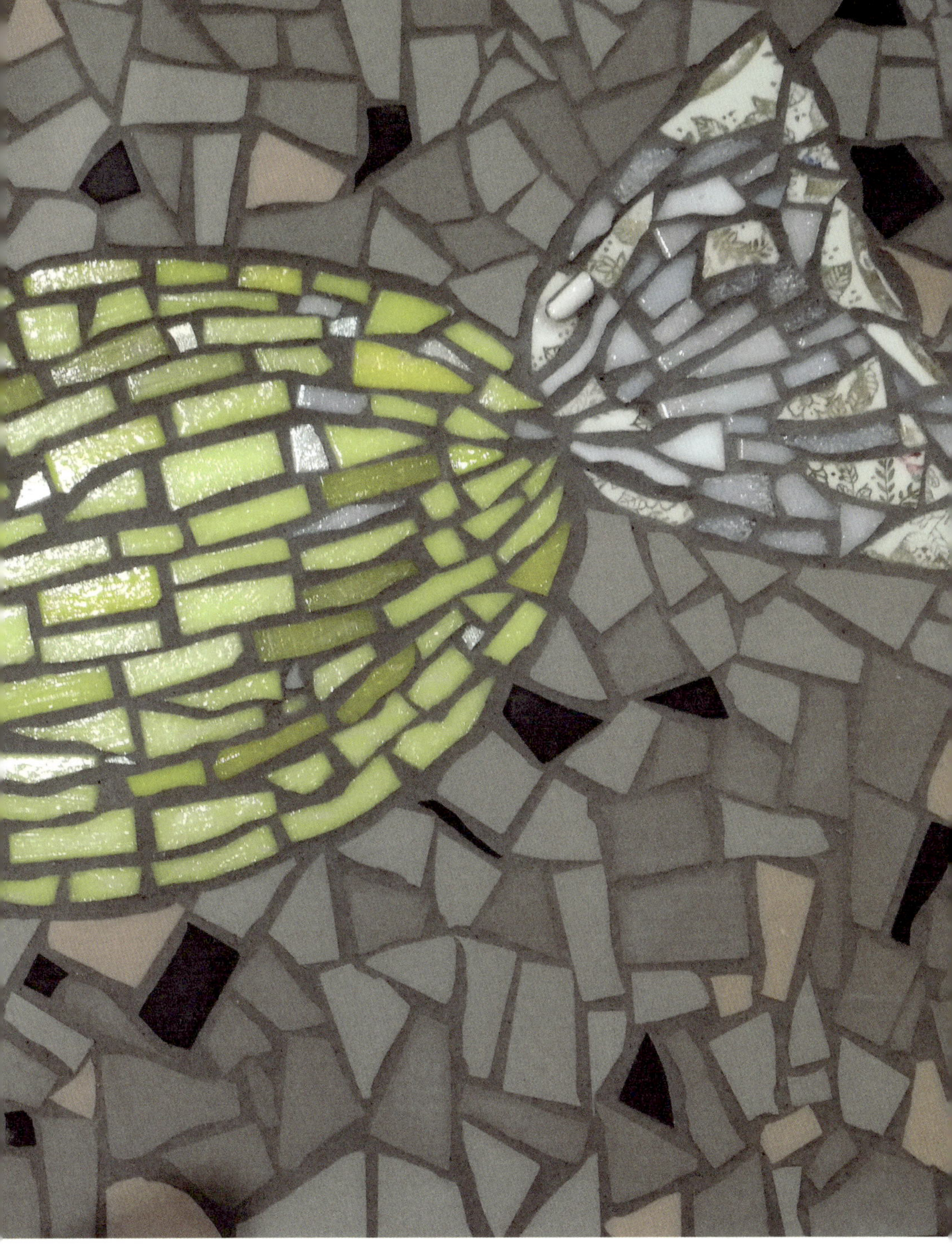

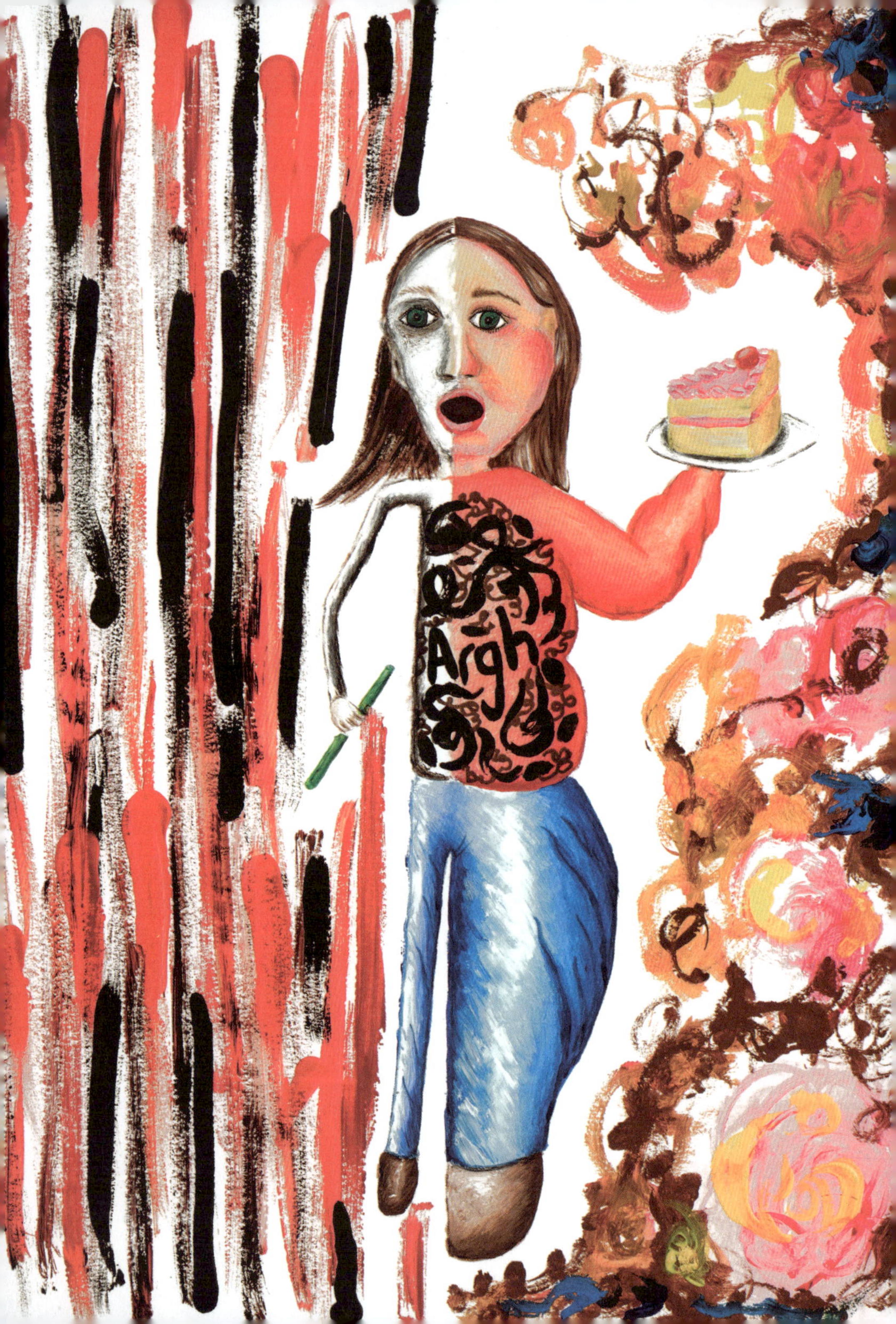
Argh

Caroline
Harvey

Inner Turmoil of an
Eating Disorder

Caroline Harvey

Acrylic paint on paper
Courtesy of the artist

"When I think of the topic of food, I sadly think of how it has become such a torturous thing for so many people. I have attended many eating disorder groups where half of the people were very overweight and the other half were very underweight. At the start everyone thinks they will be really different. Instead we discover that we are all struggling with exactly the same things. Both strategies helped to numb and cope with difficult emotions. Everyone looks at appearance and makes judgements. The actual root of an eating disorder is the pain and turmoil that is going on inside and they do not know how to cope with it. I wanted to capture that it is this inner pain that leads to an eating disorder. They need some love, understanding and support.

Being creative is important to me as it helps to express my emotions. It can be easier to express it with art than with writing or talking. Sometimes you can communicate more clearly and powerfully with a picture than with words. Making art during lockdown was especially helpful when spending time with friends and having an opportunity to chat was greatly reduced!"

Art has
helped us
through this

Fish and Chips

David Read

Collage – magazine cuttings
and paint on paper
Courtesy of the artist

"While one night watching Grayson,
Thoughts flowed I'd have to hasten.
Of things to eat and yummy food,
I thought of grub and then I stewed.

Of all the food that we all love,
The one that stands out well above.
Is fish and chips for me and you,
The nations favourite through and through.

So off I set and worked and planned,
With cuttings, scissors and glue in hand.
Old magazines and paper too,
I snipped and cut and glued so true.

And when all done and sent to Grayson,
Sue Perkins picked it, well how amazin.
And now it's here in front of you,
I hope you like it just like Sue."

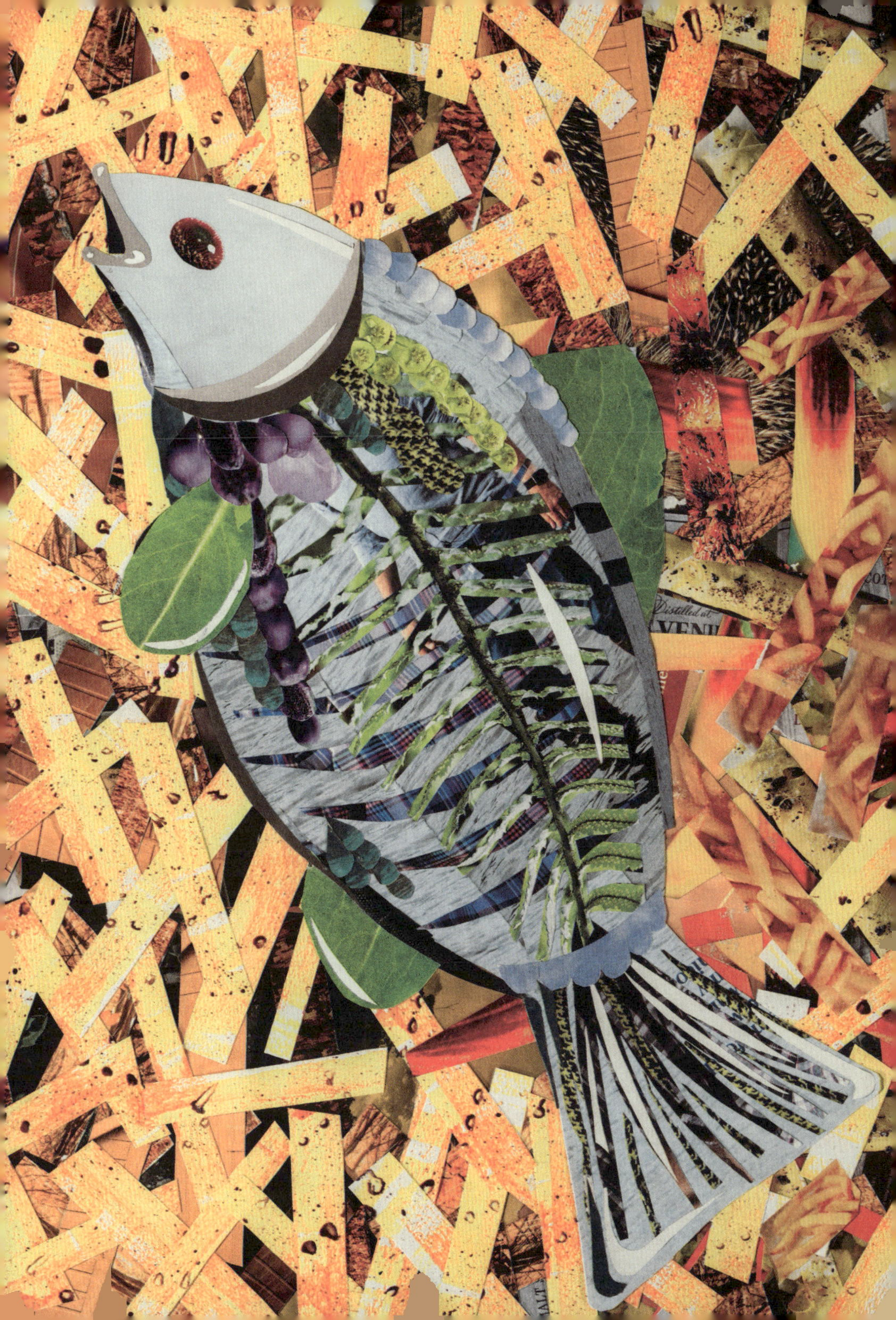

Triple Art Bypass

Lucy Sparrow

Hand-sewn felt installation
Courtesy of the artist

"My fascination with all things
medical is represented here
by this life-size felt realisation
of a patient on the operating
table, surrounded by the
paraphernalia of surgery
and towering walls
of prescription drugs.

I use the medium of felt –
a comforting and tactile
material – to initiate a
conversation about difficult
subjects such as mortality,
physical and mental health
and the importance of
our NHS.

Created as part of the
National Felt Service (NFS)
body of work, Triple Art
Bypass is a companion
piece to the Bourdon
Street Chemist exhibition
that opened in London in
April 2021, developing the
medical theme into a fully
stocked chemist where I
appeared daily to administer
prescriptions to customers."

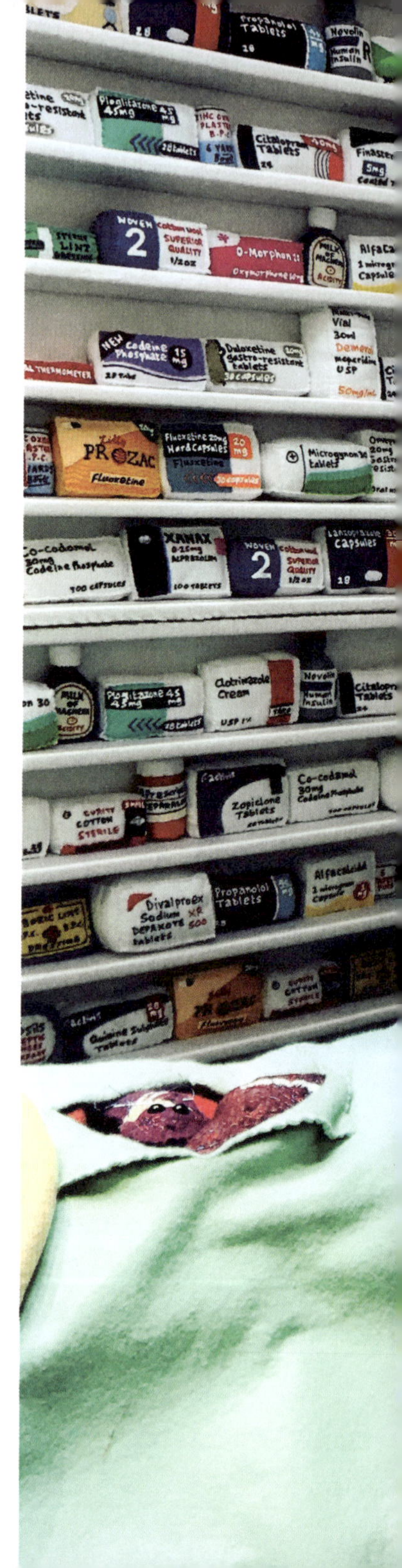

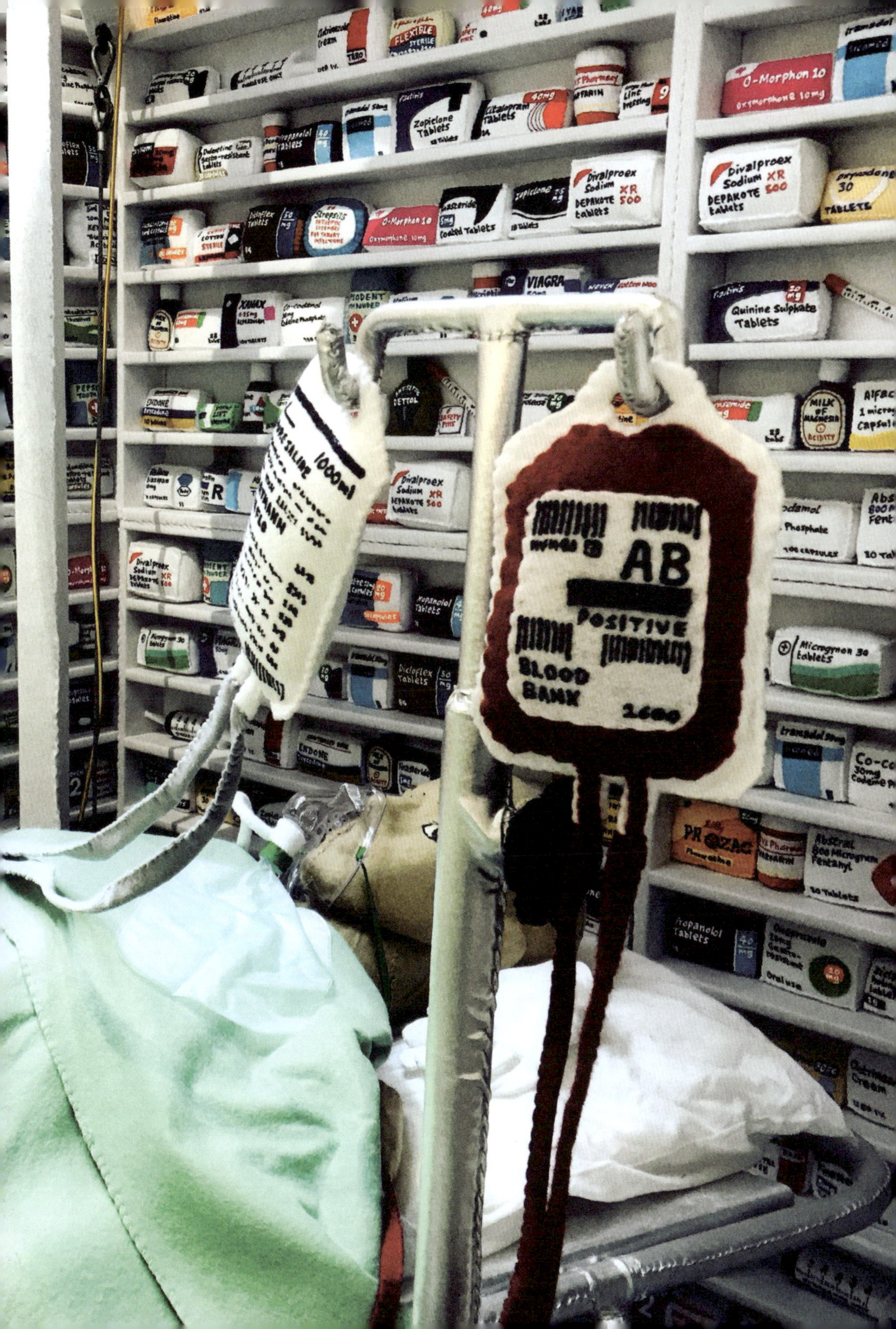

1000ml
SALINE
AB
POSITIVE
BLOOD
BANK
2600
O-Morphon 10
Oxymorphone 10mg
Divalproex Sodium XR
DEPAKOTE tablets
Zopiclone Tablets
Quinine Sulphate Tablets
MILK OF MAGNESIA
VIAGRA
XANAX
PROZAC
Fluoxetine
Propanolol Tablets
Micrognon 30 tablets
Diclofex Tablets
ENDONE
Co-codamol

Too Early for Breakfast

Sudjadi Widjaja

Acrylic paint on canvas
Courtesy of the artist

"One morning, I gave my
partner Robert his breakfast
in bed. I guess he was still
tired, even though it was
already 9am! But I never
thought that he would fall
asleep with his breakfast tray
on his lap. I decided to paint
him from the picture I took.

Being creative was more
liberating during lockdown.
I didn't have to think about
going to work the next day.
I had all the time I needed
to paint or create."

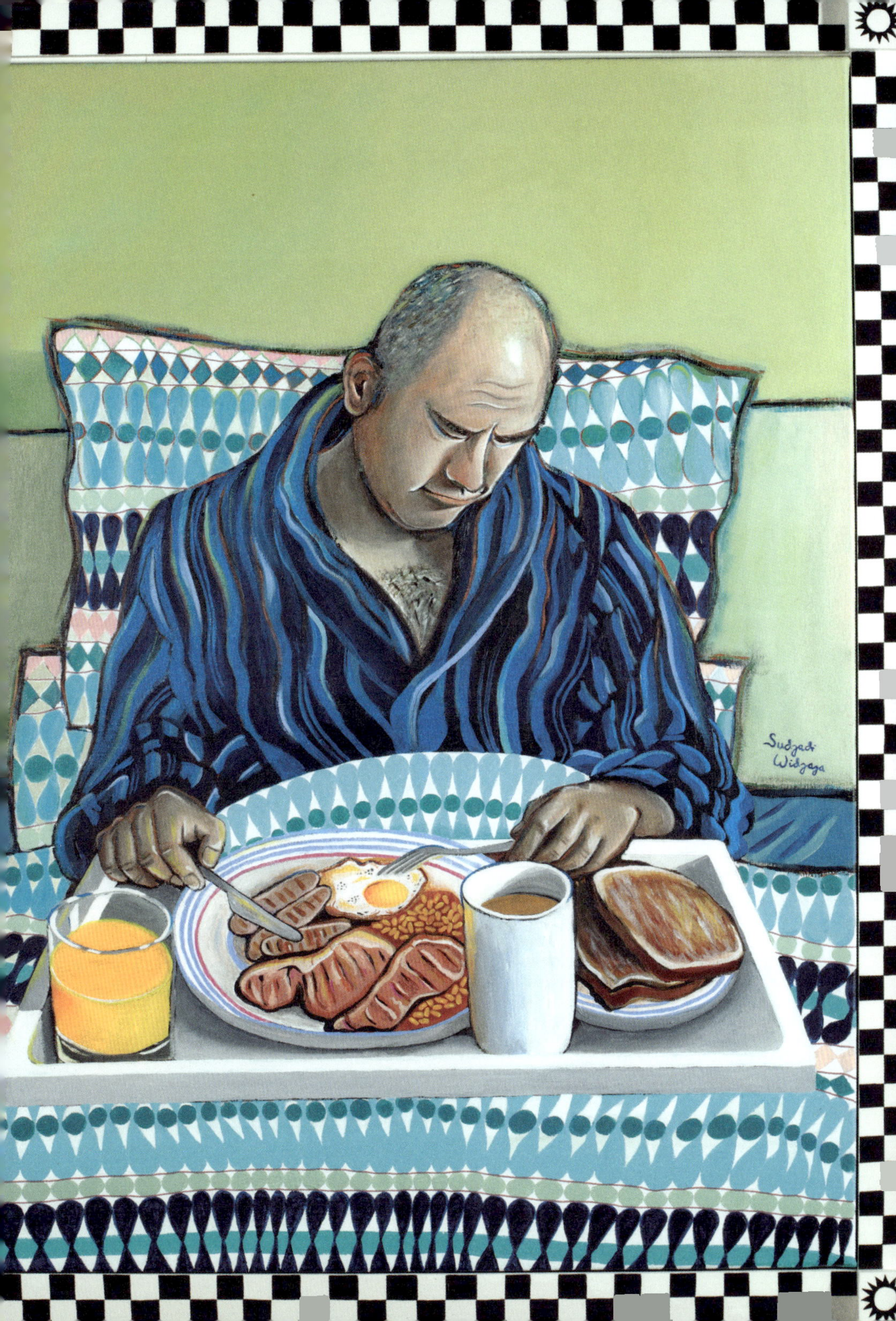

Sudjadi
Widjaya

'Vegan' Minced Steak

Ian Withall

Acrylic paint on canvas
Courtesy of the artist

"I wanted to find something
that was really rubbish or
ordinary, but then paint it
beautifully as a piece of art.
I thought about the pack of
minced beef we were going
to use for burgers for tea.
Although we are not vegan,
we do eat vegetarian and
vegan meals. I weaved this
into the artwork by having
some fun with the food
labelling. It was fun and made
me smile whilst painting."

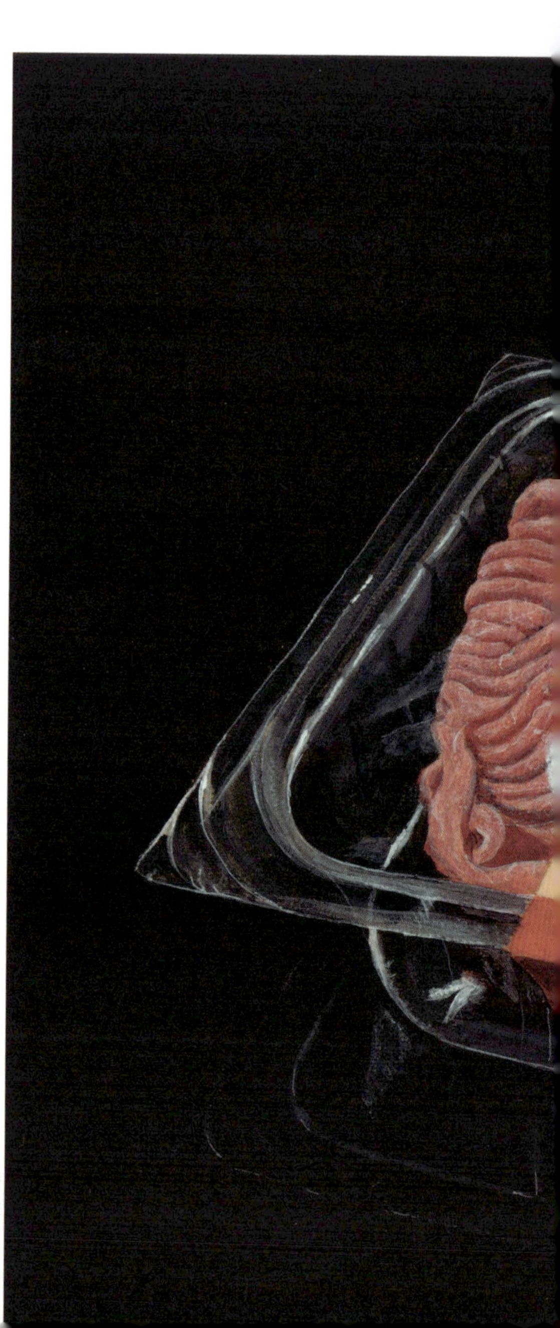

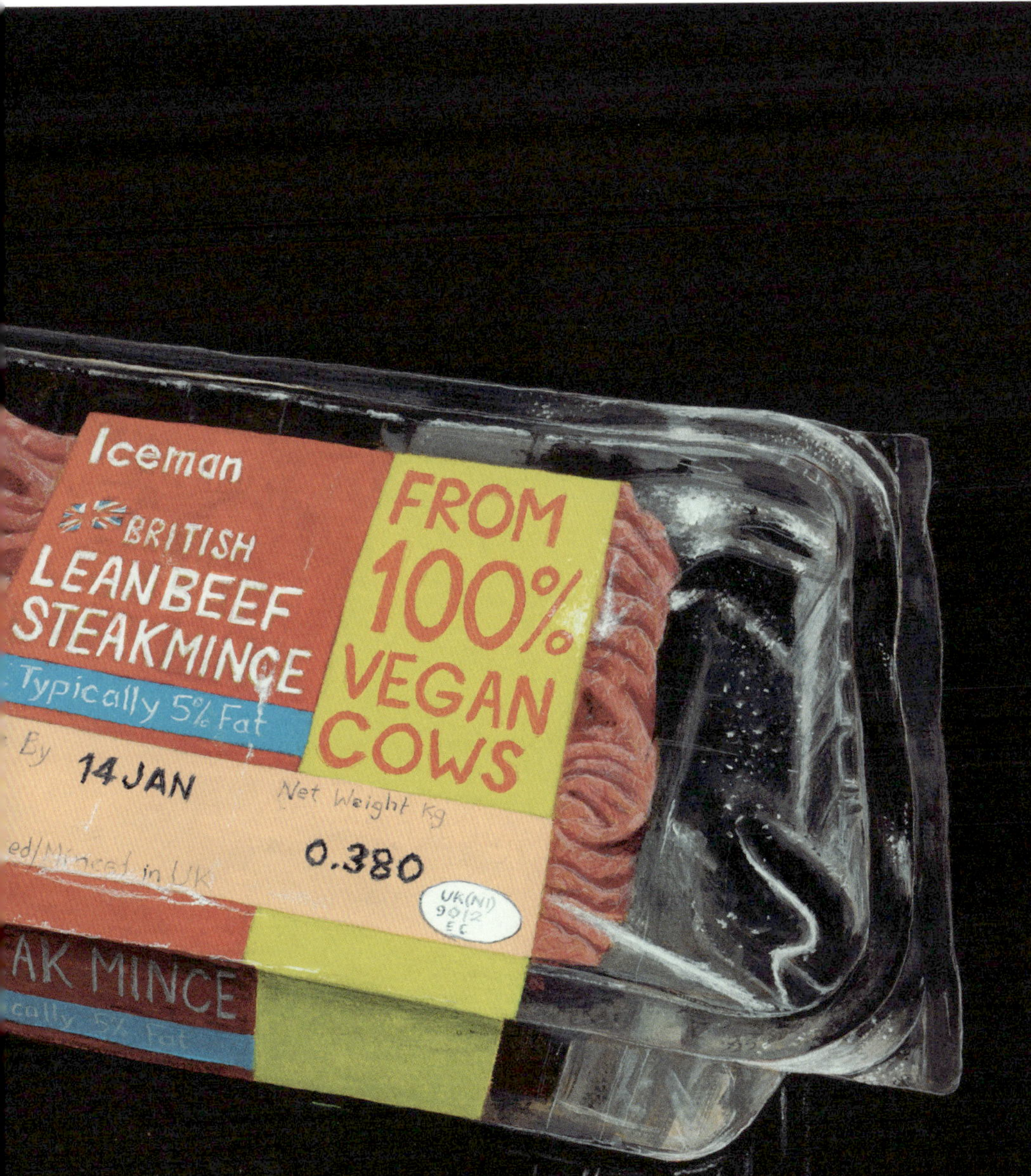

Iceman
BRITISH
LEAN BEEF
STEAK MINCE
Typically 5% Fat
By 14 JAN
ed/Minced in UK
FROM 100% VEGAN COWS
Net Weight Kg
0.380
UK(NI) 9012 EC
AK MINCE
cally 5% Fat

Daily Bread

Wendy Allen

Charcoal on paper
Courtesy of the artist

"My husband was starting
to weigh out ingredients for
our bread. This ritual has
taken on extra significance
during Covid. Making bread
is so universal. It unites
all cultures. In lockdown
this action linked us with
many people throughout
the world."

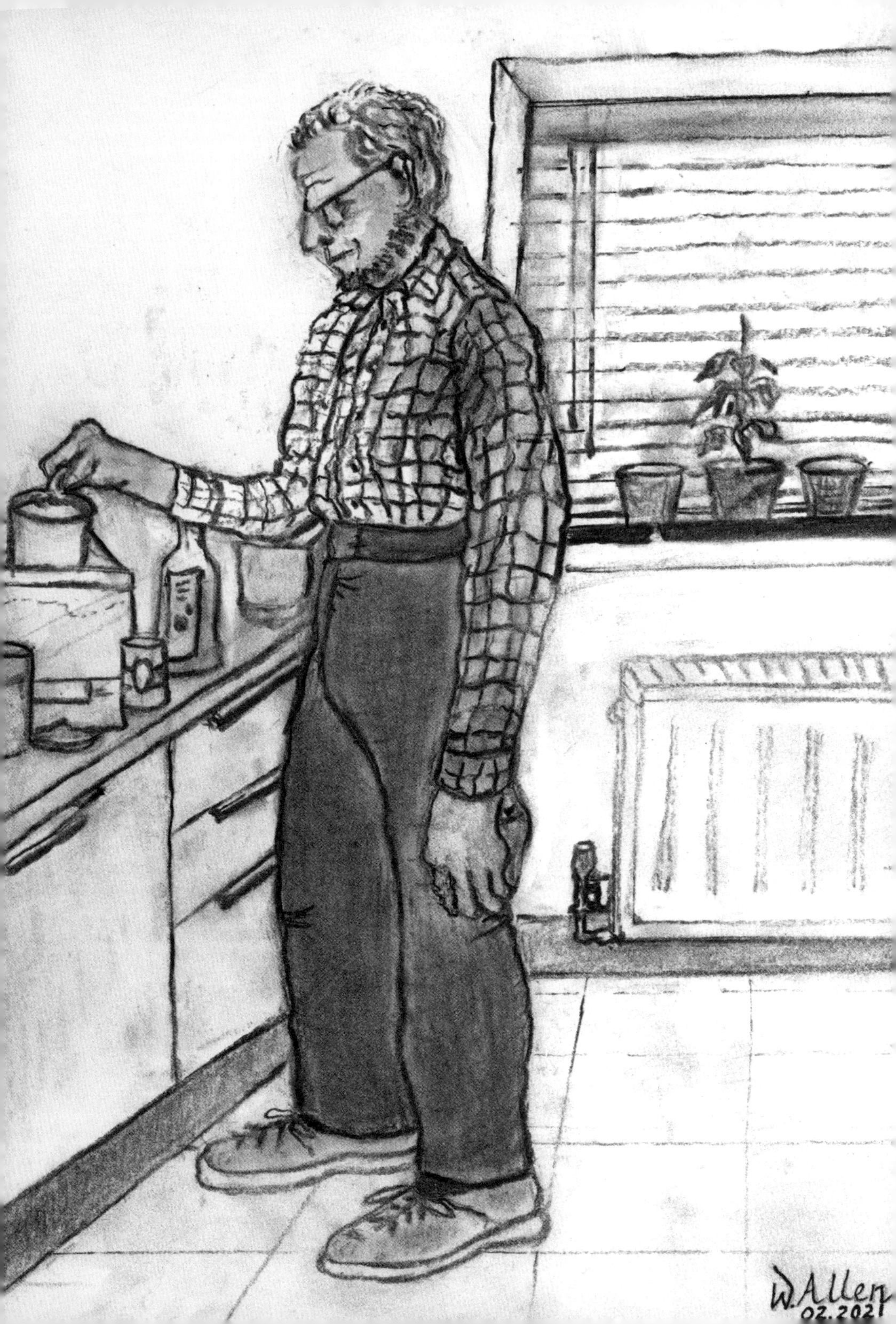

W.Allen
02.2021

Favourable Chicken

MAWAAN

Acrylic paint on canvas
Courtesy of the artist

"I grew up as a Muslim kid
who couldn't go to the pub.
In a chicken shop you buy
a packet of chips and sit in
there for two hours to do
all your catching up. This
chicken shop is the one I used
to go to. Favourable Fried
Chicken. I just love that they
went for 'Favourable'. I'm
quite proud of the painting.
It's not the best, it's not the
worst. But it's favourable."

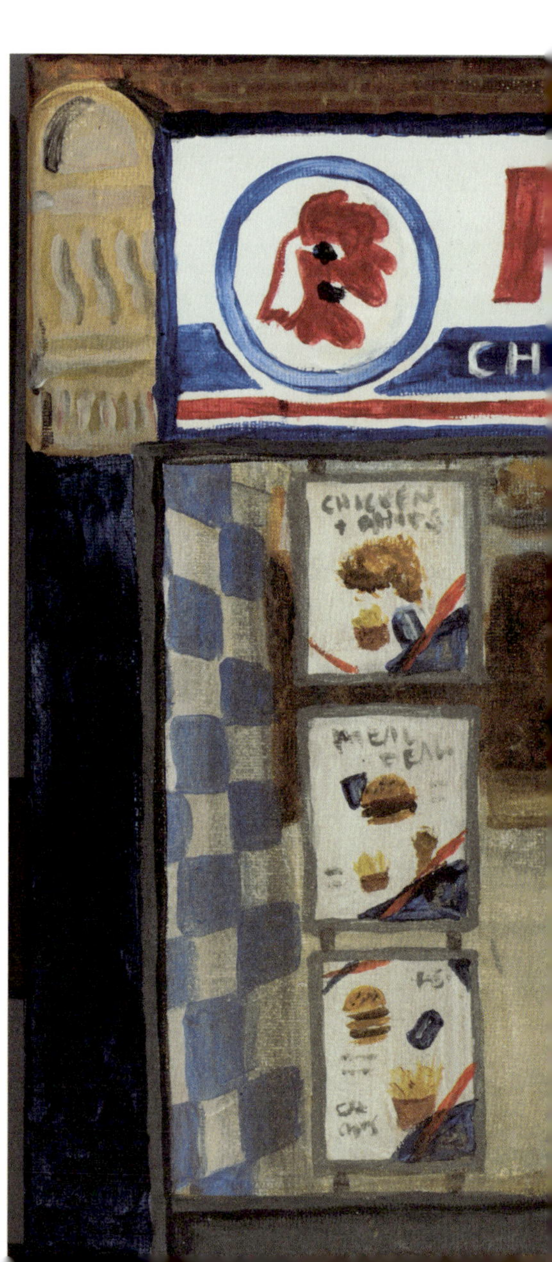

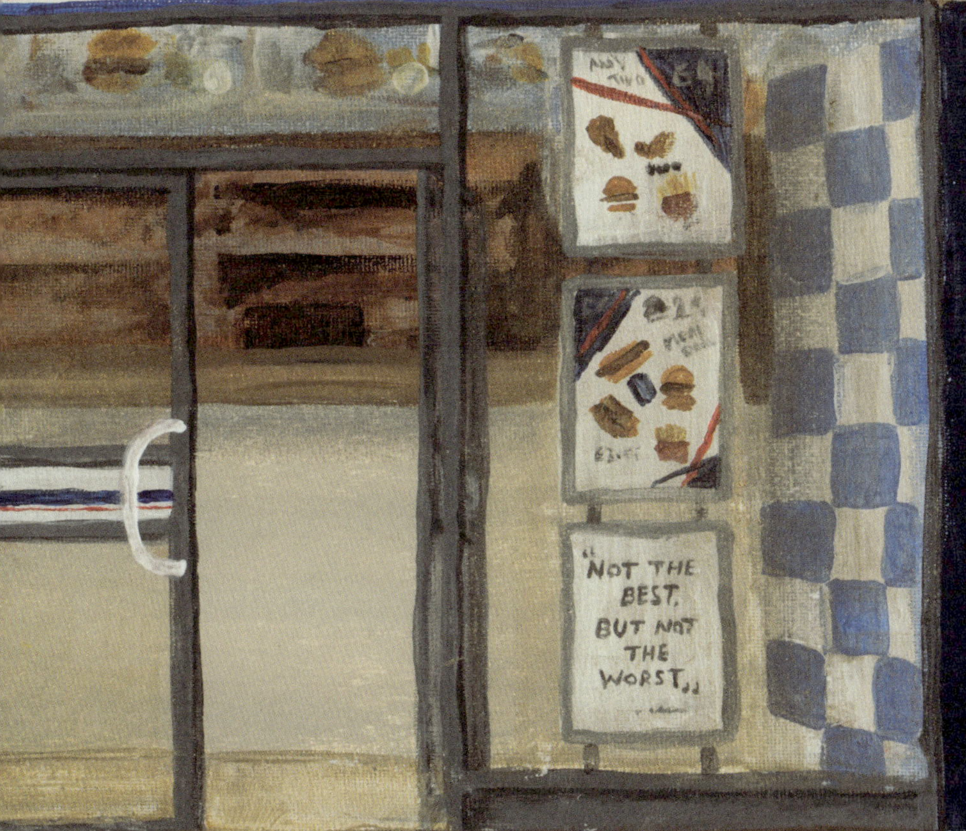
AVOURABLE
EN • RIBS • SANDWICHES
"NOT THE
BEST,
BUT NOT
THE
WORST"

In My Fridge

Cathy Sherring

Acrylic paint on board
Courtesy of the artist

"I decided to clean and
organise our fridge. I was
pleased with my efforts.
My husband then returned
from the supermarket and
crammed extra items on top.
This annoyed me! However,
I felt like it had potential for a
painting. After serving twenty
years as a mental health
nurse, I quit in lockdown.
Mainly for health reasons
and also I yearned to get back
to being creative. Painting
is a good way to focus. I am
pleased that I started this
new chapter."

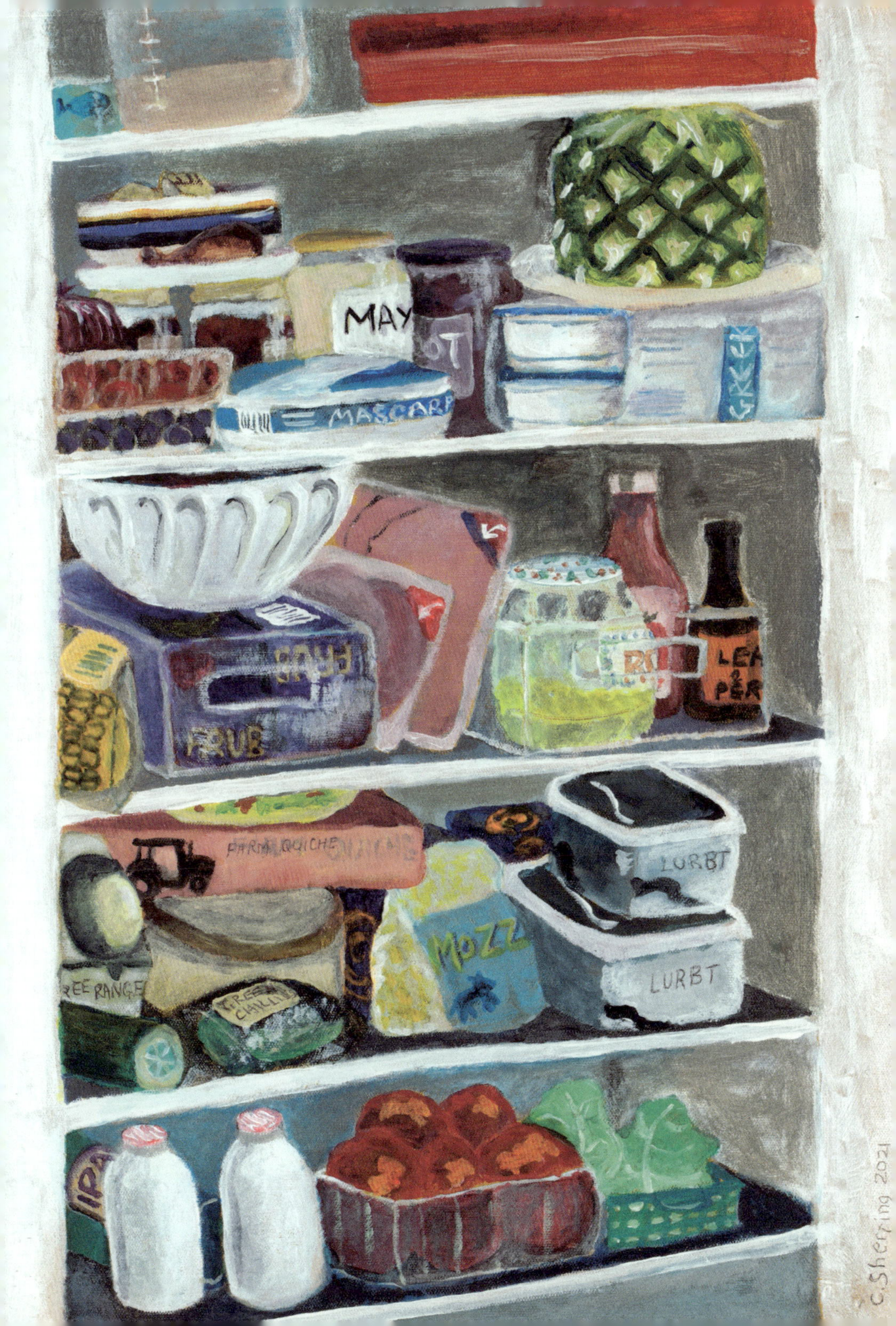

MAY
MASCARP
GREE
FRUB
GAYH
LEA
& PER
RI
PARMA QUICHE
MOZZ
LURBT
LURBT
FREE RANGE
FRESH CHILLI
IPA
C. Sheering 2021

Burger

Sue Perkins

Crocheted yarn
Courtesy of the artist

"Over lockdown I challenged
myself to learn crochet.
I love that you can make
stuff happen with a simple
little stick. This type of
crochet is called amigurumi,
which is Japanese for stuffed
toy. Crafting in general
calms me down because it
tends to be very repetitious
and methodical.

If you think of a hamburger,
it's something that's gone
in a second. Usually you're
starving and it barely touches
the sides. So it tickled me
that I would create that
most disposable of foodstuffs
in such a loving and
painstaking way."

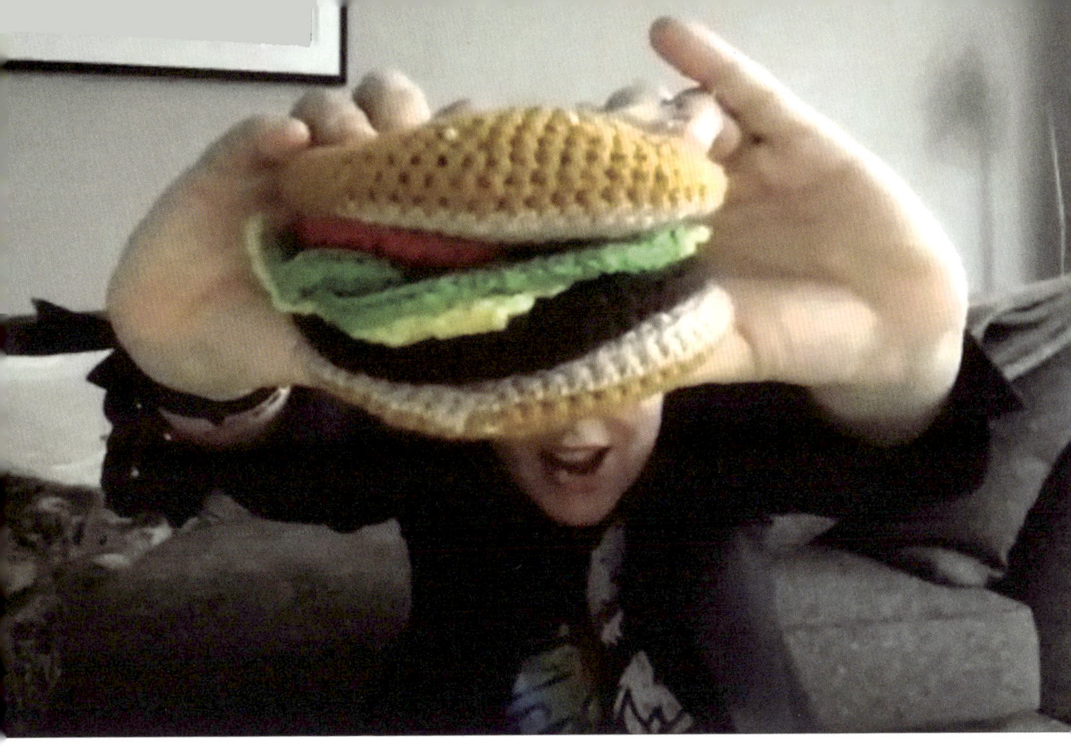

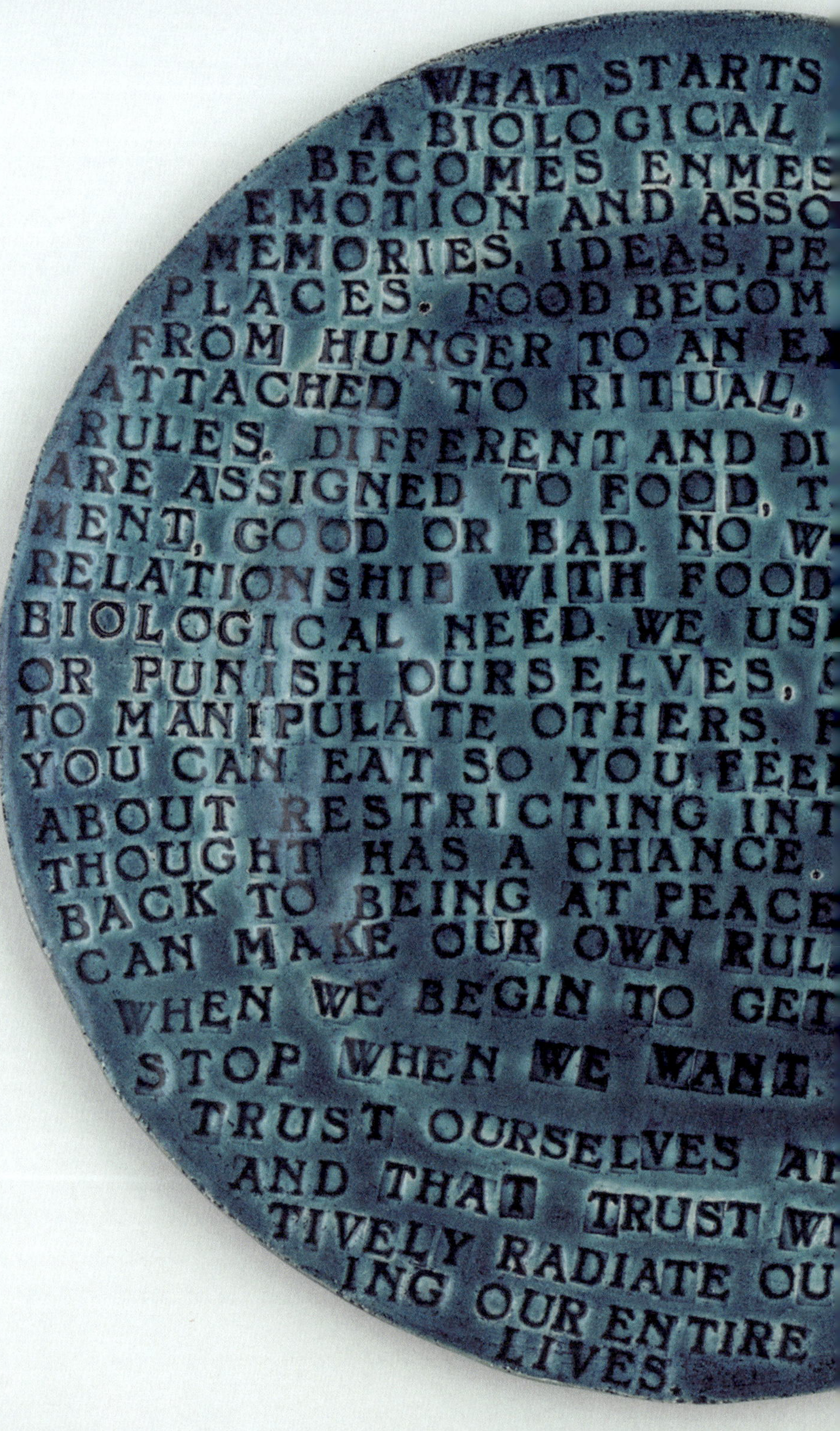

WHAT STARTS
A BIOLOGICAL
BECOMES ENMES
EMOTION AND ASSO
MEMORIES, IDEAS, PE
PLACES. FOOD BECOM
FROM HUNGER TO AN EX
ATTACHED TO RITUAL,
RULES. DIFFERENT AND DI
ARE ASSIGNED TO FOOD, T
MENT, GOOD OR BAD. NO W
RELATIONSHIP WITH FOOD
BIOLOGICAL NEED. WE US
OR PUNISH OURSELVES,
TO MANIPULATE OTHERS.
YOU CAN EAT SO YOU FEE
ABOUT RESTRICTING INT
THOUGHT HAS A CHANCE.
BACK TO BEING AT PEACE
CAN MAKE OUR OWN RUL
WHEN WE BEGIN TO GET
STOP WHEN WE WANT.
TRUST OURSELVES A
AND THAT TRUST W
TIVELY RADIATE OU
ING OUR ENTIRE
LIVES.

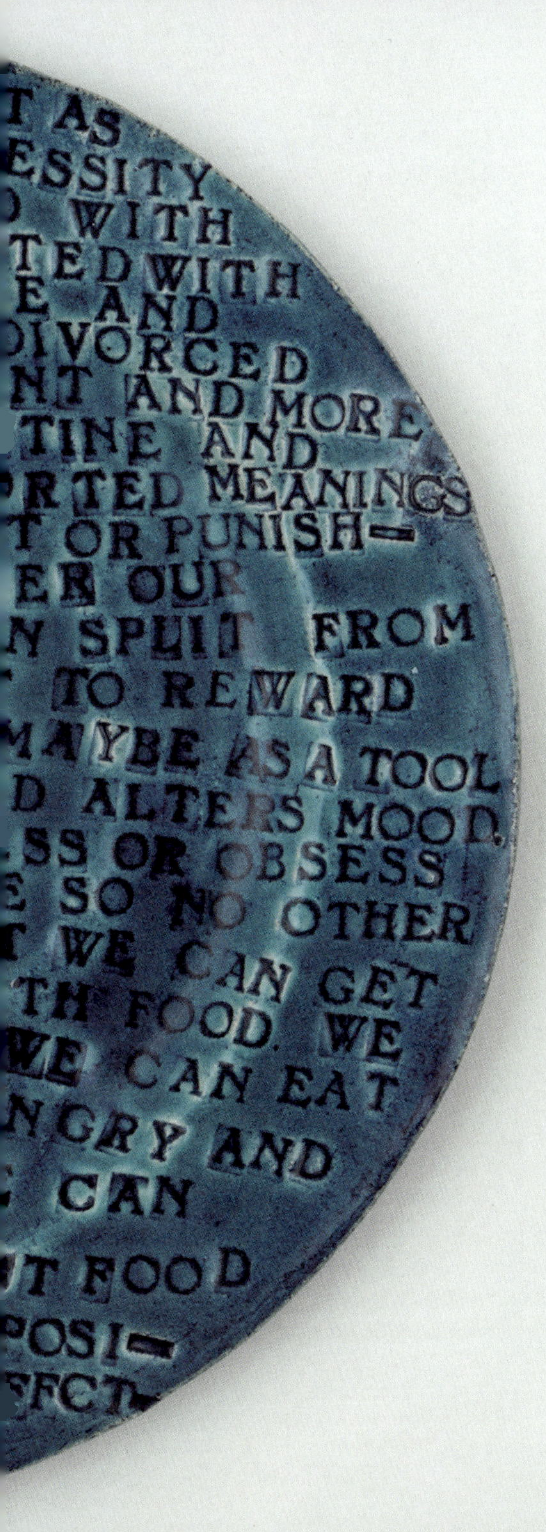

Food Plates

Philippa Perry

Glazed ceramic
Courtesy of the artist

"I wanted to talk about our
tricky relationship with
food and the culture of food.
It's very, very delicate.
Rather than regarding food
merely as nutrition, we may
treat food as punishment or
reward. What starts out as a
biological necessity becomes
enmeshed with emotion.
It's associated with memories,
ideas, people, and places."

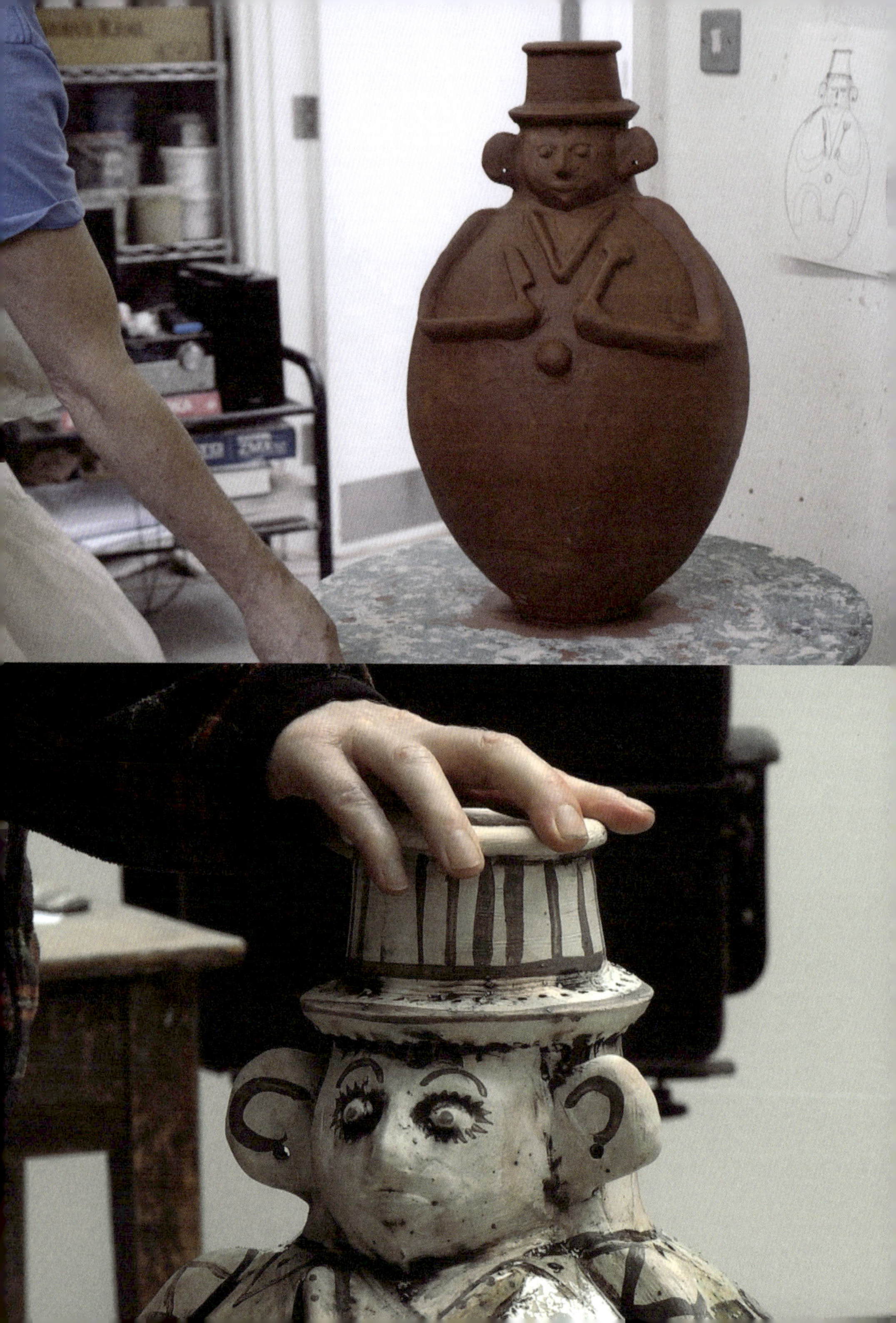

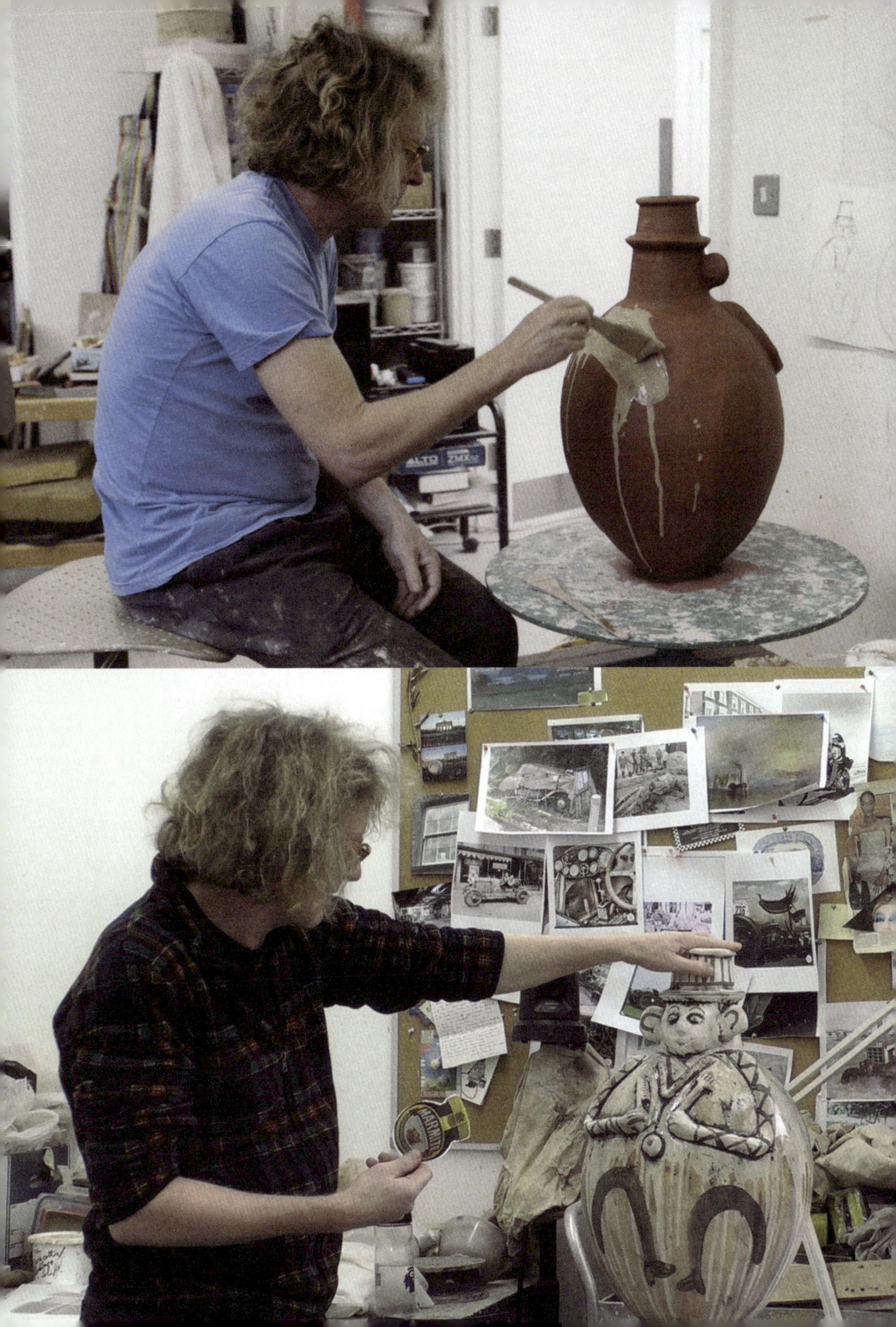

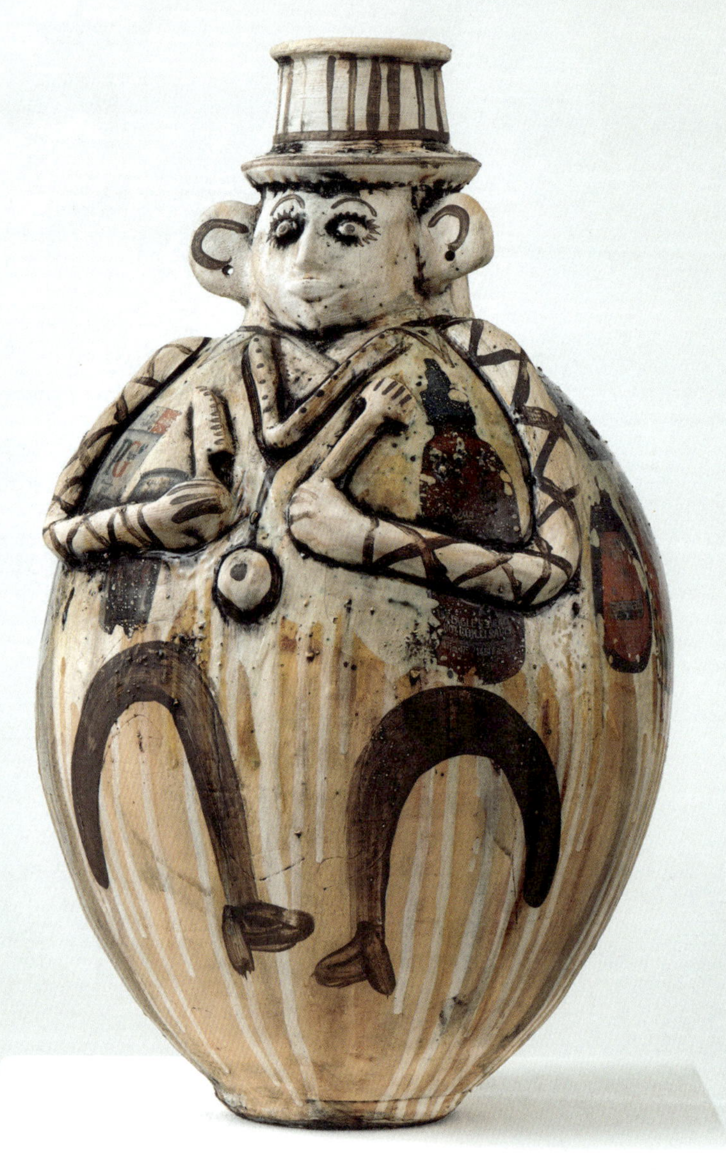

Mr Chonky Chonk
2021

Grayson Perry

Glazed ceramic
Courtesy of the artist
and Victoria Miro

"My inspiration was looking
at the person in front when
you're in the supermarket.
You're making a character
assessment from their basket.
I found this pre-Columbian,
Peruvian ceramic pot. He's a
chunky kind of guy. A good
starting point for a pot about
food. I fired on transfers
from photos of things in my
kitchen. My auntie could
spread the perfect Marmite
toast. That was a big part of
my childhood."

Face

Space

Hands ?

Space

Hands

Face?

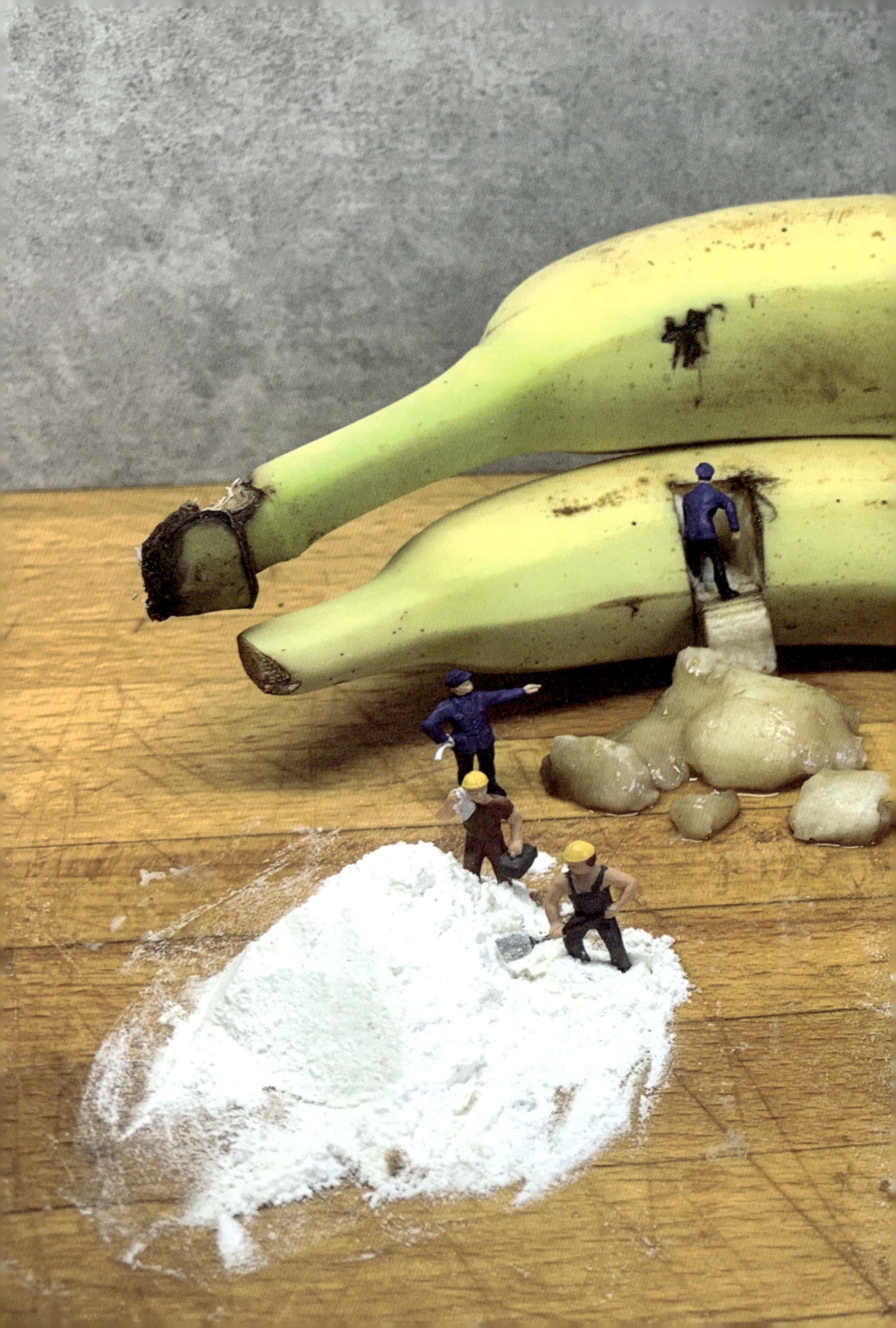

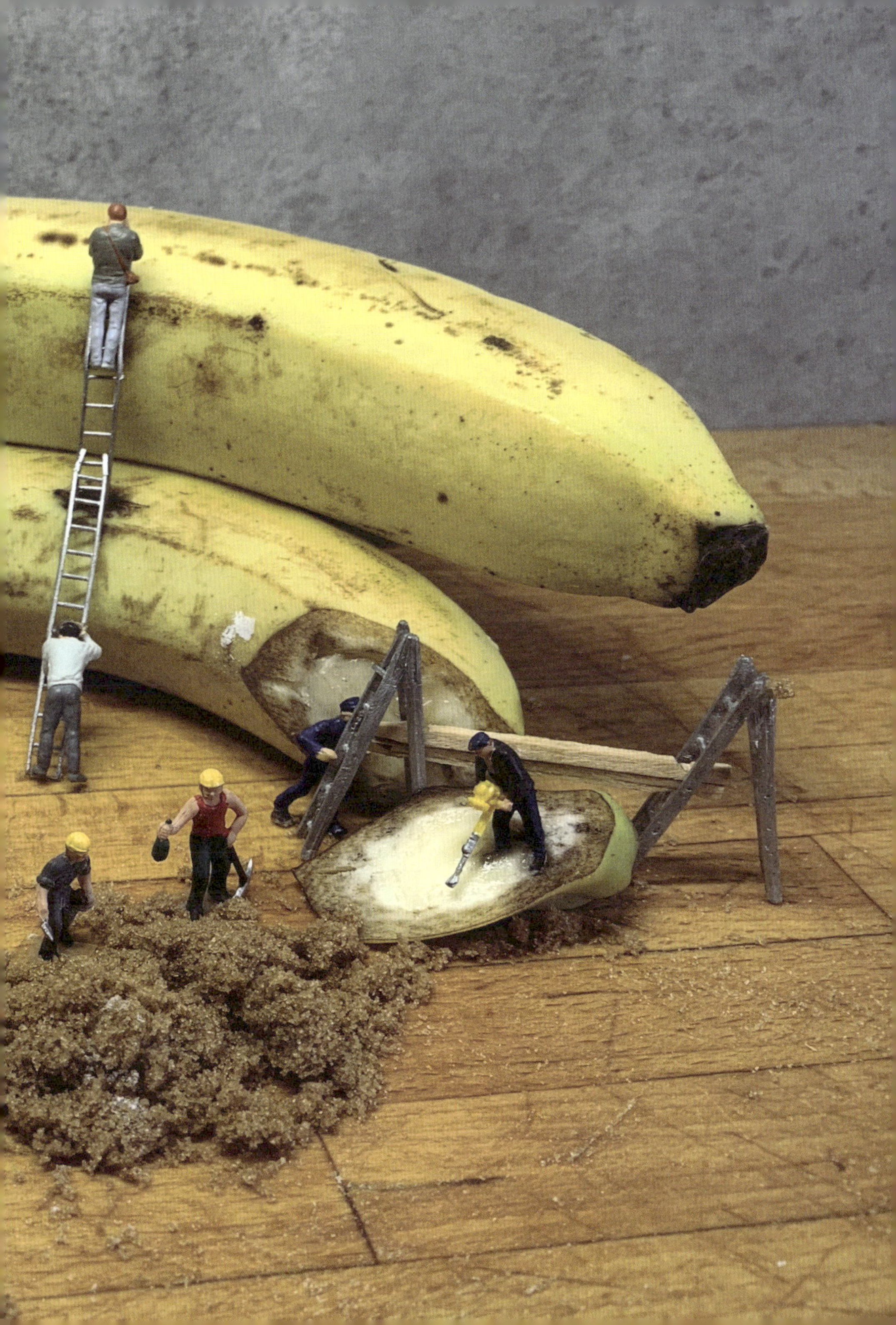

Previous:
Deconstructed Banana Bread

Greg Cook

Photograph of mixed media
diorama
Courtesy of the artist

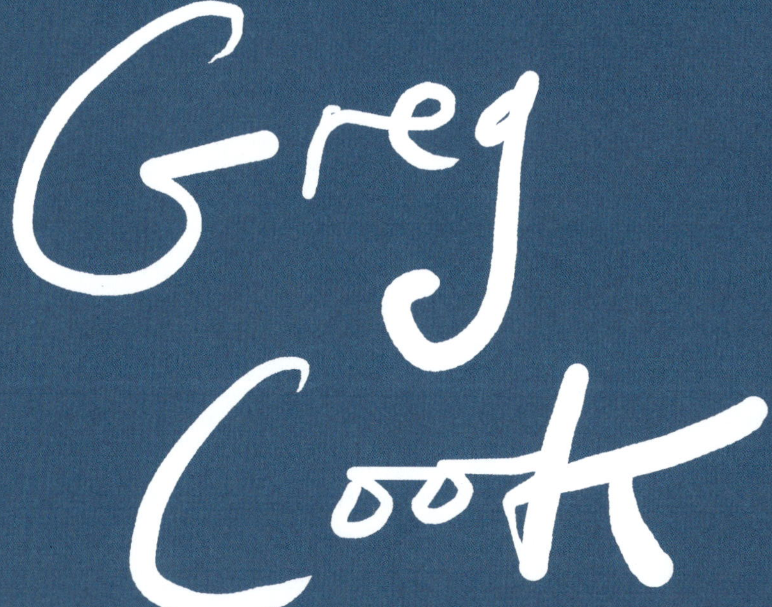

Greg
Cook

"For most of us our relationship with food changed during lock-down. In many households food transformed from being a pit-stop to refuel to the focus of the day. Food became an enormous part of our lives.

There is an irony in all this. Despite my name being Mr Cook, I am a lazy and incompetent cook. When left to fend for myself, it is usually a cold picnic, made up of whatever is in the fridge, plus mayonnaise.

I wanted to create an image to reflect this transformation of food in our lives. An image which showed how during lockdown we viewed food through a different lens. I did not feel capable, good enough or brave enough to do a drawing or painting.

So, I created a diorama, with food as the centre of attention. An image which encapsulates how food grew in our consciousness during this period. How it became the focal point of the day.

It dawned on me that food most synonymous with lockdown was of course 'banana bread'.

I initially used 'family figures', when I swapped to 'workmen' it added humour to the image, and made me smile."

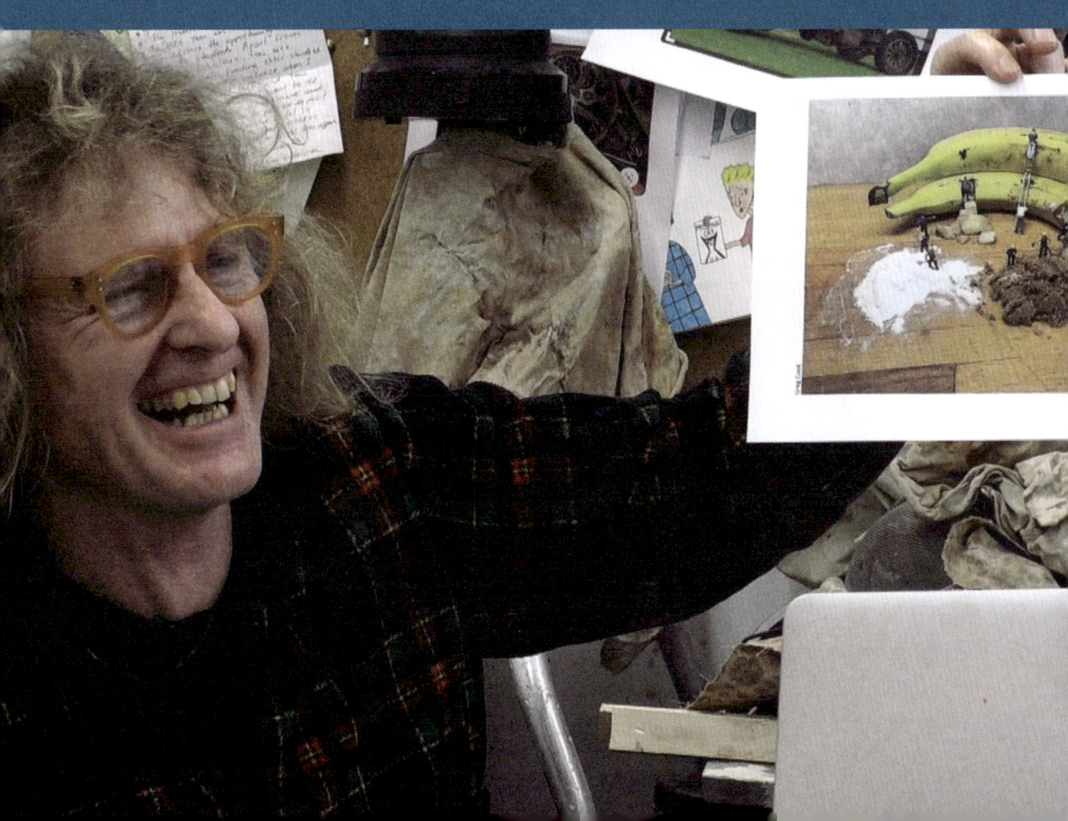

Drea

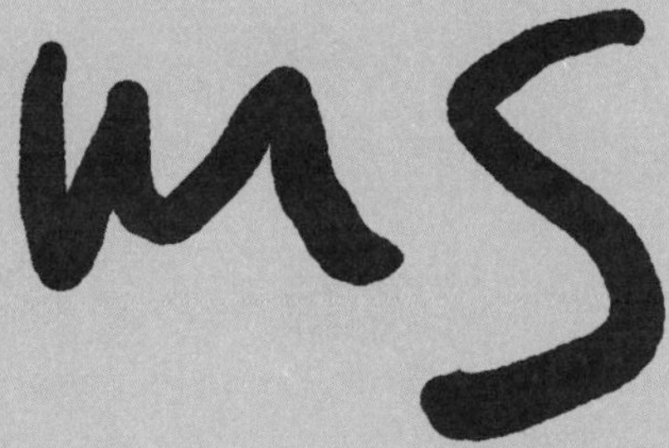

"Dreams seemed like a particularly
relevant theme because we were all
living in our imaginations during
lockdown. Perhaps more vividly
than in real life. The art of dreams
can help us understand our inner
lives and the different world we'd
like to see around us.

Our dreams tell us what's going
on in our lives emotionally,
so perhaps we need to pay attention
to them. The other sort of dreams,
the aspirational wishes and hopes,
helped us see where we wanted
to go after the pandemic.
We were dreaming of the future.
Let's keep dreaming!"

Golden Years

Robyn Ansell

Acrylic paint and gold leaf
on wood
Courtesy of the artist

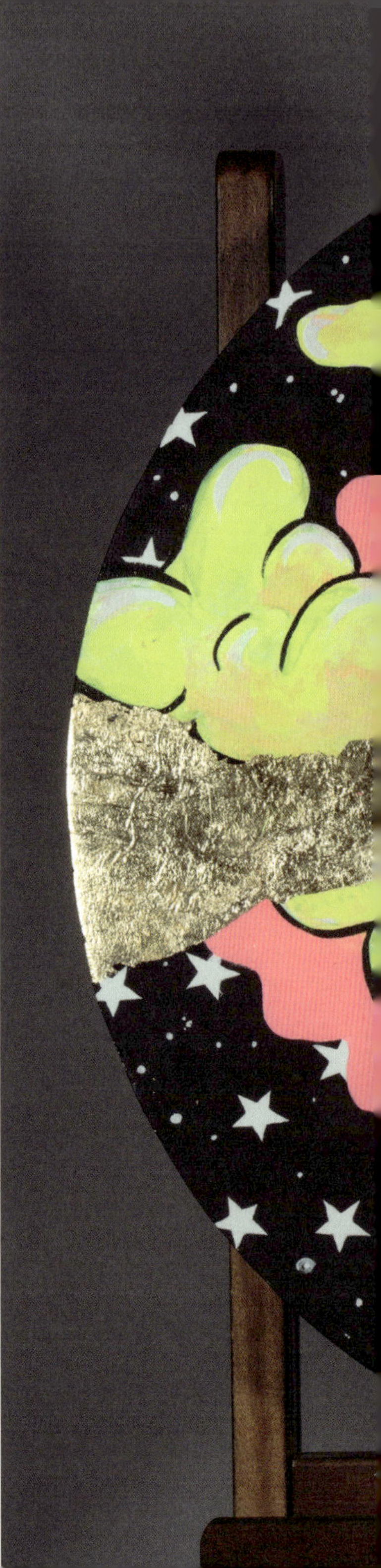

"I have a lot of nightmares.
Sometimes they're recurring,
so I thought I'd paint that.
I had a whole week of being
pregnant in my dreams.
It was a bit intense. I'm not
ready to reach that part of
my life. Nothing depends
on me and I like it this way.
The baby is drawing me in,
but I'm pulling away.
I decided to paint it. I haven't
dreamt about it since.
It gave me a chance to
confront my issues."

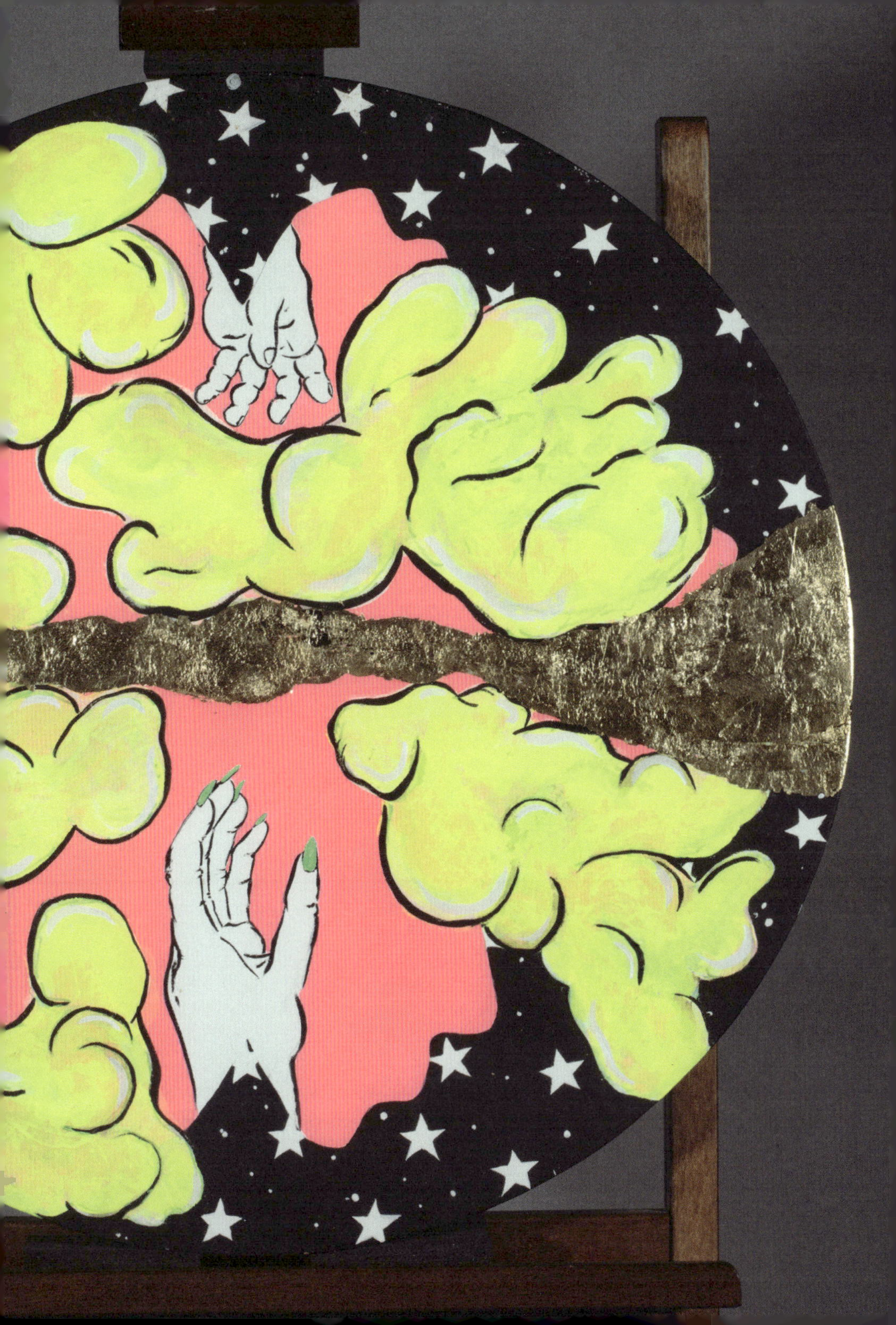

We're all Mad in Genderland

Liberty Dearsley

Digital artwork
Courtesy of the artist

"Doing my Art Foundation
was incredibly difficult during
lockdown. Most of our classes
were via Zoom. When we were
allowed on campus I really
valued the human connection
and personal expression
I saw in everyone's style.
The fluidity of genders and
clothes and characters was
what excited me. I made
this to challenge gender
stereotypes. I wanted to
satirise the familiar 'Barbie
and Ken' characters using
drag artistry to play
with my own femininity
and masculinity."

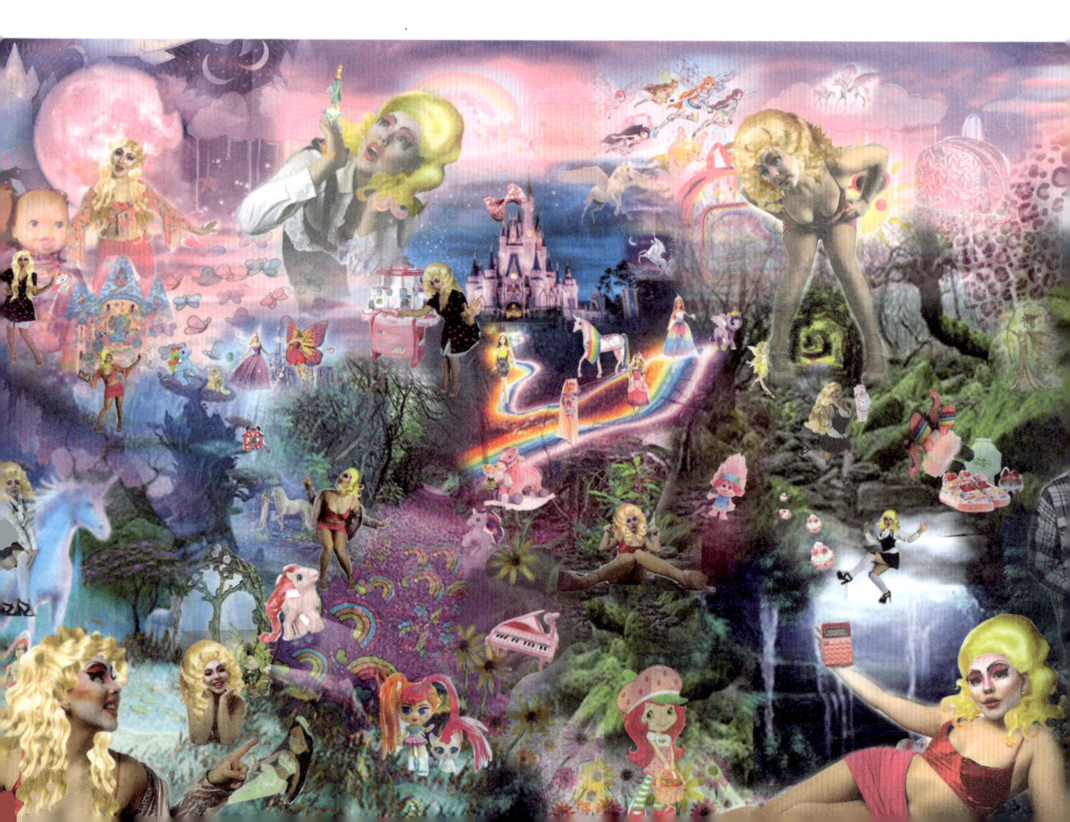

Nuts about Life

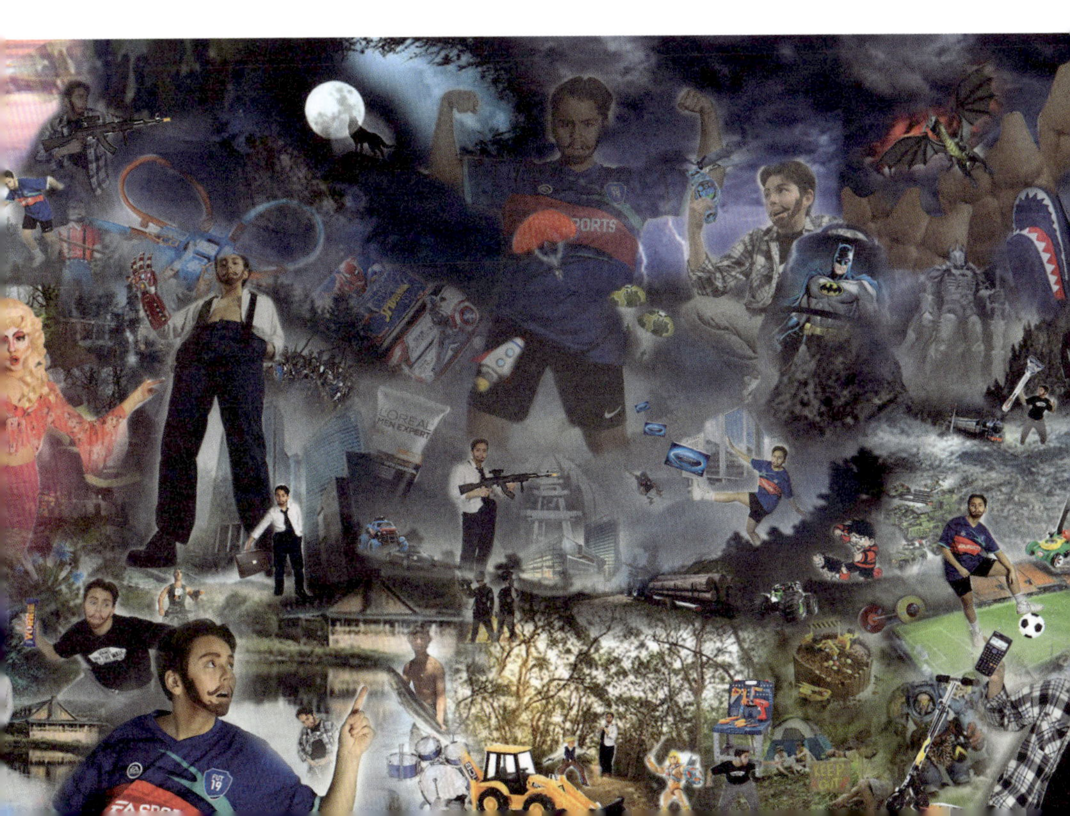

Arachnaphilia
2021

Sir Frank Bowling, Kt OBE RA

Acrylic, acrylic gel and
found objects on canvas
with marouflage
Photo: Sacha Bowling
© Frank Bowling. All Rights
Reserved, DACS 2021.
Courtesy of the artist.

"Making marks has
always been one of the
characteristics through which
we communicate with each
other. We come into the world
with this instinct. I'm all eyes,
ears and antennae.

Acrylic paint moves around.
Every time you go out there
with that stuff you're taking
a risk. Realist painting, for me,
is the paint itself. Let it drip,
let it drip, let it drip…"

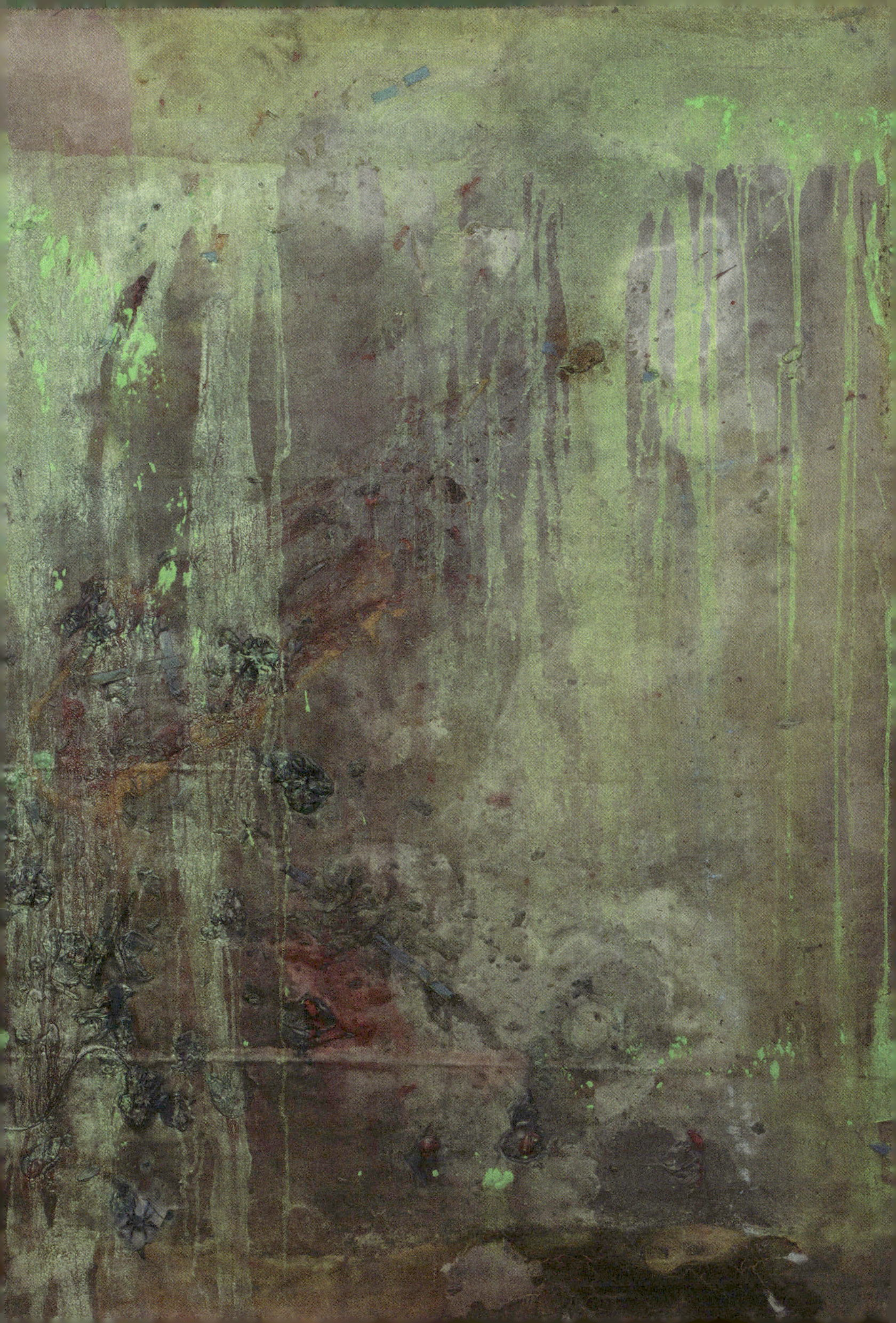

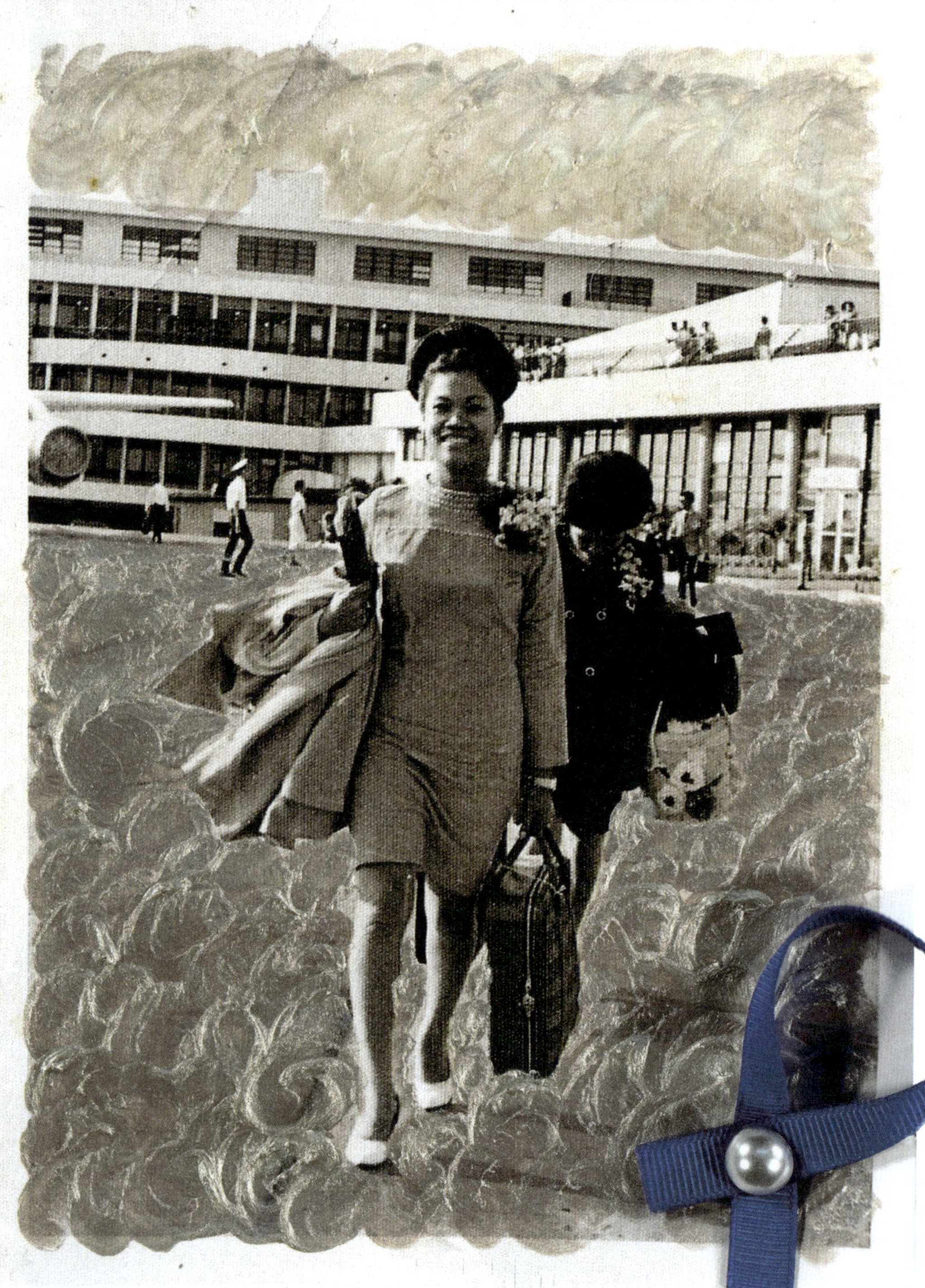

Lee Appleton

Previous:
Mum's Dream of a New Life
(Pearl of the NHS)

Lee Appleton

Collage, acrylic paint
and ink on card
Courtesy of the artist

"We had information overload in lockdown. The daily briefing, reports, graphs, diagrams, percentages, tiers, R numbers, death rates. I wanted to remember the people.

Mum was one of the first Nurses from the Philippines to come here in 1969 to work in the NHS. During the pandemic we were seeing just how many NHS and healthcare workers were immigrants. I had a conversation with Mum. She was upset that so many Filipino Nurses had died "They were just like me, they wanted to work and have a better life and they're gone.

Mum's dream was to have an adventure, and work towards a better life. In this photo taken at Manila International Airport she is on her way to England and the NHS. Walking towards the unknown, full of hope and utter joy.

I express myself through creativity. It's so important to me because I'm naturally very shy and introverted. Exploring how I feel about something through a collage gives me time to think and respond in a private way. Creating art has helped with my mental health in the past, so during lockdown it was a real comfort to focus on my project exploring Mum's story."

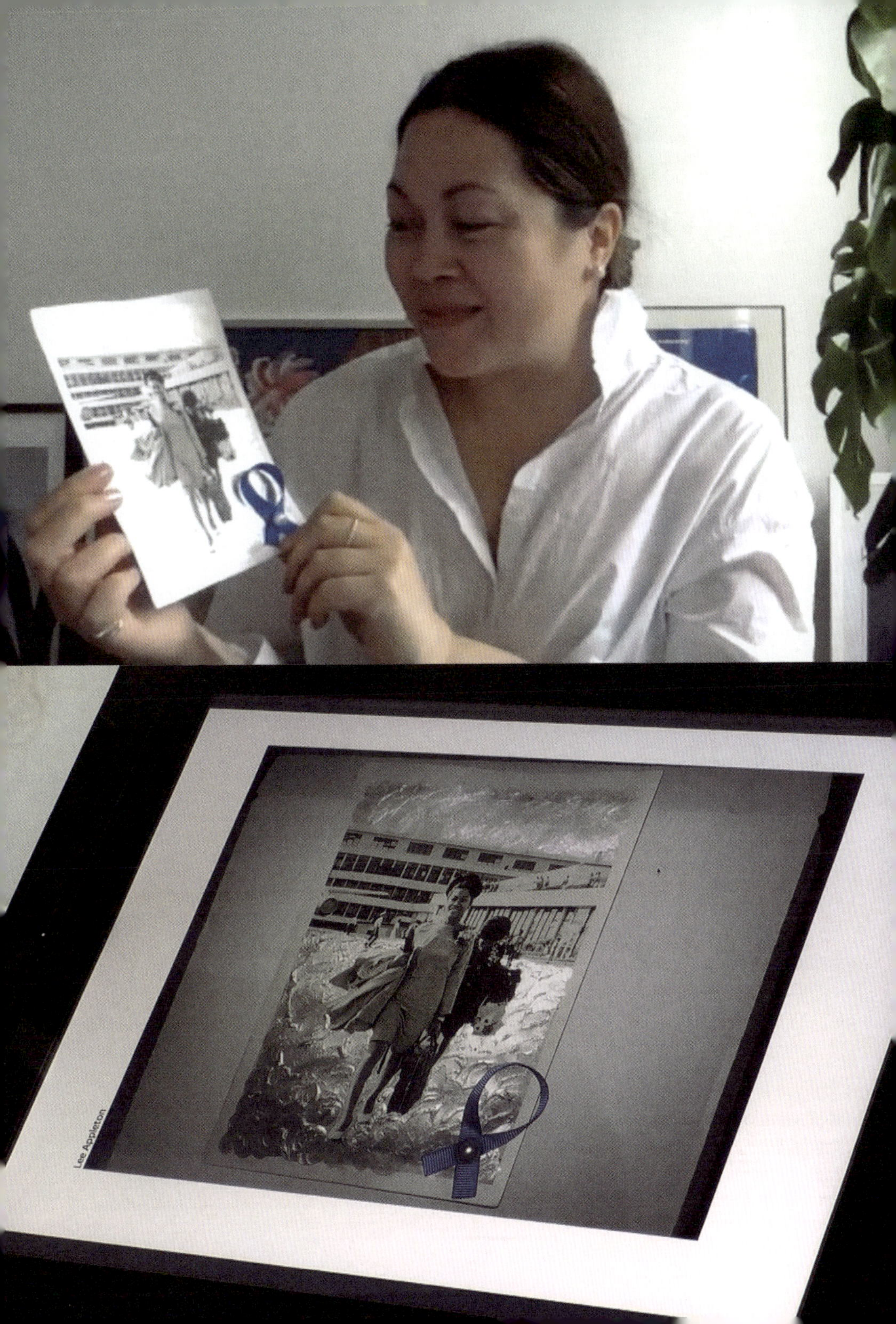
Lee Appleton

Twin Set and Pearls

Anthony Klej

Pastel on paper
Courtesy of the artist

"I've always had a fascination
with drag queens. The sense
of control they emit is unlike
any other. On the surface they
seem invincible, but what we
present to the outside world
is usually not what's hidden
beneath. Art in lockdown
was a lifesaver. Literally.
I was surrounded by periods
of depression and anxiety,
something I've suffered with
in the past. The experience
of learning to draw was
healing and cathartic.
Drawing allowed moments
of mental peace."

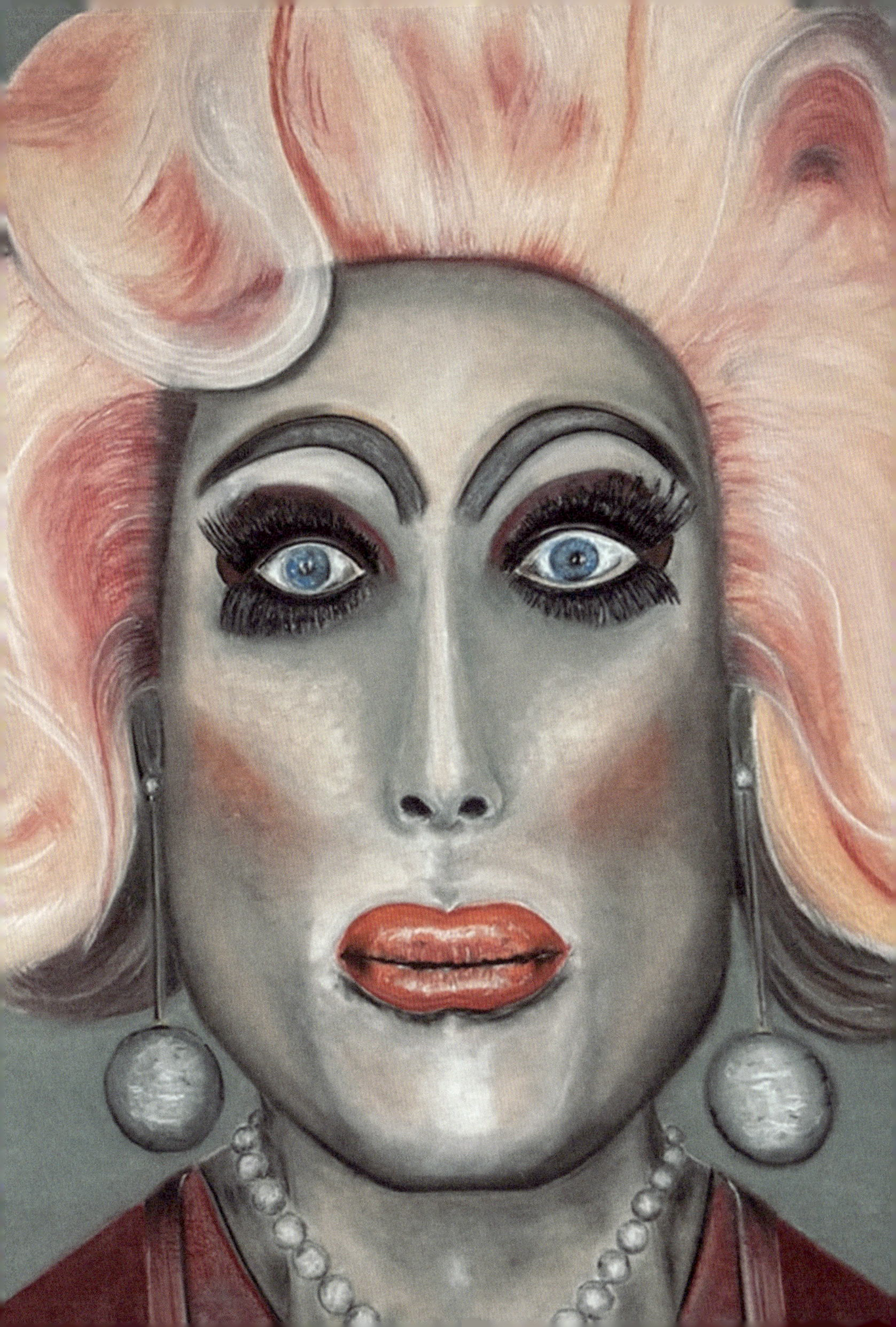

BLACK
LIVES
MATTER
everything
feels emp
now

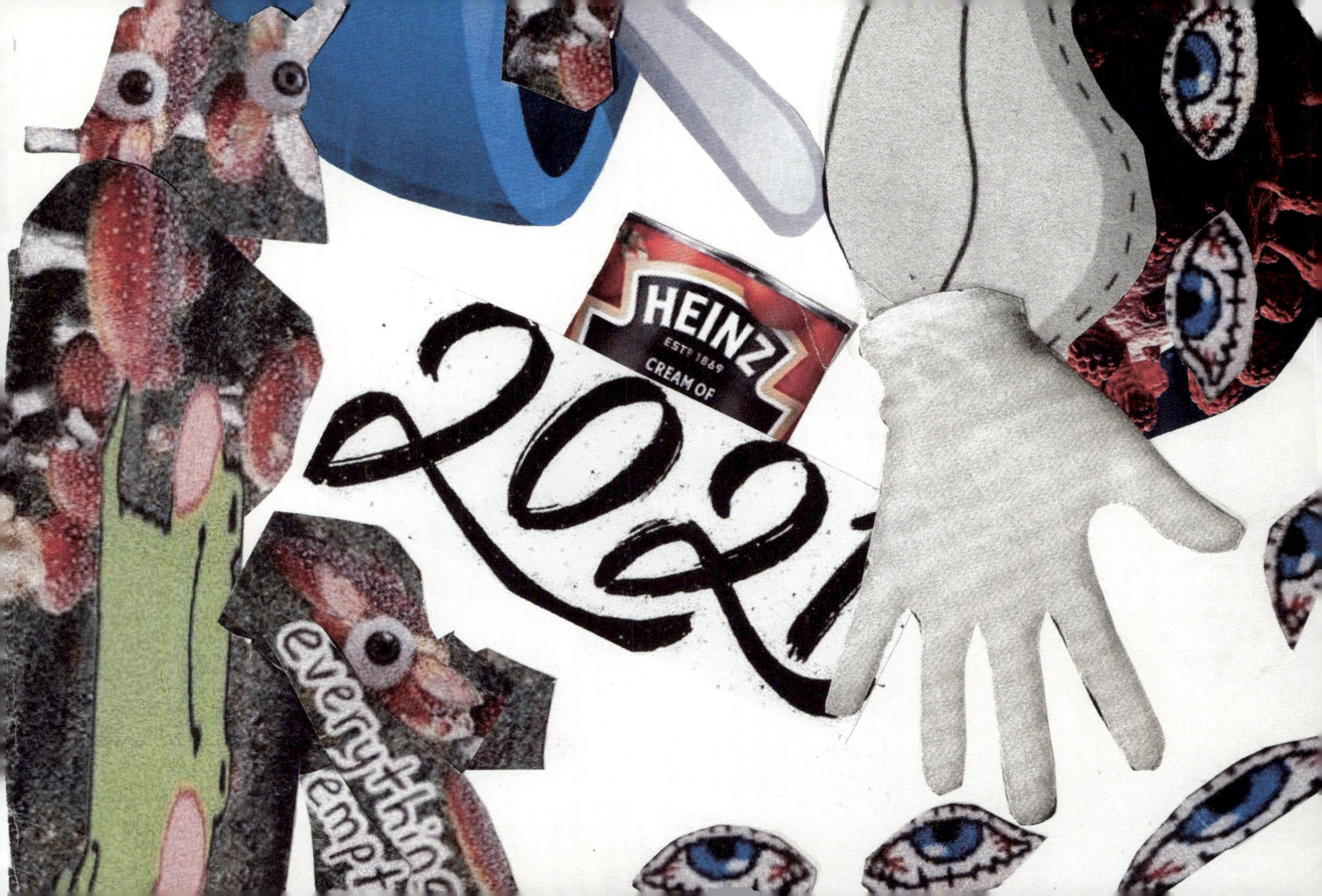

HEINZ
EST. 1869
CREAM OF
2021
everything empt

Previous:
Hopes & Dreams

April Onomakpome

Collage on paper
Courtesy of the artist

"I was inspired to make this
artwork because of a dream
I had. I was surrounded
by art canvases and I was
eating a bowl of soup. When
I woke up I wanted my piece
to represent my hopes and
dreams for the year ahead.
The eyes represent the world
eagerly anticipating the
events of the year ahead such
as more attention towards the
Black Lives Matter movement
and the reduction/increase
of Covid cases."

Synaptic Connections

Isabelle Ewing

Mixed media: papier mâché,
wire, bandages, gold leaf,
electric lights, plastic
prism decorations
Courtesy of the artist

"My inspiration came from
the feelings of sadness and
vulnerability I felt as Covid
swept through the world.
The face has a resigned
expression with an absence
of hope. There was no sign of
a vaccine when I was working
on this bust, so I wrapped it
in bandages and chicken wire
for safety. I added the lights
because we can still choose
to have beautiful thoughts
no matter how awful outside
conditions are."

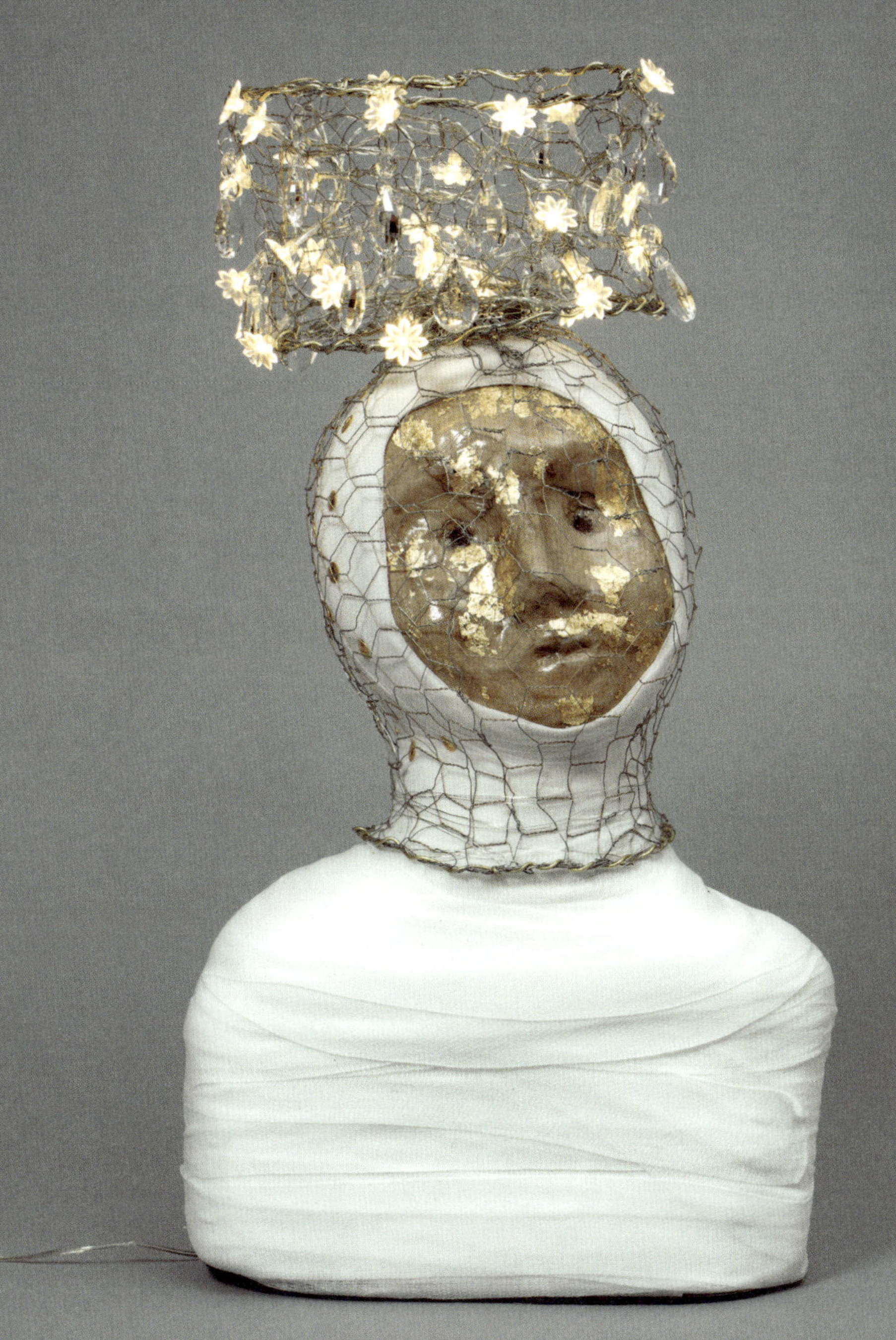

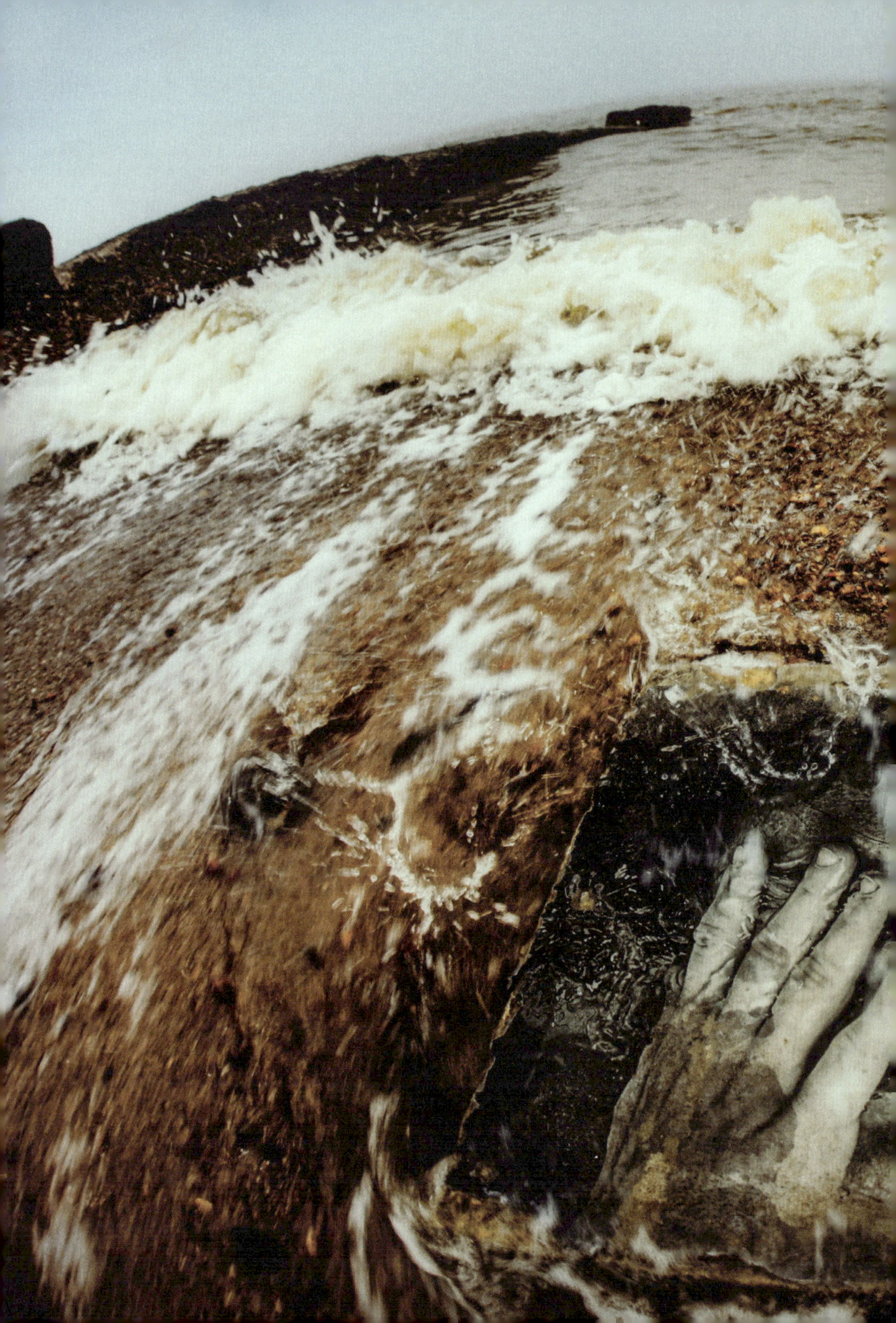

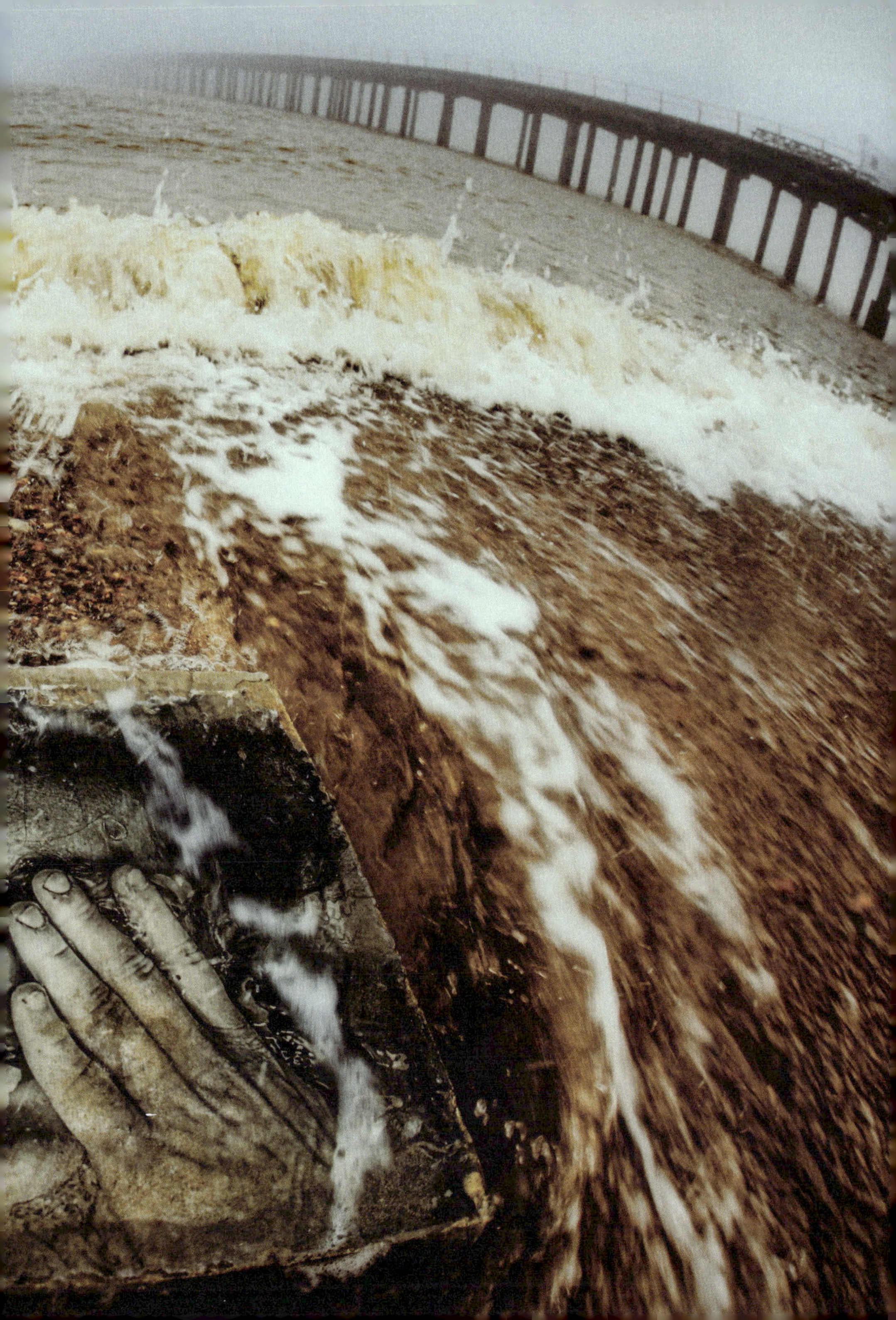

Gillian Allard

"I like to present my photographs by bonding them to surfaces such as concrete or wood. I feel that it can give more meaning to the image. It also allows me to take the photographs back in the landscape to create a type of in-camera 'collage'. This photograph was made during lockdown and involved my two boys. I think it expressed our general state of isolation.

My oldest son had been experiencing some terrifying dreams, so I tried to take a photograph that expresses this feeling. The shoot took place in our bathroom with Stan's head under water. My other son Albert was in control of the lighting. Stan was in swimming trunks.

Once I had taken the photo I later bonded it to concrete in the kitchen. I carried the slab to the sea shore and started photographing. I became aware a man observing me. I looked up and he shouted 'what are you doing?' so I pointed to the slab and carried on. He shouted dismissively 'you must be mad'. I ignored him. It would have been difficult to explain the sense of calm and purpose that using your imagination and making stuff gives you."

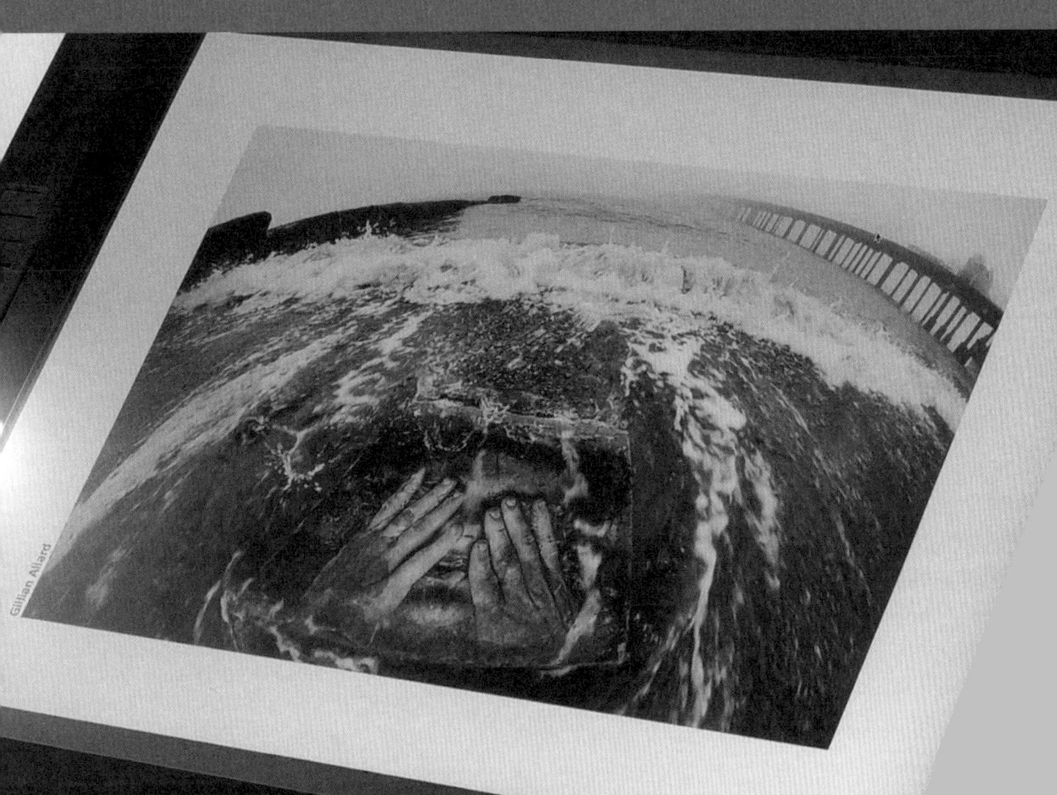

Gillian Allard

Make Small Adjustments

Polly Morgan

Taxidermied Cornsnake,
painted polyurethane,
iridescent powder, varnish
Courtesy of the artist

"Social media and the Covid
pandemic provide the context
for my recent sculptures.
I use the hides of snakes and
designs in nail artistry to
comment on the disparity
between surface and reality.
I explore how veneers are
used to deceive. The skins
of snakes offer camouflage
or warn would-be predators
away by mimicking more
poisonous breeds. I compare
them to images uploaded to
social media feeds. The filters
applied and the linguistic
contortions made allow
a particular perception
to flourish."

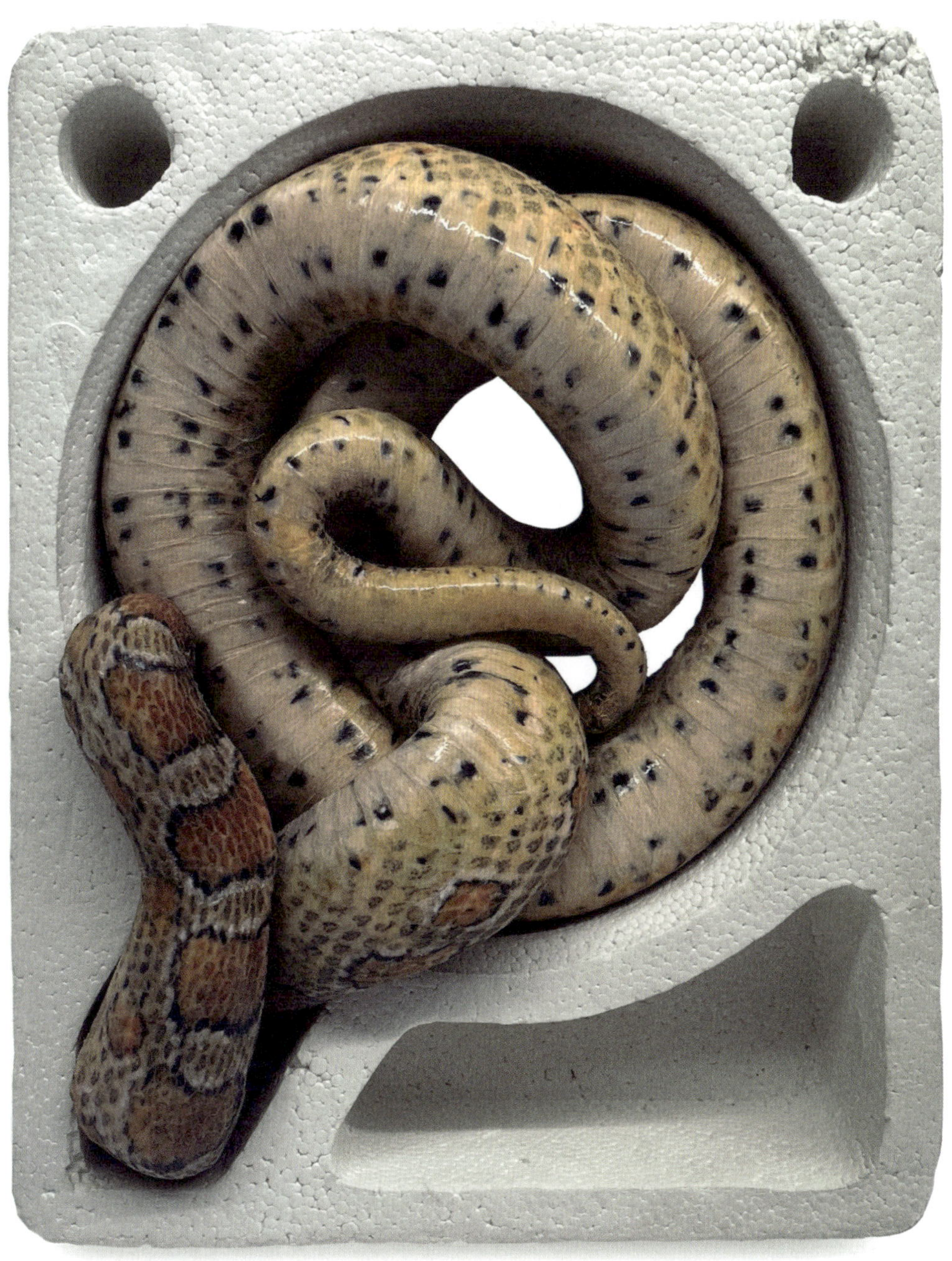

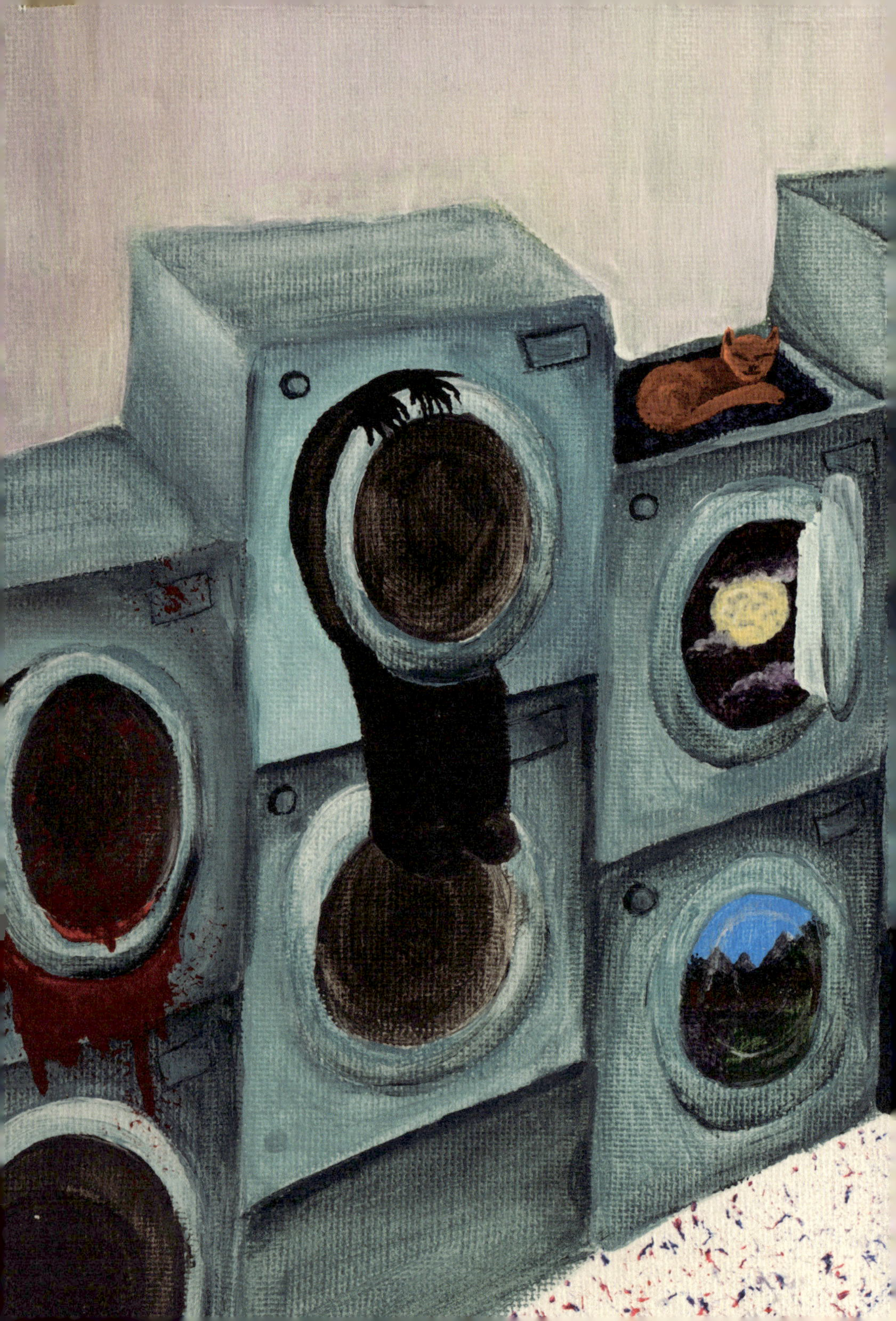

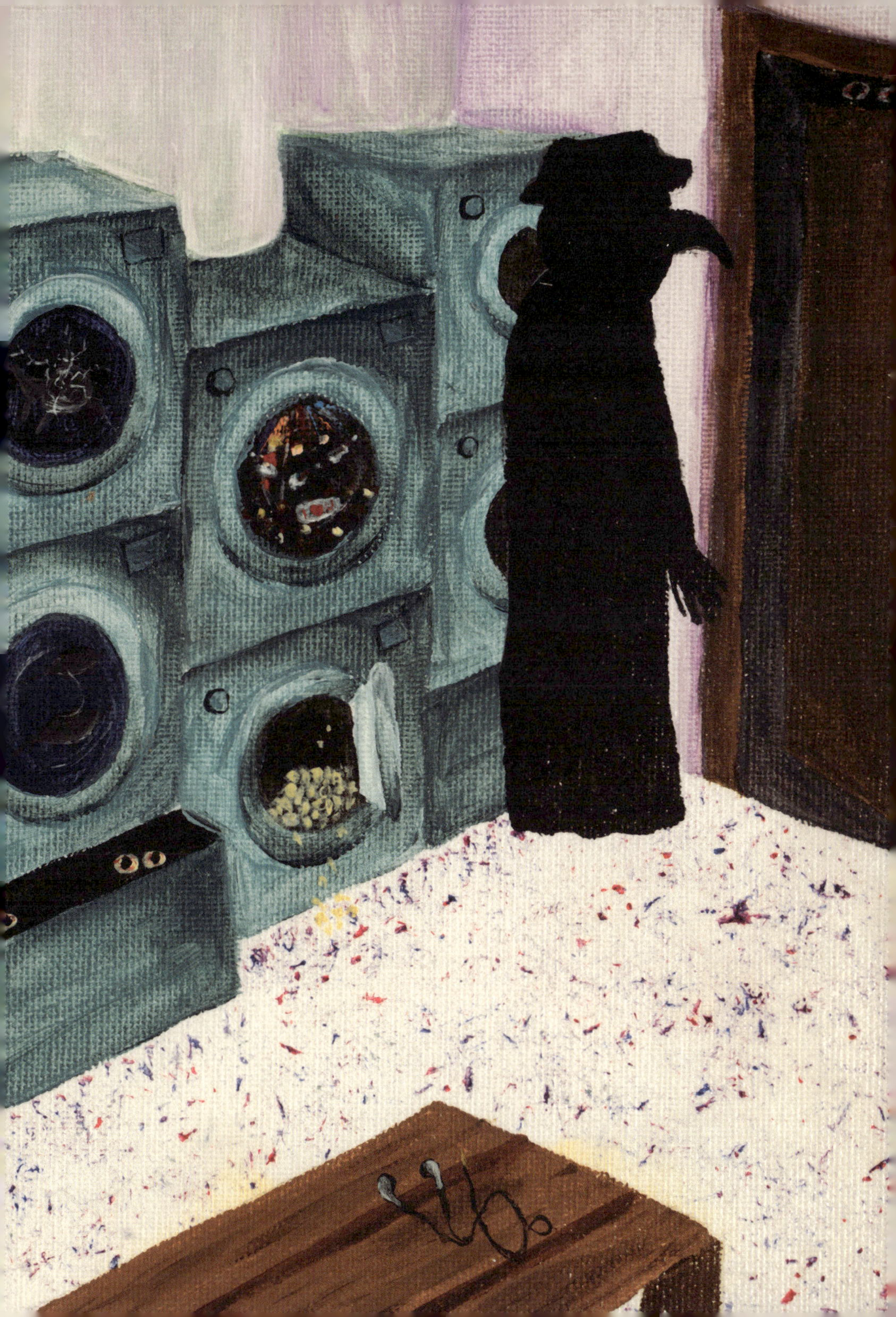

Previous:
Launder My Dreams

Jay Doughty

Acrylic paint on canvas board
Courtesy of the artist

"This is my visual remake of a
'sleepcast' from a meditation
app I was using each night.
I found a lot of peace in
meditation and sleepcasts.
However, my anxiety dreams
and sleep paralysis would
still creep in. Even when
you are doing well, your
struggles with mental health
do not just disappear.
Art is expression and brings
comfort and joy. It was a
way of communicating my
struggle with my mental
health and sleep without
having to use words."

Norman

Johnny Vegas

Glazed ceramic
Courtesy of the artist

"This is Norman. I wanted to
do something about a young
lad who I used to see on the
school run when I took my
son to school. He broke my
heart on a daily basis because
he was just *me*. I so often
wanted to stop him and say,
"Look, things do work out."
So it's about having faith in
your own dreams and quiet
ambitions. I'm smitten with
him. He got me back into
pottery. It has been a lifesaver during lockdown."

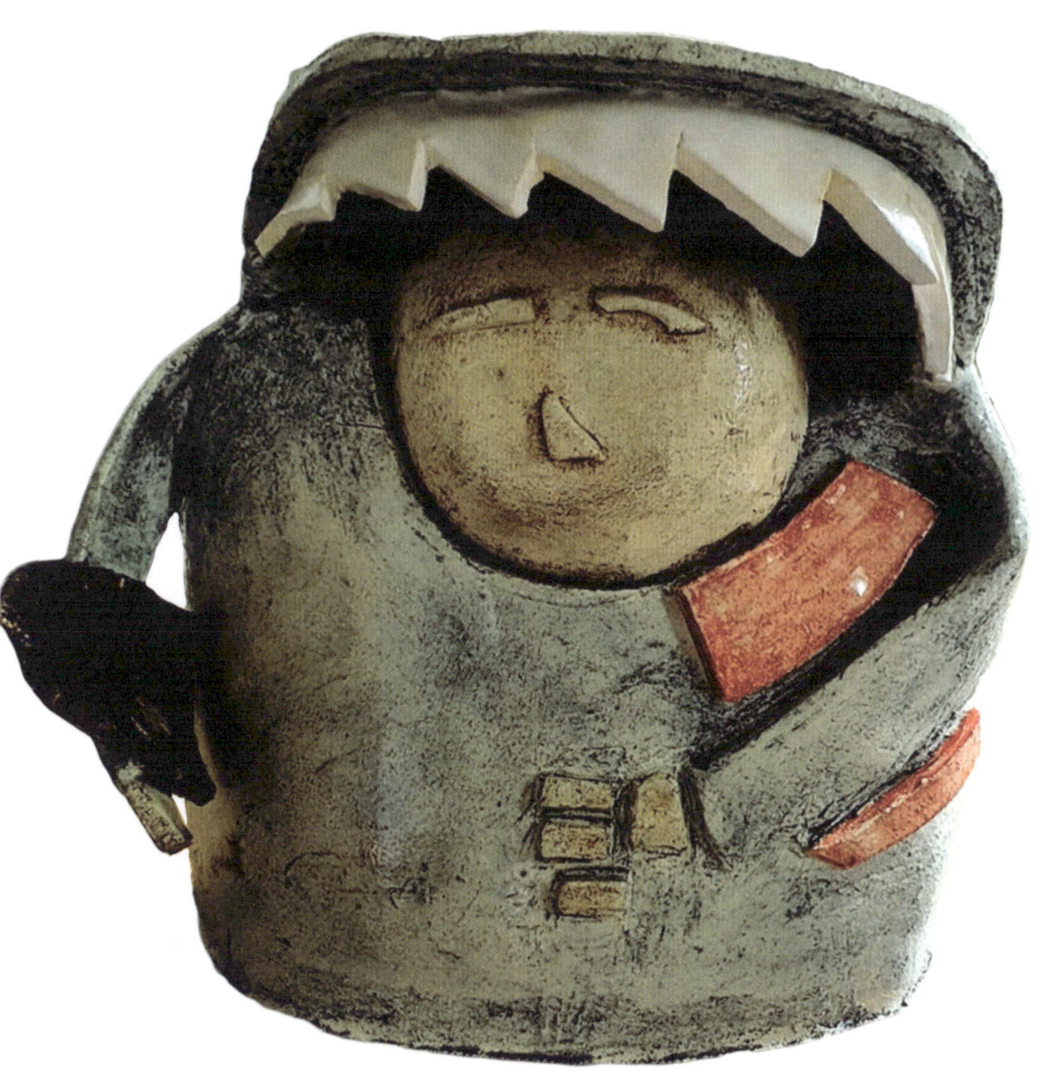

Dream Bar

Steve Nice

Painted mural
Courtesy of the artist

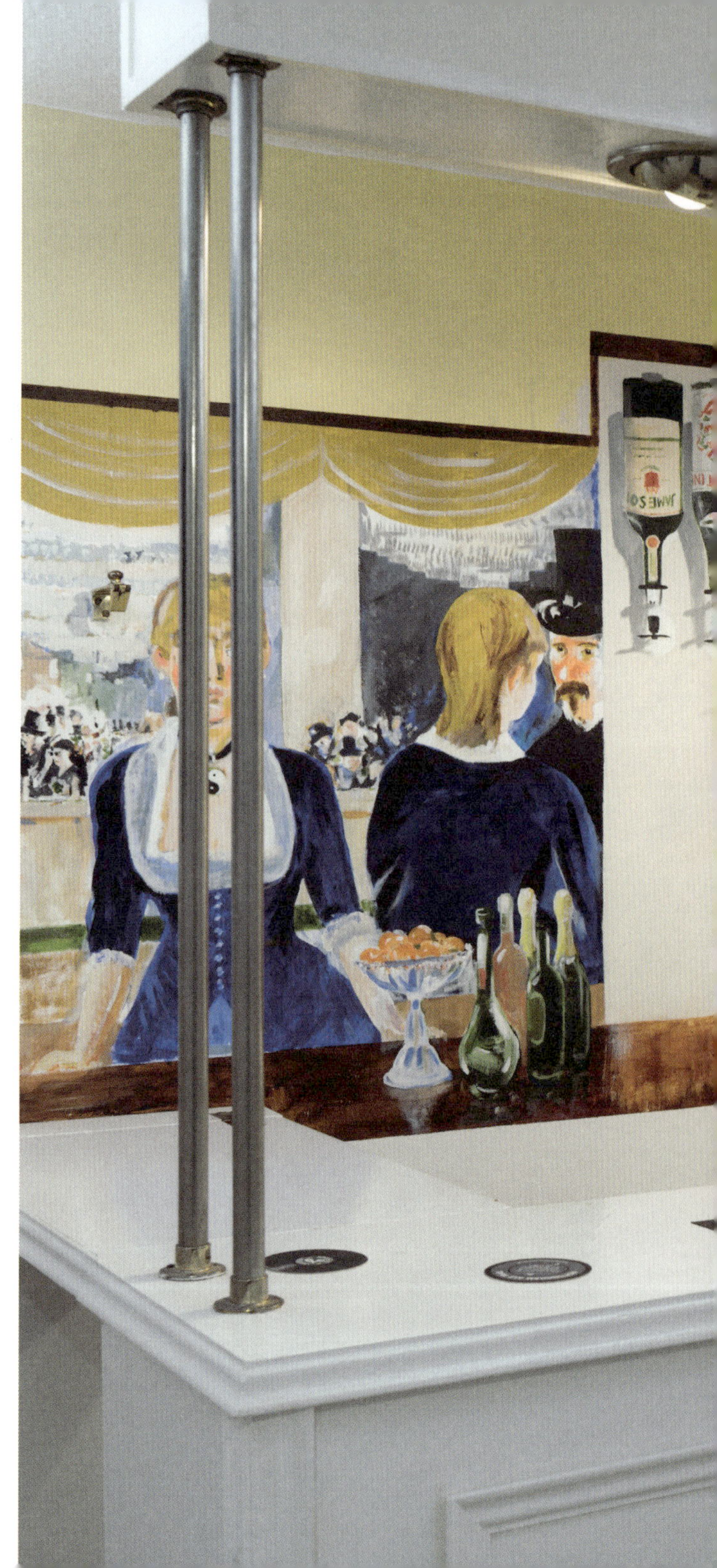

"As all the pubs were closed
during lockdown I wanted
to create an artwork which
embodied the atmosphere of
a bar. Pubs are crucial for the
wellbeing of individuals and
communities. They provide
a social environment which
is difficult to get elsewhere.
An obvious choice was a
mural behind the small bar
we have in our basement. The
artwork gave me focus during
the long days of isolation and
an optimism that we will soon
be drinking again in real pubs."

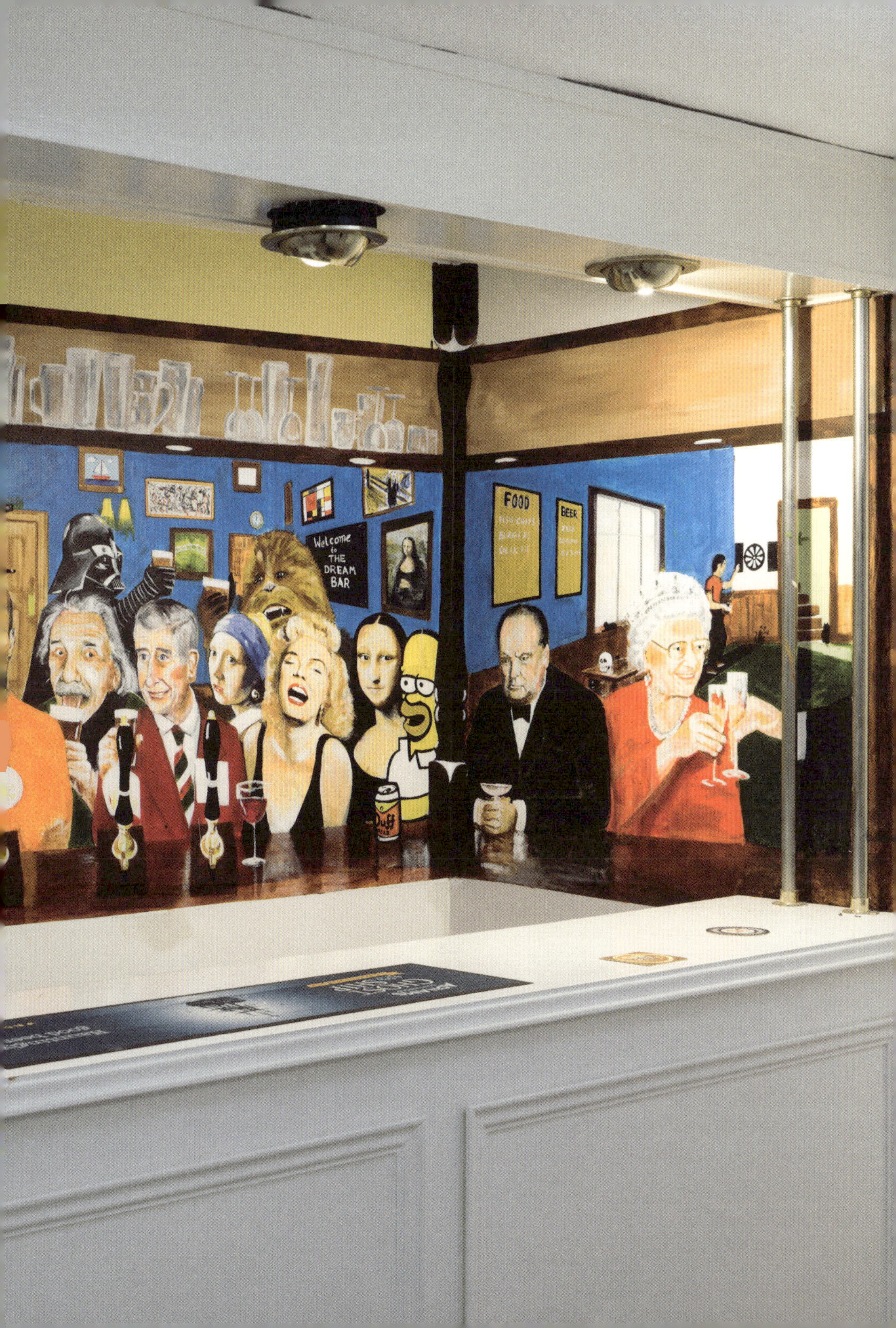

Welcome to THE DREAM BAR
FOOD
FISH CHIPS
BURGERS
STEAK PIE
BEER
Duff

Eh? What?

Patricia Oliver

Watercolour and collage
on paper
Courtesy of the artist

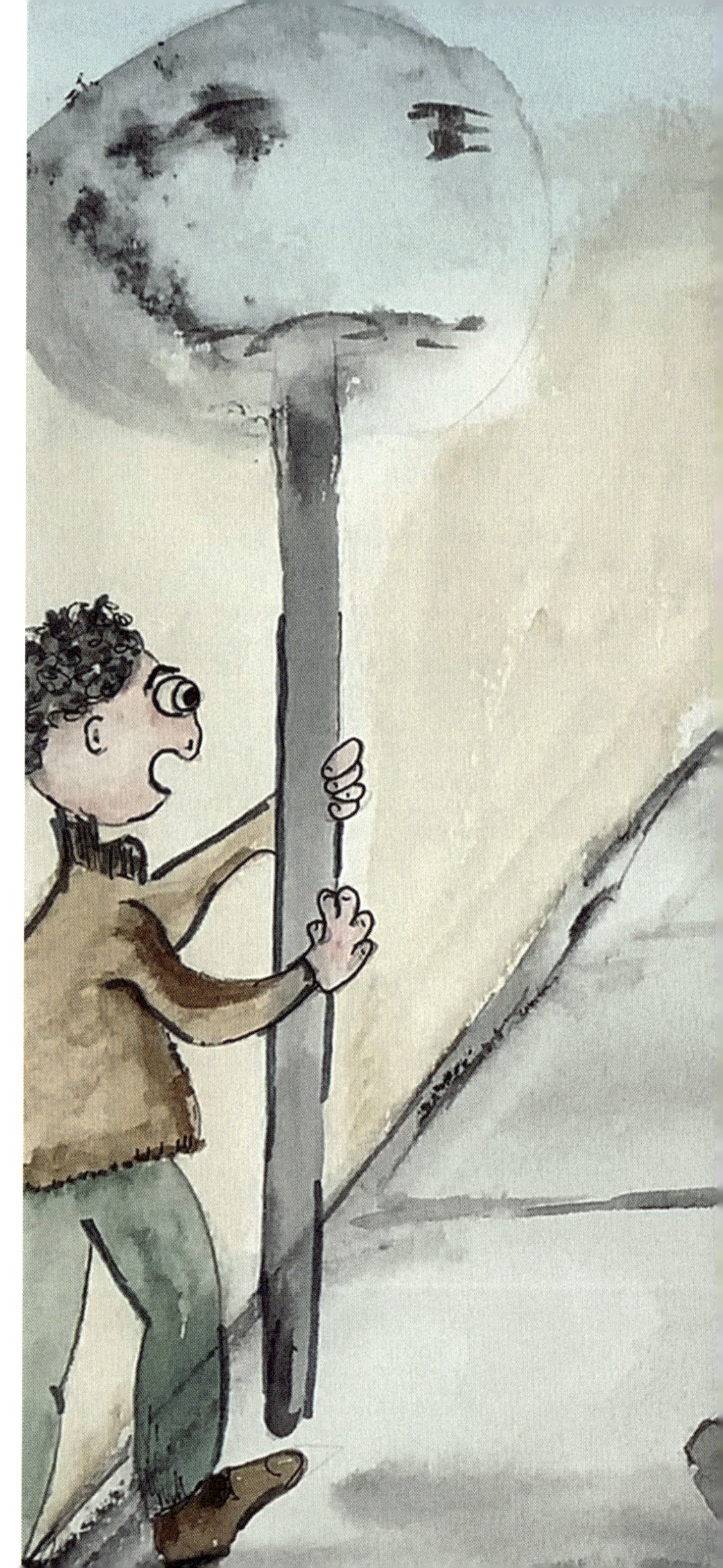

"I paint because I become
absorbed in creating a
piece of art. Lockdowns and
the ensuing isolation are
forgotten. I made this picture
to illustrate a nonsensical
dream I had. I am a giant
barcode, very bendy and
flexible. I am walking down
a street and merrily chatting
away. I am feeling very happy
and normal. I am not aware
I am something unusual.
When I tell people I dreamt
I was a giant barcode they
say 'Eh? What?'."

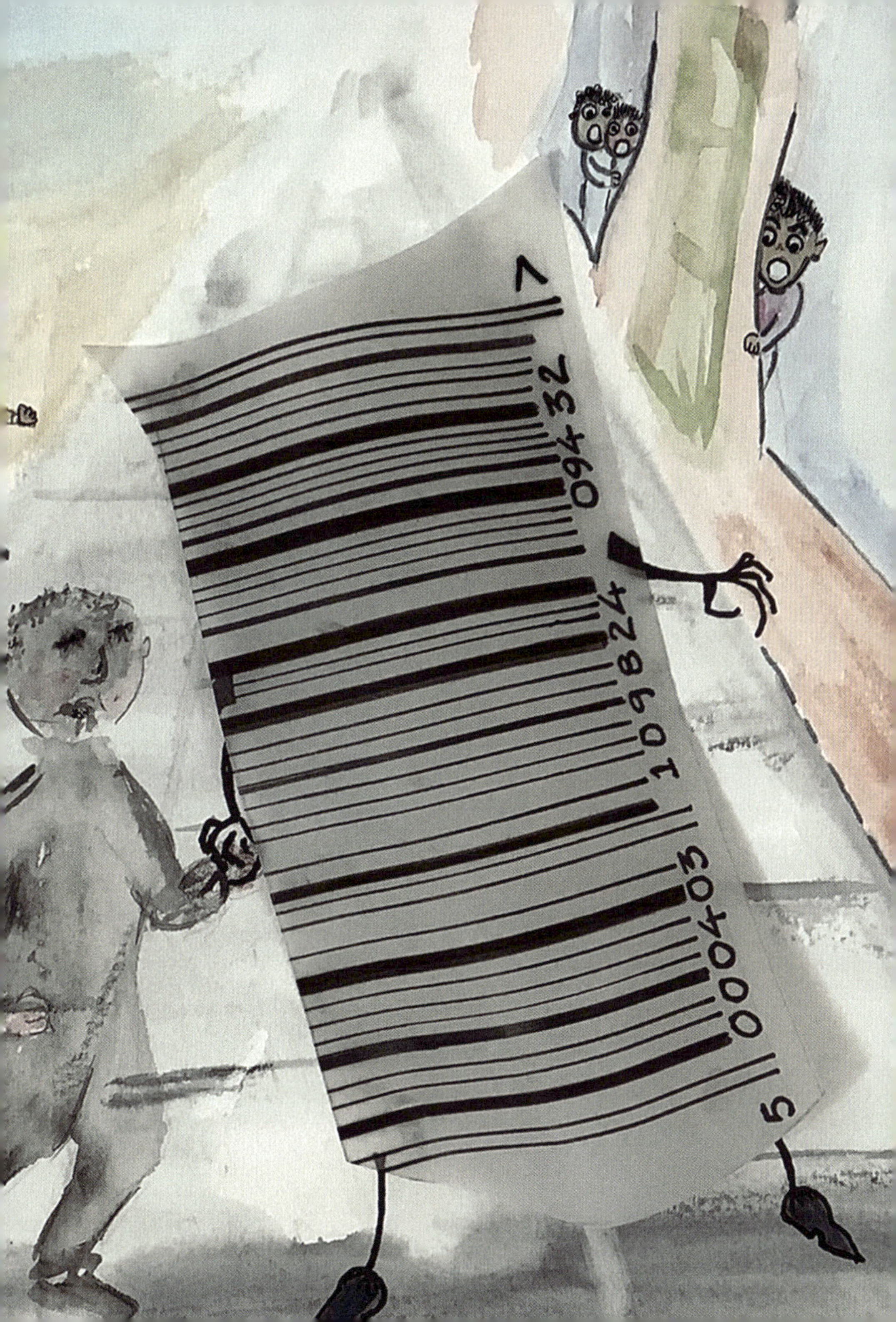

7
094 32
109824
000403
5

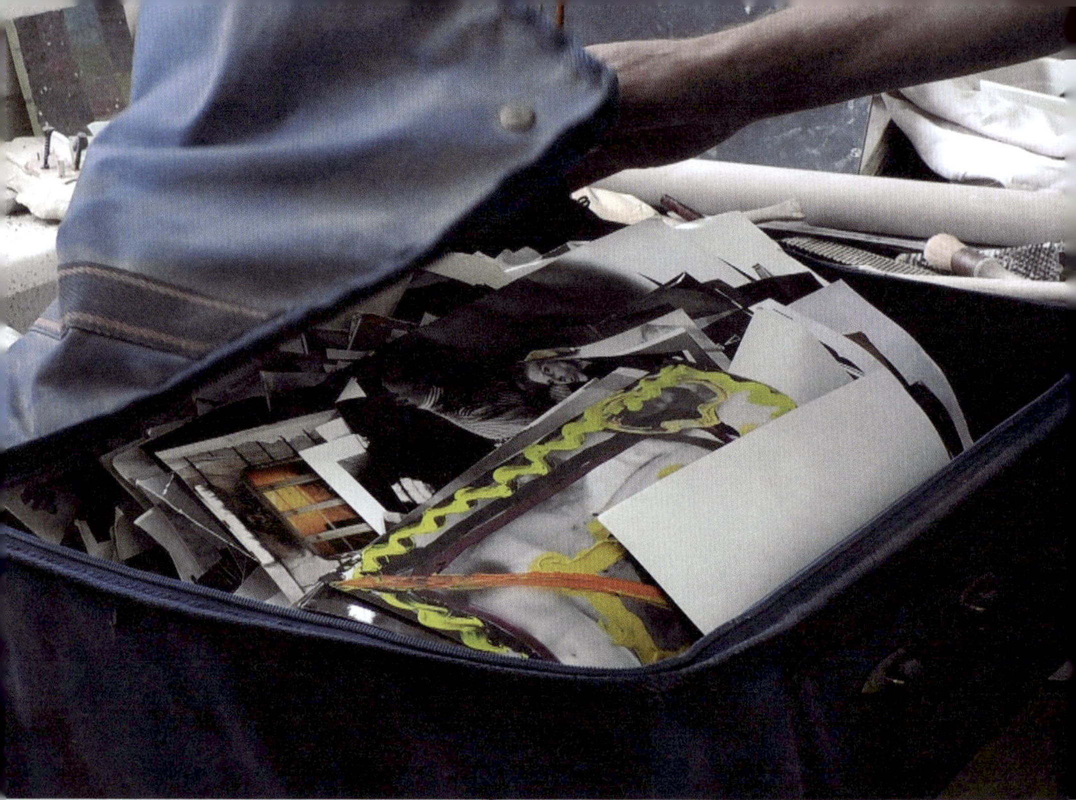

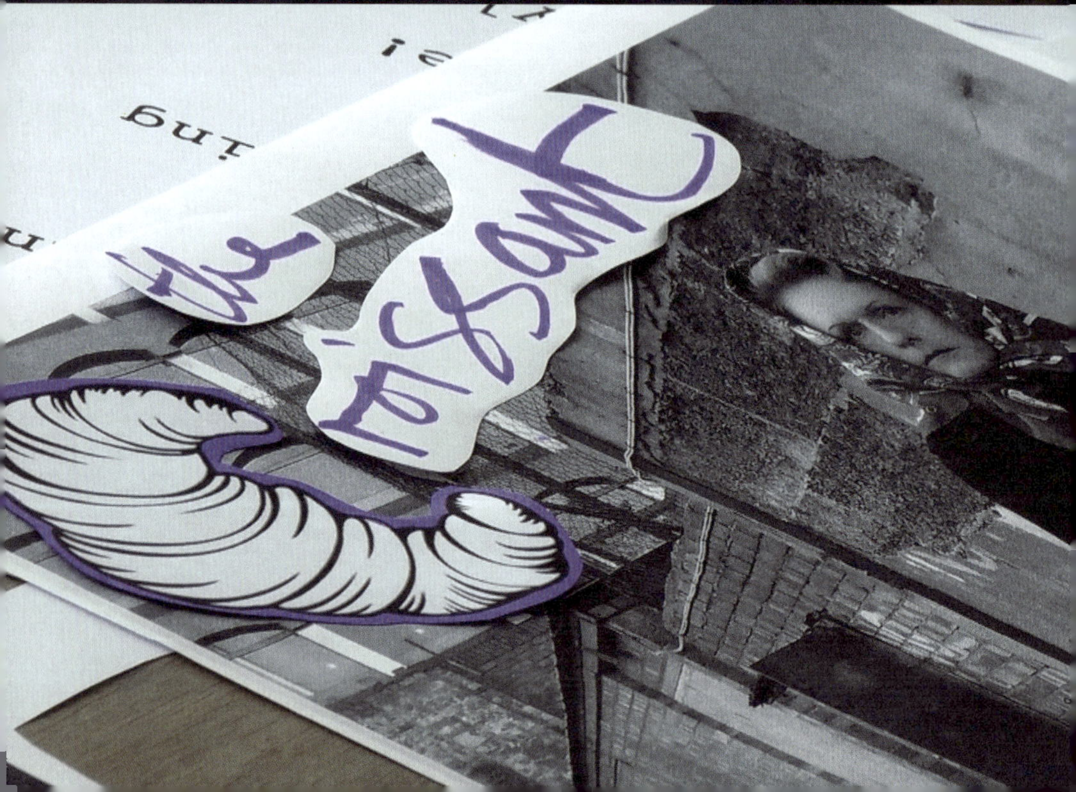

the
sam
ing

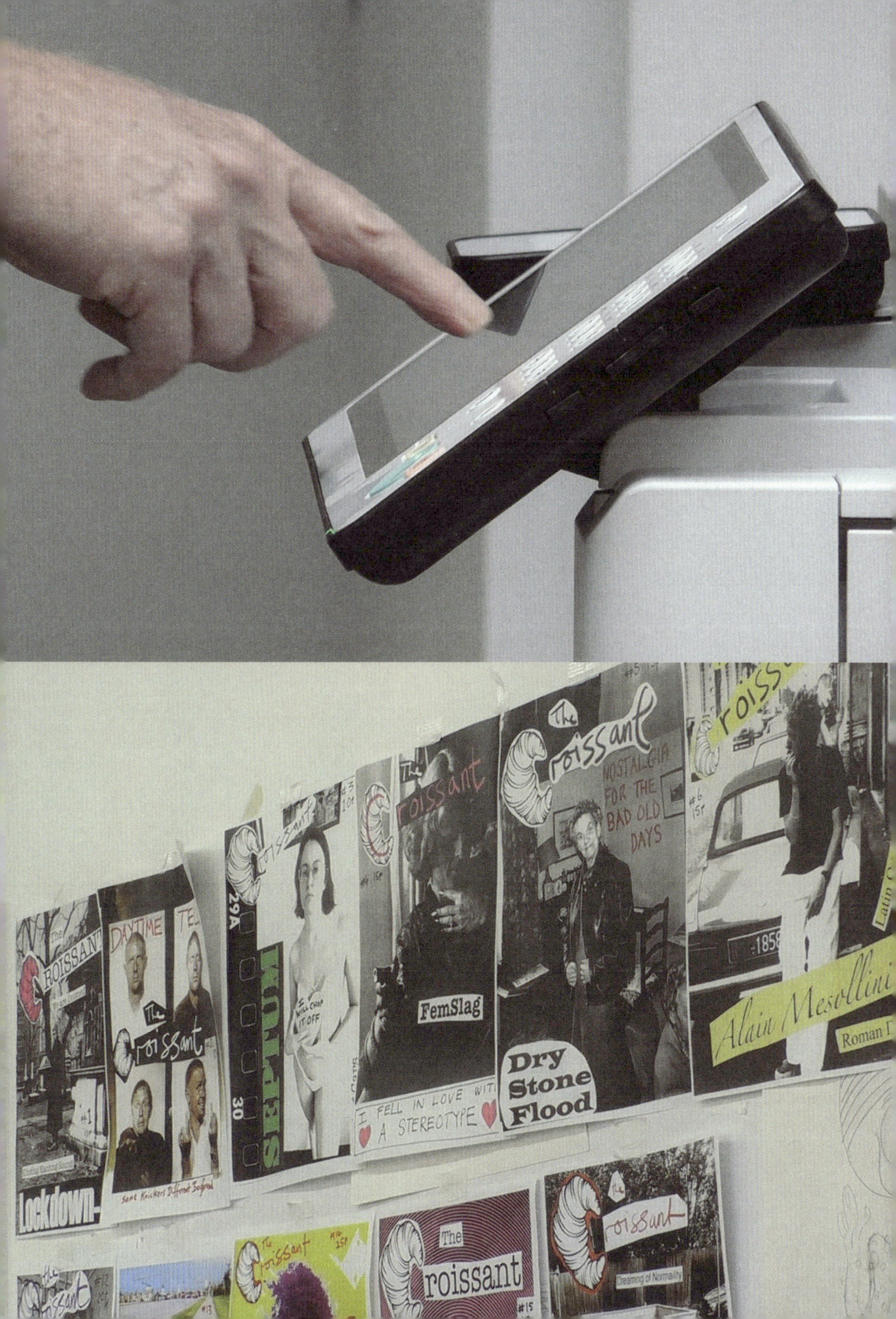
The Croissant
ROISSAN
DAYTIME
The roissant
Lockdown
Same Knickers Different Sexface
HITLERS
29A
30
roissant
The roissant
FemSlag
I FELL IN LOVE WITH A STEREOTYPE
The roissant
NOSTALGIA FOR THE BAD OLD DAYS
Dry Stone Flood
#6
roissant
Alain Mesollini
Roman
-1859
The roissant
The croissant
#19
Dreaming of Normality

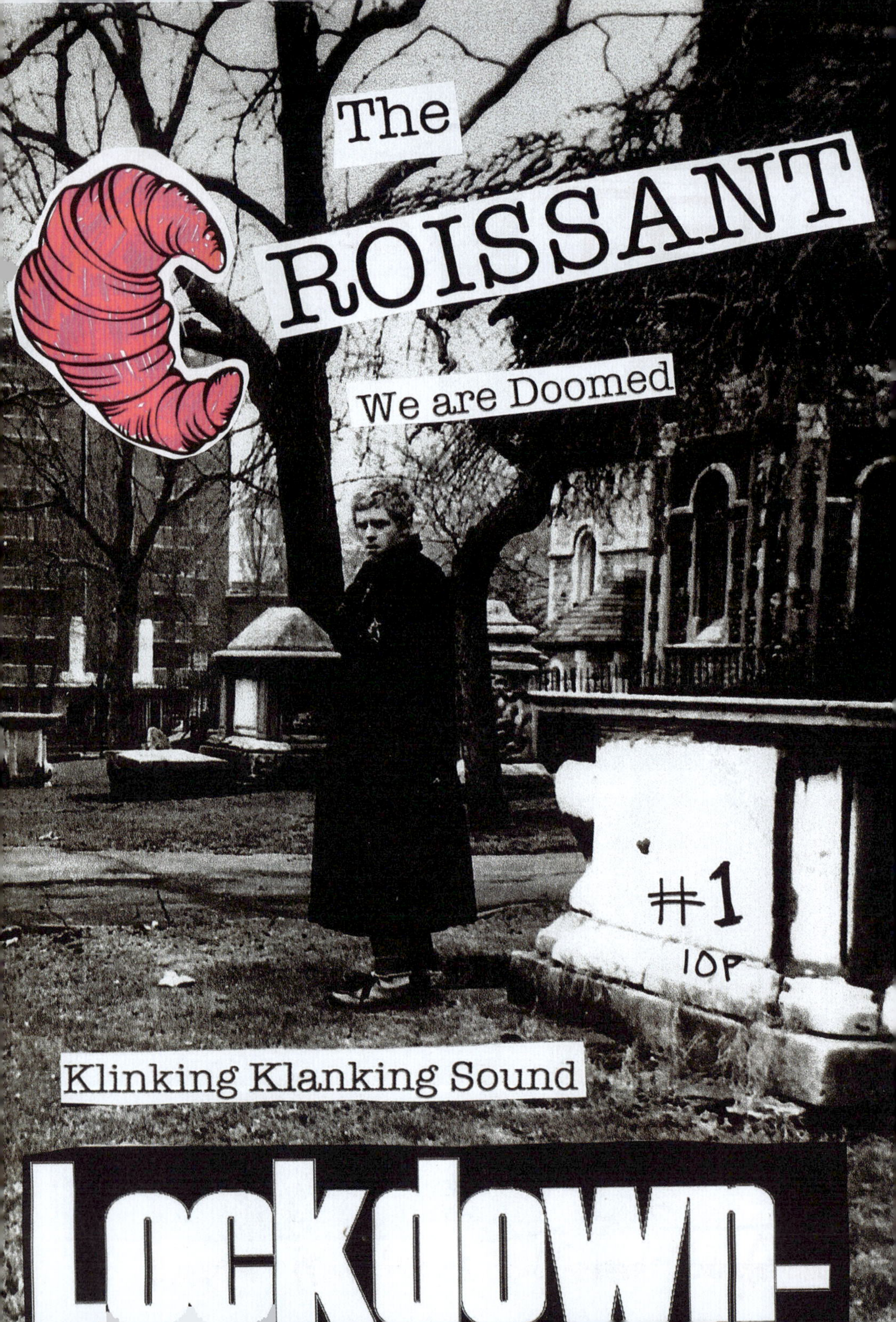

The
CROISSANT
We are Doomed
Klinking Klanking Sound
#1
10p
Lockdown

16 Croissant Fanzines
2021

Grayson Perry

Photocopies on paper
Courtesy of the artist
and Victoria Miro

"I wanted to make a fanzine
because I wanted to be a rock
star when I was young. In
some ways it's my biggest
regret, that I didn't learn
an instrument and join a
band. So I thought, "Why not
make the fanzine that would
have happened had I been
a rock star?" I think a lot of
unconscious things come out
in it because I was doing it so
fast. It's a kind of dream diary
chronological march through
the moods of my life."

Jackie
Weaver
has my
authority

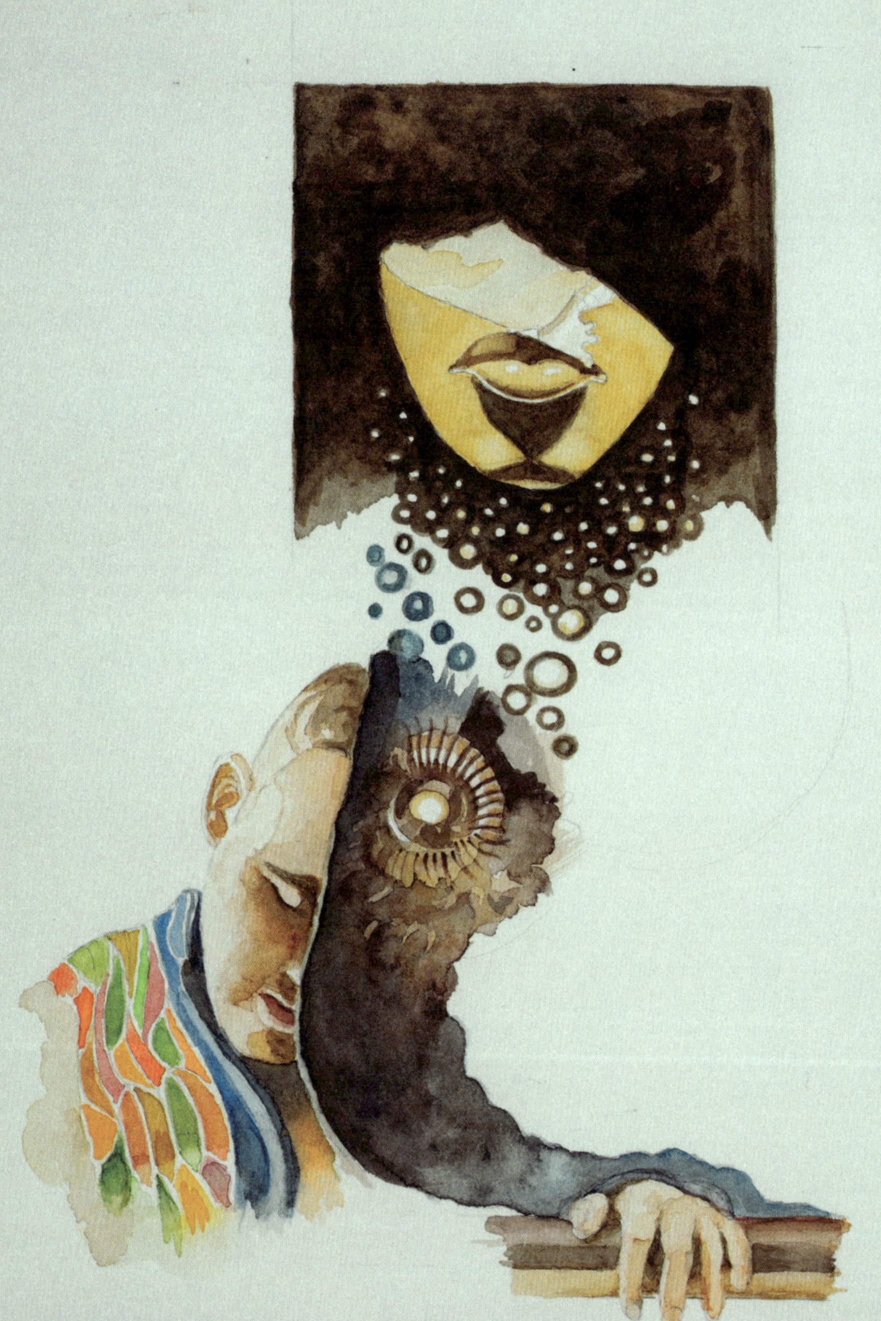

John O'Loughlin

"I decided to show all the places and things that gave me pleasure which I was prevented from experiencing by the Covid restrictions. Things like my favourite holiday destination, or a visit to my local pub for a pint, or going to the theatre. There were many images but they cluttered the painting and dwarfed the main image of the sleeper. I narrowed it down to a fragment of an Egyptian sculpture that I always go and see in the Met anytime I'm in New York. This beautiful, sensual image seemed to encapsulate all the rejected images.

Being creative is very important to me. I am an actor and I am very lucky that I am in a creative profession. When I am out of work it is a great bonus that I can fall back on my drawing and watercolour painting. It keeps the old brain ticking over till the next job comes along. When lockdown happened all the theatres were closed and work completely dried up and *Grayson's Art Club* was a 'life saver'."

you're
on
mute!

Work

"Work is the part of our lives we've all
been forced to re-evaluate over the
past two years. Art about work can
help us understand not just what
we want to get from work, but what
kind of work we think is important.

Art can help us understand what
we value about work, what we enjoy
about it and what meaning it gives
to our lives. The pandemic perhaps
gave us a chance to reassess that and
think, "Am I doing the thing I want
to do in the way I want to do it?"

Working from Home

Clare Thornthwaite

Digital collage
Courtesy of the artist

"I decided to create a digital
collage of my 'working
from home' set up. The
tropical island is my Zoom
background. I often daydream
that I'm in a far off land
rather than sitting in another
pointless meeting. The dress
is based on clothes worn
by women in paintings
by Rossetti. They are
often sitting at their desks,
twiddling their thumbs,
looking a little bit bored. That
summed up the whole vibe of
working from home for me."

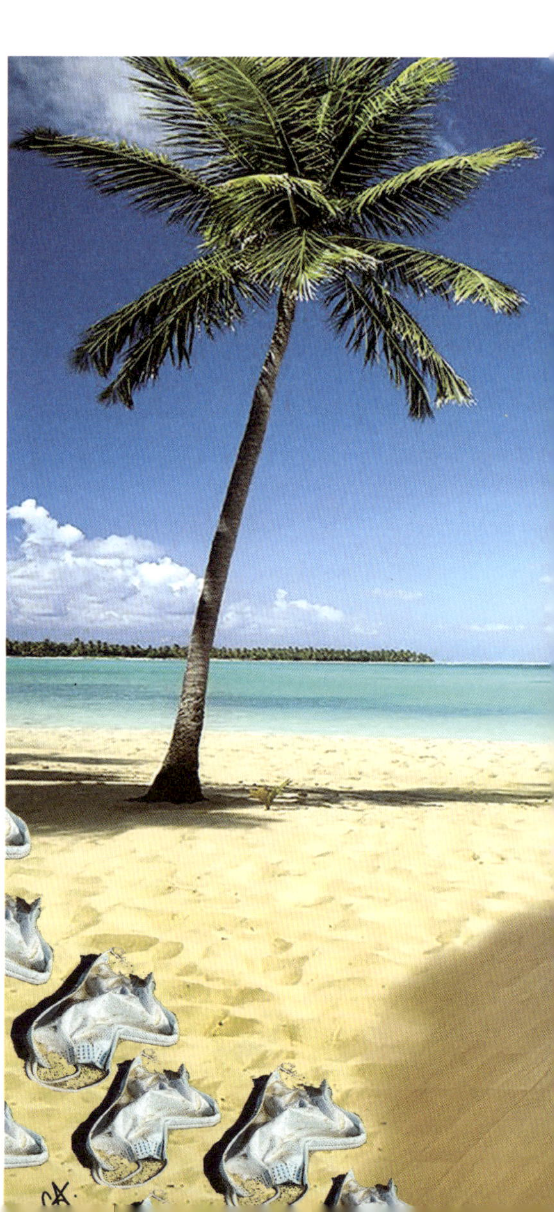

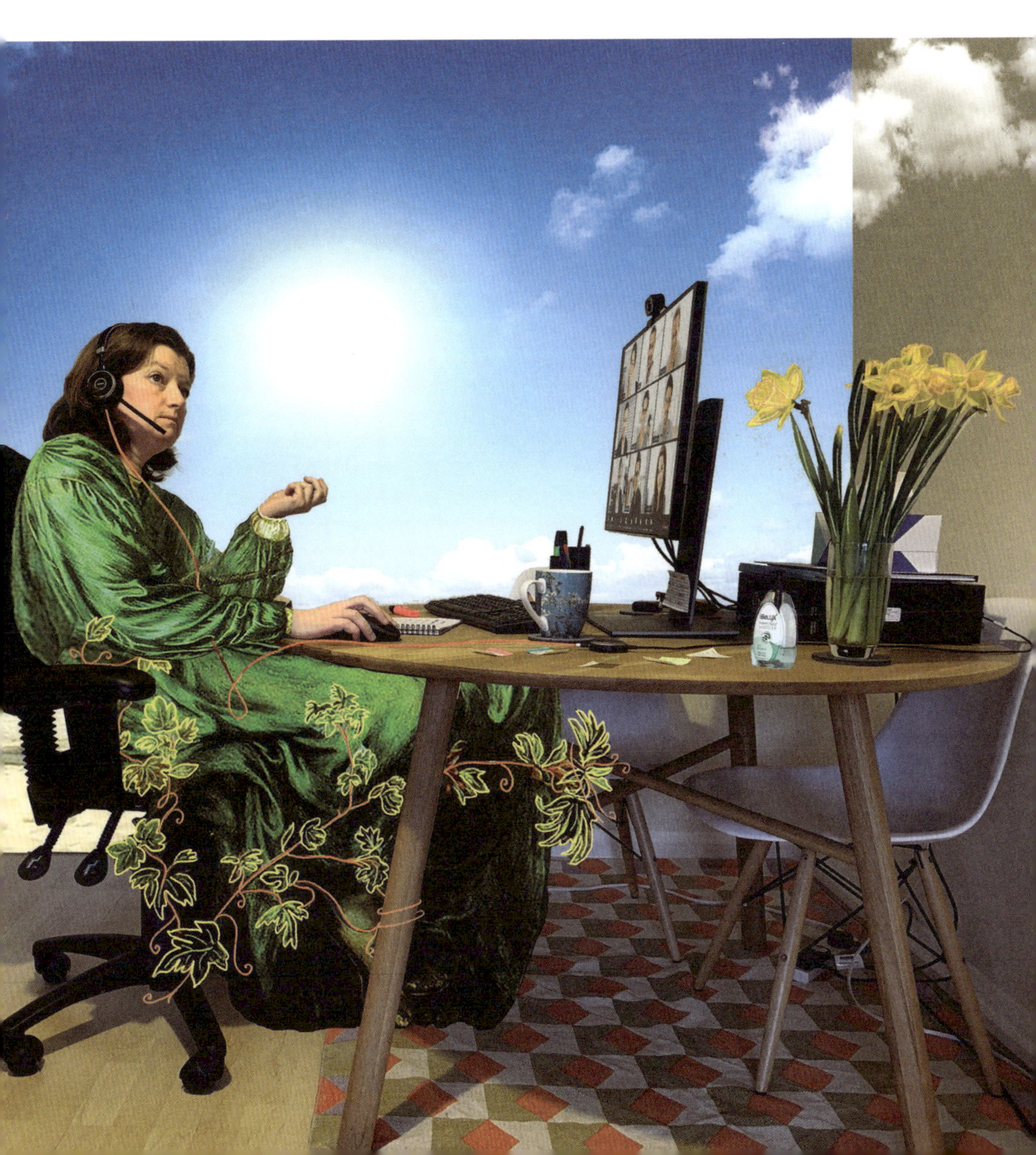
#WFH

Art Is Work

Trix Newham

Watercolour and ink on paper
Courtesy of the artist

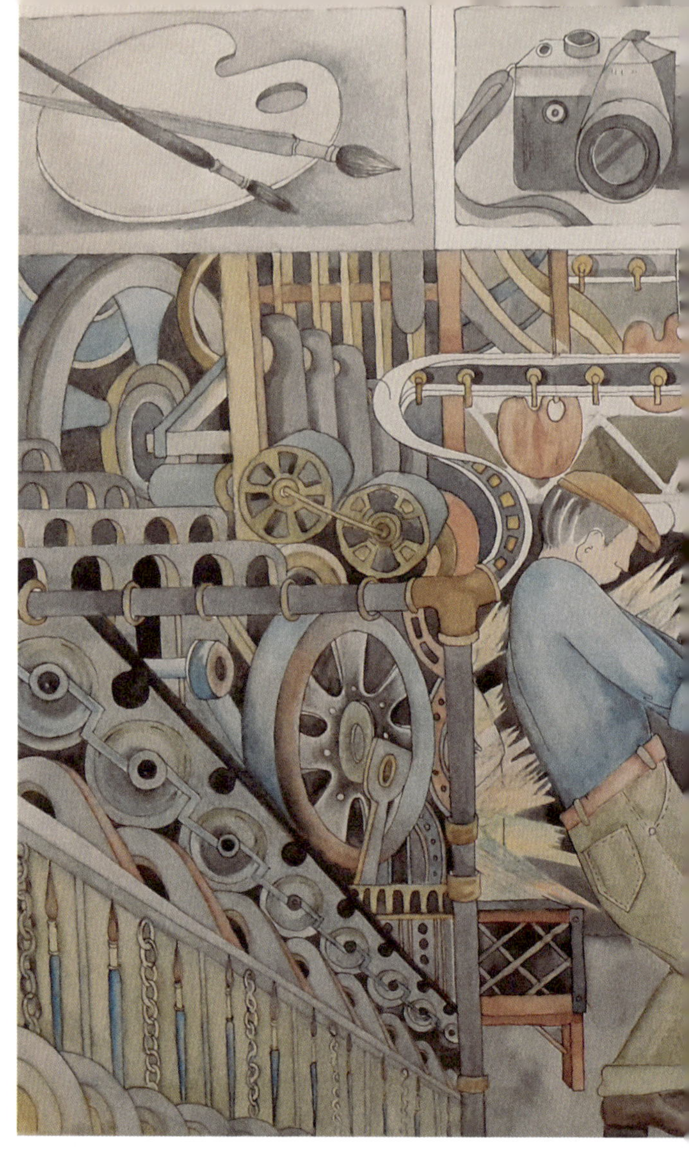

"*Art Is Work* is inspired by the
Diego Rivera Ford Factory
murals, here used to depict
the belief that art is as
fundamental to society as
car production. The creation
of which is labour. In the
original there is a viewing
gallery where the great and
good of the day could observe
the backbreaking toil of the
workers, hence the cheeky
nod to Philippa and Grayson."

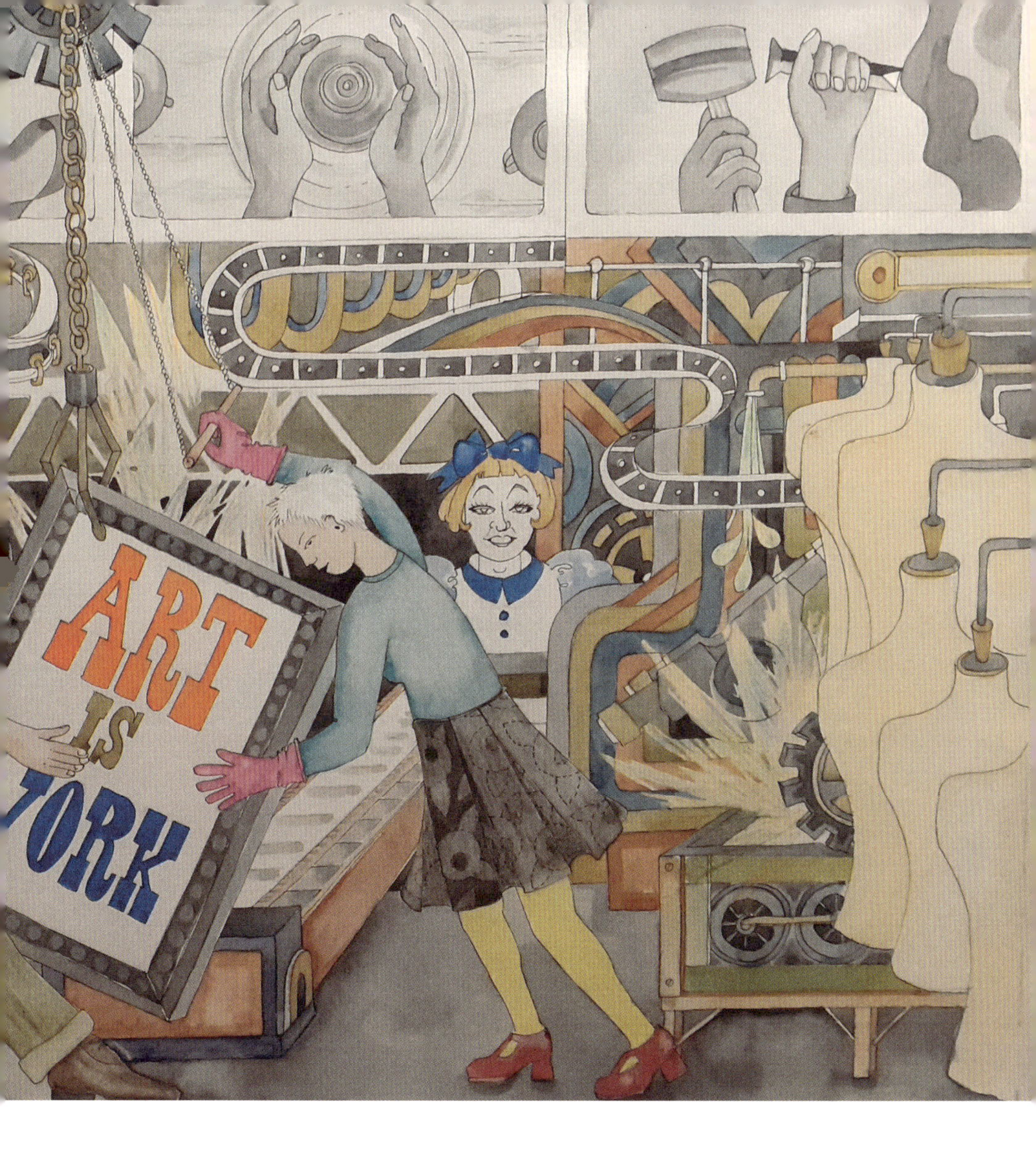

ART
IS
YORK

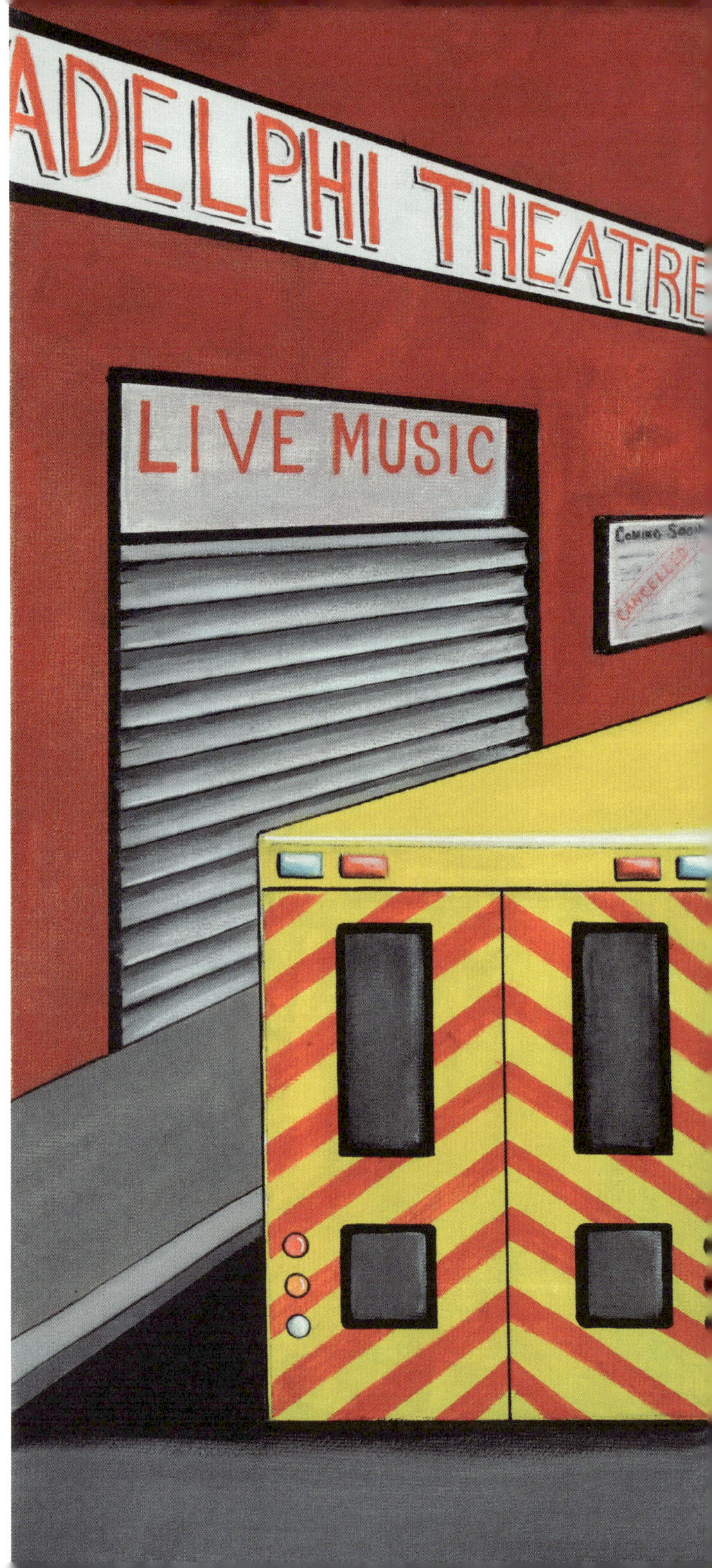

Work, During Lockdown

Enda O'Gorman

Acrylic paint on Canvas
Courtesy of the artist

"During lockdown some workplaces were completely shut down, such as live music venues, pubs and retail. Other workers were busier than they had ever been, such as emergency medical professionals and food delivery riders. Anyone who was unable to work from home depended on public transport workers so they could get to work."

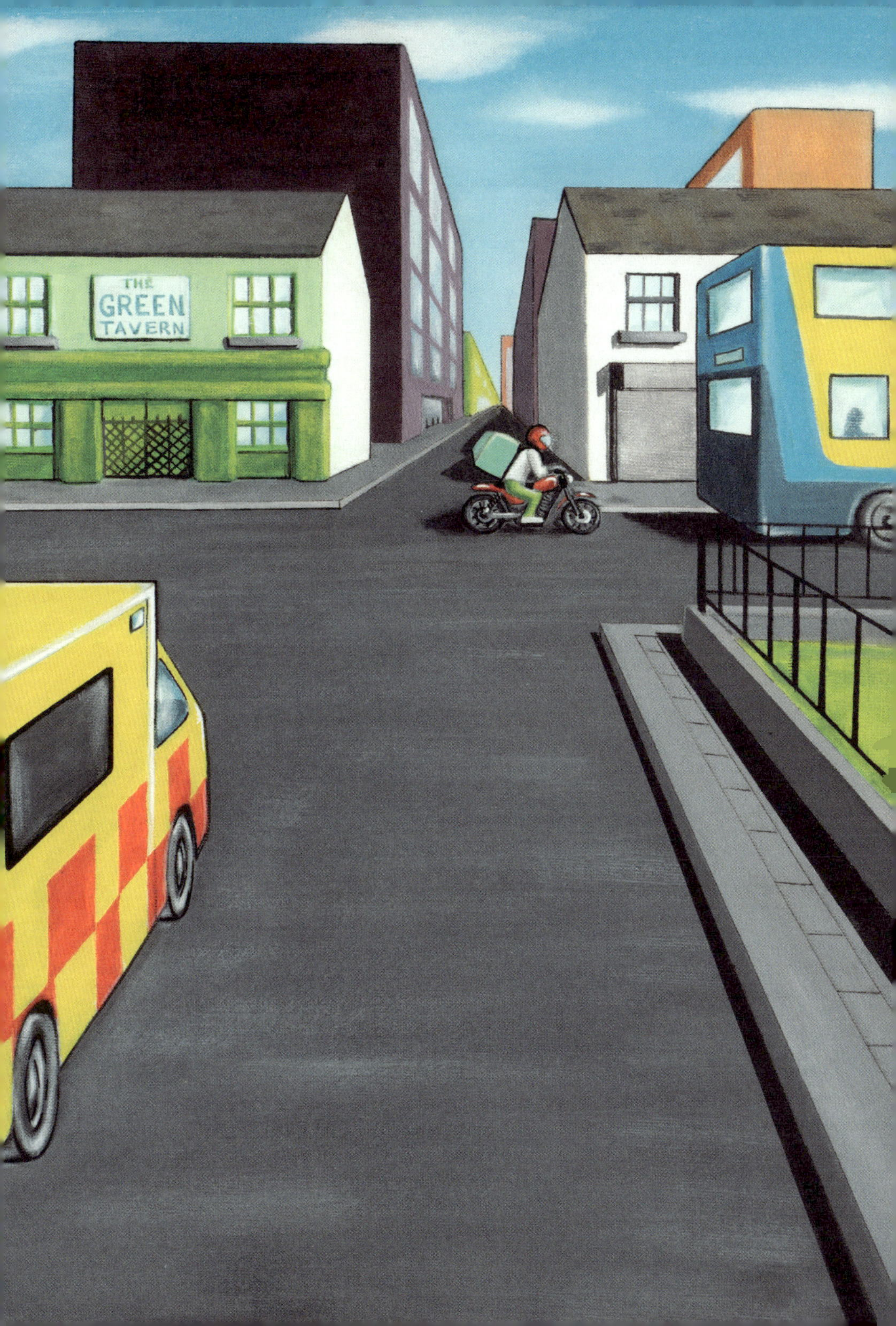

THE
GREEN
TAVERN

NHS Frontline Sketchbook:
Elderly collapse at home
during COVID-19 pandemic

Mark Robert-Blunn

Ink on paper
Courtesy of the artist

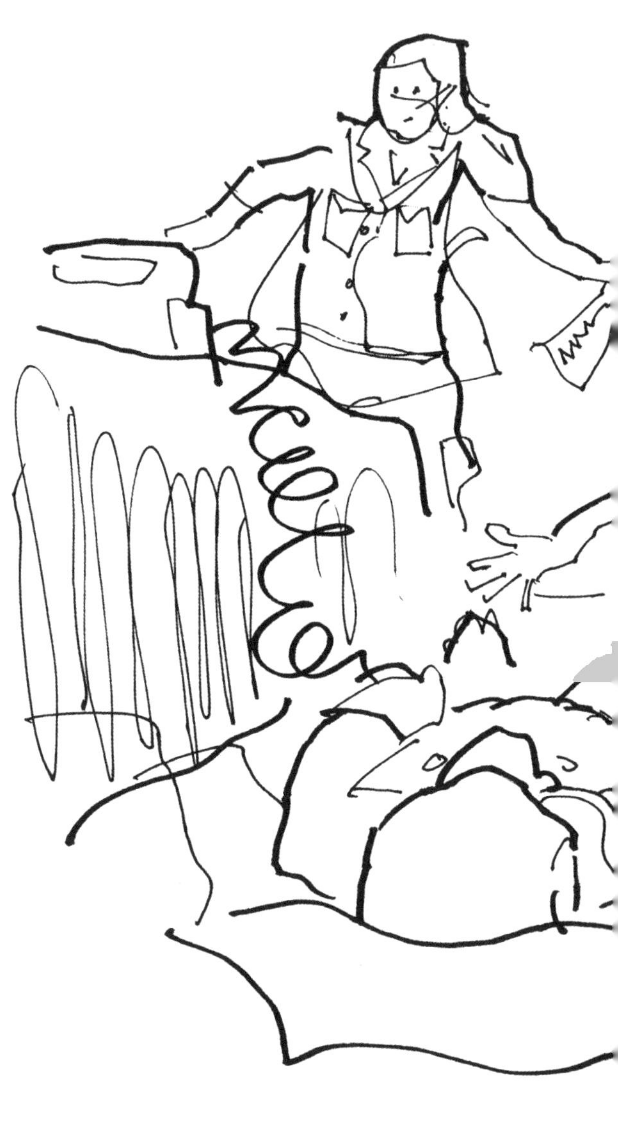

"Drawing is my way of
making sense of what I do
as a paramedic. A humbling
and privileged position
that continues to have real
meaning for me. This was
my response to dealing with
patients at the beginning
of the pandemic. An elderly
gentleman has collapsed
with acute symptoms. The
fear of infection was nerve-
wracking. I had been away
from the frontline because of
treatment for bowel cancer,
so this image is poignant for
me in all sorts of ways."

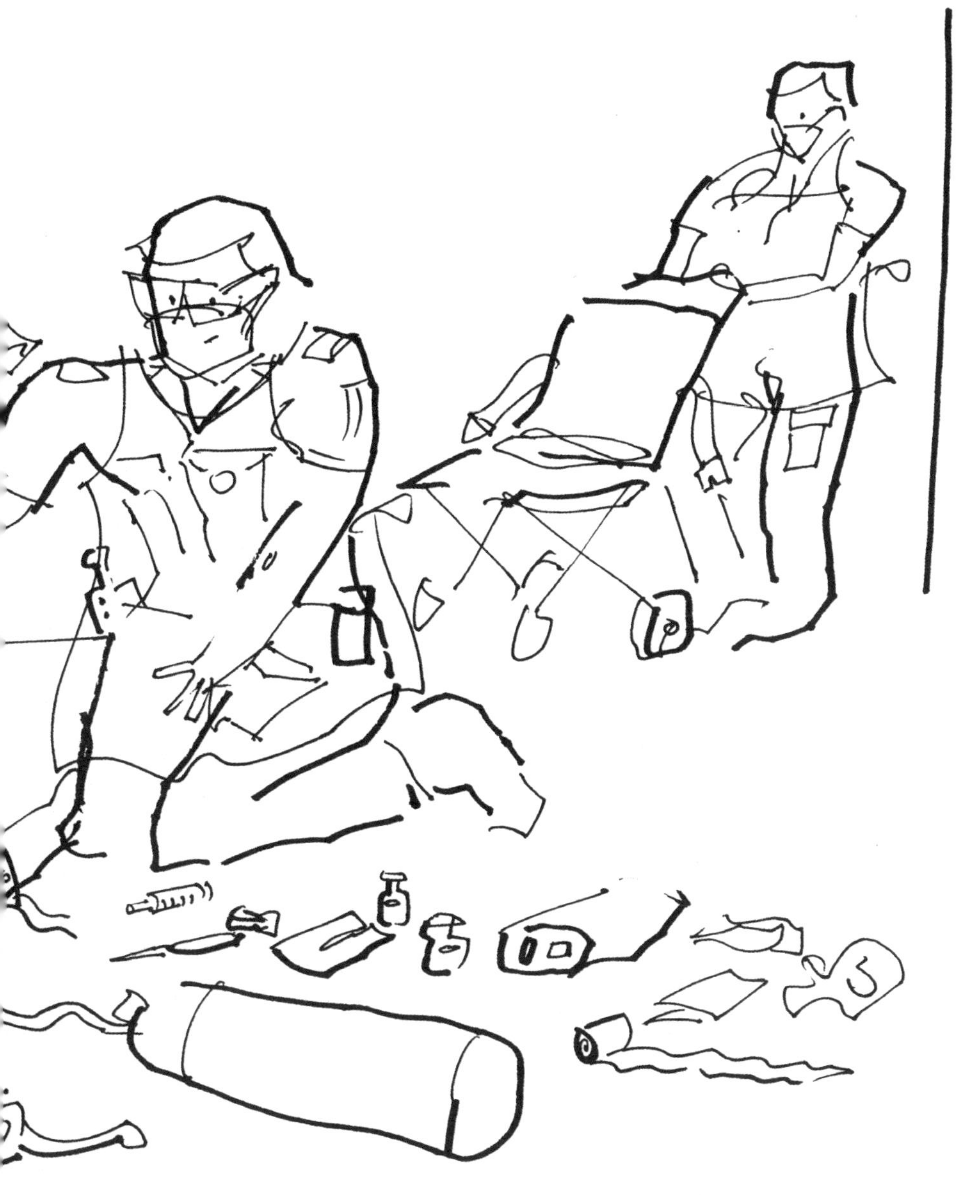

Sisyphus Works the
Night Shift

Jon Gale

Oil paint on canvas
Courtesy of the artist

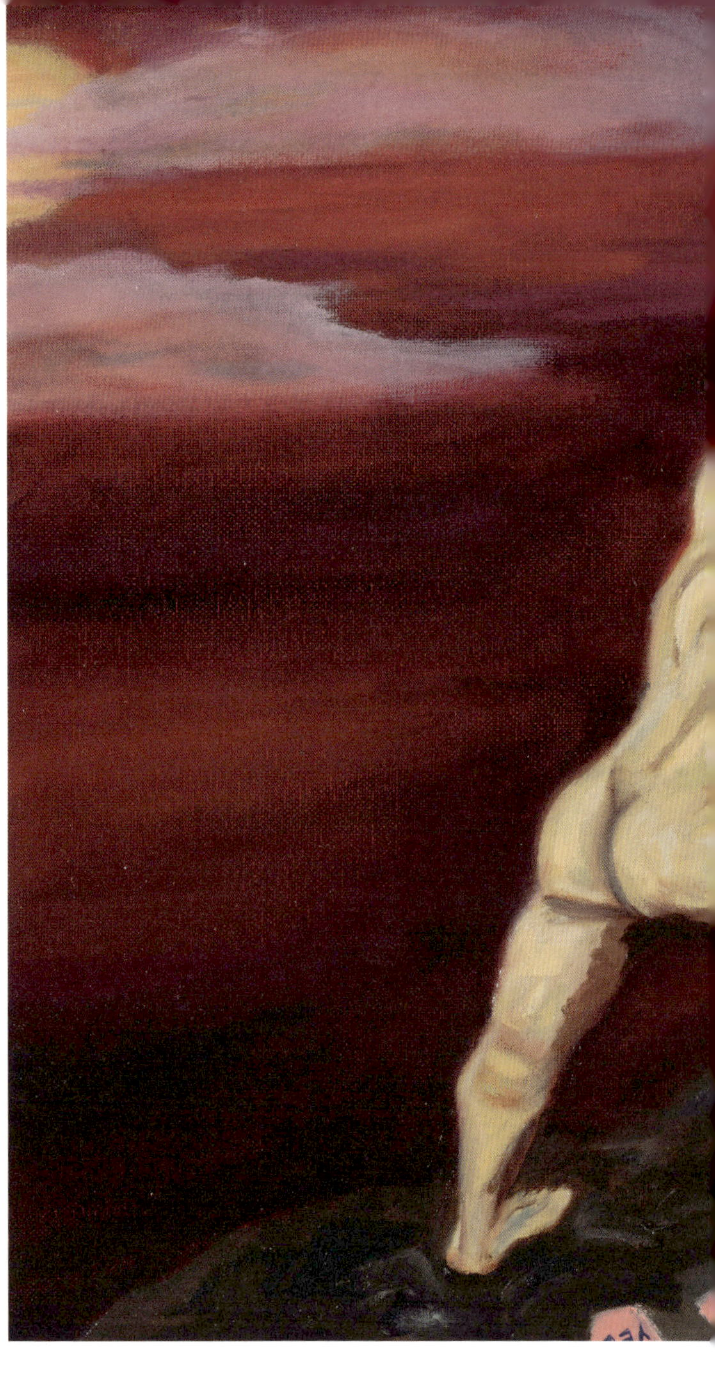

"I was working as a French
polisher. With lockdown
we couldn't go into people's
houses as much. I still had
bills to pay so went for a trial
in Tesco. I've been there six
months. I've always loved that
Victorian style when they paint
Greek myths. I wanted to do
that with a modern twist.
It's based on Sisyphus making
parallels to working dead end
jobs. I tried to merge a 21st
century working class culture
with Greek classicism."

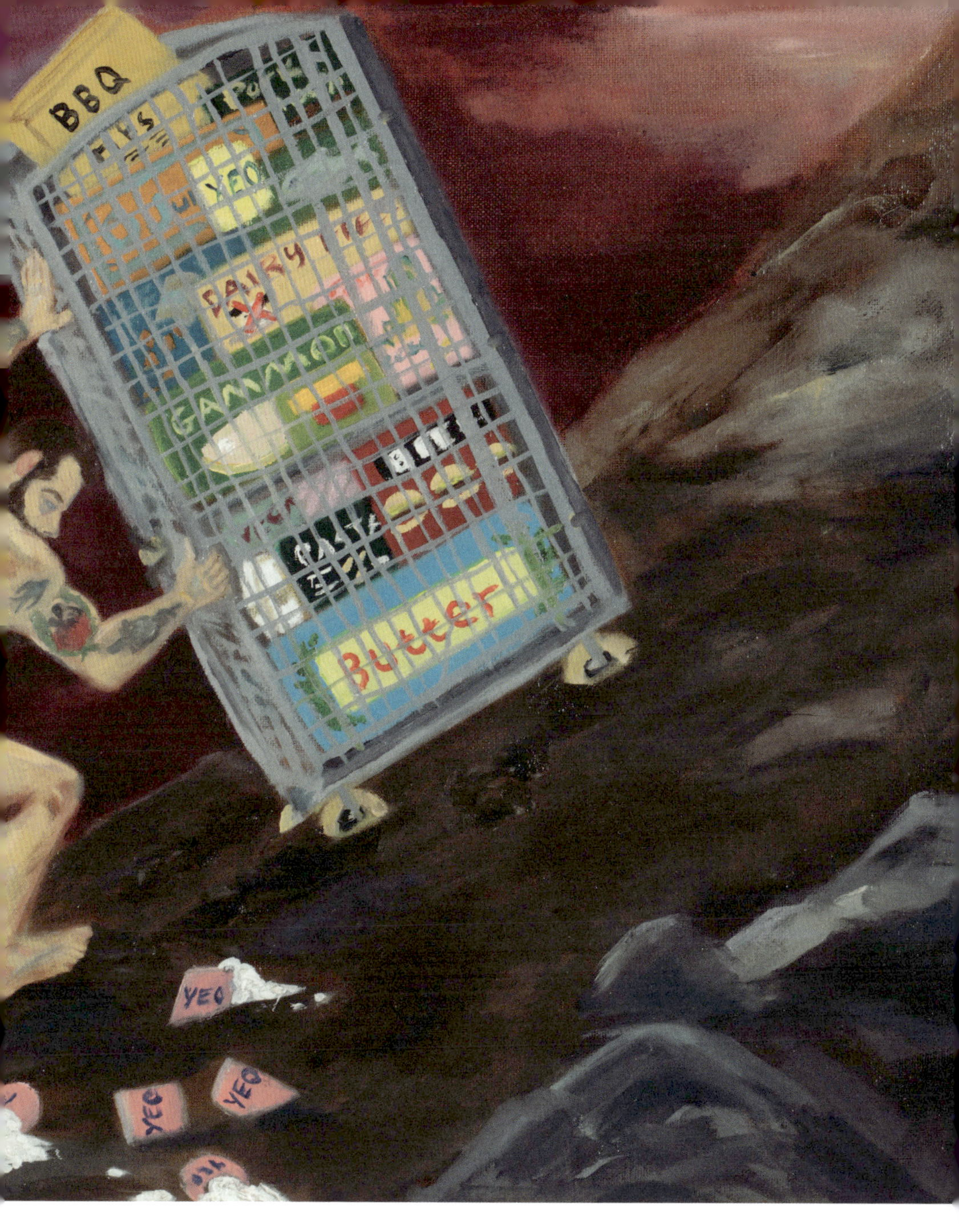

BBQ
YEO
DAIRY
GAMMON
BITE
Butter
YEO
YEO
YEO

The Covid Kids

Danny Shannon

Acrylic paint on stoneware
Courtesy of the artist

"I lost my Dad at the
beginning of lockdown and
was kind of lost. When I came
home, I sat down in front of
a ball of clay. I got lost in the
clay. The Covid Kids are the
people we once knew, once
were and still are. They are the
children of a lost education.
Dreams, potential and self
identity not yet realised.
The bully isn't here, he blew
up in the kiln. The Lord works
in mysterious ways!"

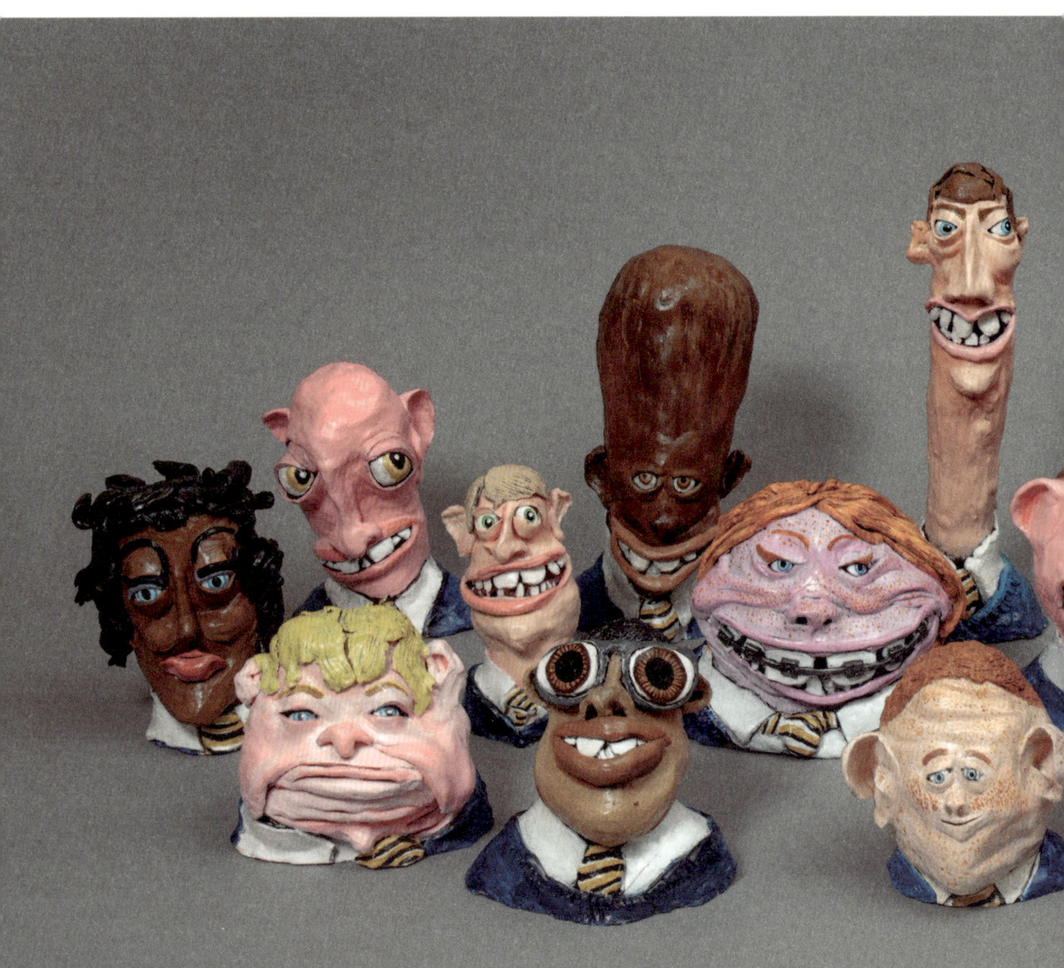

'Where's my mask?' dance

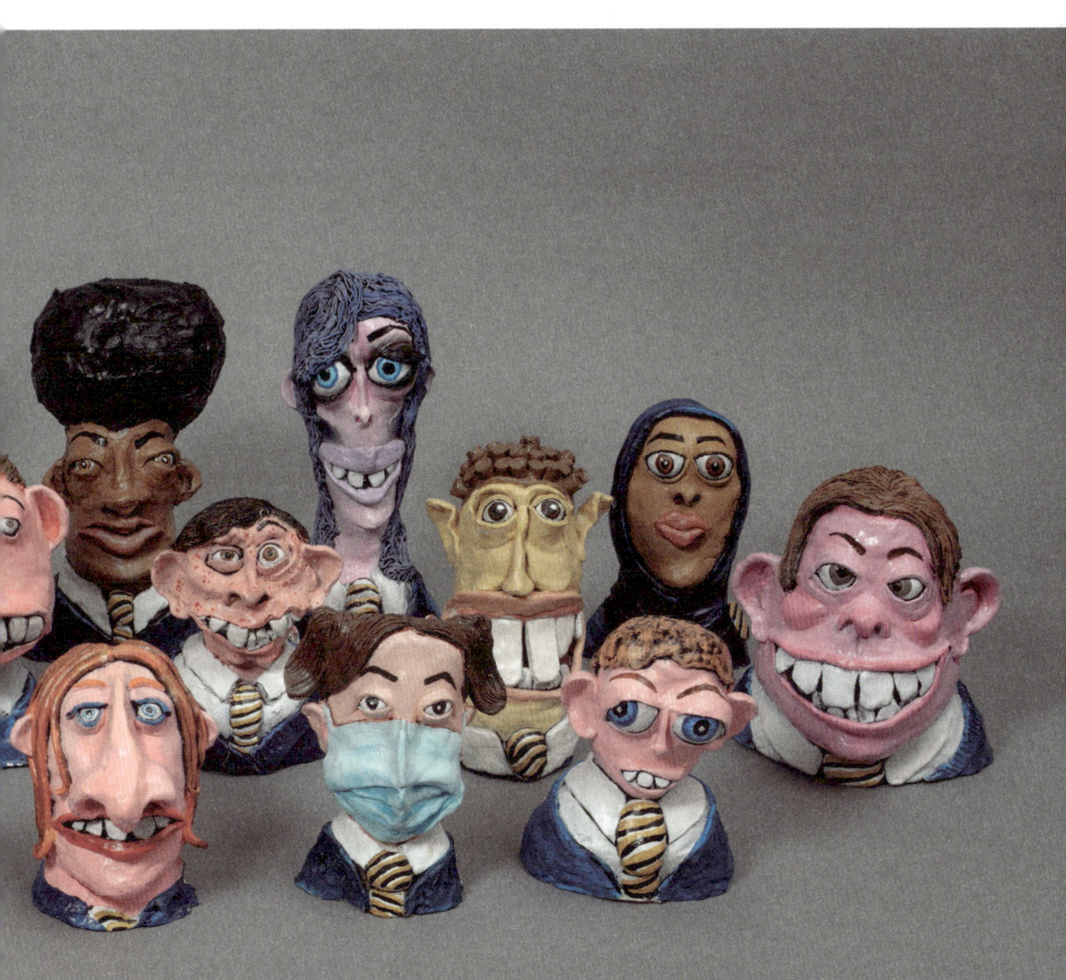

Covid Ritual Music

Madame Ceski

Coverall polypropylene suit,
decorated with buttons,
ribbons and bells,
video of performance
Courtesy of the artist

“During lockdown I bought a
coverall suit from Screwfix
with the aim to create
some Covid ritual music.
A quasi-folk costume, tune
& instructive dance to ward
away Covid. As a musician
and performer with no work,
it helped me channel
my energies and worries.
I’m really into folk customs
and rituals, so making my
‘hazmat Morris’ outfit seemed
the right thing to do. Greatly
inspired by the DIY nature of
Art Club.”

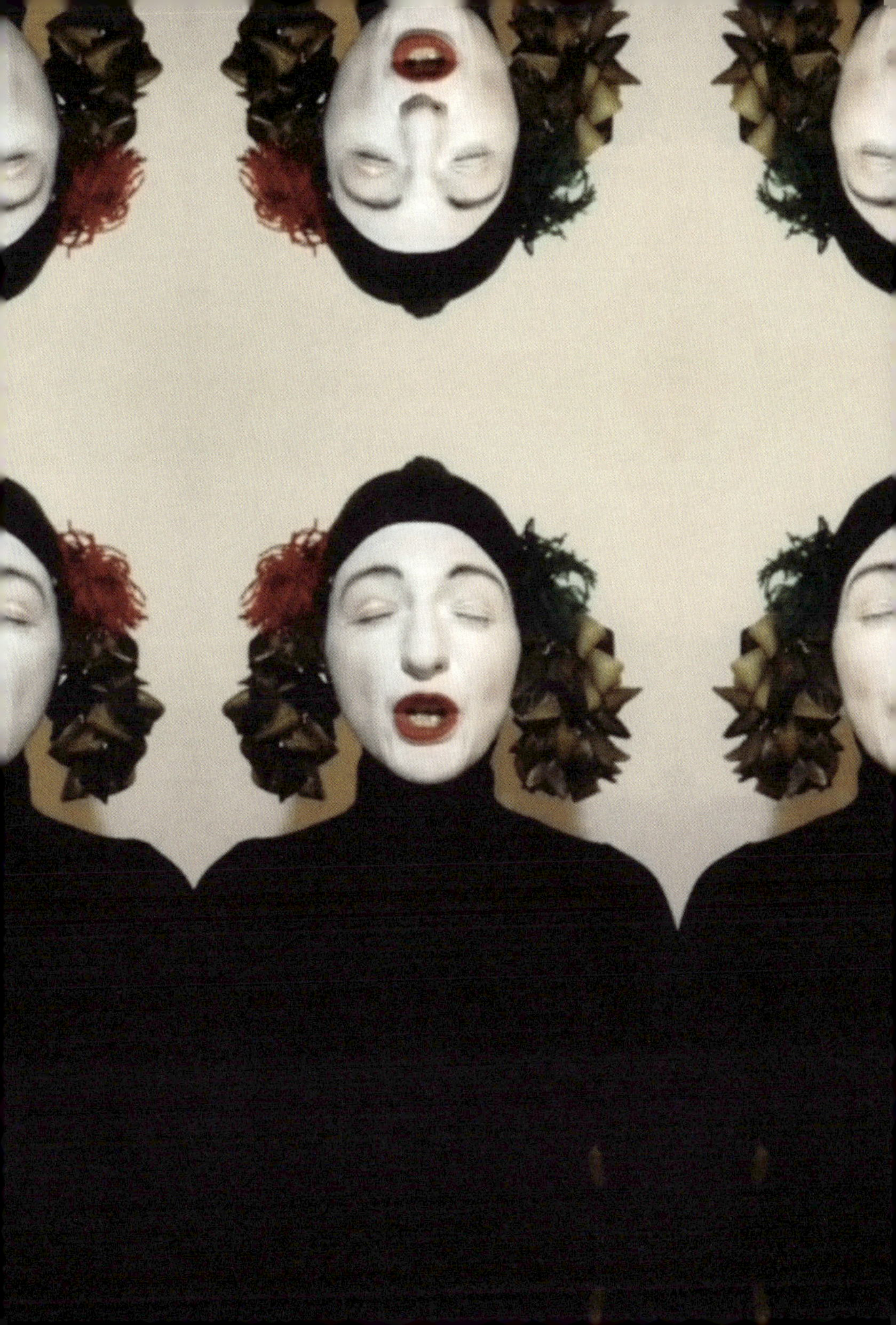

The Wave XV

Jane Seymour

Watercolour on paper
Courtesy of the artist

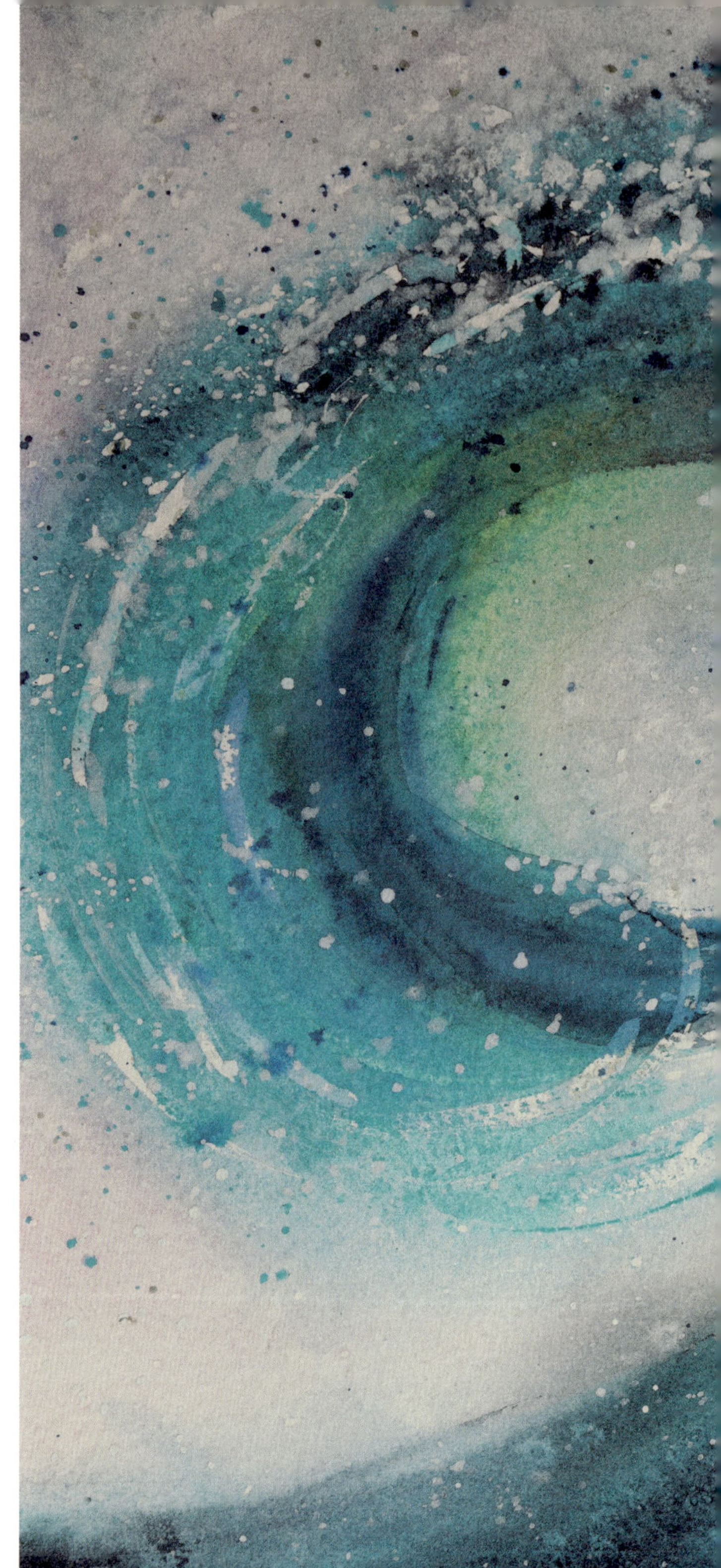

"I began painting from the
time I was forty. I'd lost
everything and basically
didn't have anything left.
A well-known artist saw the
finger paintings I'd done
with the kids, and said,"
These are really good.
I'm going to teach you
watercolour, and you'll take
it with you for the rest of your
life." That's how it all started.
Painting freed me up. It made
me feel like I could process
my feelings, whatever they
were. Art became my healing
to this day."

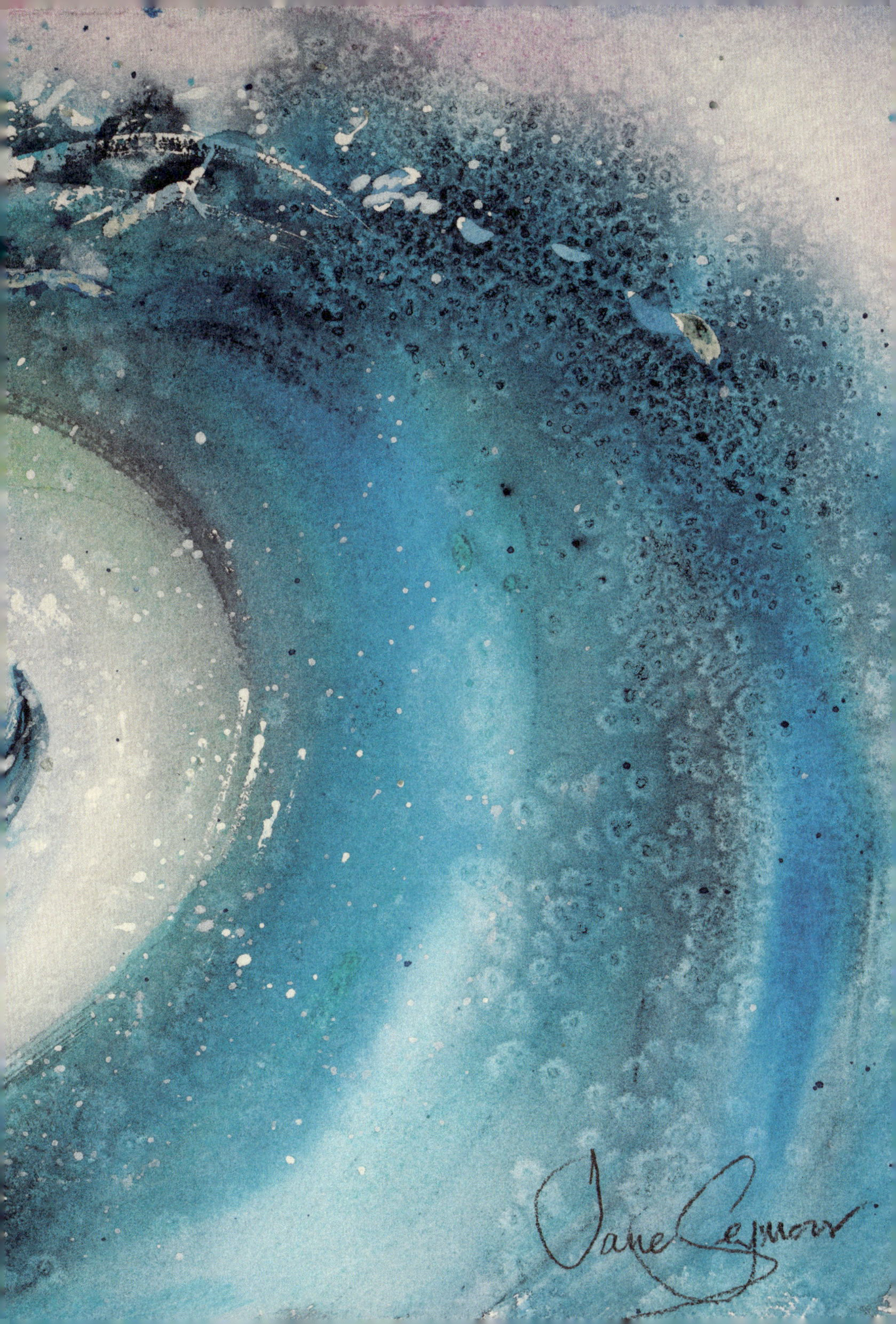

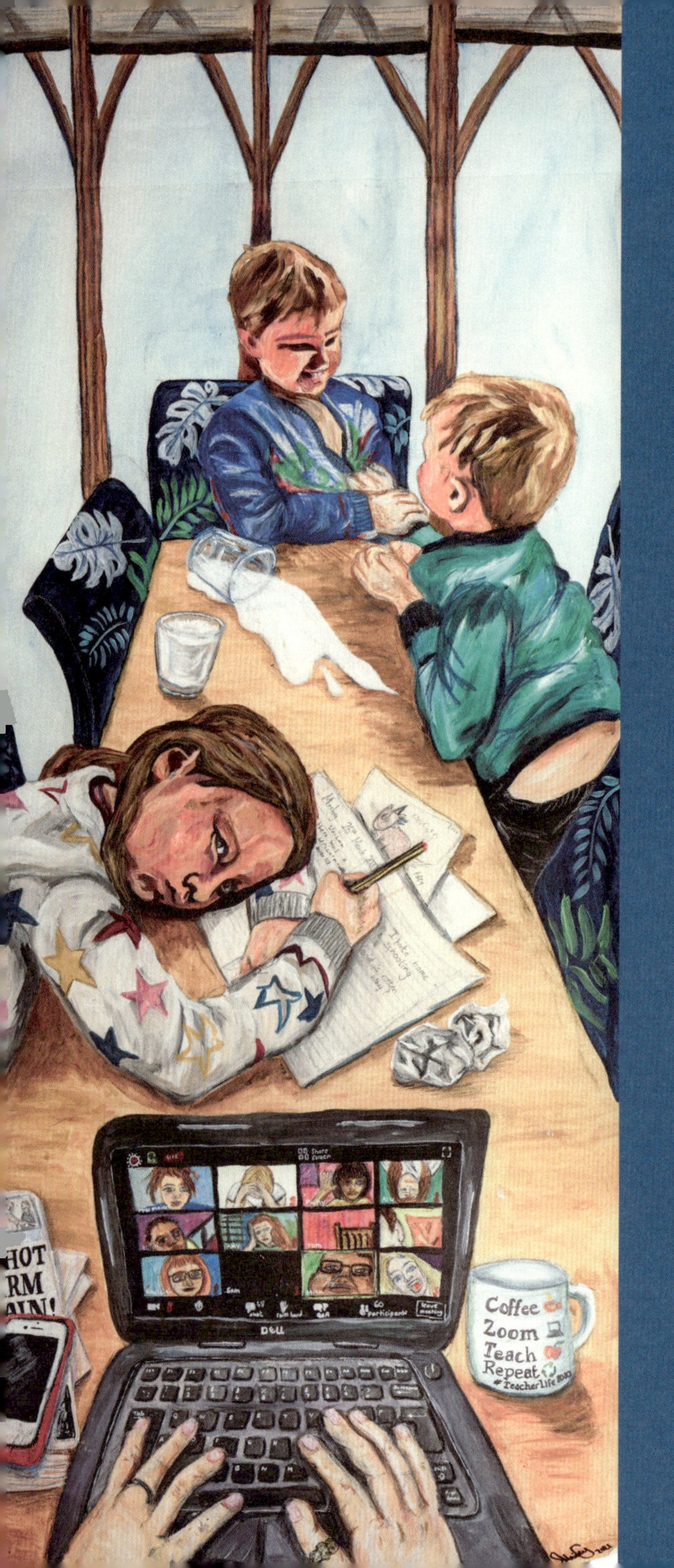

Coffee
Zoom
Teach
Repeat
#teacherlife
DELL

Sam
Mai Say

"As a teacher and a mother of three, lockdown was particularly challenging. Everyone I knew that was home-schooling was telling me 'It must be so much easier for you being a teacher. You know exactly what to do.' What they failed to realise was that teachers do not teach a range of ages in the same class, or teach three different curriculums at the same time.

So, there we were, my children, myself and 60 children (the ones I usually teach in school), muddling through as best we could. My twins trying to learn their phonics, my daughter trying to learn about the Tudors and my Year 4s trying to learn online at the same time.

At times it was chaotic. The twins would often end up fighting, my daughter deciding she hated school and the children making the best out of the hand they had been dealt.

But we got through it. We survived. And I truly believe it has made all those in education far stronger, more resilient, and able to persevere. We jumped through hoops, we completely changed the way we taught and learnt. I love my job as teacher and as mum even more so since lockdown."

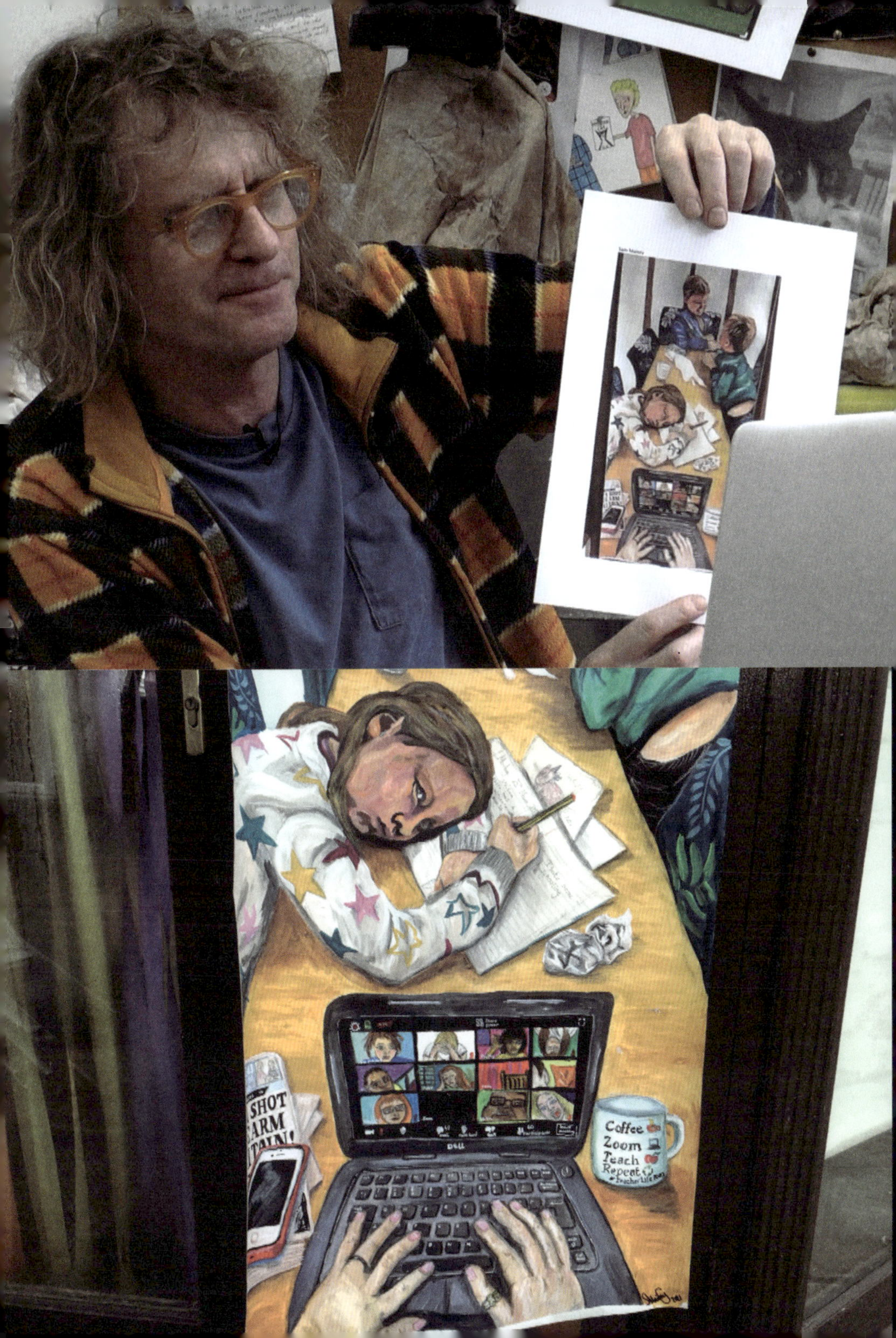

Working in the Hotel

Tom Allen

Acrylic paint on canvas
Courtesy of the artist

"I was filming in a bubble
during the lockdown. I had
to stay in a hotel for 5 weeks
without leaving. When I
was writing in my room,
I moved a table in front of a
window so I could look out
at the countryside. It can
be strange and a bit soulless
to make a workstation away
from home, particularly in a
hotel. I tried to make it my
own by changing the location
and adding eucalyptus leaves
in a jug."

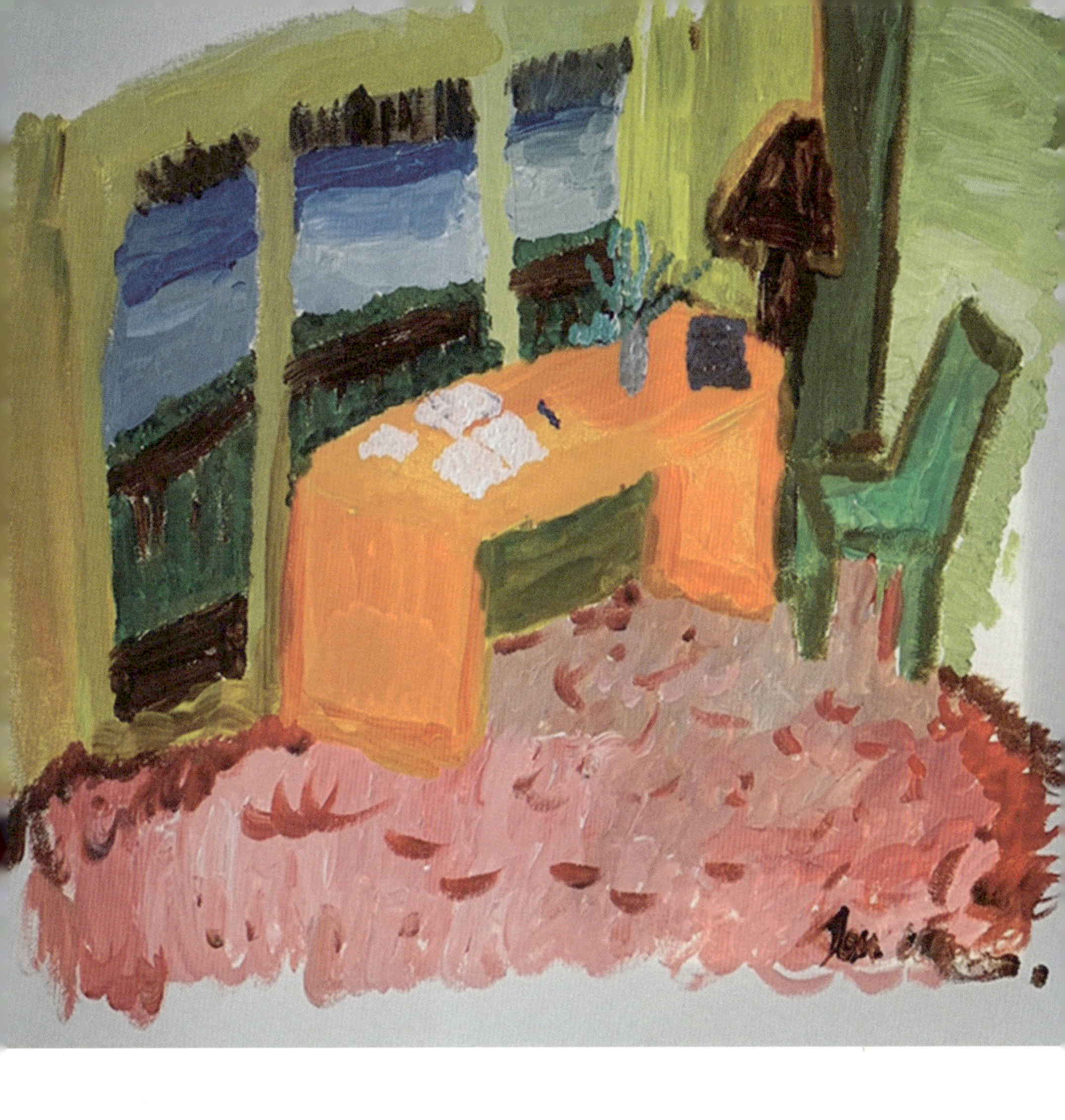

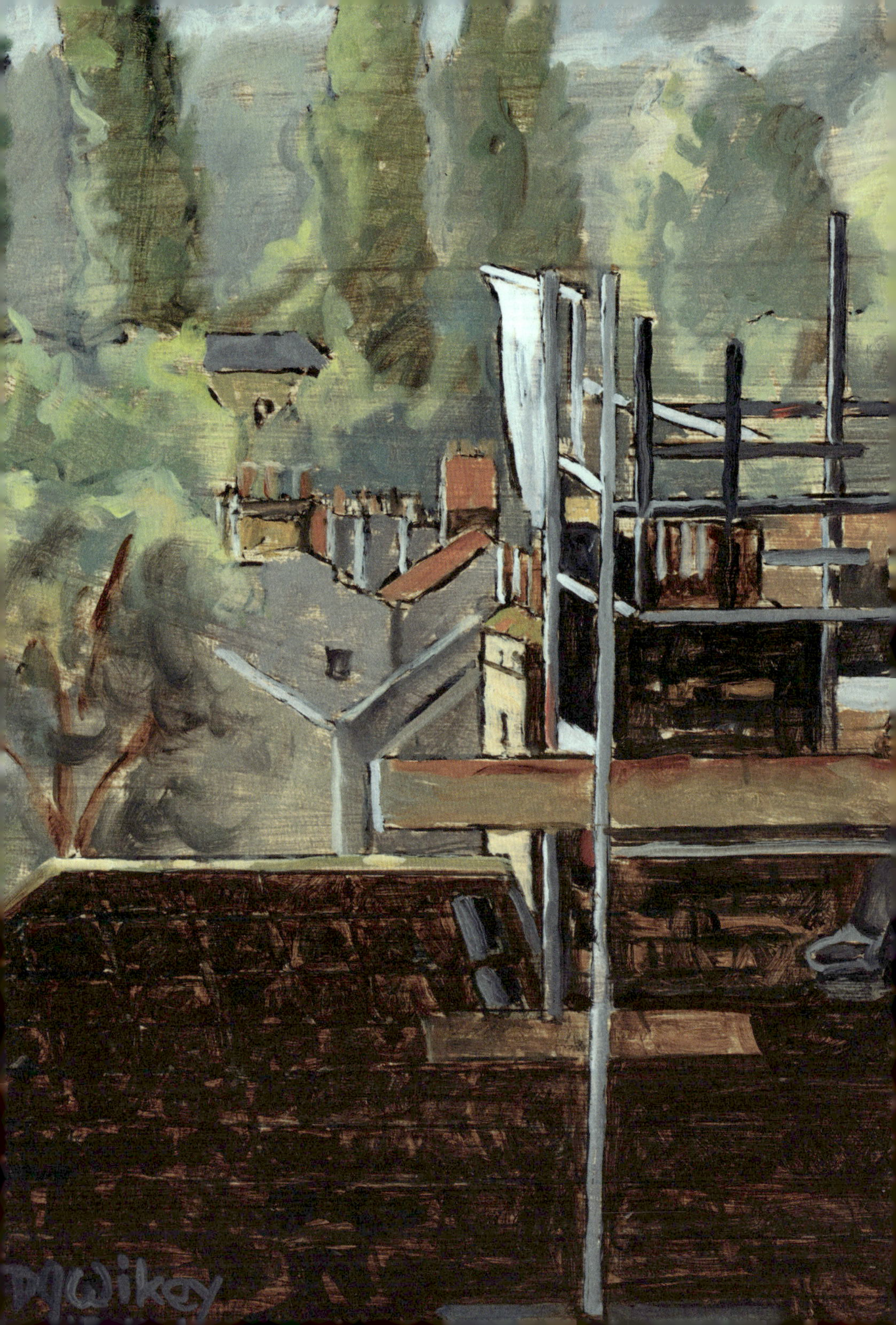
M.Wikey

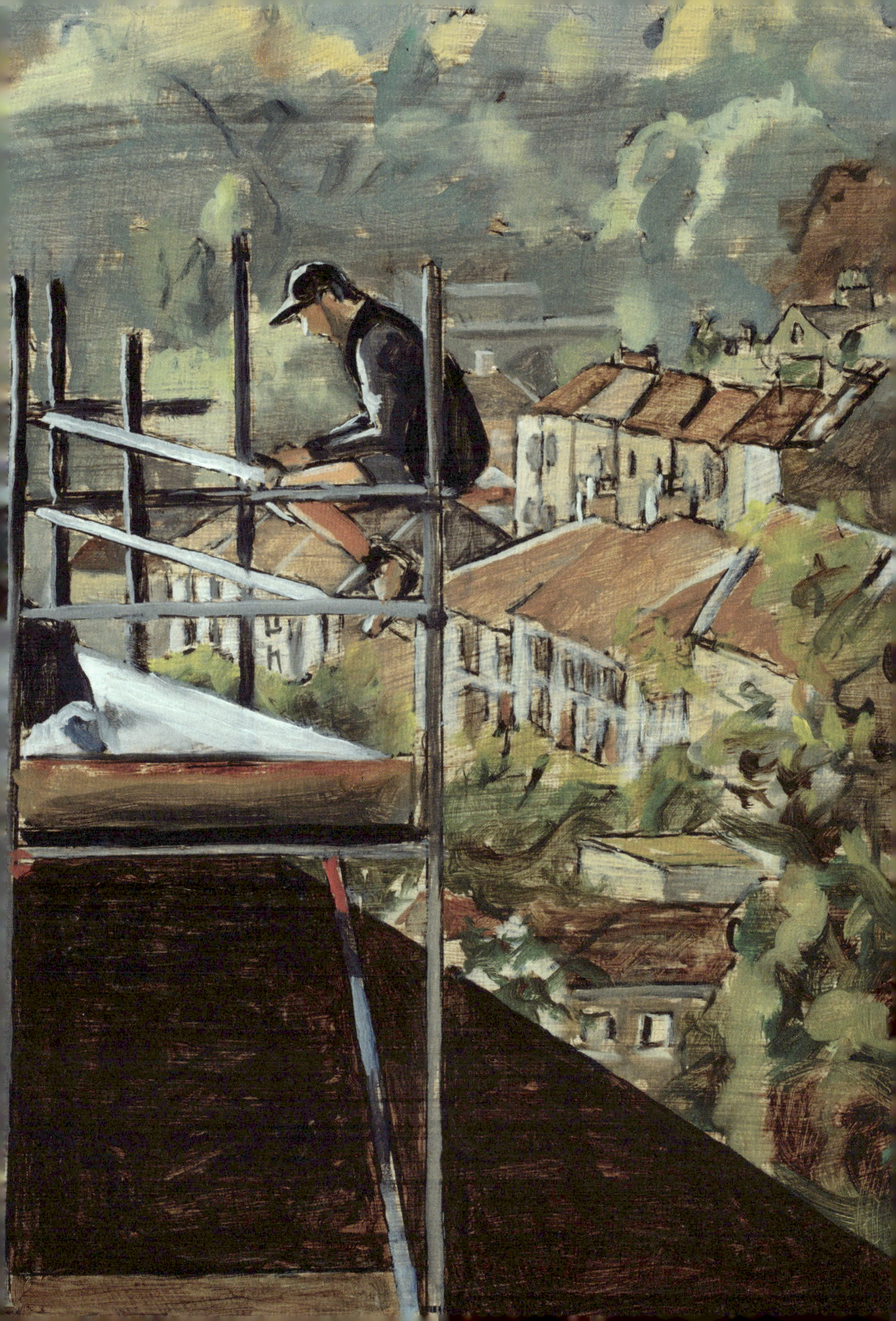

Previous:
Men at Work

David Wilkey

Oil paint on board
Courtesy of the artist

"I often paint what is around
me. I am inspired by people
and their quirks and obsession
with mobile phones. I saw this
simple scene of men at work
(on their phones) from my
garden one day and thought
'It has to be painted'."

Conditions that will reshape
you (Because you bequeath
yourself redundant
to conditions that will
reshape you)
2018

Ryan Gander

Acrylic, LED panels
© Ryan Gander;
Courtesy of the artist
and Lisson Gallery
Photography by Jack Hems.

"The thing that I love about
art is the generation of
ideas. Having ideas makes
you feel really liberated
and optimistic. I notice
anomalies, phenomenons,
then record them."

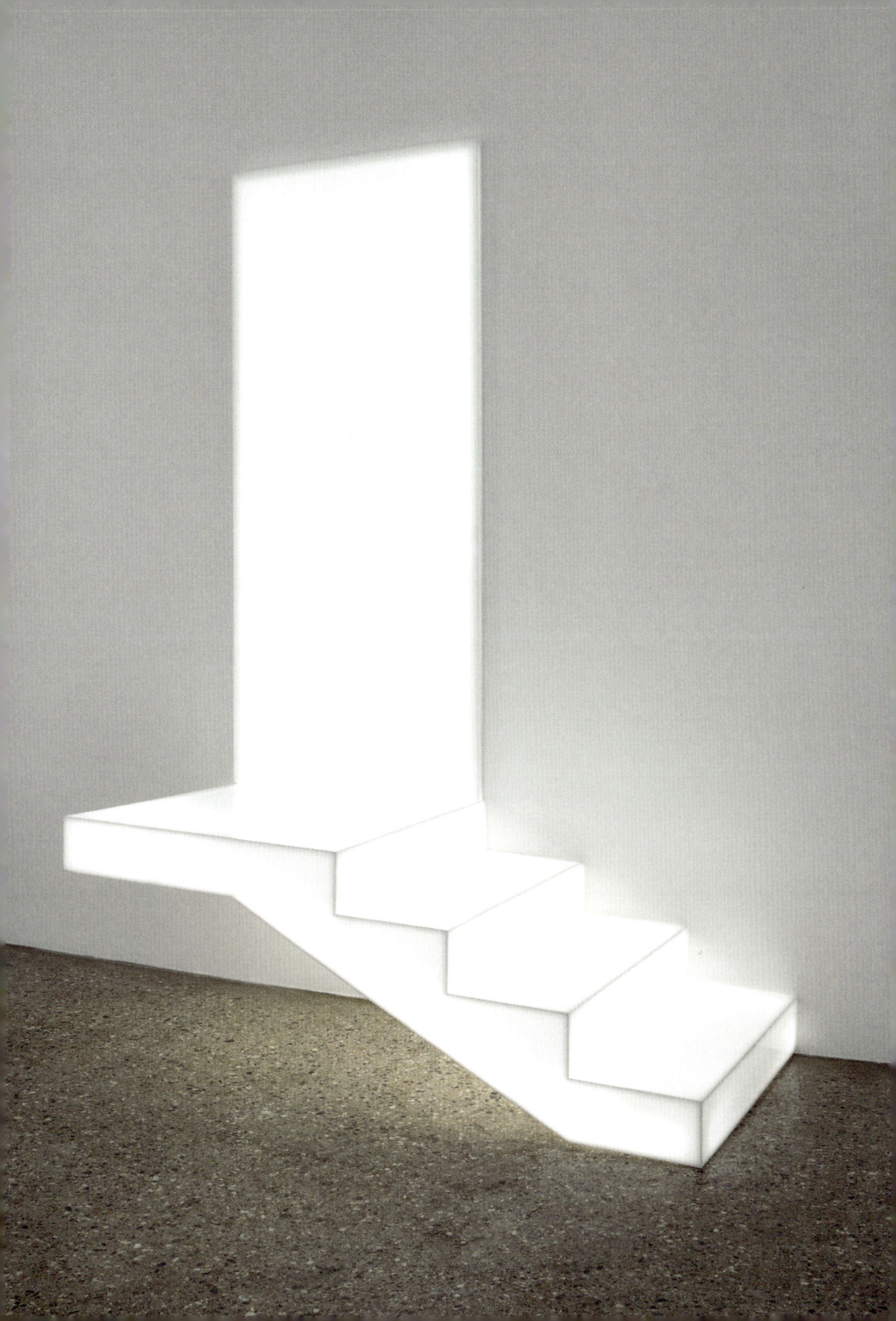

My Dad, Henry

Lianne La Havas

Pencil on paper
Courtesy of the artist

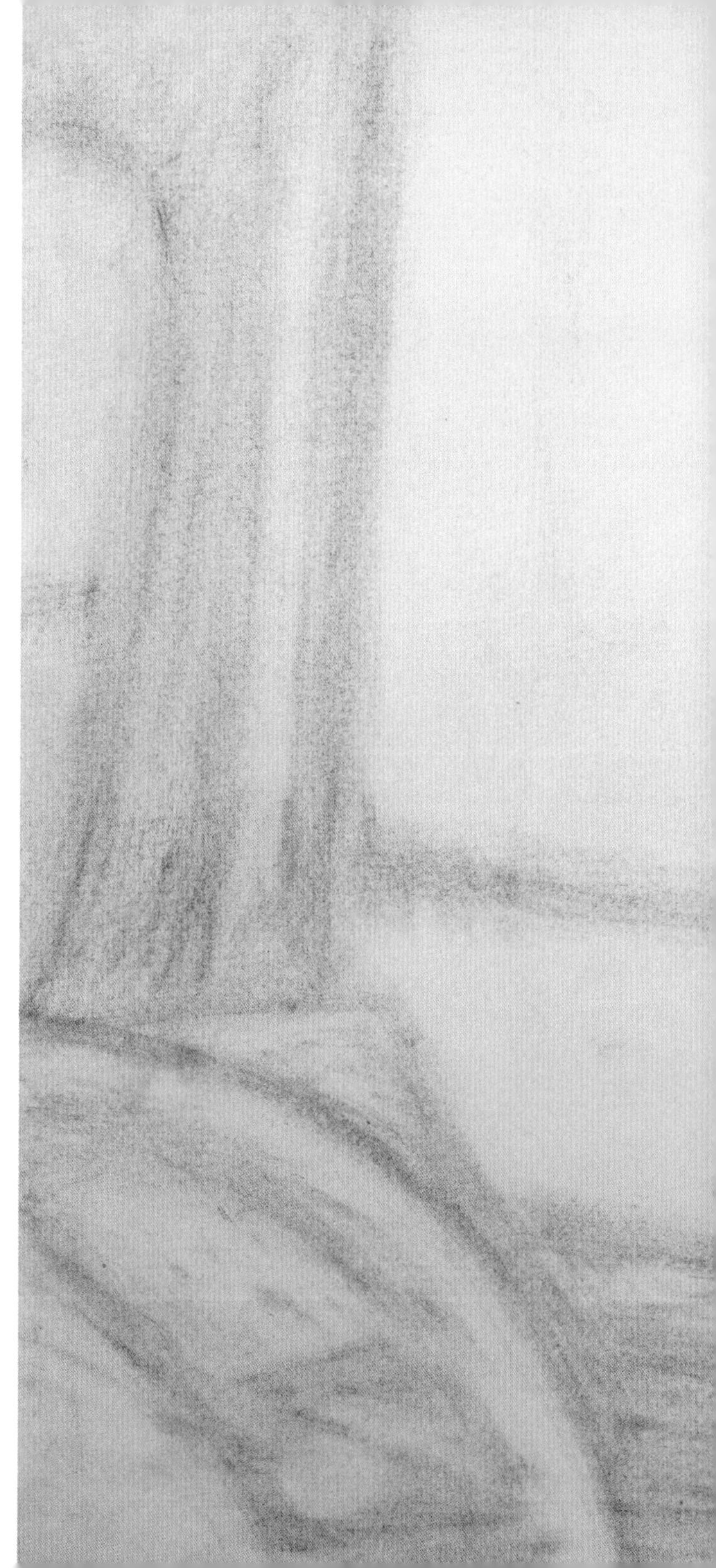

"Inspired by my father's
work as a bus driver during
lockdown. He's one of the
modern heroes. He is a
keen artist, sculptor/stone
mason, so I did this work
to acknowledge and share
how my father has inspired
my own art."

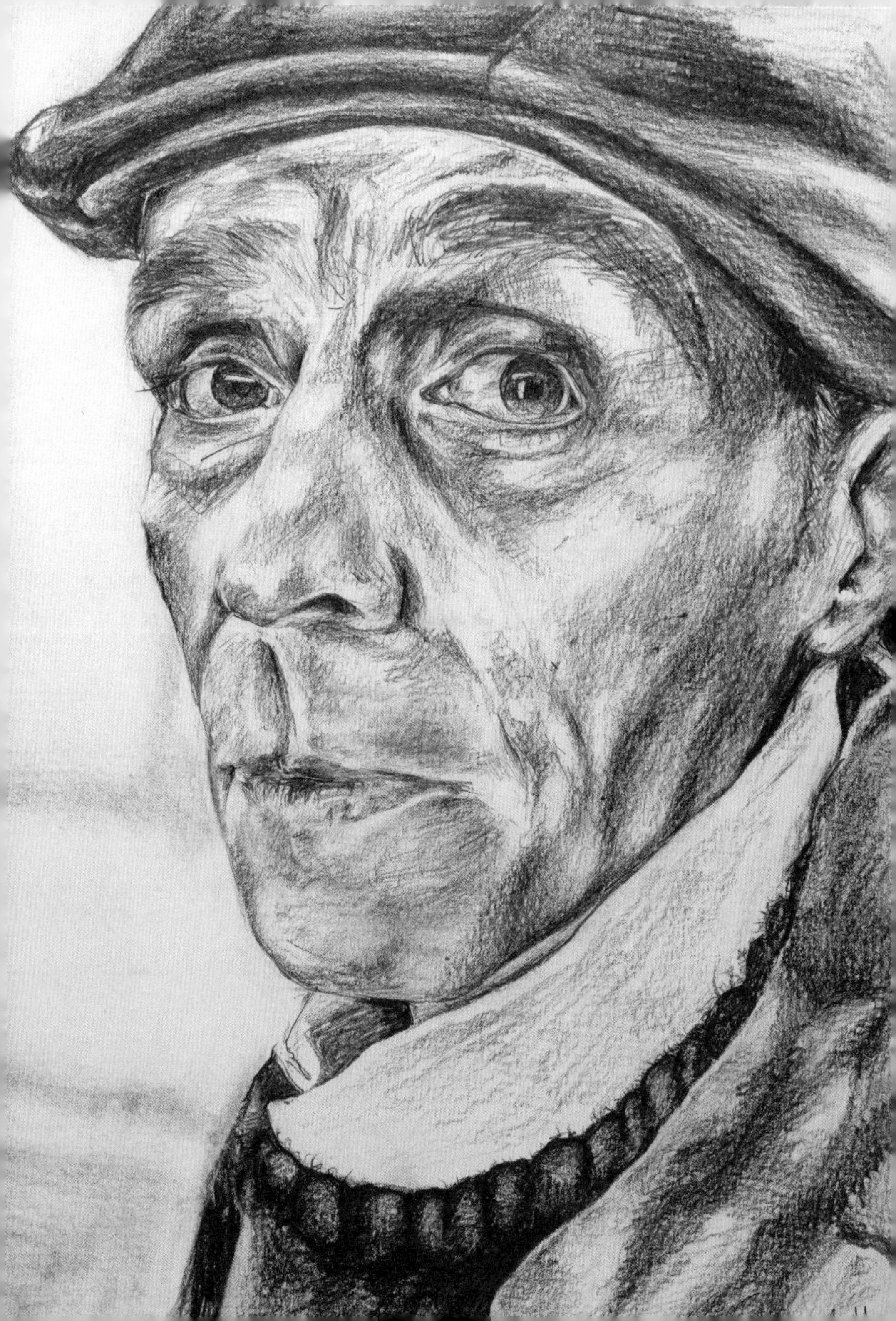

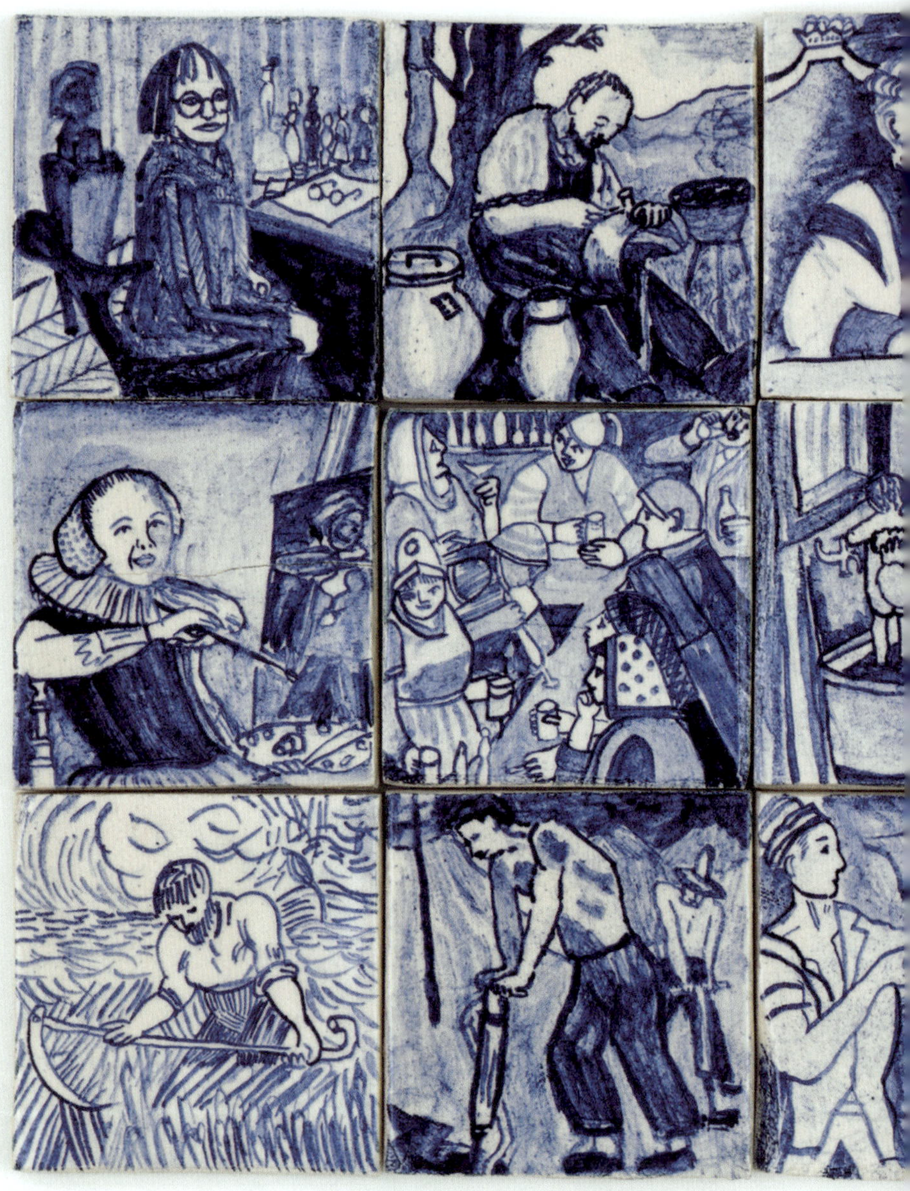

Tiles Depicting Work

Philippa Perry

Glazed ceramic tiles
Courtesy of the artist

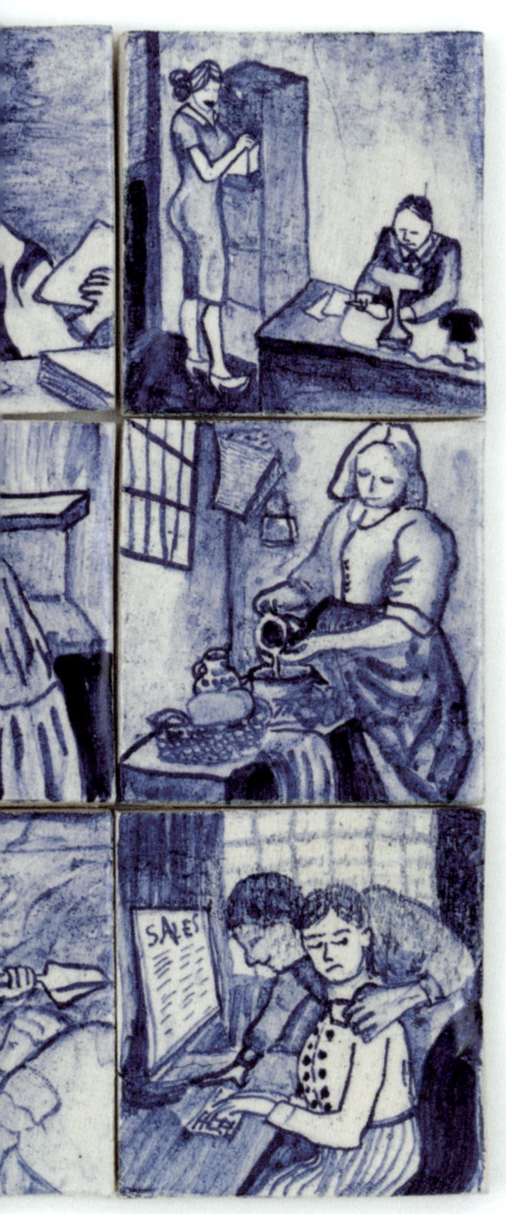

"I made a set of tiles depicting
people working and I took
the images from fine art.
Childcare is work as well.
A lot of people have been
saying they're not doing their
jobs well because they're
having to work from home.
They're having to look after
the kids. And I would like to
remind them of Hogarth's
Gin Lane. They're all doing
better than this lady."

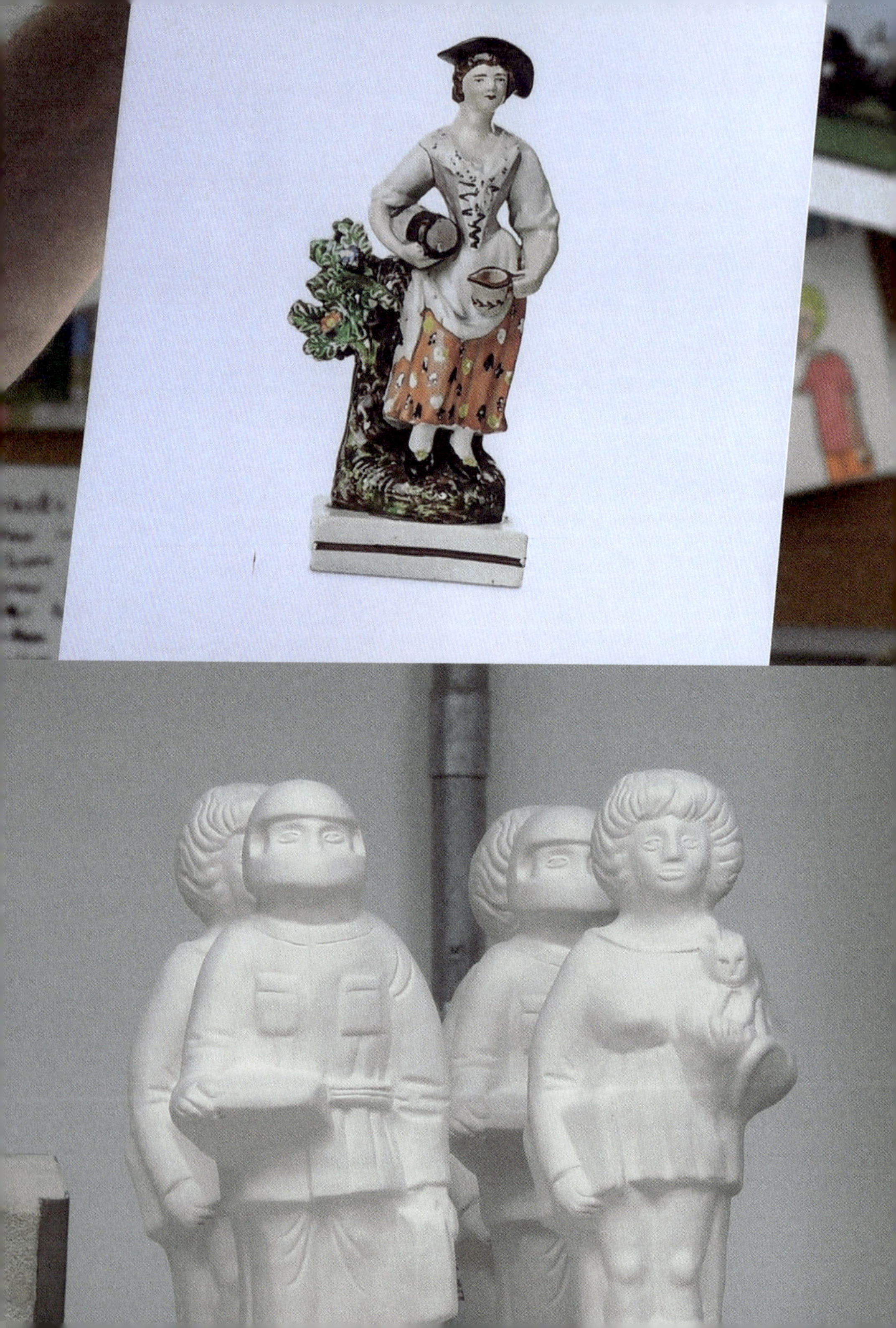

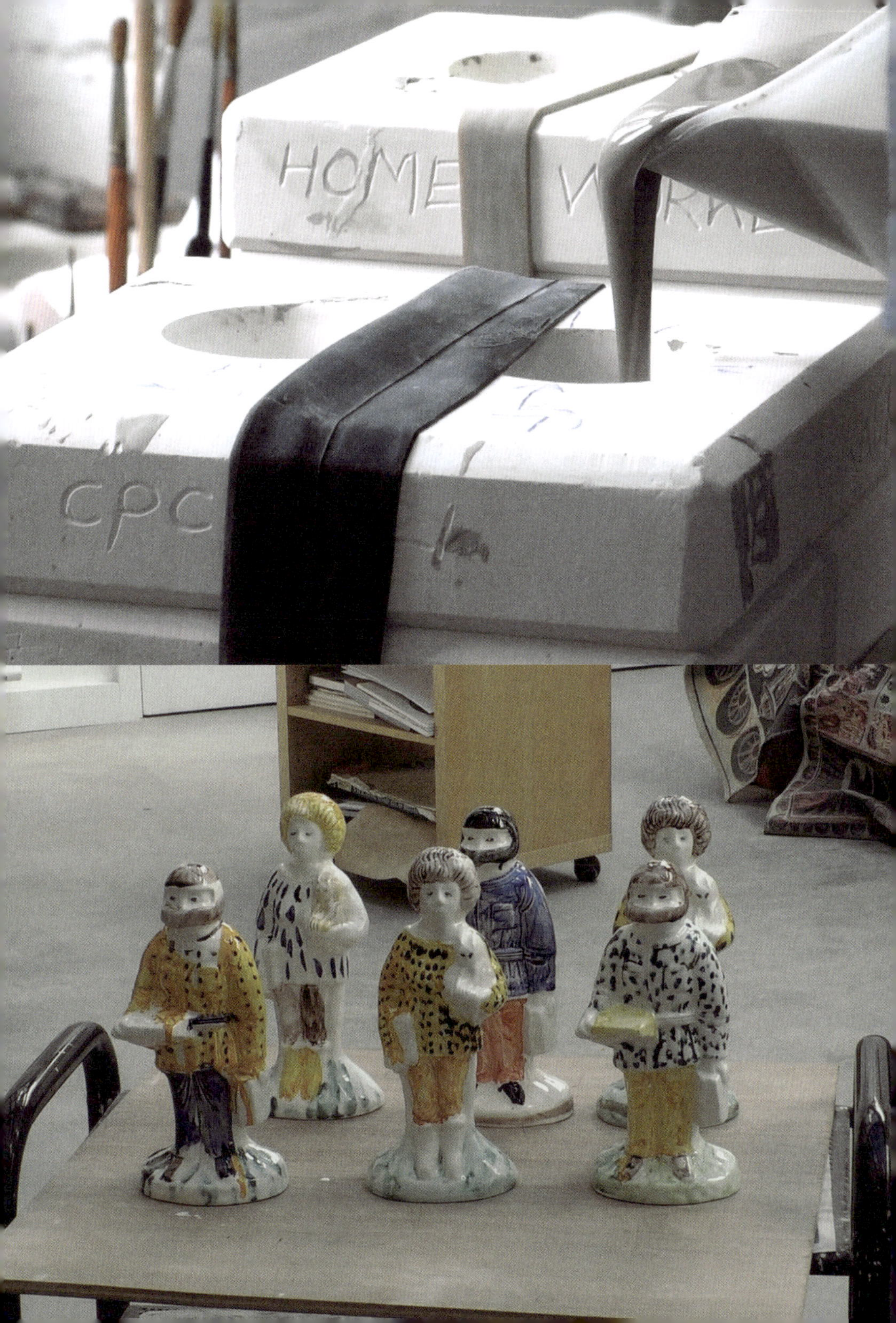

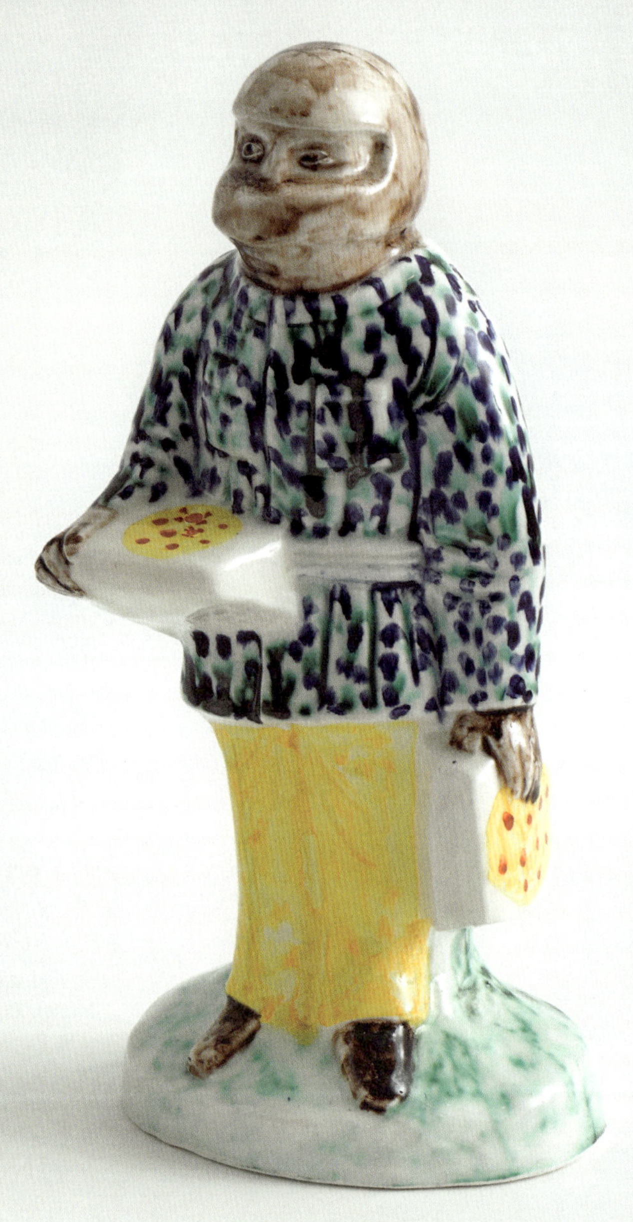

Home Worker and Key
Worker Staffordshire Figures
2021

Grayson Perry

Glazed ceramic
Courtesy of the artist
and Victoria Miro

"I was thinking about how
work has been re-evaluated
during lockdown. I saw two
phenomena happening. One
was the key worker, and the
other, people working from
home. I thought I would use
an early mass production
technique to make something
that was infused with the
theme of work. Early English
ceramic production often
depicted people at work.
I made these Staffordshire
figures with exactly the
same technique as in the
18th century."

It's NOT

coming home

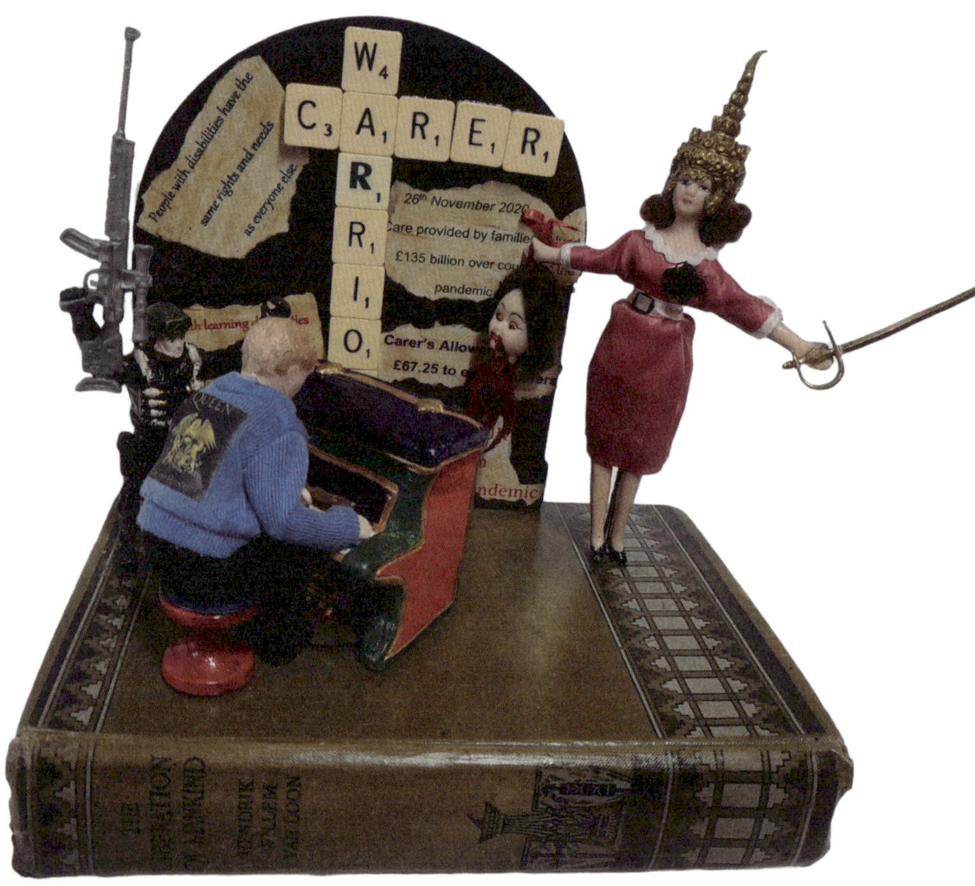

W
CARER
WARRIOR
People with disabilities have the same rights and needs as everyone else.
with learning disabilities
26th November 2020
Care provided by families
£135 billion over course of the
pandemic
Carer's Allowance
£67.25 to each carer
pandemic
QUEEN

Lulu
Willis

Previous:
Warrior Carer

Lulu Willis

Mixed media assemblage:
dolls, book, found material
Courtesy of the artist

"I am a full time carer to my 23 yr old son. He has Smith-Magenis Syndrome, which includes a learning disability, autism, behavioural, speech and language challenges. He has a balance disorder, a motor tic and epilepsy.

This artwork represents the battles we have on a daily basis with the social care system, social services and funding for his needs. We fight for the most basic things.

The piece shows myself in modern day dress carrying warrior battle gear of helmet and sword. In my right hand I have the severed head of social services, who I regularly do battle with for Matthew's right to a good and meaningful life. My husband Jim is shown in battle gear on the other side of Matthew. Matthew is doing one of the things he enjoys, playing the piano. He's oblivious to the fighting surrounding him, and the prejudice directed at him. He is wearing a Queen sweatshirt, one of his favourite bands. The work stands on a book called 'The Liberation of Mankind'. This represents the freedom people would have if they let go of the shackles of prejudice and demonstrated compassion."

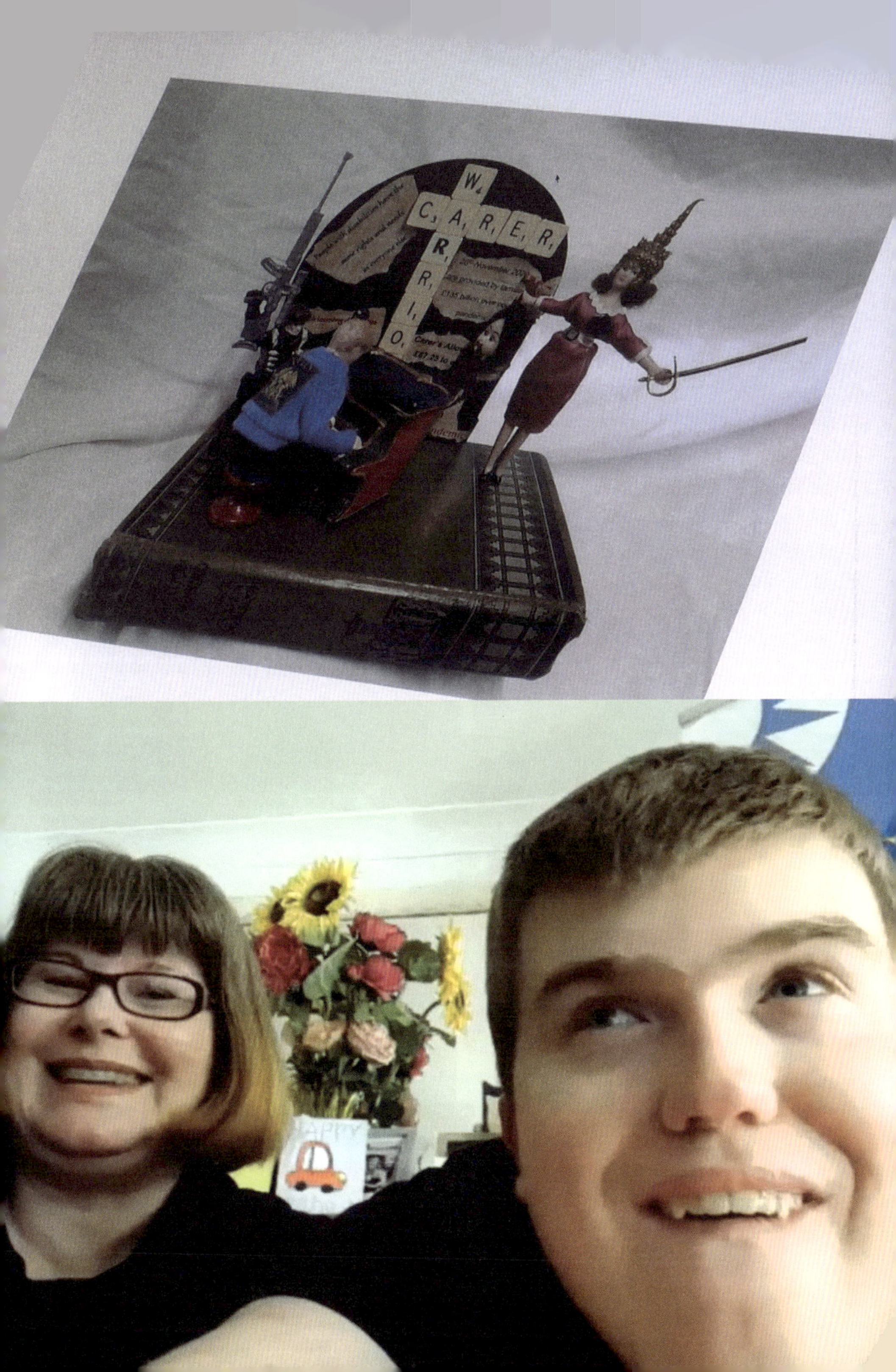

Trave

"We've probably never yearned for
travel more than we have over the
past two years. Art about travel
can give us so much more than a
geographical change of scene. It can
be a journey of the imagination,
and take us anywhere we want to go.

Whether we can travel or not,
I think we should keep travelling
in our minds and keep making
new horizons in our imagination."

The Egg

Freya Bruce

Aluminium, wood fibre
insulation and plywood
Courtesy of the artist

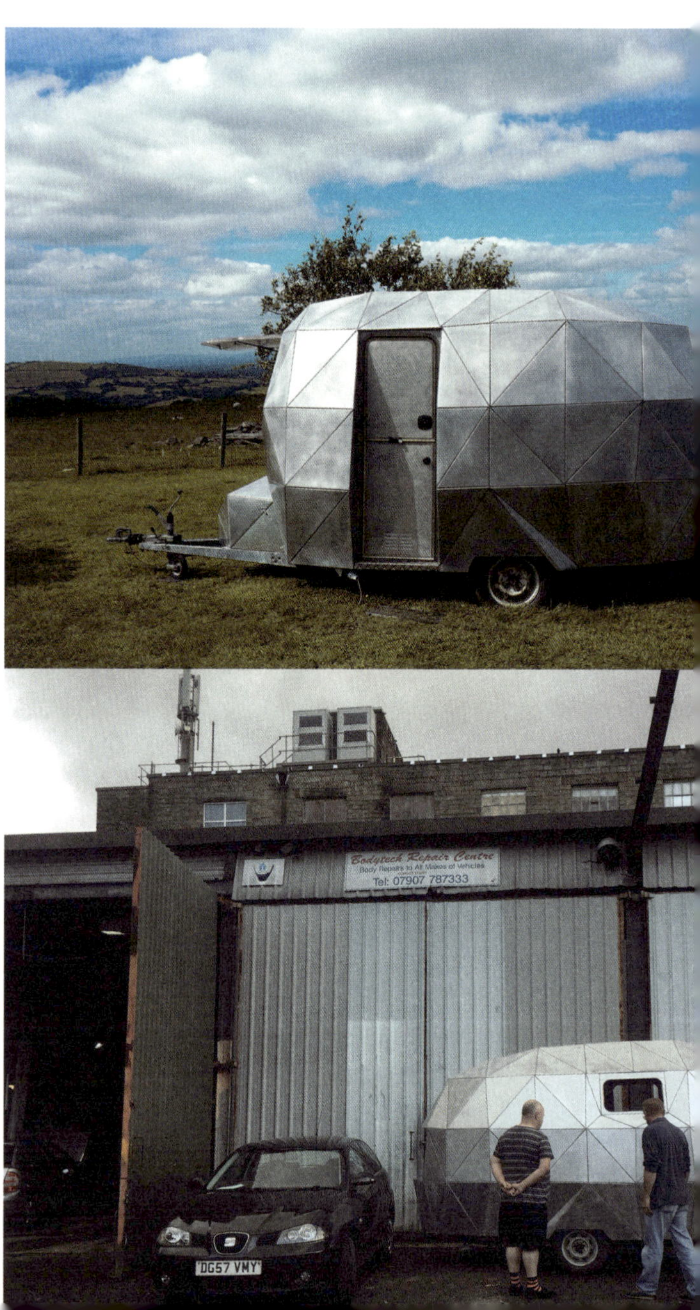

"The 'Egg' was created and
built by my Dad and I. The
shape has been in my head for
a long time. When lockdown
hit, I moved back home and
we had all of this time on
our hands. 100 individual
triangular panels were hand-
measured, cut, folded, sealed
and sanded. The process
inspired me to pursue a
Masters in Sustainable
Architecture and adopt a
more hands-on approach to
my practice. The build uses
sustainably sourced materials
to create a womb-like home."

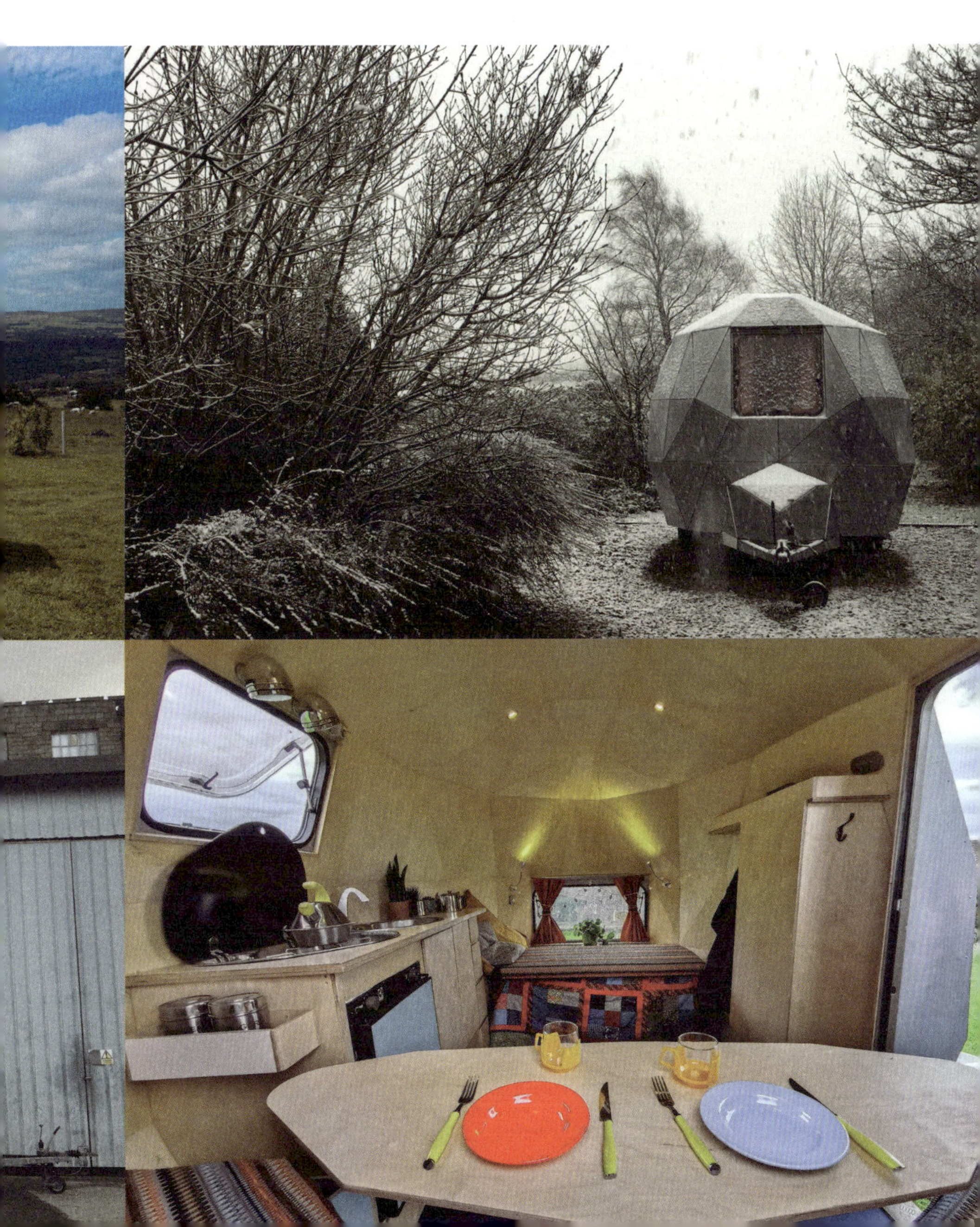

Newport Pugwash

Alex Horne

Spray-paint and plastic floor-covering on wooden pallet
Courtesy of the artist

"Motorway service stations are beacons of hope and comfort that we too often take for granted or even sneer at. This is partly a demonstration of how highly skilled the humble sign maker is and partly a celebration of the fun and relief you can find on a journey thanks to the likes of Welcome Break, Roadchef, Moto and, of course, Westmorland. Thank you all motorway service station operators."

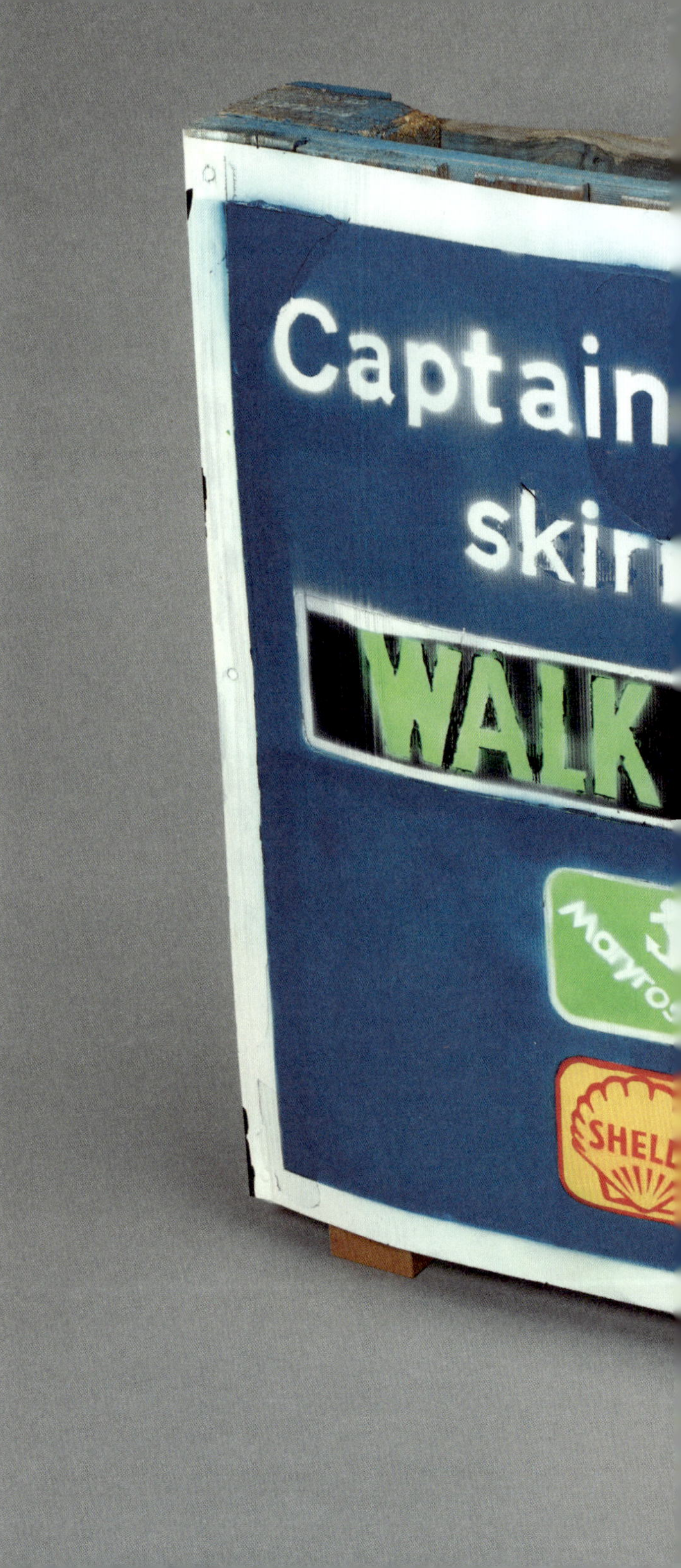

Pugwash
shes 0.4nm
HE PLANK
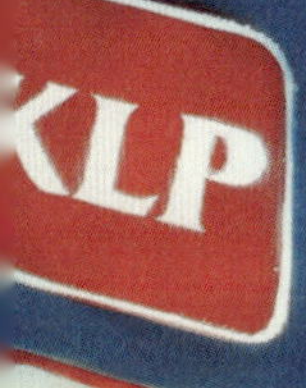
KLP

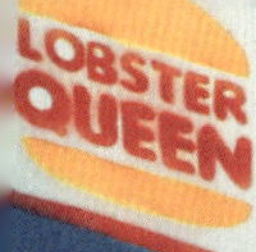
LOBSTER
QUEEN
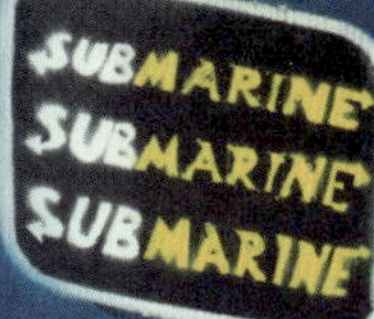
SUBMARINE
SUBMARINE
SUBMARINE

Thank you
Thank you
Thank you

Paul Weedon

Cloth, paint, stretched canvas
Courtesy of the artist

"A thank you to the monks
of Bhutan who gave us a
blessing at 'The Temple Of
The Divine Madman'. We
were struggling to conceive
at the time. They told us that
my wife would be pregnant
within 6 months and that we
would have a girl. And that's
what happened! They asked
if one of her names could be
Kinlay. The artwork now lives
in Amira Kinlay's bedroom.

To the monks of Bhutan…

Thank you
Thank you
Thank you"

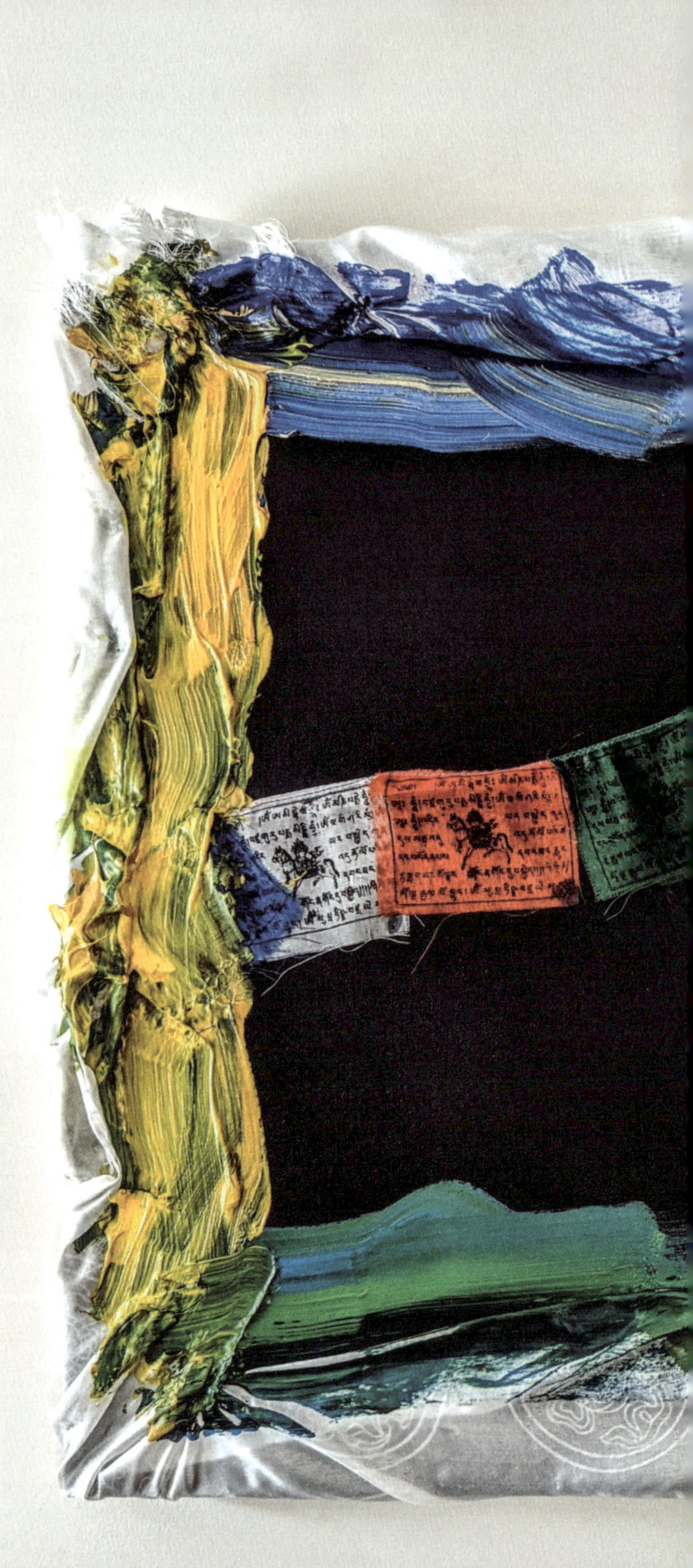

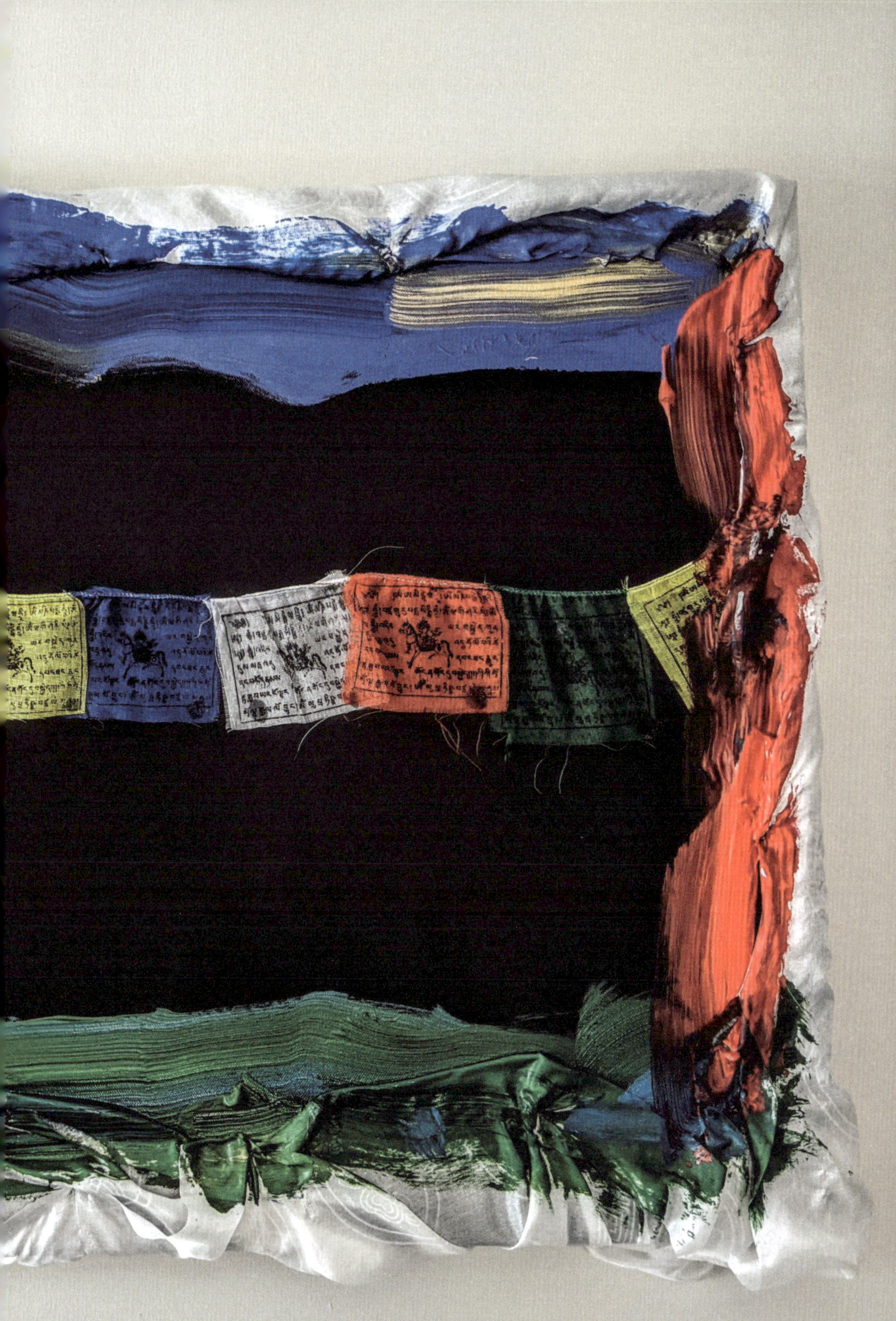

Max and Herbie Waiting
for Tall Ships

Max Mudie

Cardboard, balsa,
modelling clay
Courtesy of the artist

"I am a photographer. My
German friend Herbie and I
usually meet in some foreign
port to chase tall ships. That
didn't happen in 2020 and is
unlikely to happen this year.
That is a long time without
seeing my friend."

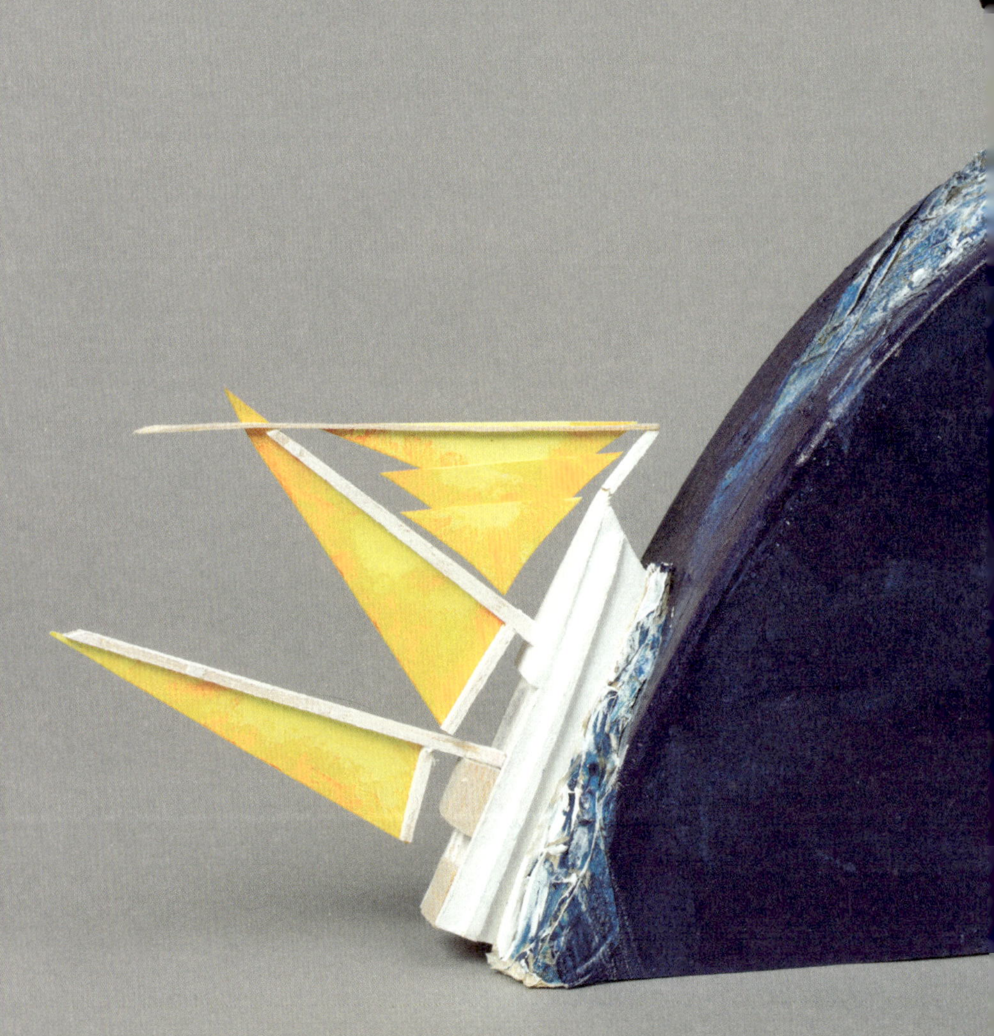

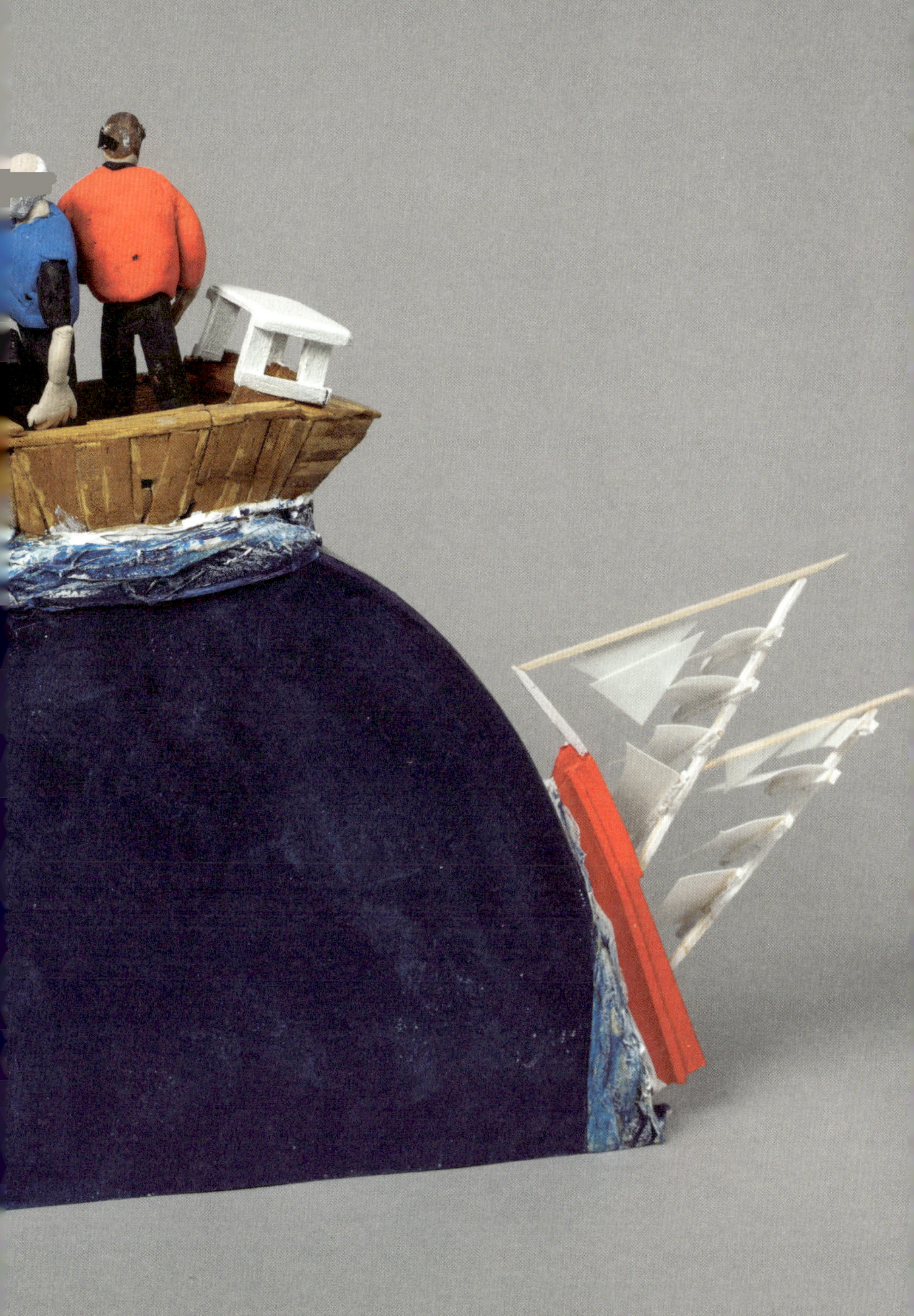

Coming Home:
Not Coming Home

Tyler Baker

Acrylic paint on canvas board
Courtesy of the artist

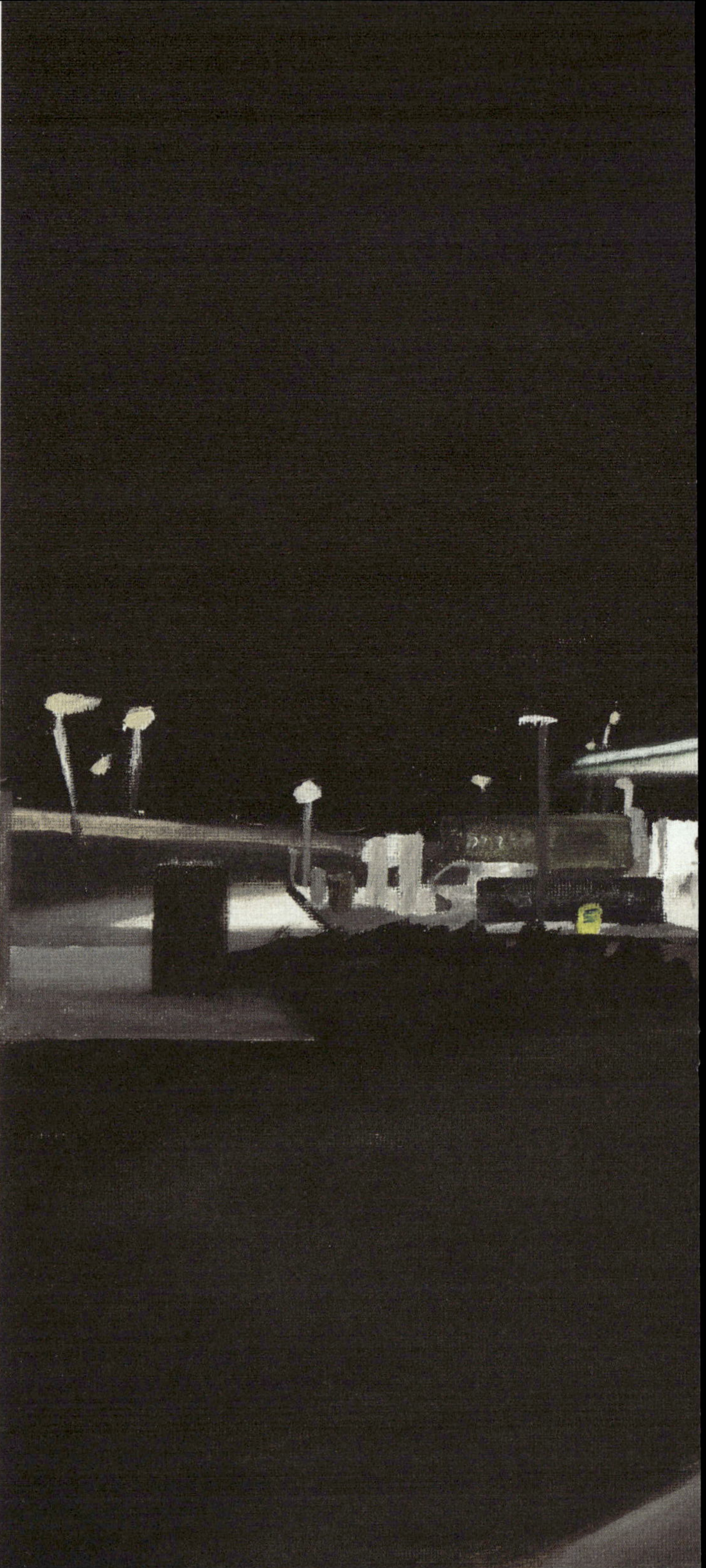

"The painting is of the petrol
station on the A12 slip road
which leads to our house.
When I travel home from
a concert or holiday late at
night, I see the light of the
petrol station and know
that I'm nearly home. So
you could say this painting
represents how I missed
being able to go out to these
types of events in lockdown."

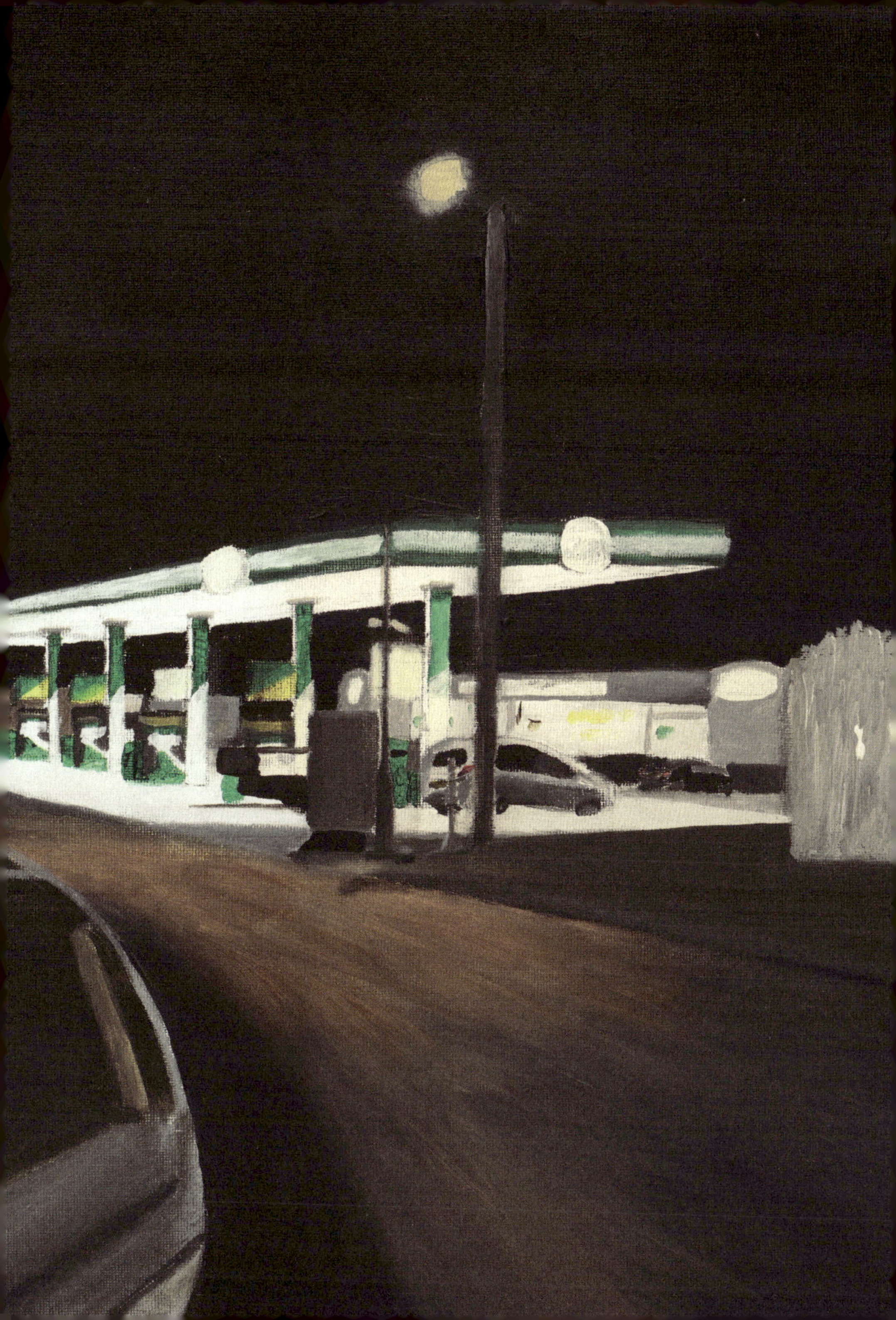

Cabin Crew –
20 Minutes to Landing

Martine Elliott

Acrylic paint on canvas
Courtesy of the artist

"In 2018, I retired from a
23-year cabin crew career.
I went from one BA to a very
different BA – a painting
degree! Unable to leave our
houses throughout lockdown,
I had to travel back through
my experiences. Could I
recapture these experiences
onto canvas? I created this
painting using memories of
coming into land after days
away on long haul trips.
I wanted to express the dream
of flying off somewhere and
my feeling whenever I was
coming home."

Freedom Day!

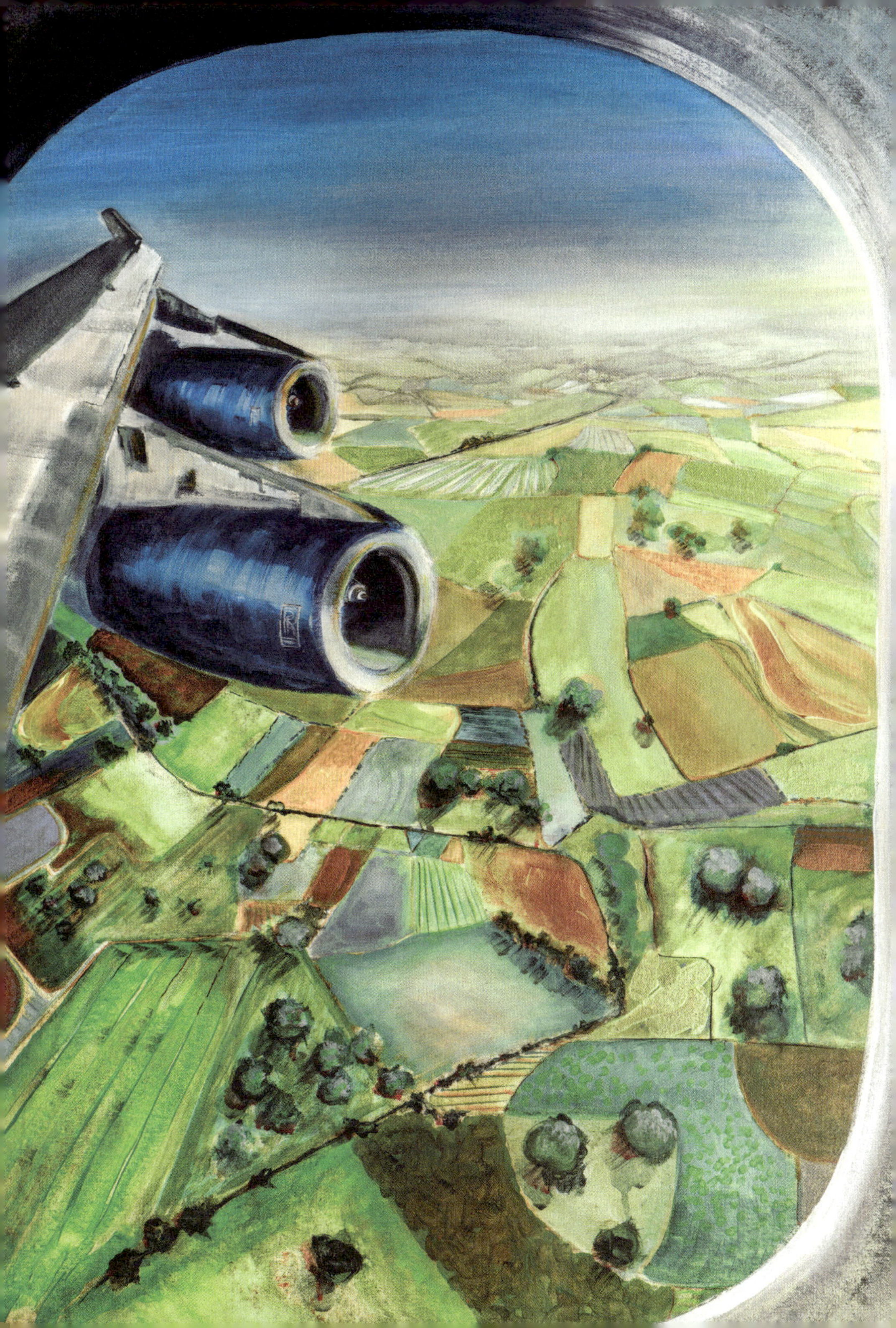

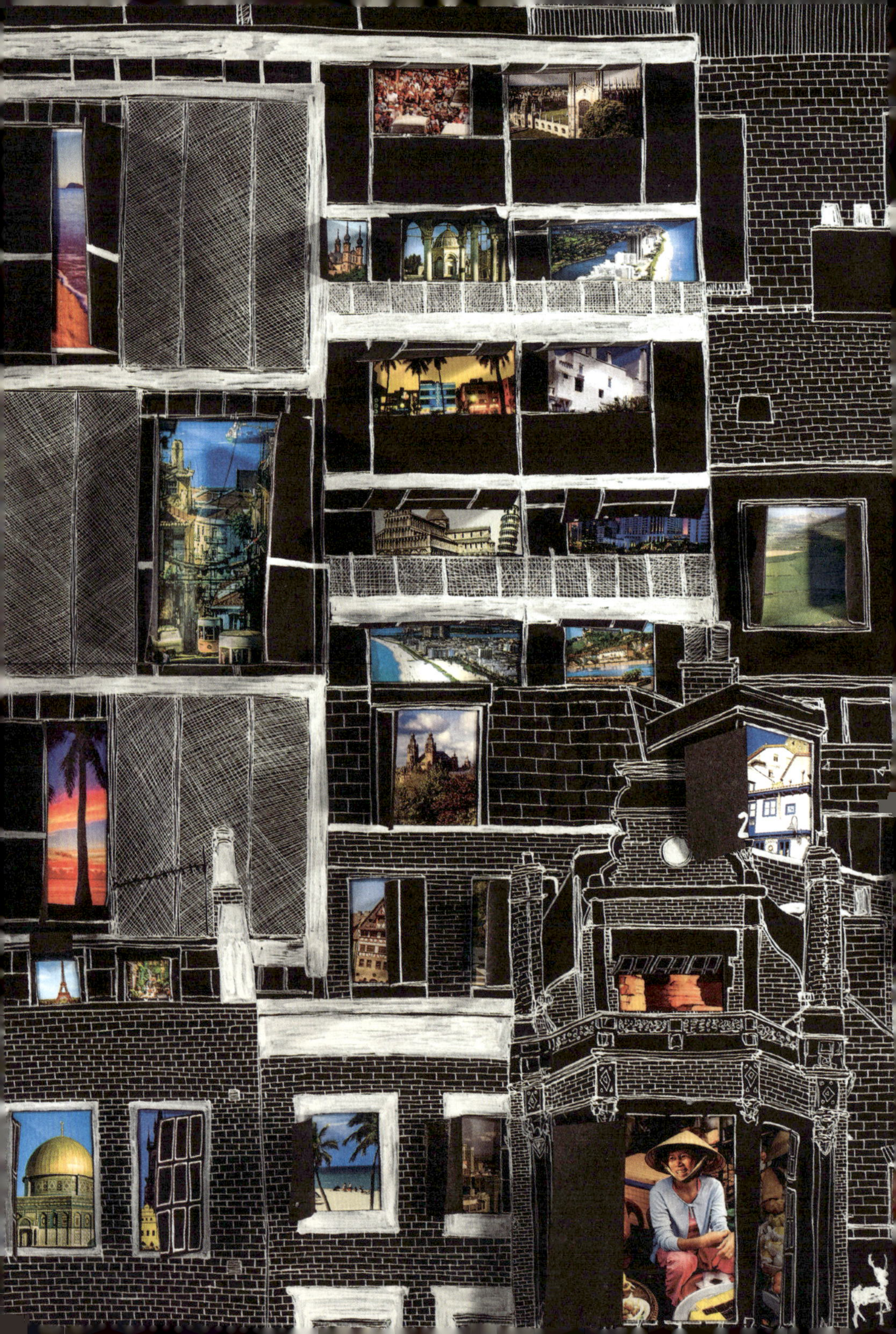

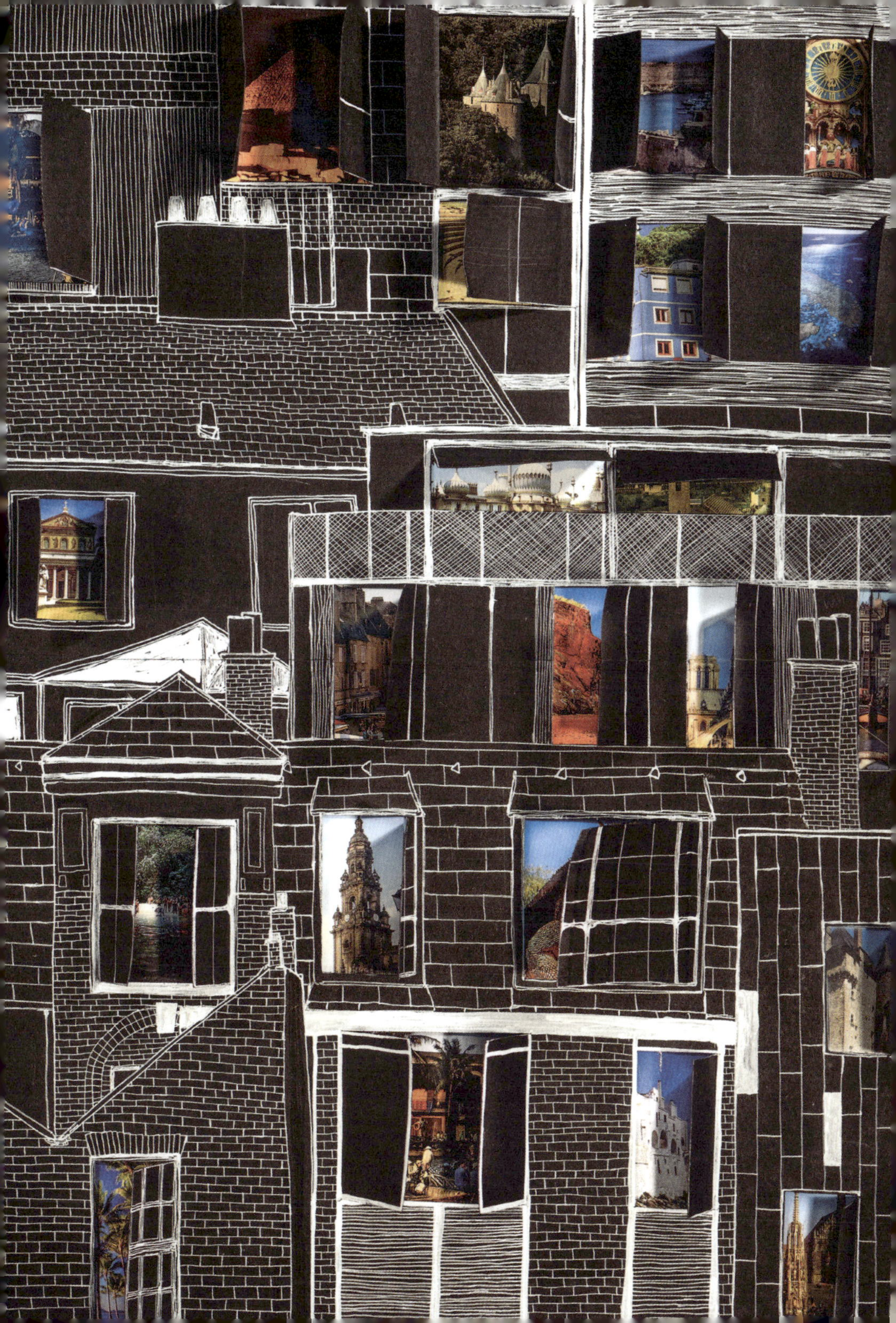

Previous:
Lockdown Travel
'Advent Calendar', SE1

Catherine Mottram

Ink on card
Courtesy of the artist

"Lockdown was particularly
hard for those of us with
small homes and no gardens.
I began to think about
the people trapped inside.
I decided to make an 'advent'
calendar using postcards
from travels. They are all the
travel hopes, dreams and
memories of the people stuck
inside in their homes. I found
the process very calming. It
helped take my mind off the
increasingly bad news as the
second wave of Covid hit."

Young Marlon

Derren Brown

Acrylic paint on canvas
Courtesy of the artist

"He's got such a lovely face.
A very old Hollywood feel. In
exaggerating the features you
get a sense of a personality.
We probably don't like to
think that our personality
is just there on the surface.
I don't consciously caricature
anything. I'm just recreating
what I'm seeing and it comes
out a bit exaggerated. When
the resemblance is there,
I can sort of hear their voice.
It's something that sort of
clicks into place."

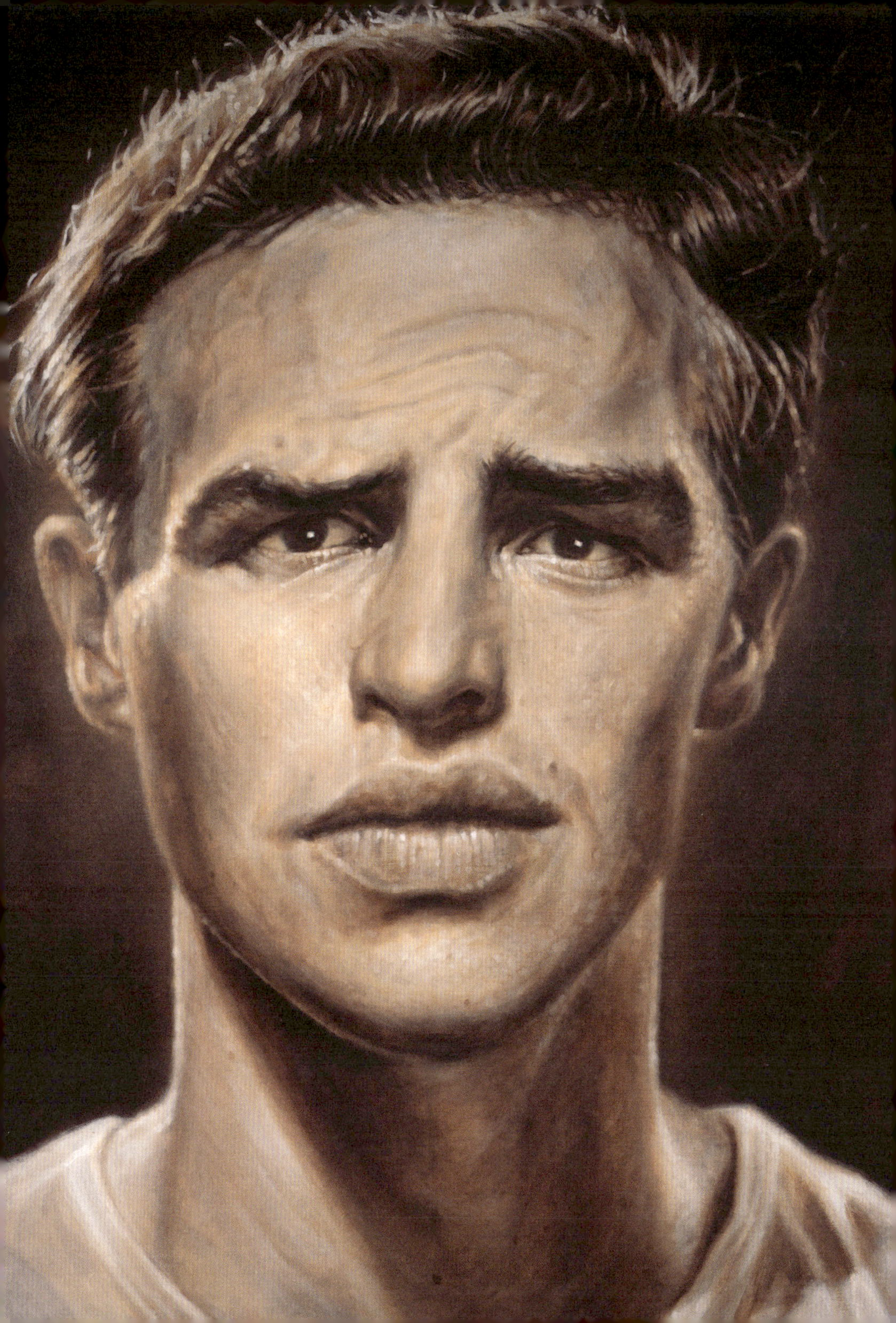

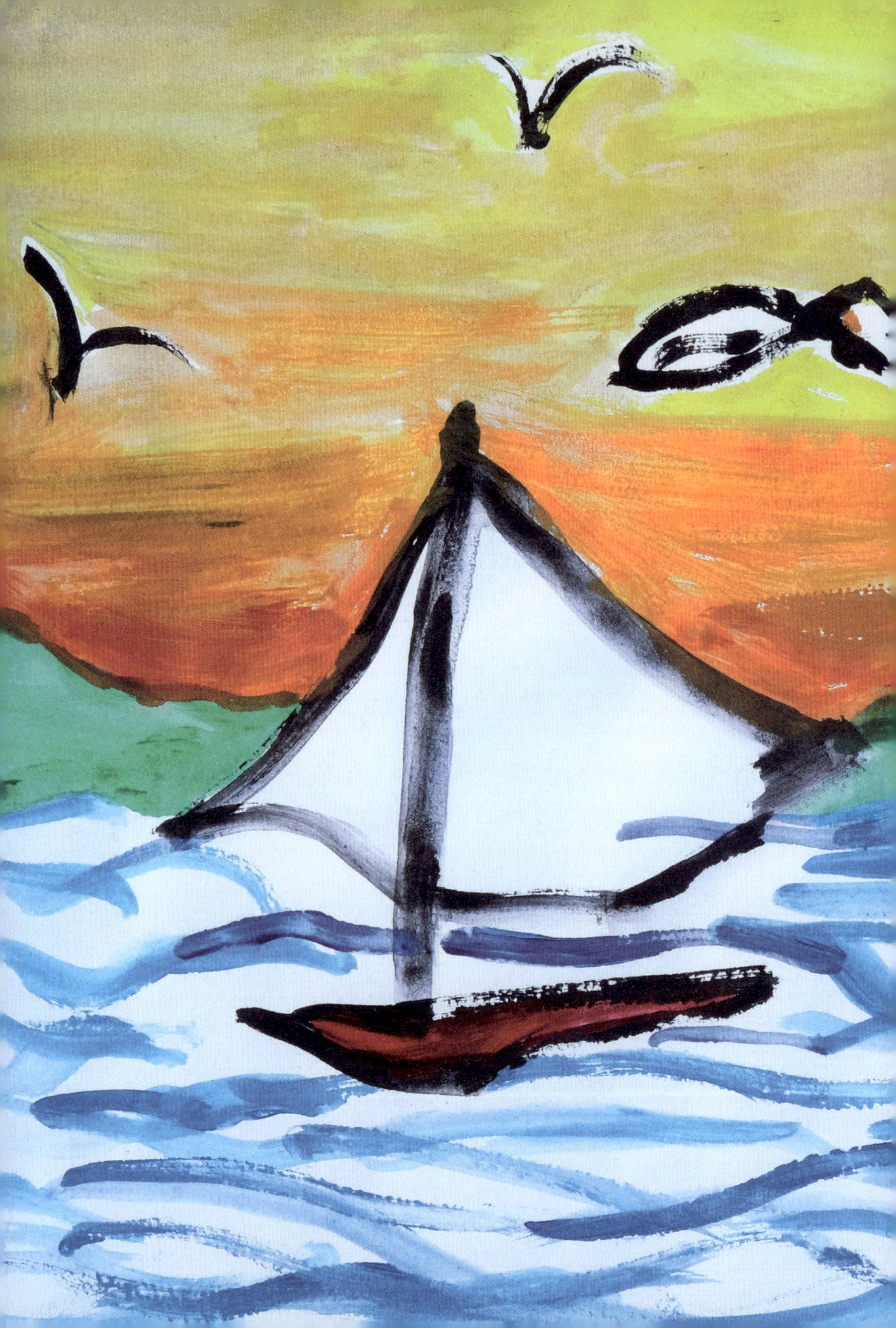

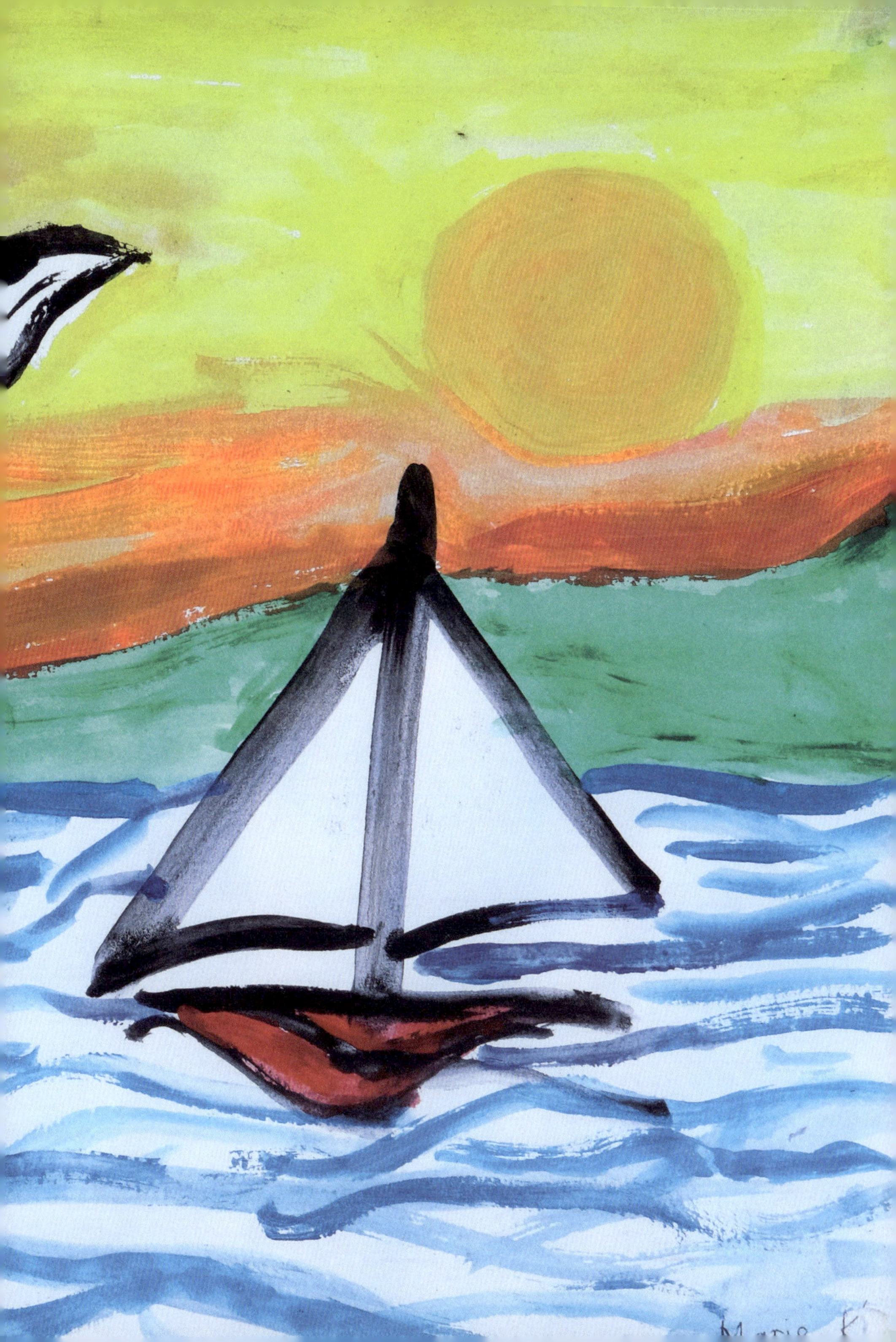

Marie Kathrens
(with encouragement
from Taylor
Kathrens Mayne)

"My grandma, Marie Kathrens, is 93. She is a former teacher and artist. She's had Alzheimers for almost 10 years. She was always original, hard working and fun. Having lived by the sea for her entire life, her paintings are predominantly seascapes.

Living with Alzheimers means Grandma doesn't experience life as she previously knew it. She can't express herself in conventional ways anymore. Her lucid moments are becoming less frequent.

When she paints she is able to communicate with her present in a different way.

She had friends in her retirement home who helped her throughout her day. They engaged in all sorts of activities that helped her remain in a semi-coherent state. Lockdown took away the only stimulation she had. The decline in her mental health was visible. Her confusion rapidly increased. It was heartbreaking. It was clear she needed a companion who could encourage her

to do the things she loves. I started going in on a daily basis. We spend two hours together being creative in any way we can.

It's amazing to see what she comes out with. Often Grandma wants to draw seascapes. She loves drawing the waves and always insists on putting a little flag on the top of her boats.

She has a playful soul with an infectious cheerful nature and she loves to paint. Some things never change."

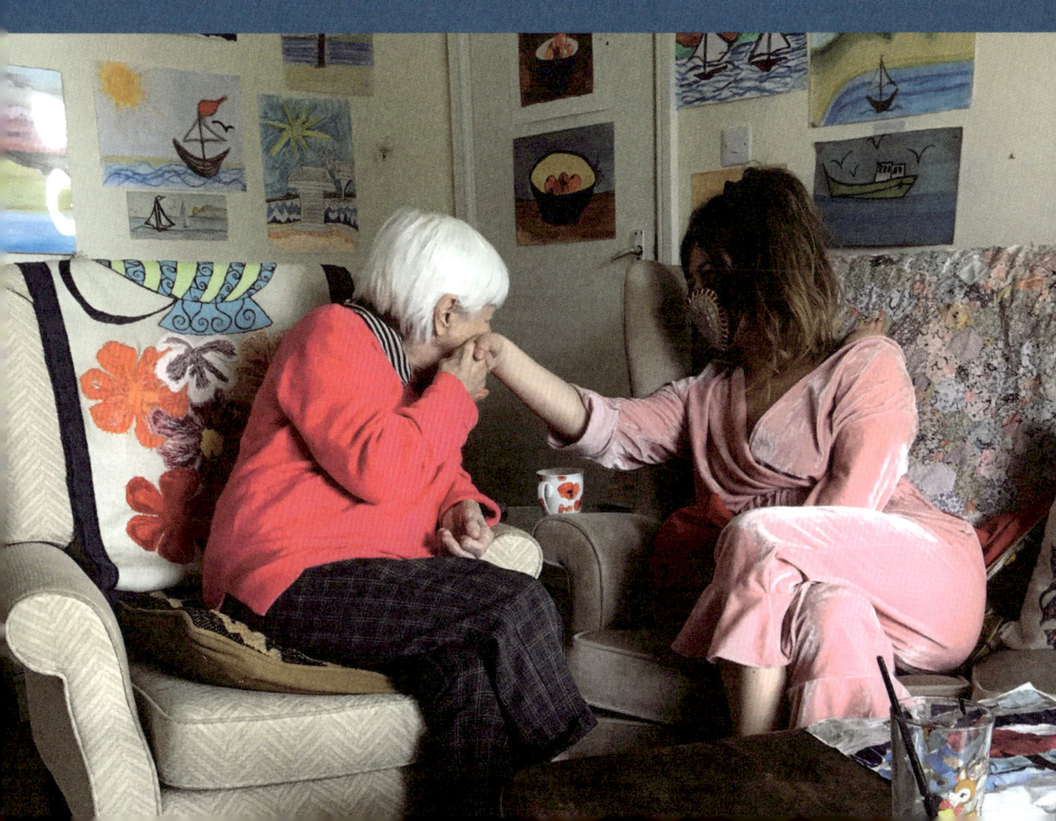

Sydney

Mary Bonner

Acrylic paint on canvas board
Courtesy of the artist

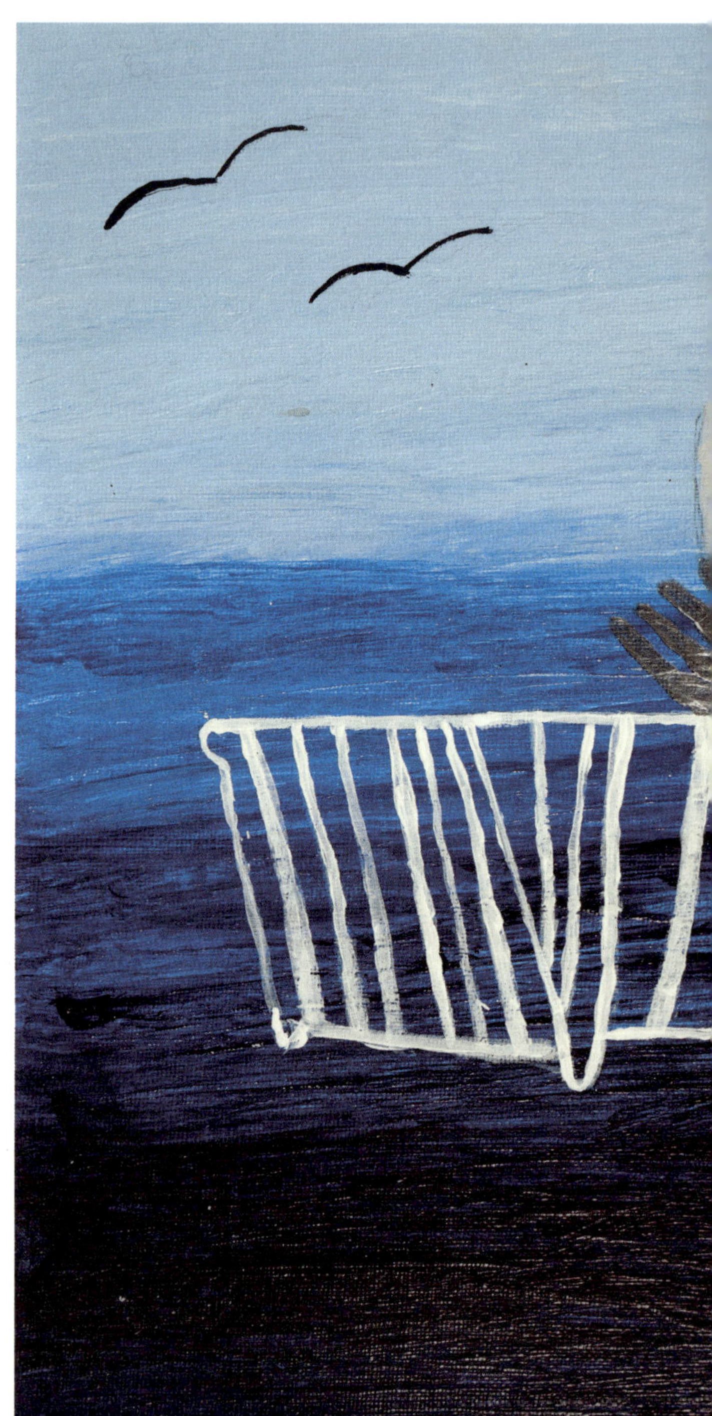

"Before the pandemic I lived
in Sydney and I miss it dearly.
I often daydream about
going back. Especially when
washing up."

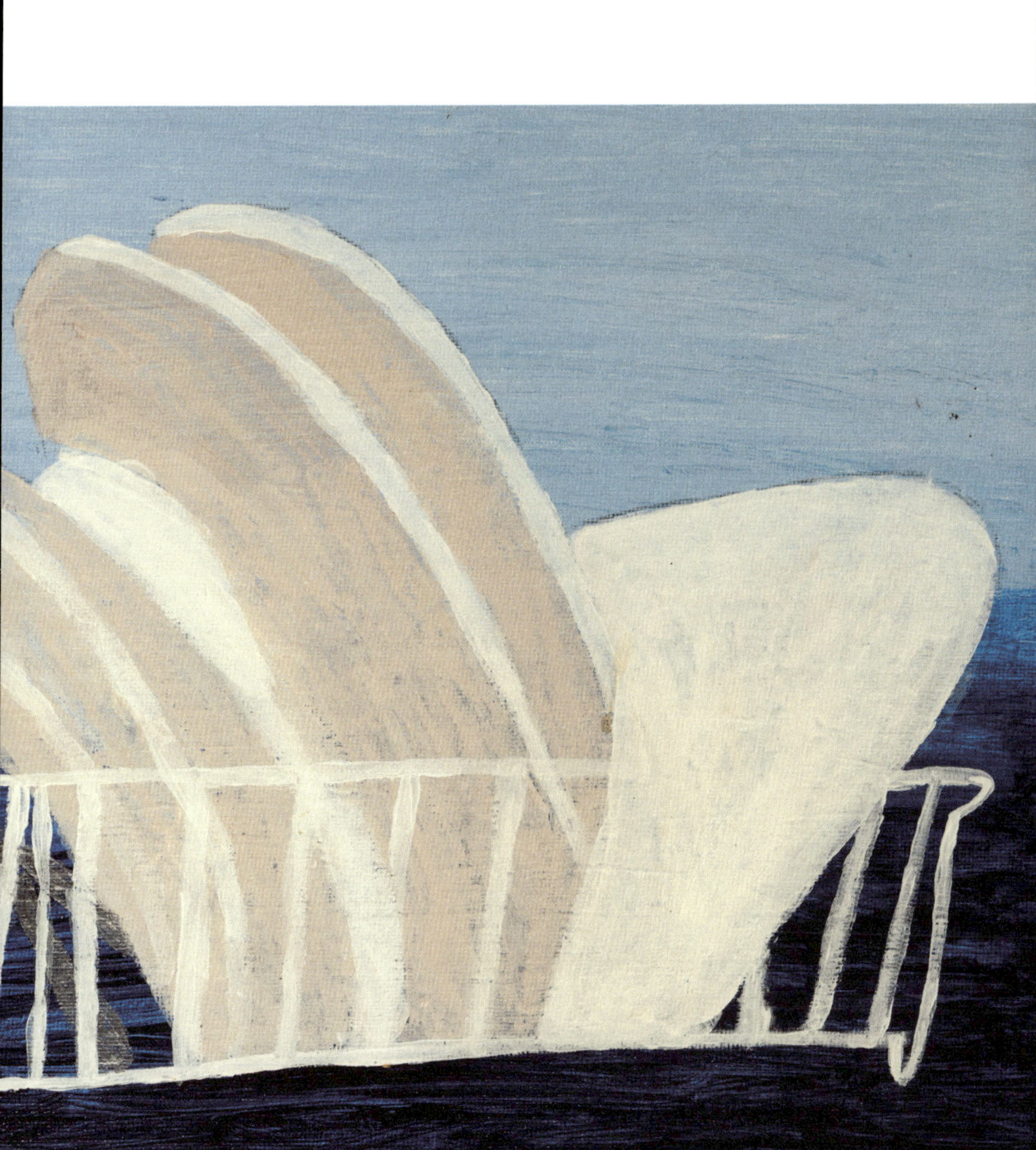

Ticket Rug

Simon Fraser

Wool on canvas backing
Courtesy of the artist

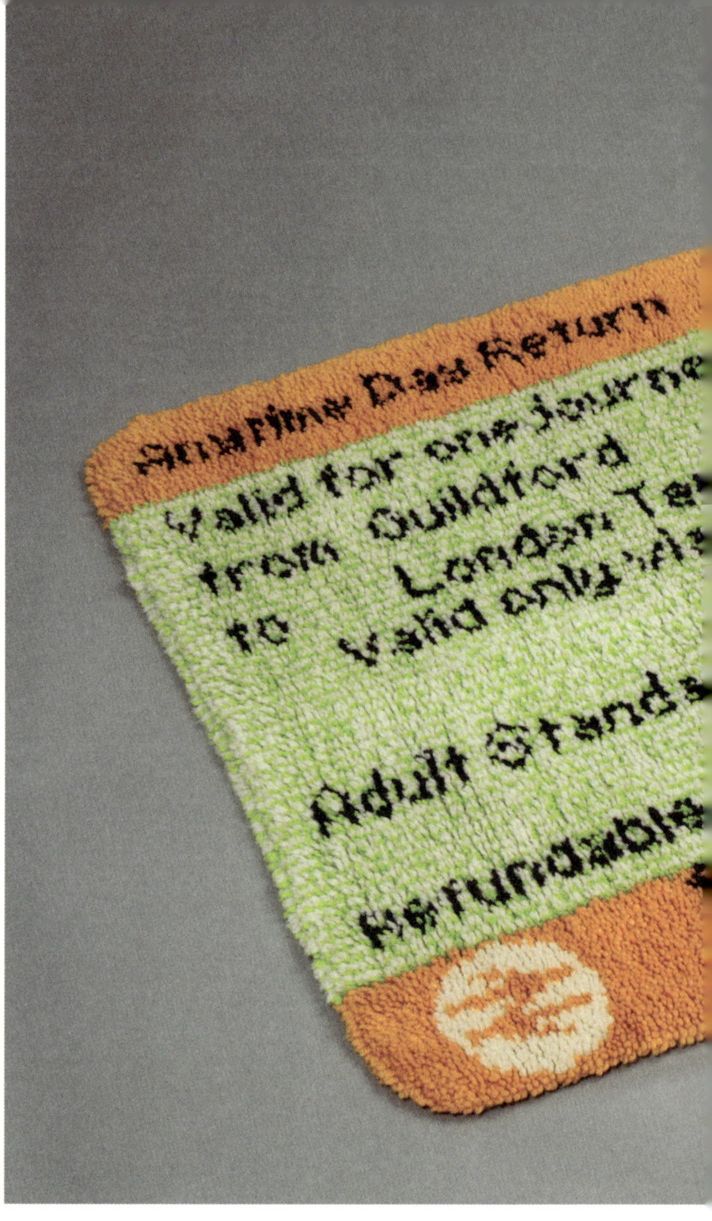

"I've always loved things that
are the wrong scale. When
I started making rugs a few
years ago, my inspiration
would come from small
items. I started the Ticket
Rug in March 2020. There are
just over 25,900 individual
threads in the rug. It took me
about 60 hours to complete
(usually while watching telly).
The ticket is dated 1st April.
It just seemed appropriate.
My next rug, currently under
construction, is based
on a Sainsbury's receipt.
It's even bigger."

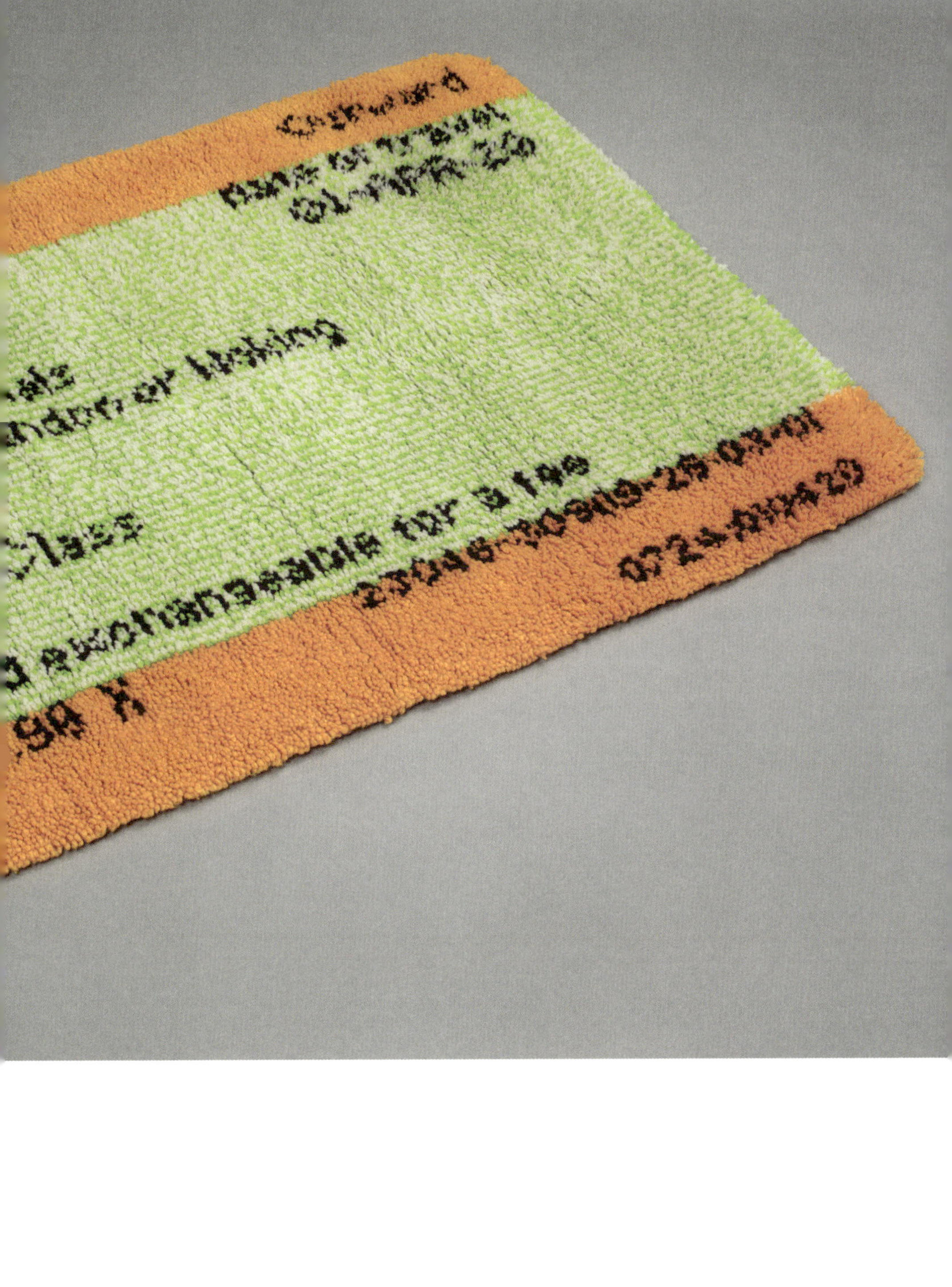

Jhansi Ki Rani
2020

Chila Kumari Singh Burman

Neon sculpture
© Chila Kumari Singh Burman
Courtesy of the artist

"Jhansi Ki Rani is one of my
heroines. She is a widely
admired figure and symbol of
Indian resistance, dressing as
a man to fight against British
forces in fierce battle. In this
piece I'm acknowledging her
significant female led act of
resistance to British colonial
rule in India."

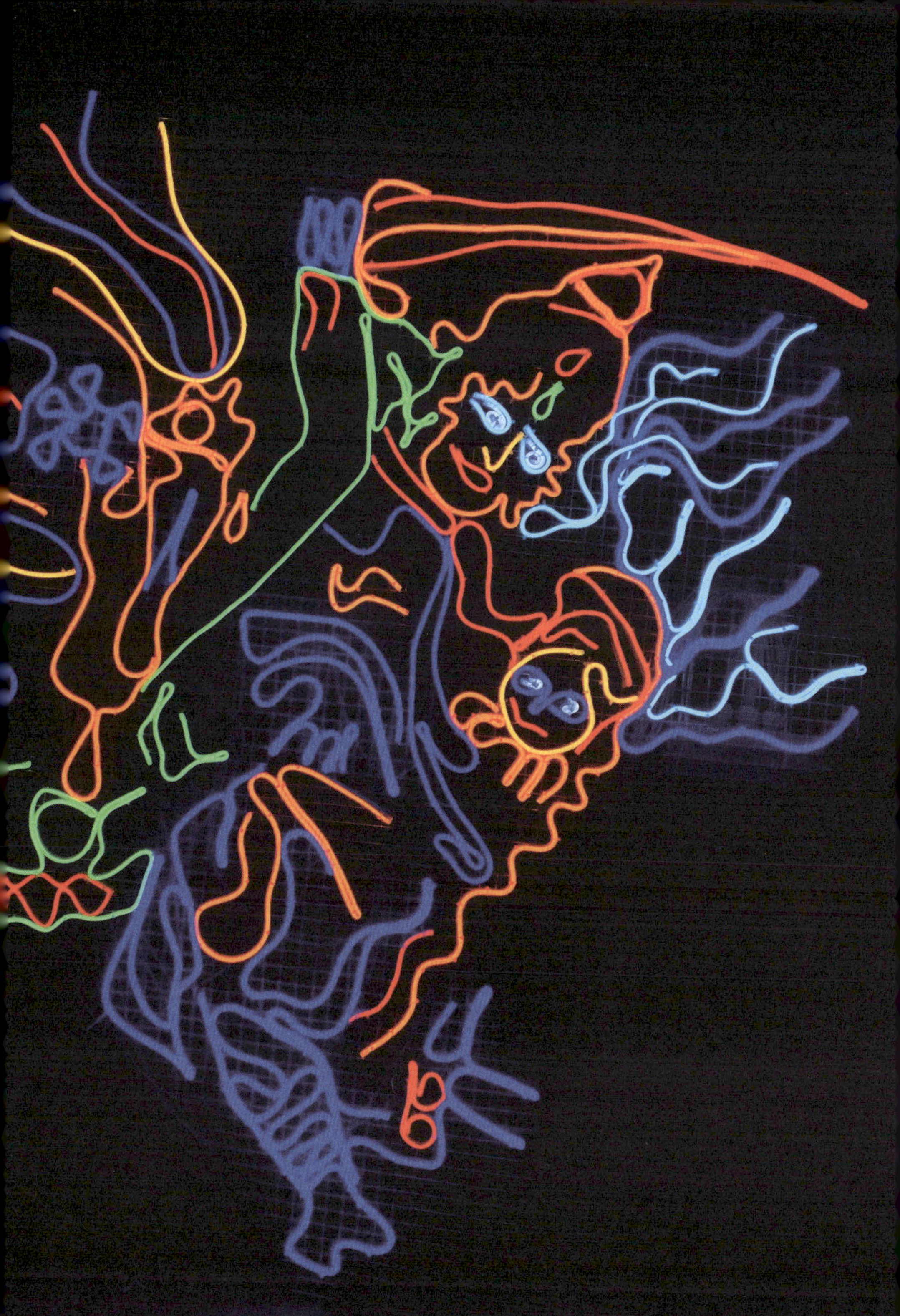

Without Us There is No Britain
2020

Chila Kumari Singh Burman

Neon sculpture
© Chila Kumari Singh Burman
Courtesy of the artist

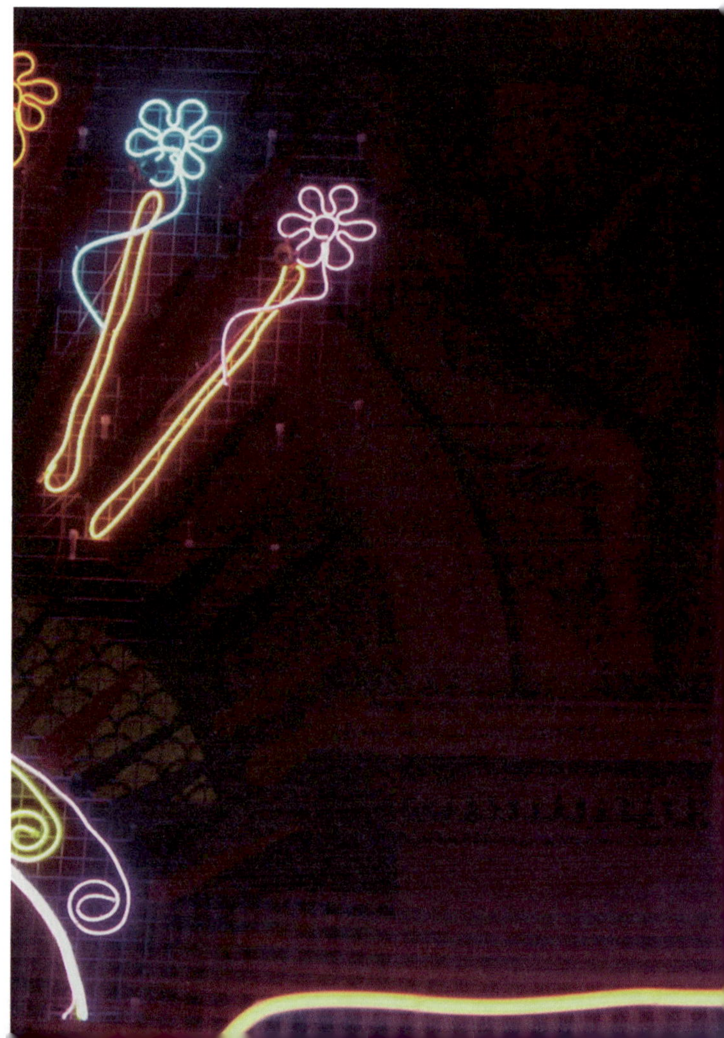

"This piece developed from
my early involvement in
a collective South Asian
women's magazine, produced
in 6 South Asian languages.
It makes a direct comment
on the legacy of colonialism,
and the significant
contribution of migrant
communities on the culture
and heritage of Britain."

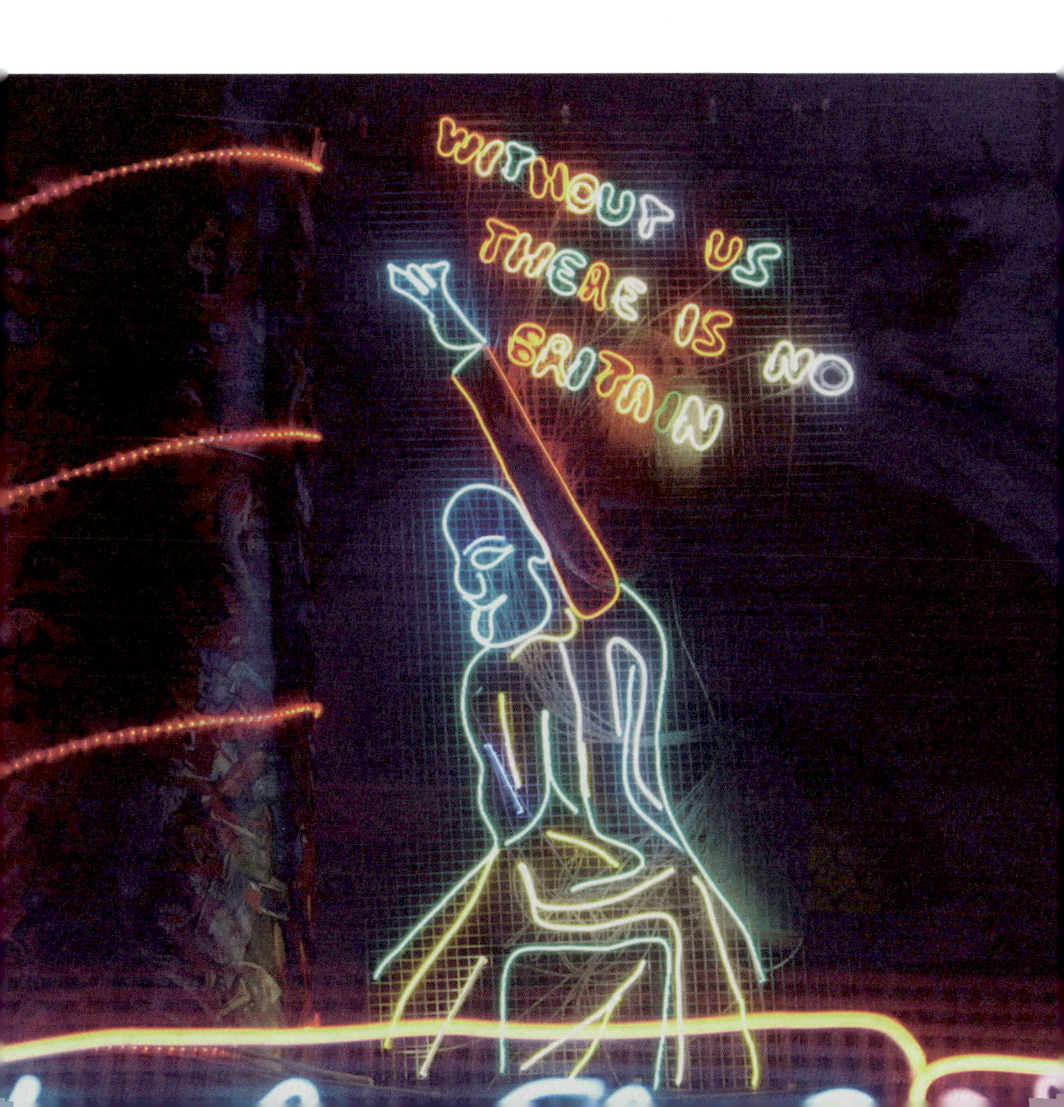
WITHOUT
US
THERE
IS
NO
BRITAIN

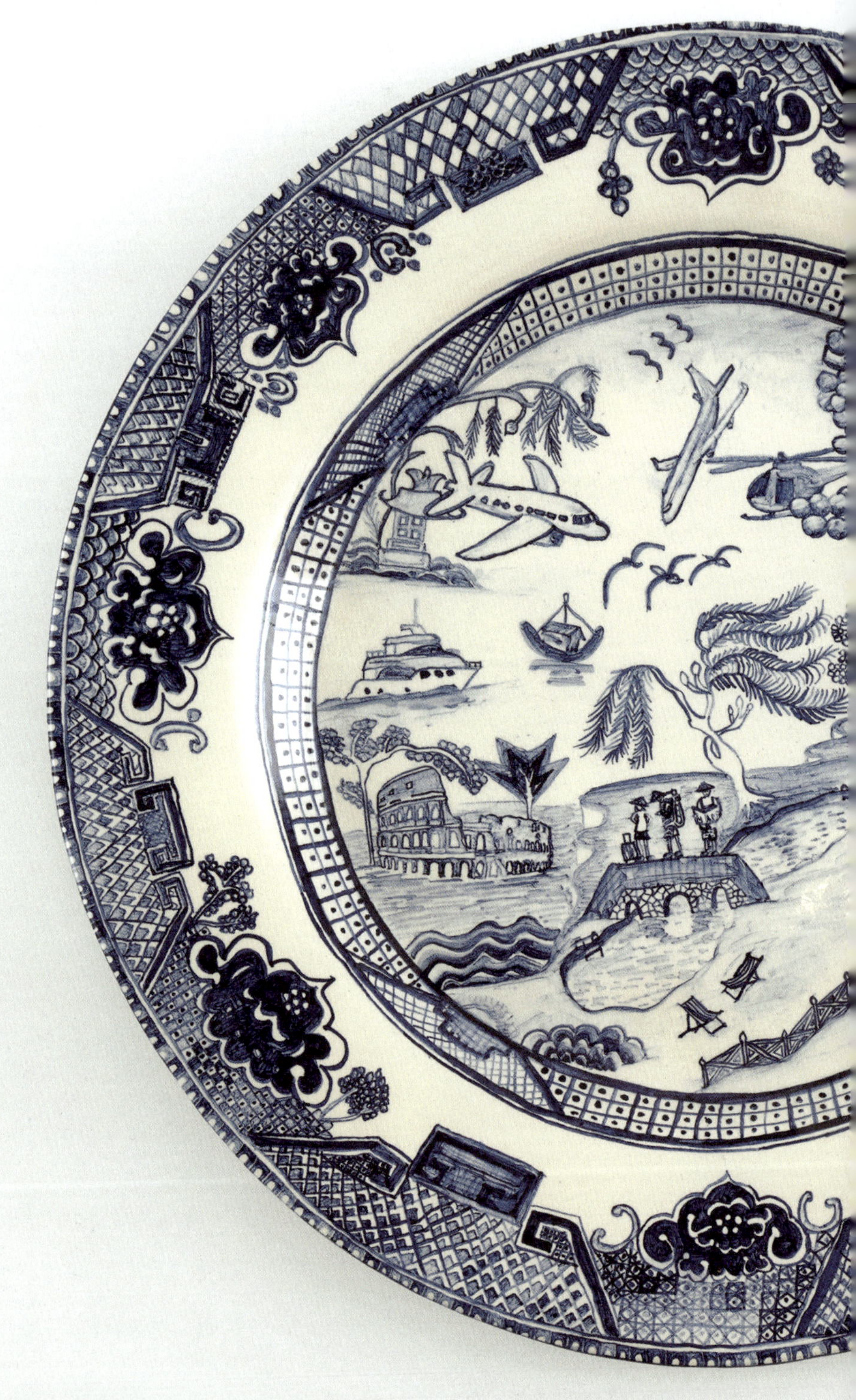

Willow Pattern Plate

Philippa Perry

Glazed ceramic plate
Courtesy of the artist

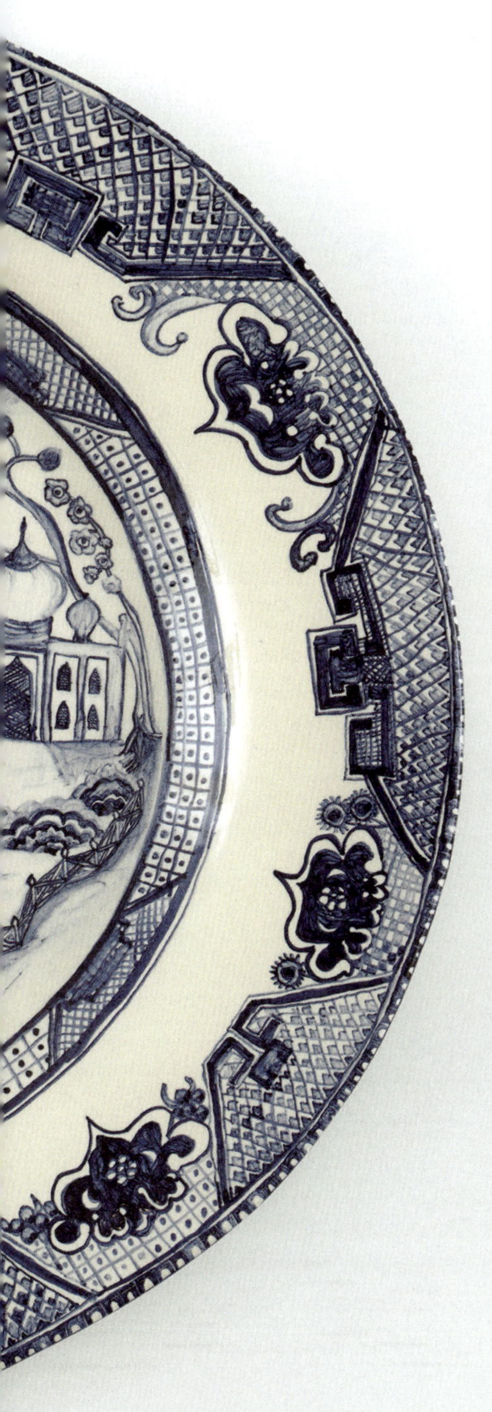

"All we can do at the moment
is fantasise about travel. If
you look closely at the centre,
you've got the woman with a
wheelie thing. She's a holiday
maker, like me. I've got my
deckchair by the pool. The
other two travellers depicted
represent the tourist who, like
the holiday maker, enjoys a
bit of relaxation but is also
interested in the culture of
the place they are visiting and
the third figure represents
the traveller. They think
themselves a bit superior
to the holiday makers and
tourist and they are looking
for cultural immersion."

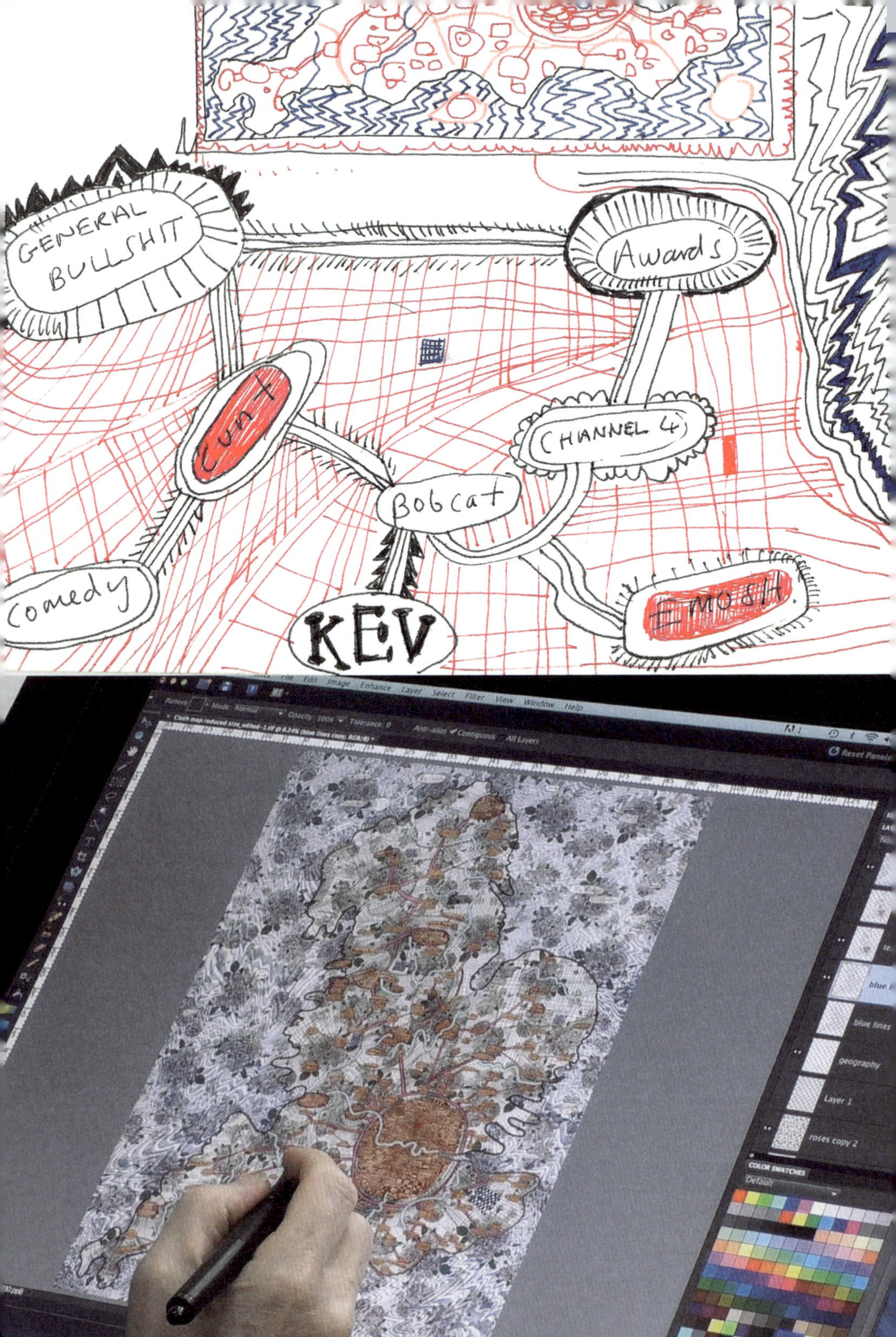

GENERAL BULLSHIT
Awards
EVENT
CHANNEL 4
Bobcat
Comedy
KEV
MOSH.

File Edit Image Enhance Layer Select Filter View Window Help
Reset Panels
blue
blue lines
geography
Layer 1
roses copy 2
COLOR SWATCHES
Default

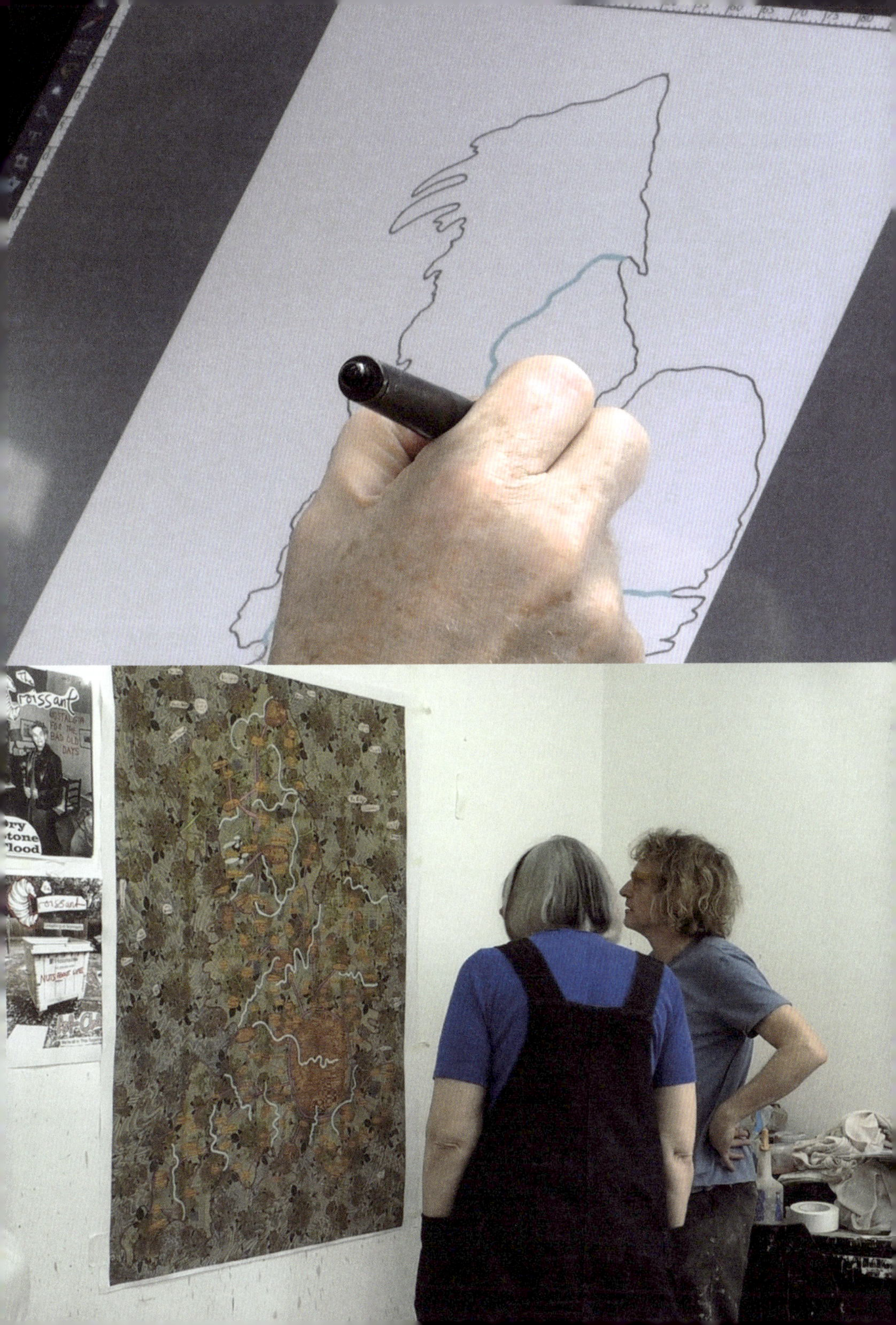

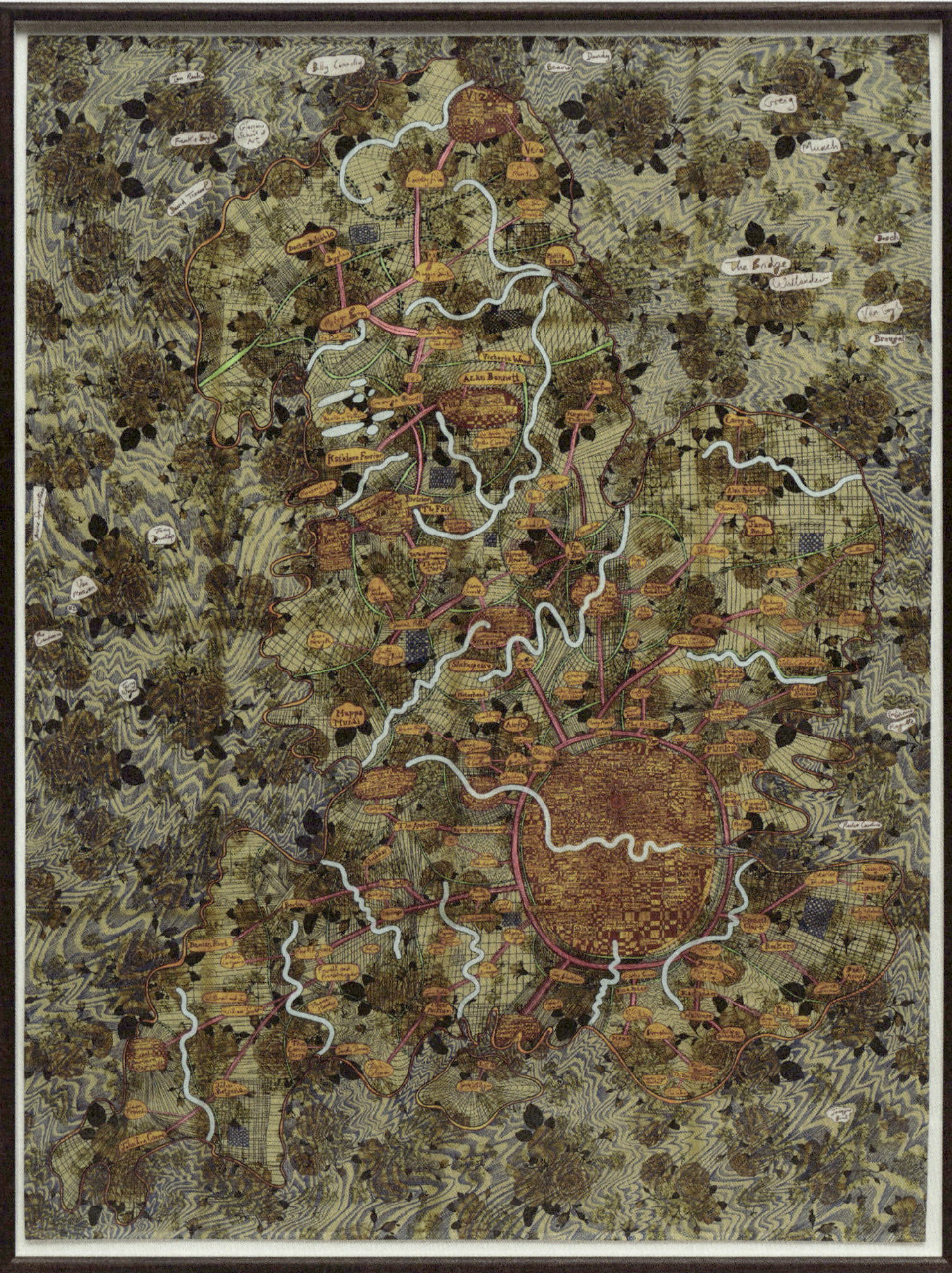

England as seen from
Lockdown in Islington
2021

Grayson Perry

Digital print on cotton
Courtesy of the artist
and Victoria Miro

"When I was working on this,
I was thinking about how
we were all travelling in
our imaginations. I've put
the floral material in the
background there. So very
English. It evokes an idea
of England, but a kind of
trapped, slightly stifling
suburban idea of England."

Double

Jabbed!

esa
LOST IN SPACEX
SOME PART OF OUR BEING KNOWS THIS IS
WHERE WE CAME FROM. WE LONG TO
RETURN. AND WE CAN. BECAUSE THE COSMOS
IS ALSO WITHIN US. WE'RE MADE OF
STAR-STUFF. WE ARE A WAY FOR THE COSMOS
TO KNOW ITSELF.
CARL SAGAN
NASA
2020
PERSEVERANCE
SATURN V APOLLO FLIGHT CONF
AT SOME POINT, EVERYTHING'S
GOING TO GO SOUTH ON YOU. YOU'RE
GOING TO SAY, 'THIS IS IT. THIS IS
HOW I END.' NOW, YOU CAN EITHER
ACCEPT THAT, OR YOU CAN GET TO
WORK.
SO IN THE FACE OF OVERWHELMING
ODDS, I'M LEFT WITH ONLY ONE
OPTION. I'M GONNA HAVE TO
SCIENCE THE SH_T OUT OF THIS.

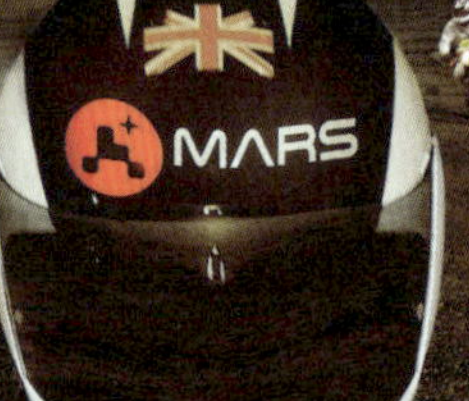

MARS

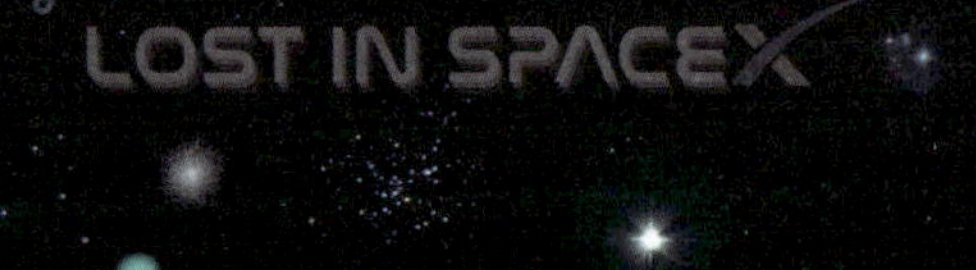

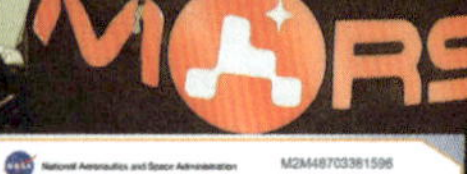

MARS

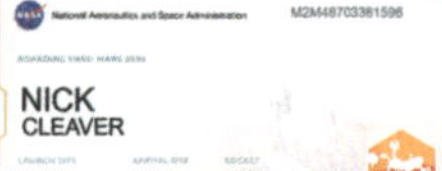

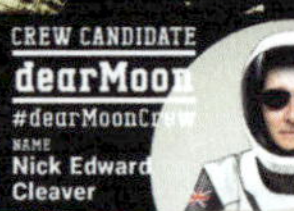

National Aeronautics and Space Administration
M2M48703361596
NICK
CLEAVER
MARS 2020

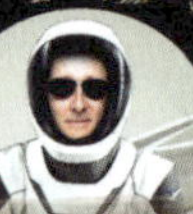

CREW CANDIDATE
dearMoon
#dearMoonCrew
NAME
Nick Edward
Cleaver
COUNTRY
United Kingdom

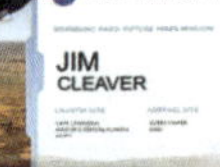

National Aeronautics and Space Administration
M2M9008187D
JIM
CLEAVER
JULY 2023

Nick
Cleaver

Previous:
Lost in Spacex

Nick Cleaver

Digital collage
Courtesy of the artist

"During lockdown, my wife Claire and I travelled through the universe by using our very own spaceship for the eyes. A 6" Dobsonian Reflector Telescope. It was a way to escape the planet and transport ourselves into the stars.

During this time my brother Jim sadly died. He was a great space and science fiction fan. As a child he collected Star Wars figures and we watched every episode together. The last and final episode was the last time I saw him in bodily form.

After he died, I mused on how when we die our atoms return to the universe. In effect we borrow atoms from the universe and return them when our allotted time here is done. As we wandered through the stars and galaxies it occurred to me that Jim was now part of all that we were seeing.

The piece includes photographs of stars and planets taken through our telescope by Claire. The other images are borrowed and focus on the theme of Claire and I travelling in space with our dog Jamie. Real and imagined spacecraft from the Star Wars movies appear. As does my brother in the form of Obi Wan now at one with the force!"

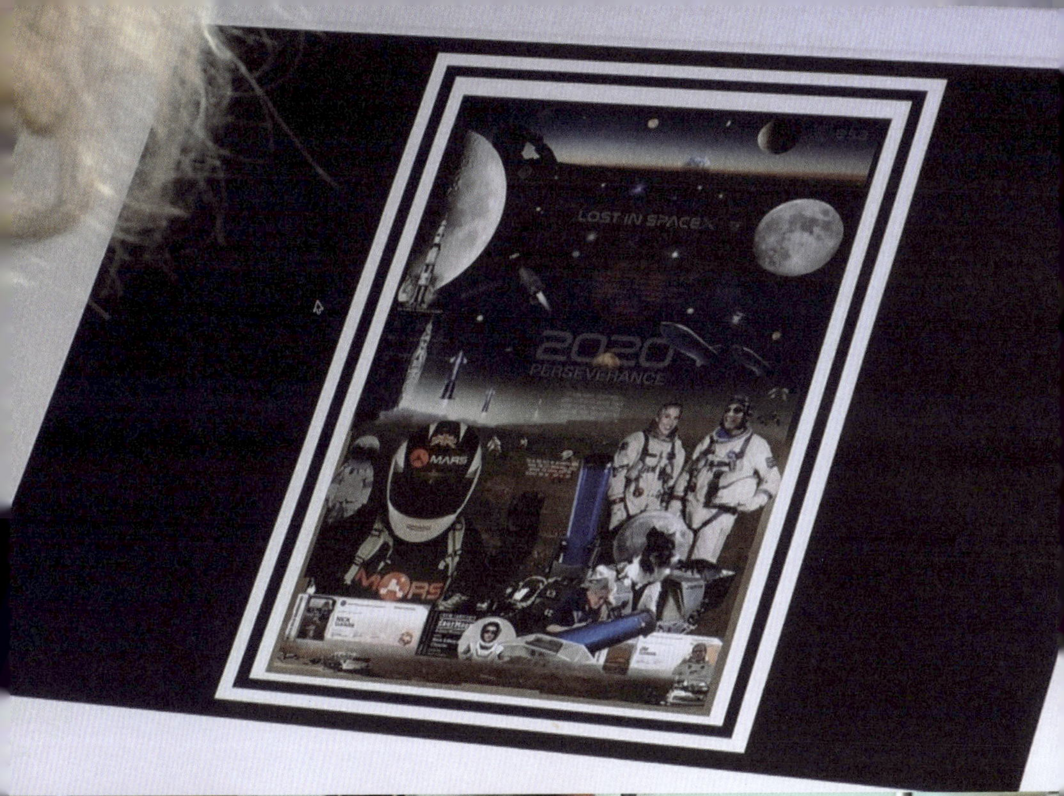
LOST IN SPACEX
2020
PERSEVERANCE
MARS

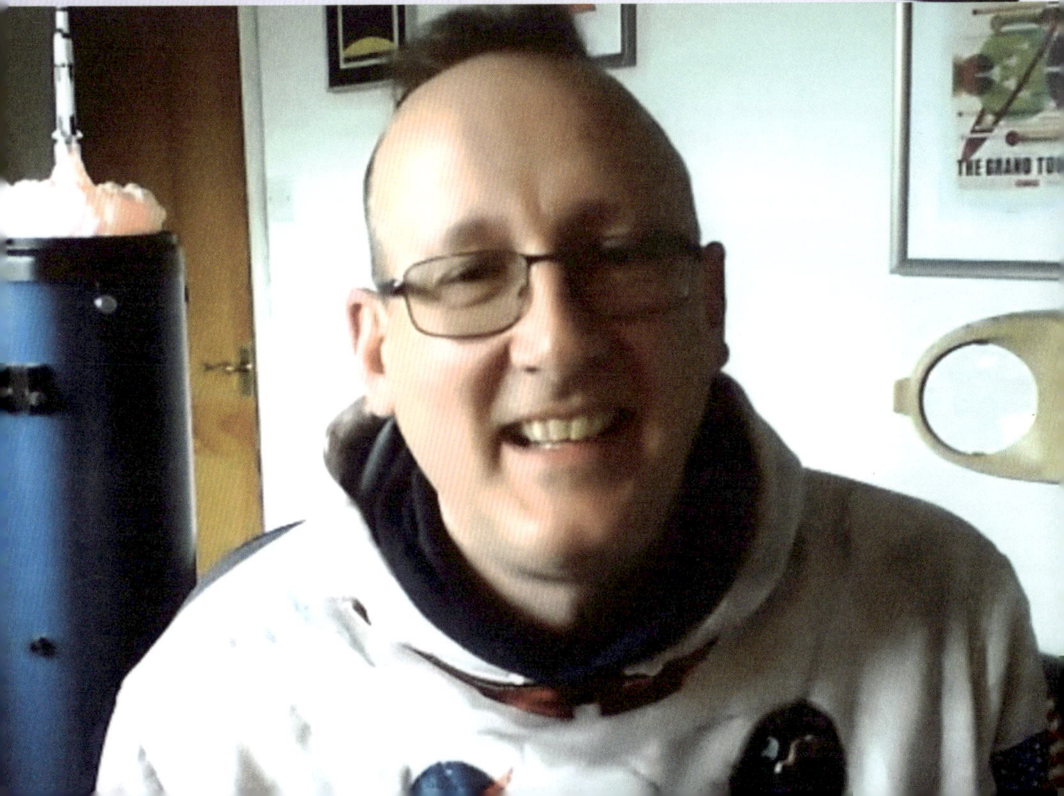
THE GRAND TOUR

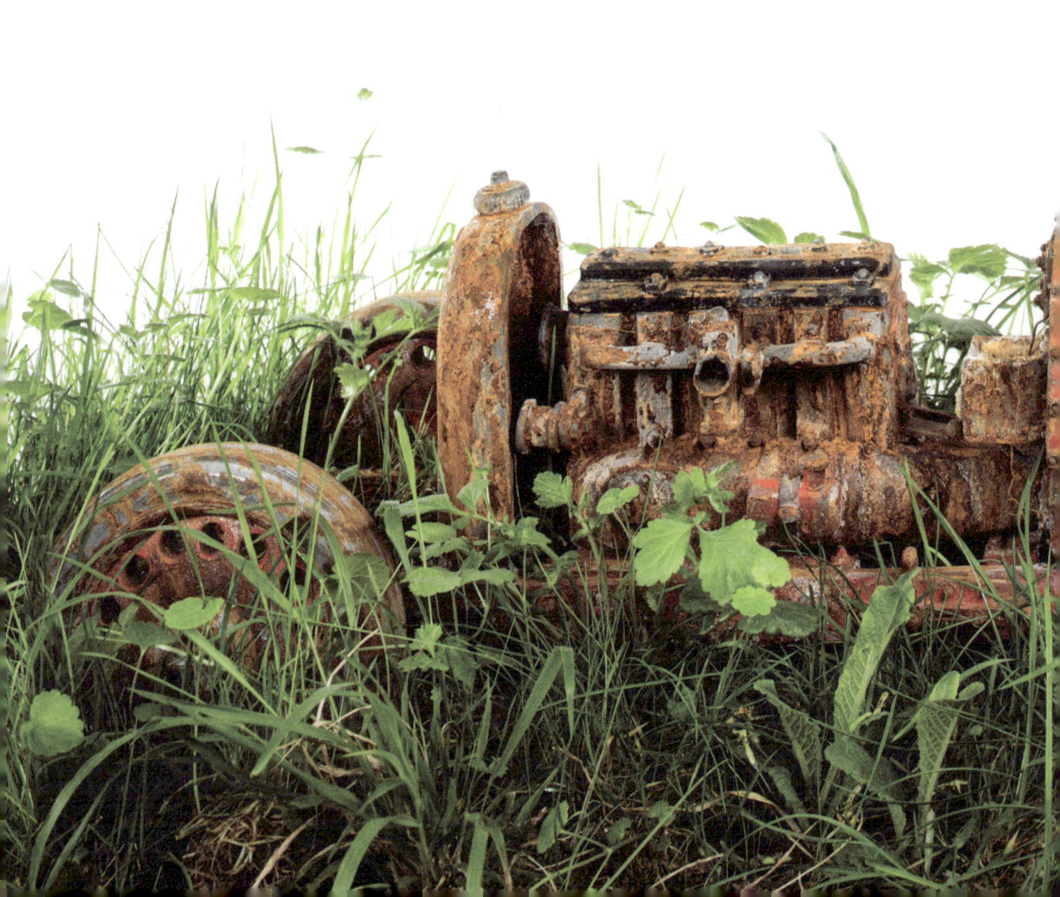

A Dream of England
2021

Grayson Perry

Cast iron
Courtesy of the artist
and Victoria Miro

"I made this car out of cast
iron. It's one of my favourite
materials to work with.
I sculpted it out of clay and
had it cast in iron. I like
the idea that it will sit there
slowly rusting.

It's a piece of England.
A memory of a mythic place
that has died. It's about a
nostalgia for masculinity
and in many ways it's a
memorial to my dad."

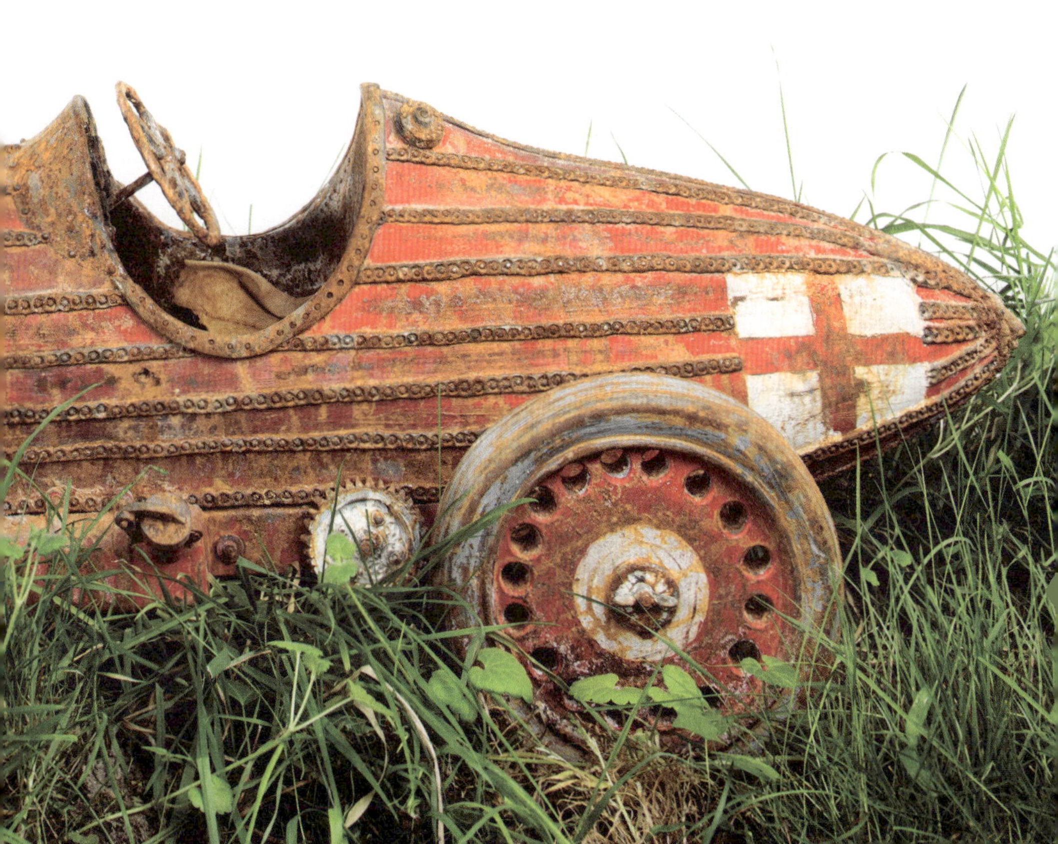

England resting in the corner of a field
glass elements
1m-10cm
wooden tray.
threaded
rod for axles. + mounts.
wood chassis with ceramic additions
then cast.
Maybe bonnet discarded next
to it
lions
knights
queen + k
boadicc

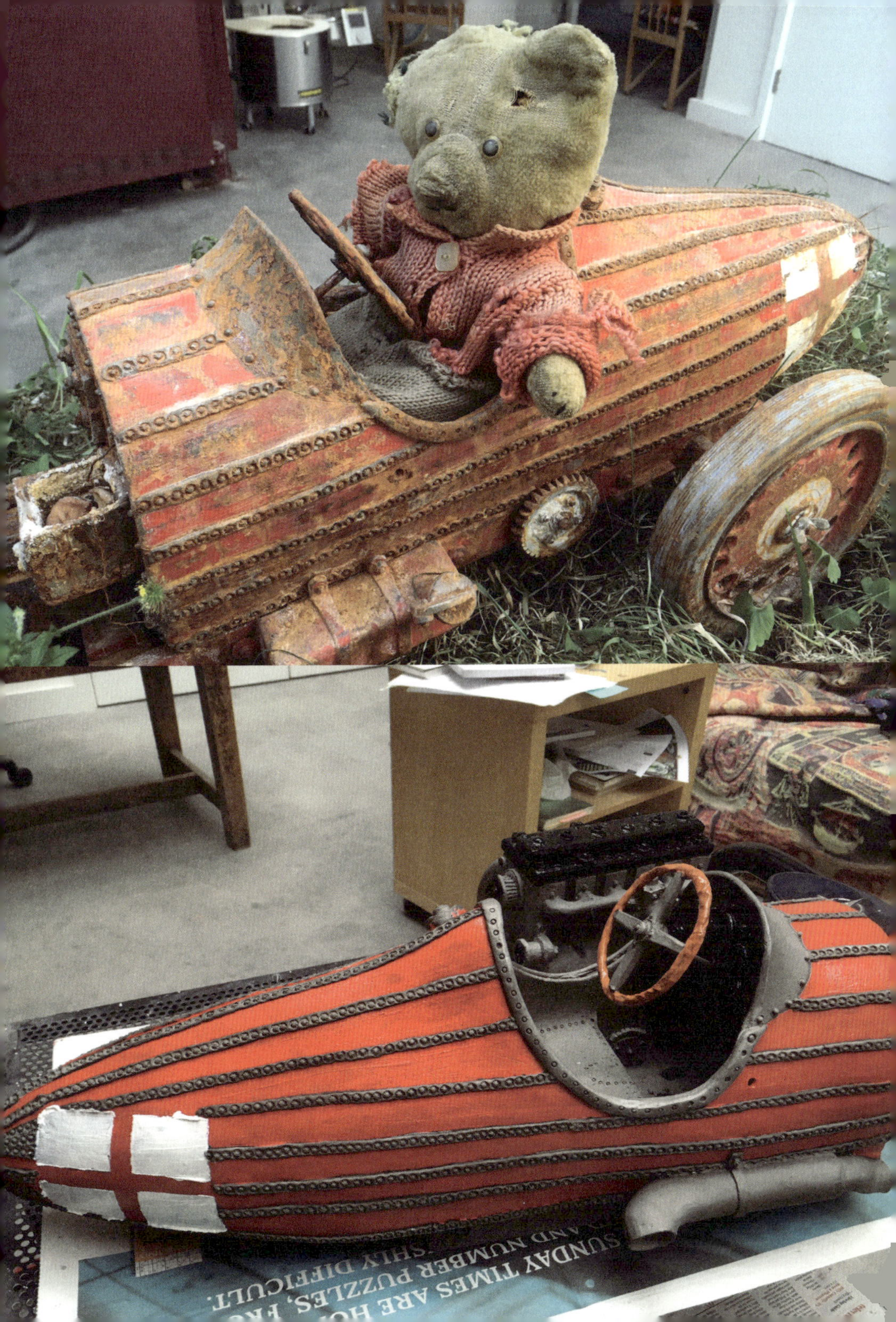

A Dream of England

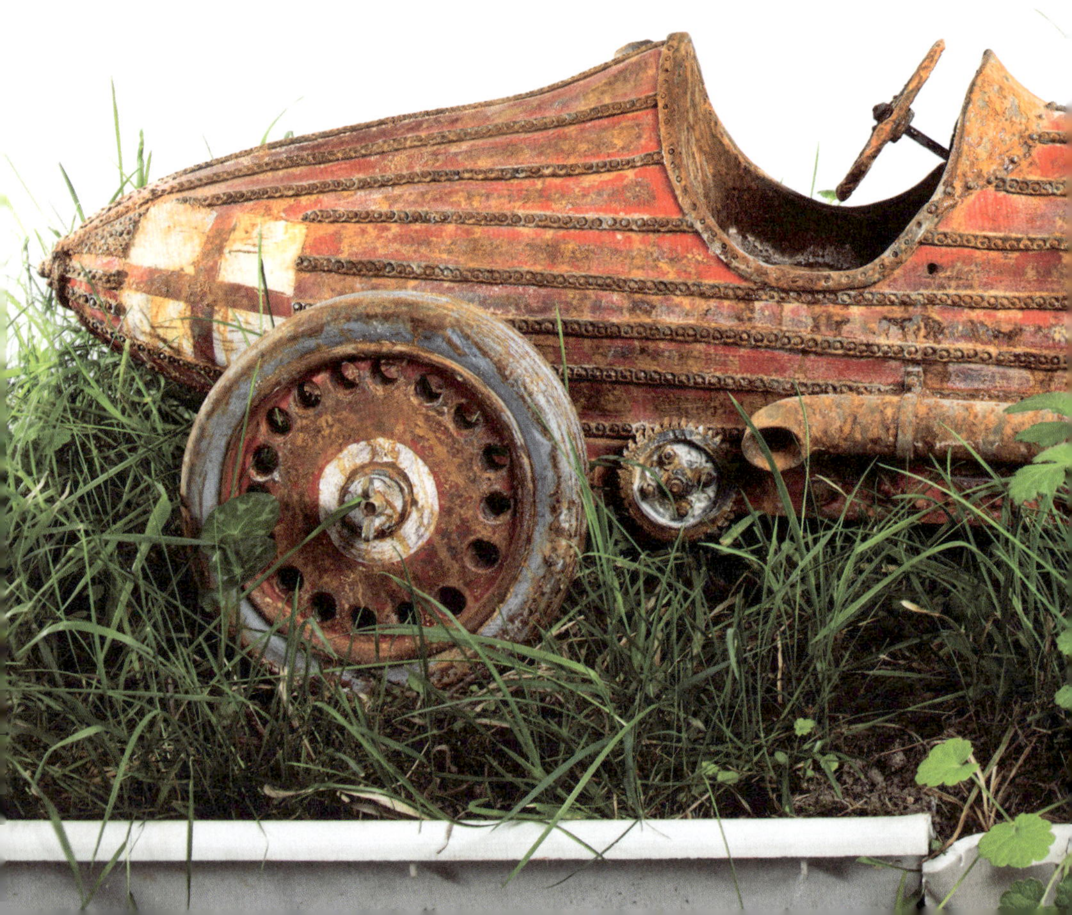

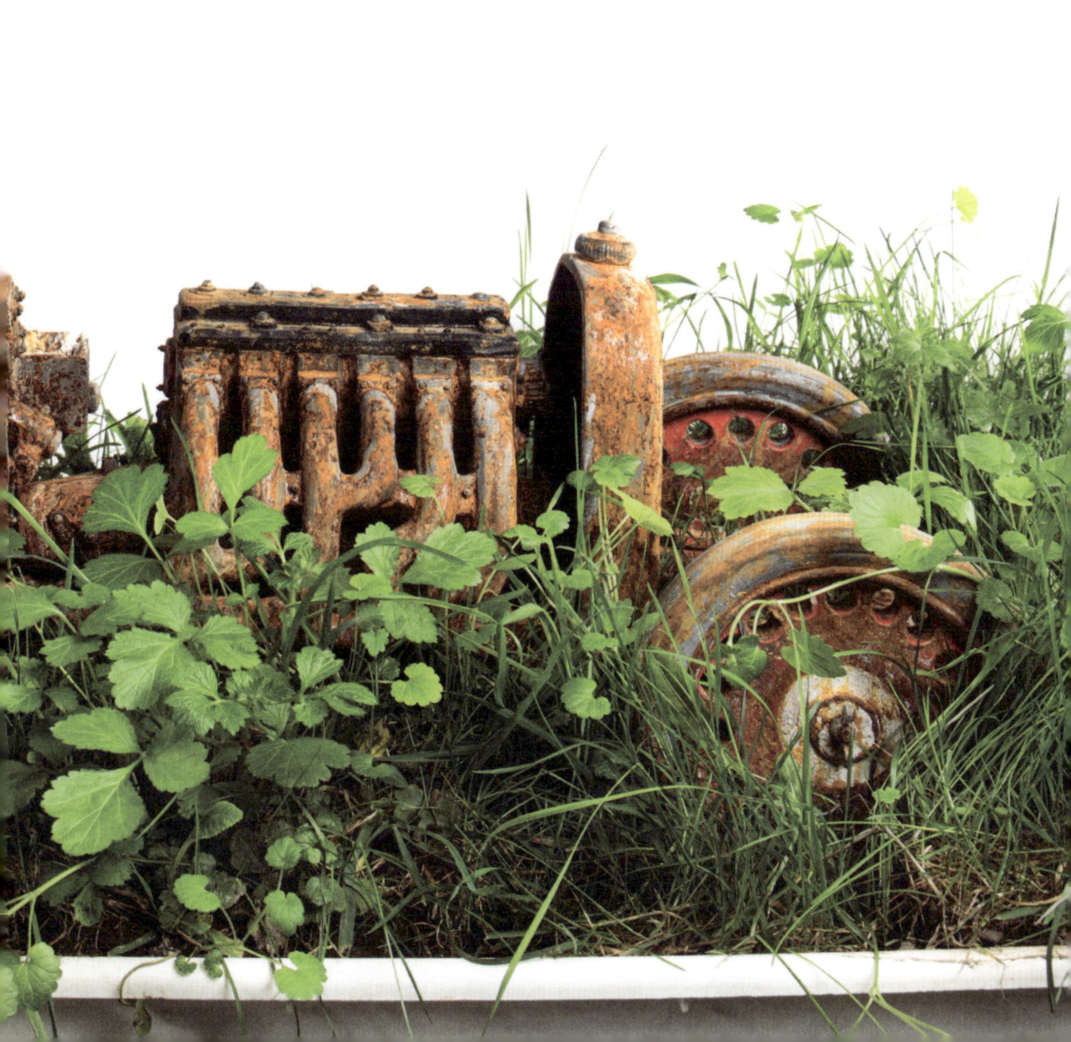

Lovely people
making lovely
art

Featured Artists

Alex Horne
Allegra Gordon
Amelia Mullins
Andy Goldsworthy
Andy Jeffrey
Anneka Rice
Anthony Klej
April Onomakpome
Banksy
Becky Tyler
Boy George
Caroline Harvey
Catherine Mottram
Cathy Sherring
Chila Kumari Singh Burman
Chloe Hänchen-Garner and Tom Hänchen
Cian McLoughlin
Clare Thornthwaite
Danny Shannon
David Bailey
David Read
David Wilkey
Derren Brown
Dora Lam, Winnie Lam and Sam Lam
Emma Ridley
Enda O'Gorman
Esther Jeanes
Freya Bruce
Gillian Allard
Gillian Mather
Grayson Perry
Greg Cook
Harry Hill
Harry Rose
Holly Walsh
Ian Withall
Imogen Paton
Isabelle Ewing
Jane Seymour
Jay Doughty
John Olohan
Johnny Vegas
Jon Gale
Julie Bennett

Laura Connelly
Lee Appleton
Leonie Brown
Lesley Woolvine
Lianne La Havas
Liberty Dearsley
Lucy Sparrow
Lulu Willis
Madame Ceski
Marie Kathrens
Mark Gee
Mark Robert-Blunn
Martine Elliott
Mary Bonner
MAWAAN
Max Mudie
Nick Cleaver
Patricia Oliver
Paul Weedon
Philippa Perry
Polly Morgan
Prabhneet Sondhi
Robyn Ansell
Russell Tovey
Ryan Gander
Sally-Anne Wilson
Sam Maisey
Simon Fraser
Sir Frank Bowling Kt OBE RA
Steve Nice
Stevyn Colgan
Sudjadi Widjaja
Sue Perkins
Suzanne Bull MBE
Sweet and Maurizio D'Apollonio
Toby Bain
Tom Allen
Trix Newham
Tyler Baker
Wendy Allen
Yinka Ilori MBE
Zoë Pyne

Marcus Rashford Feeds the Kids

Acknowledgements

With thanks to:
Grayson Perry, Channel 4, Swan Films,
Victoria Miro, Bristol City Council,
Arts Council England.

Bristol Museum & Art Gallery
would also like to thank:
Fine Art Transport provided by Jayhawk Ltd.
Niche Frames, Bristol Design,
Manchester Art Gallery, all the contributing
artists and everyone involved in making the
exhibition such a success.

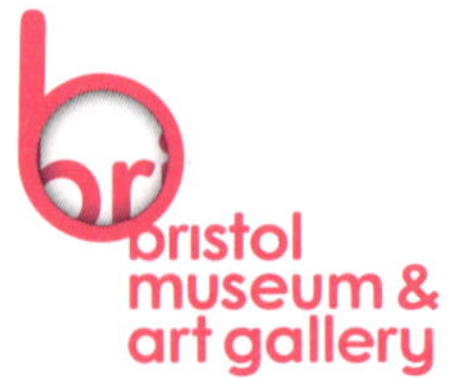

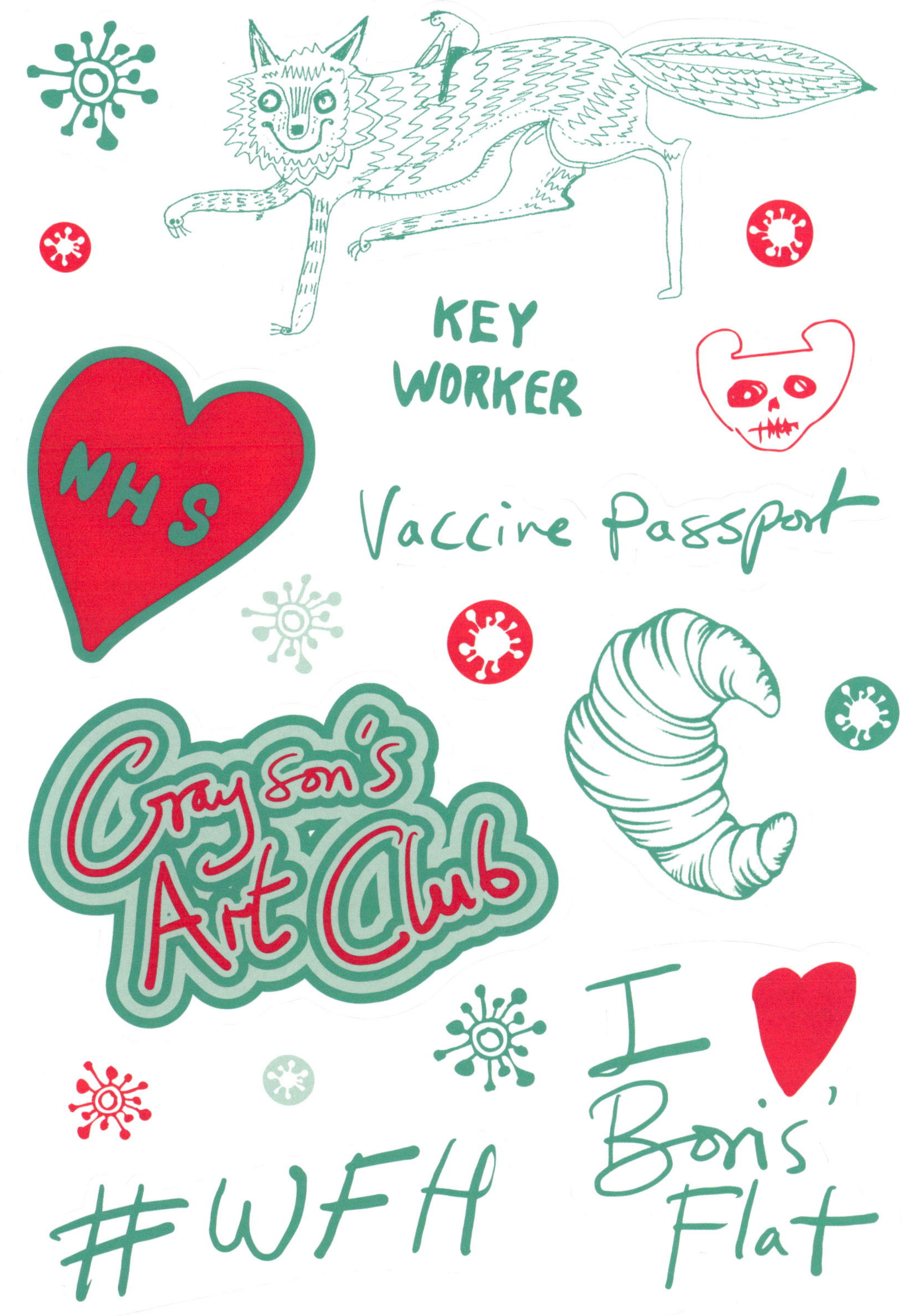

KEY
WORKER
NHS
Vaccine Passport
Grayson's
Art Club
#WFH
I ♥ Boris' Flat